A Commentary on
JEREMIAH

A Commentary on
JEREMIAH

David Pawson

Anchor Recordings

First published in Great Britain in 2017 by
Anchor Recordings Ltd
DPTT, Synegis House, 21 Crockhamwell Road,
Woodley, Reading RG5 3LE

**For more of David Pawson's teaching,
including DVDs and CDs, go to
www.davidpawson.com**

**FOR FREE DOWNLOADS
www.davidpawson.org**

**For further information, email
info@davidpawsonministry.org**

ISBN 978-1-911173-76-2

Printed by Ingram Spark

Contents

1:1-3	9
1:4–19	31
2:1–3:5	51
3:6–4:31	73
5–6	85
7:1–8:3	99
8:4–9:26	111
10:1–12:6	129
12:7–13:27	147
14–15	163
16–17	181
18–19	199
20–21:10	217
21:11–23:8	235
23:9–24:10	249
25–26	267
27–28	287
29–30	307
31	325
32–33	345
34–35	359
36 & 45	375
37–38	389
39–41	403
42–44	419
46–49	439
50–51	457
52	475

This book is based on a series of talks. Originating as it does from the spoken word, its style will be found by many readers to be somewhat different from my usual written style. It is hoped that this will not detract from the substance of the biblical teaching found here.

As always, I ask the reader to compare everything I say or write with what is written in the Bible and, if at any point a conflict is found, always to rely upon the clear teaching of scripture.

David Pawson

READ JEREMIAH 1:1–3

In this introductory study of Jeremiah's words and deeds, his character and life, we begin with the first three verses. Before I taught on the book, I had thought that one could skip over them fairly quickly, but they need more attention than might be expected.

The book of Jeremiah is not the most frequently read part of Holy Scripture. Some people don't read it because it is a big book of fifty-two chapters. If you studied a chapter a week you would take a whole year to get through it. Then there are others who find it a bit of a boring book because there is quite a lot of repetition in it. There are still others who find it a baffling book because it is an anthology, a collection of prophecies, and various other things, and it has been put together in an apparently haphazard way so that the prophecies are not even in chronological order, so it is not the easiest book to study.

Nevertheless, the whole of the Bible was inspired by God and is profitable and able to make us wise. Since Christians only have one book to study we should dig into every part of it so that we know it all. I remember a converted communist coming to our church's young people's fellowship in Newcastle. He was converted through seeing the film *Quo Vadis* because until he saw that film he had never known that anybody except communists would die for their faith. This converted him. He came to our fellowship and he asked all our young people, "How many of you have read the Bible right through?" There were a number who were embarrassed to say they had never done so. He continued, "That's amazing! I would never dare to call myself a communist if I'd never read *Das Kapital* right through," which is quite a challenge. We Christians only have one book to master, so we should study every part of it, and there is no more relevant part of God's Word to our national situation than the book of Jeremiah. You will see this as we look at some of the background. We will see that he was God's man for a nation going to pieces.

Jeremiah was God's man for a nation declining from having been one of the first powers to being a very third-rate power, a nation losing its empire, losing its territory, a nation getting involved in all sorts of relationships with other nations to try to survive by joining larger power units, a nation that was doing exactly what ours is doing, and that was becoming weak in its external and political relationships because it was becoming weak morally and spiritually inside. As we go through this prophecy you will think you are reading the Sunday newspapers. It is a most relevant part of God's Word. People used to bring me newspaper cuttings during our studies of Jeremiah. They were taking the Word of God, then picking up their newspaper the next morning and relating God's eternal Word with man's word. It becomes possible to see how it all fits.

What is there for us in the first three verses? We shall take each phrase in turn. I am not trying to press a meaning out of them but it is so exciting when you get right into God's Word. Here is the first: *to whom the Word of the Lord came*.

Opinion polls tell us that many people still believe in God and many of them talk to God, especially when they are in trouble. But the privilege we have as the people of God is that we have a God who talks to us—that is the difference. Most people in the world have believed in God, and most people in the world say prayers, but to have a God who talks is exciting. Yet I am not sure whether it is good news or bad news. There are times when one would prefer to have a God who would just listen and who would not speak. You see, it is good news that God will talk in the sense that you can relate to someone who will talk to you. You can believe in their existence before they talk to you, but you can't relate to them unless they are willing to communicate and make a two-way conversation and a two-way relationship.

If God sat up there in heaven and we just had to believe in him and talk to him but we never got any response, never heard anything, never had him talk to us, we could never say that we are related to God. You could say, "I believe in his existence, I say my prayers," but when you can say, "God has spoken to me," it is exciting, but whether it is good news or bad news depends on what he says, doesn't it?

If God is a God who talks, he is a God who will speak to us from what he thinks. He will not just say to us what we want him to say. That is the difficulty, and that is the bad news. If God is going to speak his mind, his mind may not be what my mind is. His ways and thoughts are higher than mine and maybe even contrary to mine. I am not always sure that I want him to speak especially if he is going to rebuke me or criticise me or say something that will hurt. You know, most of the Bible is unwelcomed news. Did you realise that? If you don't believe me, go through your Bible and just put a little cross on every page that contains words that are not congenial to human nature—you will be staggered.

Most of this book is bad news to fallen human nature — from the very beginning of the Old Testament. What is one of the first things God says? "You shall not eat from the tree of knowledge of good and evil. The day you eat, you die." Now is that good news? Is that a nice thing to hear, when all of us have nibbled at that fruit in one way or another and tried both good and evil so that we can have some personal knowledge of both? It has left us ashamed and guilty and not fit to meet God. You turn through the pages of the Old Testament. The very last words of the Old Testament are these: "Lest I come and smite the earth with a curse" — not very nice; I wish God hadn't said that.

You start the New Testament and you are not into it very long before you find this God is saying to a young couple, "You shall call his name Jesus because he shall save his people from their sins" — not from their fears or their doubts or their problems or their perplexities, but from their sins. That is the last thing we want to be saved from. We want to be saved from so many other things. Then you come to the Sermon on the Mount and if you can read that through without feeling uncomfortable you are a better person than I am. We go through to the final book of the New Testament, and the greater part of the book of Revelation is not welcomed by many people. It is about plagues, disasters and horrors, and it is a part we don't like to read.

So, what do we do? We pick out bits. We have a promise box made out to look like a nice box of chocolates and we have some nice little promises inside which you can pick out with tweezers and read. Or else we read this bit and that bit which are nice. We love the 23rd Psalm; even unbelievers like it, but do they read the other psalms in front of it and behind it? Never!

Now look at the edge of your Bible, look at the pages, and see where the dirty pages are. Have you ever done that? See how dirty the edge of the pages of Jeremiah are, see if the gold leaf has worn off there. God says so many things in this book of Jeremiah that people have taken his very name — and they say of someone who is depressing, "Oh don't be a Jeremiah." It is almost as proverbial as the expression "a Job's comforter". A "Jeremiah" is a doom and gloom person, so we don't like reading it. We don't want to listen to what God has to say, because God is saying: If you carry on the way you are as a nation it is inevitable that your nation will crack up.

But Jeremiah is not all doom and gloom. God never gives his Word in an unbalanced way — just as, in any bed of nettles, very near it you will find a dock leaf to rub into the sting. Throughout the book of Jeremiah, you will find little glimpses of hope, little gleams of dawn. Every so often, the very fact that God is still speaking in this disastrous situation is cause for hope, because if it were finished entirely God would just wash his hands of it and would remain silent and let it happen.

The fact is that Jeremiah went on prophesying until the captivity, and it took him over forty years, and he went on speaking—right to the day of disaster. Why should God go on speaking? The answer is that he never gives up. God is going to go on speaking and saying: I still warn you till the day it happens, so that if just one listens to my Word and does something about it, then that would gladden my heart.

It would be nice to jump through Jeremiah and say, "I'm going to talk about some texts in the book." Then I could pick all the nice bits out and leave you comforted. But no, we are going to go through Jeremiah. You have got to go through it. But it is when you have been knocked down and when you have been humbled that God can tenderly lift.

The Word of the Lord came—and that is better than no word at all. In fact, there had been seventy years of silence and now God was talking again. There are periods in our life like that when the heavens seem like brass and we don't hear anything. Then God begins to speak again. It is not always a comfortable word, but wouldn't you rather have God saying anything to you than not speaking at all? Wouldn't you rather have God rebuking you than saying nothing? It means he still loves and he still cares and he is still concerned.

The next phrase I want to emphasise is in v. 1 — *The words of Jeremiah*. Here is the miracle and the mystery of inspiration. The Word of the Lord; the words of Jeremiah — which is it? The answer is both, and don't ask me to explain how. The Bible is a miracle in itself. It is the words of Jeremiah and Isaiah, Paul, John and so on, but at the same time, it is the Word of the Lord and if you treat it as either then you misinterpret the book. There are those scholars and others who read the Bible purely as a book by human authors, and therefore as a fallible book full of contradictions and mistakes, purely to be studied as history or literature, in the same way as you study any other book—and that is a mistake. Equally, there are Christians who treat this book as if the people were simply machines and as if there were no trace of any human character in these books. But you find that Jeremiah's personality comes through, Paul's grammar comes through, John's heart of love comes through, and so there are the two aspects. It isn't as if this bit is the Word of the Lord and then we get a bit of human word— as if they are all mixed up and you have to ask the scholar, "Which came from God and which came from Jeremiah? Which bit can we trust and which bit can't we?" All of it is both. That is the mystery of inspiration— that God can take a human personality and pass his truth through that personality without denying that personality; using that person, his temperament, his experience —using that person's very grammar. Paul's grammar comes unstuck at times. It flows so much like rapids in a river that sometimes he starts a sentence and you get to the end of it and realise there is no primary clause and no main verb. Then he just stops and starts again. He is just so full that it is pouring out like a torrent. God can use that so that the result is the infallible Word of the Lord. Don't ask me to explain it. Just hold both things together.

When you are reading the book of Jeremiah you need to get both—the human situation, the human background, the human feelings, the human prophet, and to remember that the result of what has come through that human situation is God's infallible Word to us. Now that is all there in the first three verses. The Word of the Lord came, the words of Jeremiah, and we are reading both.

Now I want to pick out two characteristics of the words of Jeremiah which are different in degree from every other prophet. First of all, he is a man who speaks in pictures. Someone who speaks in pictures will always be an effective speaker because people will say, when they listen to him, "Oh, I see!" When I mentioned nettles and dock leaves, did a little picture come into your mind? Perhaps you remembered a time when you rubbed a dock leaf onto your stung finger. You *saw*. Jeremiah is doing this the whole time: drawing pictures. Therefore, you will never forget some of the things he says because you see them: *Can an Ethiopian change his skin or a leopard his spots? Then you can begin to do good, you who are used to doing evil*. Now doesn't that really hit you? What a picture! Think of a leopard trying to rub his spots off, scratching and scratching, and they won't go. An Ethiopian? If you have ever seen an Ethiopian, you will know that is the most beautiful skin in the world—golden. An Ethiopian's skin is perfect. Can an Ethiopian change that? He can't. So, in vivid pictures, Jeremiah is saying: imagine an Ethiopian trying to change the colour of his skin; you imagine a leopard trying to scratch his spots off — then if they can do that, you can change from being bad people to being good people. That is the death knell of all human reformation. It is saying you will never make yourself good. God needs to do something radical with you. You need to have a surgical operation. You need to be born again, created anew.

There are many other pictures: a girl and her ornaments; a man and his waist cloth—thus Jeremiah depicts what ought to be the clinging relations between Israel and God. The stunted desert shrub in contrast to the riverside oaks; the incomparable olive; the dropped sheaf; and even the dung upon the fields; the vulture, the stork, the crane, the swift, the lion, the wolf, the spotted leopard coming up from the desert or the jungles of Jordan; the whinnying stallions and the heifer in heat; the black Ethiopian already familiar in the streets of Jerusalem; the potter and his wheel, the shepherd, ploughman, and the vinedresser; the driver with his oxen yoke upon his shoulders; the harlot by the wayside; the light in the home, the sound of the hand mill—all everyday objects of his people's sight and hearing as they herded, ploughed, sowed, reaped, or went to market in the city— that's Jeremiah.

You find that sometimes he uses these pictures in speech to get a point across. As the birds migrate back to the same nest, why don't my people find their way back to God? Isn't it vivid? Sometimes God uses pictures to speak to Jeremiah and says, "Jeremiah, what do you see?"

He says, "I see an almond tree."

"Jeremiah, what do you see?"

"I see a boiling cauldron tipping over."

What do you *see*? Sometimes, when the people wouldn't listen to Jeremiah with their ears, what he did was to give them a picture: he would take a jar and break it; he would take a stone and bury it. He would take his old, dirty underwear and leave it under a rock until it was full of maggots and then bring it out and say, "That's what you were like. You were once as close to God as my underwear is to me, but this is what has happened to you." They saw where they wouldn't hear. It is very vivid and it is picture language. I hope that in the deeper sense you enjoy the clear pictures that God gives through Jeremiah. But Jeremiah had gifts of observation and imagination, which our Lord Jesus had. His teaching, too, is full of pictures from everyday life.

Now the problem we have with this is that the culture and the country and the background from which all these pictures are taken is the Middle East, not England. Therefore, we have to translate them into pictures of today, or we have to try to get back into that culture, and I will try to help you to do that. But picture language was part of Jeremiah's words. The Word of the Lord came through the words of Jeremiah so it came in picture language.

The second thing about Jeremiah, as far as his words are concerned, is this: Jeremiah is the finest poet among all the prophets—lyrical, he would have been a great songwriter. His songs would have been top of the charts again and again. He has taken the folk song style and most of his prophecies are in verse. Now this doesn't come out in the Living Bible or even in the Authorized, I think, but in the Revised Standard Version you find that wherever his words are in poetry the lines are broken. There are more spaces between; they are not just in straight lines of prose. You will find that much of the prophecy is in poetry. It is like going down a river. Sometimes it is running flat and smooth in prose, then you come to a cataract and you are rushing down and the white water is all around you—the poetry comes out.

We need to know a little about Hebrew poetry in order to understand. It is impossible to translate into English—that is the problem. Therefore, we are again at a disadvantage. Just as the pictures of Jeremiah come from a bygone day, the poems are also in a rhythm and a language that are strange to us. Hebrew poetry did not rhyme. Now most English poetry does, or it did until recently, so we are used to rhyme. Hebrew poetry depends not upon rhyme but upon rhythm, the beat; the sense of stress; accent. Here is a silly little poem, which will help you to realise what is happening: "There was a young lady of Deal who was stung on the nose by a wasp. When asked if it hurt she replied, 'No it doesn't, but I'm jolly glad it wasn't a hornet.'" There is a perfect example of rhythm without rhyme. You expected rhyme but you didn't get it. But you got the rhythm, didn't you? That is a limerick rhythm but not a rhyme. Hebrew poetry is like that. There have been some valiant attempts to translate Jeremiah's poetry which don't quite come off. There is a characteristic rhythm there which may vary in the number of beats, but I want you to notice something else now. There is not only a rhythm of sound, there is also a rhythm of sense, and this is the key to Hebrew poetry. It is nearly all what is called "parallelism", whereby you say a thing twice. The second line, which is usually shorter than the first, repeats the thought of the first line. Have you noticed this? Can a maiden forget her adorning or a bride her girdle? Have you got it? The same thought is repeated in different words. Sometimes the second line simply repeats the first line in different words. Sometimes it says something opposite to the first line. Sometimes it adds something to the first line, but there is a very definite two-line pattern all the way through.

If you study the Psalms you will find that they are nearly all in this rhythm: "Bless the Lord, O my soul, and forget not all his benefits" —you find it running all the way through. Now I am afraid we are going to miss a lot of this poetry, but why do you think that God gave words in pictures and poems and chose a man with a vivid imagination and with a great poetic gift? It was because he wanted his Word to be remembered. You remember pictures and poems better than you remember any prose. If a preacher gives an illustration, paints a picture in your mind, that is what will stick. Or if you quote a little poem, that is what will stick.

If I quoted the poem, "How odd of God to choose the

Jews, but odder still for those who choose the Jewish God and scorn the Jews", then you might think, later on, "Now what was that he was saying? 'How odd of God,'" and then you will get it. God wanted his Word to be remembered until it was applied. Therefore, he put it in pictures and in poems and the words of Jeremiah are full of both. Of course, he also gave us one other gift. He didn't just give us a Jeremiah who could speak, he gave us a man called Barak who could write. Jeremiah was a prophet with a secretary. Barak wrote down the poems and some of the biography of Jeremiah, which is important to have. The poor man had just finished writing down the first lot when the king took a penknife and sliced it into pieces, throwing it on the fire bit by bit as he read it. So, Barak had to write it all out again. But out of revenge he wrote even more fully and wrote even more down, and the king had a bigger book to cope with. So, we have the book of Jeremiah – the words of Jeremiah written down by Barak.

Now the third phrase I want to look at is this: son of Hilkiah of the priests. It is at this stage that you have to begin to dig and get back into the man's upbringing. Jeremiah was called to begin his ministry when he was still in his late teens, a shy, diffident youth, full of excuses.

He seems the most unlikely young man to challenge not only one nation but, as God said to him, "all the nations" — "I've set you over all the nations." His words would have international effect. Why did he choose this shy, diffident boy? God knows what he is doing. He doesn't choose haphazardly. He chooses a man for what he can see in him and for what he can put into him; for what is already there and for what God knows he can add. He often chooses someone because of their background. There is no doubt that you can read a lot into the background. When you get into it, it is fascinating. Jeremiah is living in a little village about an hour's walk (three to four miles) north-east of Jerusalem and just off the beaten track, so no tourist goes there today.

When I started this study I thought, "I must go to see the little village." It is now the little Arab village of Anata; it was then Anathoth. He was of the priests. Why was he living there? Why wasn't he living nearer Jerusalem? Why weren't they near enough to the Temple for the whole family to be involved as priests? The answer is that Jeremiah was of a priestly family that had been excommunicated, which had been turned out of priestly service. They had a long family tree that went back to the days of Moses and even earlier. In that family tree was the great priest Eli of Shiloh. Do you remember Eli and Samuel? Then, coming a bit further down, there was a priest called Abiathar, whom Solomon for various reasons had turned out of the Temple and said, "You may be a priest but you are not going to worship or lead the worship in my Temple any more, and none of your line will." He banished them to that little village called Anathoth.

There this family lived, knowing they were called of God, that they had the right to serve God in his Temple and yet were shut off from it. That is the background, and here was a devout family keeping their relationship with God but unable to exercise their ministry, with all the frustration that included. It was a devout home. By this time, people had stopped choosing religious names for their children. In the nation at large, when a boy or girl was born they usually chose a name they liked for the sound of it. They didn't choose a name that tried to relate that child to God. But in many of the names of the Bible you get the thought that the parents wanted their child in some way to be used by God. So, the name Hilkiah—his father—means "God is my portion," or "God is all I want." What a lovely name to give your baby. He would have that name to live with for the rest of his life. Can you imagine living with that name when God was not all you wanted?

Lax of Poplar, a famous Methodist minister of many years ago, was one day christening a baby and he asked the parents, "Name this child."

The parents said, "Genius."

He said, "Pardon?"

They repeated their request: "Genius."

He said, "You mean a brilliant person?"

"Yes."

"Oh, don't saddle the child with that," he whispered. "That's an awful name to give a child. What will he do at school?"

Again, they said, "Call him Genius." The cockney father said, "We want to give him something to live up to." So they called him Genius.

Now that was simple biblical practice. But it was symptomatic of the nation's decline that no longer did the people want to give their children names that might link them to God or remind them of him.

The name Jeremiah means, "God hurls, God fights, God throws." I wonder if they realised when they used such a name that this young man was going to throw God's Word at a whole nation, and at the whole world. But they called him that in a devout home. It was a home in which he obviously knew his Torah because in the earliest prophecies he gave there are constant references to the Ten Commandments and to the prophets who had preceded him.

His home situation prepared Jeremiah because this was to be his ministry: he was to be a prophet of God and yet he was constantly to be refused a hearing. He was to be imprisoned, beaten, ridiculed, mocked, and so he was not going to be welcomed in his ministry. He was brought up in a background of people who were called of God to minister and were not allowed to—that he might be able to cope with the frustration of later years. Isn't it fascinating? "Son of

21

Hilkiah of the priests."

The next phrase to consider is: "In Anathoth in the land of Benjamin." In between the coast and the river is the Holy Land—Judea. It consists (in an oversimplified way) of a line of hills running up and down north and south between the river and the coast, nearer the river than the coast. Near the top of the line of hills, Jerusalem is just a little down on the west side, which is the green side, which is the side the rain comes to, because it comes from the Mediterranean. On the dry side there is the wilderness, the desert, with barren rocks right down to the river, which is way below sea level—the Jordan and the Dead Sea. The village of Anathoth is right on the ridge so it is between town and country, between green fields and desert, and in the far distance, over the great gulf, there was a beautiful green land where the hills came up again and a little rain from the west could fall again and there you had the meadows and the pastures of Gilead.

Jeremiah would look over to that barren desert, to the green hills of Gilead, and he would say, "Is there no balm in Gilead? Is there nothing sweet or beautiful to help us there? No medicine there? No herbs there to cure our complaint?" You see how vividly it comes. So, all through the book you get this sense of him being between the fertility and the barrenness, between the grass and the sand. Living in those two places he knew that he lived between the two conditions in which the people could live. They could either live with the blessing of rain, fertility and food, or they could live in the barrenness of the desert. The way God could do it would be this: if he switched the wind from the west to the east it came off the desert. Then the wilderness got no rain and the western slopes got no rain. Famine came, water was scarce—there is a vivid description again of this condition in 14:1–7.

I remember one summer of drought when we saw brown

grass as the hay crop failed, and we drove to Scotland and saw cattle being fed with hay in August. Do you realise the implication of this? That is what Jeremiah was seeing. He realised that it is in the hand of God to give and withhold. It is within the hand of God to bring drought and to send rain. He learned this from having been born in Anathoth where he had seen plenty on the one hand and barrenness on the other—and Anathoth was a perfect background. But Anathoth was not only the border between east and west, it was a political border between north and south, and this too brought Jeremiah to see it.

The political boundary was this—in the south, below the line at Anathoth were two tribes: the big one called Judah from which we get the word Jew, and a little one called Benjamin, to the north, which was right up against this border. North of the border were the ten tribes of the rest of the people. But by Jeremiah's day those ten tribes had been lost. They had ceased to be, for after Solomon, many years earlier, there had been a civil war; there had been a split between north and south—two tribes in the south, ten in the north. It was the ten in the north that went to pieces first and they collapsed. They were invaded, the Assyrians took them away and they came right down as far as Anathoth and stopped there.

So as the boy Jeremiah stood in the village street, if he looked north he looked into a land that was barren of his people, with perhaps only a few hiding in the hills, occupied by enemies; it is a city lying in ruins, and he knew from reading the prophet Isaiah that it was entirely their fault. He looked south and saw the beautiful city of Jerusalem still standing, but he saw in its streets the very same moral and spiritual collapse which had led Samaria to collapse. Living in Anathoth, he looked naturally to the desert and the fields and he looked politically to the occupied and the south. It was as if he had lived on the border between Vichy and Free France.

He had seen what had happened in the north and he knew it could so easily happen in the south. The boy was brought up living on the border. Are you getting the feel now? All through his little head as he grew up were thoughts and questions. Why did those ten tribes lose their land? Why were they taken away? "Daddy, can you tell me why? Why are those hills so barren and why are these so green? Daddy, why?" You can imagine him drinking all this in until one day, when he was about twenty years of age, God said, "Jeremiah, I want you."

God knew what he was doing. In fact, we shall see that while Jeremiah was still a bulge in his mother's tummy, God was preparing him—that is what God says: "I was getting you ready. I'd set my hand on you. I was predestining you to this." Poor Jeremiah was a man who had to wrestle with the problem of predestination. He was trapped and there were times when he wished he had never been born. There were times when he cursed the day he was born. There were times when he said, "God, why have you done this to me? If I try not to speak of you any more there is a hidden fire in my bones. I'm weary and I can't contain it. Why did you do this to me?"

But, when God calls, you have no option. Any preacher or teacher or prophet of God will tell you this: if God has called, you have no choice. Many ministers would leave the ministry tomorrow if they had any choice about it. But they can't. Why not? Because they remember a day when God said, "You." They have no choice and that is what happened to Jeremiah. So, God prepared this boy even before he knew and then one day he told him, "You're just the man I want."

We have two more phrases to pick up. Let us take the next. "In the days of Josiah, Jehoiakim, and Zedekiah"—now I don't expect that excites you, unless you have read the books of Kings lately. You see how the Bible hangs together. You will never understand that unless you read the books of Kings and Chronicles. Whilst studying Jeremiah, I suggest that you also read the relevant parts of Kings and Chronicles as well as the whole of Jeremiah (again and again) until you are with me all the way. Then you will understand the drama.

Now I never liked history at school. I hated it in fact. I thought it was the most boring subject and it still can be. But the important thing is that when God speaks he always speaks in time and in space at a particular period, at a particular place. We have to get back into that time and into that space, and understand what he was saying, before we can extract the principles and apply them to today. So, we are going to have to do a bit of history. As I read these three names—Josiah, Jehoiakim, Zedekiah—they begin to take flesh and blood. They were real people.

Funnily enough, he actually lived in the days of five kings, or even six. But he doesn't mention some of them. He was born in the days of Manasseh and I'll tell you a little about him. When Jeremiah was a boy the king was Amon, and when Jeremiah was called of God to be a prophet, Josiah was king. Then there was another whose name was not mentioned here—Jehoahaz—who only reigned for three months and then he was gone. Then came Jehoiakim, who managed eleven years, then another man Jehoiachin (Jeconiah) who managed three months, and then finally Zedekiah who reigned for another eleven years. So that two kings who reigned for three months are not mentioned, and the two kings of his boyhood are not mentioned because he didn't prophesy during their reigns. But let me just give you a very quick thumbnail sketch. The name Manasseh should make you shudder. It was he who corrupted the nation and he was on the throne when little Jeremiah was born. That man

25

introduced political intrigue, moral corruption, and spiritual pluralism until there were all kinds of things happening in the villages and streets of Jerusalem. It was in Manasseh's day that they began to take little children and burn them alive to God—that is what was happening. Indeed, had Jeremiah not been born in a family out of town he might well have ended his life as a human sacrifice. But Manasseh died and Amon came on the throne and he was overthrown. So, an eight-year-old boy called Josiah came to the throne. Jeremiah was eight years old when Josiah was eight and came to the throne. These two boys grew up together and Josiah was a good man—a good boy—at first. As Josiah came to his teens he said, "You know, it's time we spring cleaned the Temple. It's in a terrible state. Let's get it put right." They spring cleaned the Temple, and while they did so they found in an old bricked-up cupboard, a copy of the Law of Moses. Now such was the state of the nation that it had not been read in years. It is as if when spring cleaning someone came across an old family Bible, which they received at their wedding and they never looked at. They read the Law and Josiah said, "Unless we put things right and spring clean the nation, we're finished."

He began to try to reform the nation but he did it the wrong way. He did it in utter sincerity but being the king he ordered people to be good. You can't change human nature by act of parliament. Jeremiah, who spoke very highly of Josiah, never worked with him because Jeremiah could see that you can make all the new laws you like (these days you might get the parliament to tell everybody they must observe Sunday and all the rest), but you won't have changed the situation. So, Jeremiah saw that Josiah's reform had not worked. I want you to get this message. It is too easy for us to blame the government for the state of the nation and to say that if only they made the proper laws we would put the situation right—don't you believe it. Jeremiah's word is more relevant. Josiah's reform was a failure in the long term and Jeremiah carried on. Because, after Josiah went, then you had these tumbledown kings, especially the two he mentioned—Jehoiakim and Zedekiah.

During that time, they were rushing around joining this alliance and that, trying to save the nation by getting united to stronger nations, and God's word was, "Why don't you come to me? Your greatness came from me. Your power came from me. I made you a stable power among the nations. I wanted to use you among the nations. Why didn't you come back to me? Why do you run to these other nations?"

It was partly that which led me not to vote for going into the Common Market, because I was indifferent to it in the sense that I don't believe the salvation of Britain lies there and we are discovering that. It seems to me sheer hypocrisy to join a Common Market and then cry out, "Buy British." It is ludicrous and it just underlines that our salvation lies elsewhere. Jeremiah had to say this and Jehoiakim took the nation lower down and Zedekiah took it lower down still, and he was just a puppet instead of a king.

During Jeremiah's time there were three decisive battles. The battle of Megiddo was between Egypt and Judah, and in it the young boy king Josiah died. Then the battle of Carchemish between Babylon and Egypt took place. Babylon won. Finally, there was the battle of Jerusalem, between Babylon and Judah, and Babylon won. Or to put it in a word if you forget the details, from being a major nation, Israel was now a shuttlecock between great powers struggling for supremacy, backing the wrong one each time, and being swallowed up in the whole boiling cauldron of political affairs. I believe that is exactly what was happening to Britain in the twentieth century, and so Jeremiah speaks to us.

Finally, let me take the last phrase: "until the captivity".

You know, Jeremiah was at times the only one who believed that disaster would come. Everybody else said, "It will turn out all right." That used to be the typical British attitude: "We'll muddle through. We'll get by. We'll have a bad time for a year and then things will pick up and we'll be all right." That is what they said in Jeremiah's day. Jeremiah had to say, "You will never again be what you were. You can't pick yourselves up any more than the leopard can change his spots." He had the lonely task of preaching doom and gloom when people didn't want to know. They wanted prophets who would cheer them up. They wanted people with good news. They wanted people to say that things weren't as bad as they seemed to be.

So, our Jeremiah preached; the politicians tried to paint it as not so bad, and that was the situation. Isn't it real? Isn't it relevant? I think the thing that strikes me is that Jeremiah had to bear a tragic pain in his heart. He had to watch his own nation go down and down, and I have had that sense increasingly. Have you? I had the sense that my children would never grow up in the Britain I knew. He had to watch his nation go to bits and go to pieces and become a weak nation with no influence.

Furthermore, he not only had to watch that but he had to tell the people it was going to happen before it happened, which made them suffer before the disaster came. More than that, he had to tell them when all the other prophets were saying, "Jeremiah's wrong. It's going to be alright. We'll muddle through." He had to face the loneliness of standing on his own.

God even said, "Jeremiah, don't you marry." A wife and children would be a liability. So, he had no one. Even his own family plotted to kill him at one stage and he was alone with God. In that loneliness with God and in the agony of it when sometimes he blamed God for it all, he cried out to

God in utter honesty. "Why, why God did you push me into this? I loathe the job." In that solitary walk with God he discovered the secret of personal religion. Out of the agony and suffering there came some of the finest scriptures you can find on how to stand alone with God. It is a most moving story and he did it not just for one year or two years or ten years or even twenty, but forty-five, until the captivity.

Then he had to say something that made him appear to be a traitor. He had to say to the nation, "Accept captivity willingly. Go with them, don't fight it." They said, "You're a traitor against your country." He said, "No, it's no use fighting. God says it's no use, so accept it. Go with them." He had to see it through. It is because of this that there is one chapter in Jeremiah that brings you straight to the cross, that is almost a description of our Lord's trial. It is an astonishing thing that Jeremiah understood the sufferings of Jesus.

I finish with this: "to whom the Word of the Lord came". God went on speaking and that is the remarkable thing. Down and down went the nation, but God went on speaking. This is the most important thing in a nation's life. When Josiah was king, when Jehoiakim was king, when Zedekiah was on the throne, when those battles were taking place, what is the most significant feature in the text? "The Word of the Lord came". You find that in Luke, chapter 3—you remember when so and so was Caesar and so and so was governor and so and so was high priest, the Word of the Lord came to John. The most important event that will happen in Britain is that the word of the Lord will come.

Prophecies are already coming from God about this nation. God is still speaking to Britain in words that read almost identically to Jeremiah. There is an astonishing parallel in some of the prophecies that are being given. So, as we study Jeremiah we are going to listen to what God is saying today as well. The fact that God is still speaking means that in his mercy and grace he has not finished with us and he has not wiped us out. He is still waiting for people who will listen and obey the words of Jeremiah, the Word of the Lord.

When I was in Vancouver, one of the most interesting things I saw was James Cunningham's wall. Seven miles long, it was built around the main park there, a beautiful area, a thousand acres of forest with a thousand trees a thousand years old. It is right in the middle of the city but it is almost completely surrounded by the sea. As a teenager, James Cunningham began to build a sea wall around the park to protect it from the ravages of the ocean. Fifty-nine years later he had nearly completed it when he died. Heavy stone by heavy stone he had cemented that wall. It stands about four to five feet high. It was completed by someone else shortly after his death.

What remarkable patience and persistence—keeping it up all those years, devoting his whole life to just one wall. He is remembered for it. Of course, he had encouragement. He had the encouragement of having the whole city backing him and he became quite a well-known character. People encouraged him to go on with the work and to complete it, and the city was paying him to do it. As far as I know, no vandals ever broke down the wall that he had built. So, he could look back with pride and see what he had done and know that it would last long after he had gone.

Jeremiah prophesied for the Lord for about forty-five years. He, too, began in his teens, and year after year he went on, and what he was hoping to do all those years was to build a bulwark around his nation (made up of the two tribes of Judah and Benjamin) that would save it from the ravages of a world in turmoil, of nations all around waiting to attack; a bulwark against the forces of moral as well as military evil.

But the difference between Jeremiah and Cunningham was that not one single person encouraged Jeremiah. Nobody paid him to do it. Furthermore, vandals would break down his work again and again. He would finish up in prison, his life would be in danger, and yet for forty-five years Jeremiah kept at it, which makes him even greater than Cunningham. What kept him at his work of trying to build that bulwark? For most of the time, Jeremiah realised that there would one day be a great storm which would wreck the entire wall and apparently destroy his life's work. What kept him at it?

There was only one thing and, as I have already mentioned, this is what keeps servants of God going when they are experiencing discouragement: *God called*. If you are sure of that, you have no choice. You cannot run away, you cannot get out of the situation, God has called and that is why the call is so important. When I offered for the ministry I went along to the minister of our church and I said, "I want to go into the ministry." He looked at me and his first comment was, "Stay out of the ministry if you possibly can. Go away, don't come back to see me for another eighteen months," which I thought was wrong tactics. After all, don't we want as many people in Christian service as possible? Why discourage?

But I knew later why he had said that to me. I went back after eighteen months and said, "God tells me I must. He's called." Time is a good test of God's call. Jeremiah knew that unless God was in this, he couldn't stick it. He was being called to the most thankless task any servant of God has ever faced, the most discouraging situation any prophet of the Old Testament ever faced; God knew that the call had to be strong, clear, firm, so definite that for forty-five years it would hold Jeremiah at his post. Once God has called, you have to stay with that until he cancels the call or calls you to something else. God never did change Jeremiah's call.

Now we are going to study that call. There are three notes that are sounded. The first is the note of *predestination*. I know that is an offence to our human pride—that God should have free will and have the right to decide what to do with my life. Nevertheless, predestination is a fundamental truth. Those who believe in predestination always have a stronger sense that God can keep them; that God has called them because it was his decision and not theirs. If it were our decision, we would waver, but if it is his decision then we can't.

Next there is the note of *prediction*, and that again is something only God can do, because only he knows the future and only he can unveil it. In Jeremiah's life, the call revealed that God spoke the future, writing history before it happened.

The third note is *protection*: that God is able to deliver those whom he calls from the situations in which they are going to find themselves.

To put it at a deeper theological level, in these three notes right at the beginning Jeremiah was learning of three great attributes of God: his omnipotence, omniscience and omnipresence. Because these were right in the call, they held Jeremiah for forty-five years. Firstly, his omnipotence—God has absolute power and therefore he is able to decide what a person should be before they are even conceived. He is able to form them in their mother's womb. He is able to get them ready for the job. He is able to do this because he is omnipotent. He is in charge of everything.

Secondly, there is God's omniscience: he is able to say what is going to happen precisely because he knows the future and who shapes it. He knows the future as well as we know the past.

Thirdly, there is God's omnipresence. Think of this phrase in the words of the Lord to Jeremiah in the final section of this chapter: "I will be with you" (see 1:19). The Psalmist can say, "If I take the wings of morning and dwell in the uttermost parts of the sea even there your hand shall lead me. I can make my bed in hell, you'll be there." The word is *Sheol*, meaning the world of the departed, which means frankly and in simple terms that someone could commit suicide and still have to face God.

It is only if you have a constant sense that God is all-powerful, all-knowing, and all-present that you are able to face any situation that is likely to occur. If we waver, if we become shaken, it is because we have forgotten one of those three things—we have forgotten that God can predestine and order affairs; we have forgotten that God knows everything, that we don't have to explain anything to him; or we have forgotten that God is right there with us because, 'In him we live and move and have our being.'

First of all, then, divine omnipotence, the note of predestination. Literally, predestination means to decide someone's destiny before they do. The fact is that God has already decided your destiny. Predestination is primarily to *service*, not to salvation. Have you noticed how often in the Bible we are predestined to service? In other words, God has decided what your calling in life should be. How important it is that you find it because you have only one life to live, and you can never have it over again. To think that God has taken the trouble to plan my life, to predestine me beforehand! My earthly father nearly predestined me. He knew I wanted to be a farmer and he was making arrangements for me to have a farm when I was old enough to take it over, and had I taken it over I could have said, "My earthly father predestined me to this," but my heavenly Father had other ideas. He had predestined me to something else and I was born to it.

Prince Charles was born to be King of England. Sometimes you feel sorry for him—he has no choice. He can't say, "Well, I'd rather like to be a plumber." He might play at it for a few months to get experience, but basically, he was born to be a prince. He was predestined, and he has had to accept that predestination. In the same way, a baby boy who was born at the same time as Jeremiah was born to be king. His name was Josiah, and he and Jeremiah grew up together. They were the same age, they played as boys, but at eight years of age Josiah became king; he was predestined. In the same way as Josiah was predestined to be king, Jeremiah was born to be a prophet. Jeremiah was no afterthought, he was a forethought of God's. God doesn't make his plans haphazardly.

God had Jeremiah lined up for the situation long before he was even conceived. "I knew you before you were formed in your mother's womb". The word "knew" there alludes to a very deep relationship. It is the same as Adam knew Eve and she bore a son. I was related to you long before you were related to me; before you were even thought of I was related to you. You know, one of the great discoveries you make when you become a Christian, and get into God's will and into his plan, is that he was related to you long before you were related to him. He was watching over you and he stepped into your life and he was guiding circumstances so surely.

You look back and say, "Predestined according to the foreknowledge of God—hallelujah". To think that it wasn't all me, to think that he was seeking me, to think that he loved me, to think that he planned my life—that is exciting. So, predestination to me is not an intellectual problem, it is an emotional uplift. Therefore, Jeremiah was the result of a planned birth. No biological accident, he was planned, and he was formed. God was shaping him, not just physically but temperamentally within the womb. Before he was even born, God had set his career apart from other careers. When he was born, God appointed him to be a prophet, and now God informs him of the situation. God is simply telling him what has already been decided.

You know, there is no room for two first person singulars in a life. I mean by that the little word "I" which is the keyword of chapter one of Jeremiah. If you underline your Bible, underline the word "I" and you'll be startled at the pattern that emerges. God says, "I knew you, I formed you, I consecrated you, I appointed you," and then comes a little voice saying, "But I am only a youth and I cannot speak." Now there is no room for two first person singulars in a life and Jeremiah is making a somewhat feeble attempt to assert his first person singular against a very strong first person singular. The great *I am* has spoken. God got four "I"'s in to two of Jeremiah's, which is perhaps significant because later you find in chapter twenty Jeremiah says, "God, you are too strong for me. You fought me and you won." I think that is the story of every servant of God. We didn't choose where we would be.

Having been offered a post as a pastor, twice I wrote a letter saying, "No, I will not come." God had to humble me until the third time when I had to say yes. That is the testimony of so many. You try and get your "I" in. There's only room for one "I" in my life. It's either the great "I am" or it is me. Jeremiah was learning this when God called him: which was going to be the "I" who decided his life? I knew you, I formed you, I consecrated, I appointed you—and Jeremiah's first response is: I'm afraid you've got the wrong one Lord. It is almost cheeky when you realise that it is rather like saying: Lord, you really don't know your job—you've got quite the wrong kind of person.

Considering what God was wanting to do with him, I can understand Jeremiah. It is a natural reaction. God wanted him, as it were, to be his spokesman to the United Nations, and remember Jeremiah was eighteen or nineteen years of age: I want you to be my mouthpiece to all the nations; I want to speak through you to the whole world. This teenage boy was not a brash extrovert. He was a shy, sensitive boy who shrank from people, felt things keenly and was easily hurt. His response is: You've got the wrong person, I'm not old enough, I've got no ability in speaking—I'm just not right, Lord. Often that is our first reaction when we are called by God to do something—I'm not the right one; here am I, send *him*. We try to put the "I" back in and we don't get very far.

God is so gracious that he will listen to an argument and he loves people to argue with him. They mean business. He would far rather you argue with him than you didn't answer him. But I tell you this: you will never win an argument with God. But he loves people who have wrestled with him. He loved Jacob because he had wrestled him and had said, "I'm not going to let you go until you bless me." He loved Moses because Moses tried this and he argued and argued until finally God won the argument. Gideon tried the same thing. You try arguing with God, but at least you are talking to God—and he will win the argument.

There are two things about Jeremiah's reply, which I want you to notice. First, he seems to have forgotten who he was speaking to. How could he? But God did listen and did reply.

The other thing is to ask why Jeremiah said it. Was he saying it in order to try and help God or in order to protect himself? Do you think he was genuinely saying: "Now God, I really want you to have a spokesman. I really want you to speak. I really want you to speak to the world. I really want to help you, so I am just going to suggest someone even better than me"? Do you think he was really doing that, or do you not think this was an excuse—anyone but me? In other words, was it genuine weakness or was it an unwillingness to be used? There is no doubt in my mind from God's reply that it was unwillingness. Jeremiah wasn't really concerned about God's work being done efficiently by a more able person. He was concerned that he should not get involved. When we say, "Oh, there's somebody else I'm sure who can do this better than I can," we ought to ask: am I saying that because I really want the work done well or am I saying it because I'm a bit afraid of being involved, especially publicly? That is what really lay behind Jeremiah's excuse. I deduce that from what God said. God wasn't inviting him to do that job and wasn't discussing it with him. He was *telling* him. "You must go to everyone I send you to and say whatever I command you." God informs people, he doesn't invite them. He tells them: this is what you shall do; this is where you shall go. You have no choice but to rebel or submit; you don't discuss. So, in a very firm but gentle way God boosts Jeremiah's morale by being firm.

Sensitively, God sees right through to the heart of Jeremiah and says, "Do not be afraid of them" or, literally, don't be afraid of their faces—which is very telling. It is people's faces we are afraid of, never their backs. Have you noticed that? This is why people much prefer to sit in straight rows, just looking at the backs of heads in front. That is why sometimes when I have asked someone to take part in a service they say, "I could never face all those faces." It is people's faces that we can get afraid of and the expression on them, how they look at us, because that may reveal how they are thinking. Frankly, if I took too much notice of people's faces I would have been out of the ministry a long time ago, and I guess some left the congregation because they took notice of mine!

You know, three hundred and sixty-six times in the Bible God has to say to someone, "Don't be afraid"—because fear paralyses action. Service for the Lord is often crippled by fear, shyness or self-consciousness. We are afraid that if we start praying in that prayer meeting we will choke up or forget what we are going to say. There can be fear of people and what they might think of our prayer. They might think it's a very foolish prayer. So, we are afraid of people and God has to deal with this. He could not use someone who is afraid of people. If you are afraid of people you will never make it, so don't be afraid, get rid of that fear.

It was a healthy fear because the career of a prophet was not a safe one. No insurance agent would have given a life policy to a prophet in those days. Too many of them had come unstuck and had been persecuted—threatened or killed—so it is no wonder Jeremiah was afraid. Now God touched Jeremiah's mouth. Jeremiah must have felt a physical sensation on his lips at that point. You know, you can feel physically the touch of God. Some have told me that they have had that. Jeremiah felt a finger on his lips. You know, when somebody puts a finger on your lips it means first: be quiet, shut up, stop it. Jeremiah stop talking! "I have put my words in your mouth." So who says you can't speak?

The one part of Jeremiah that God wanted to have was his mouth and it is the hardest thing to get hold of in anyone. It is the easiest thing to get hold of for evil purposes because we are born in the kingdom of Satan and the tongue (says James) is set on fire by hell. It is like a spark that can start a prairie fire, and in Canada that really does come home to you. Canadian forest fires are started with one spark, one little flame, and James says, "Your tongue is like one flame, one little spark," and it can do so much, for good or evil. You know, God finds this is the hardest thing in people to get hold of: their tongue.

But when God really gets hold of people he shows it by getting hold of their tongue because that is the hardest thing to control. It is like a little rudder that can move a whole big ship around. It is like a little bit in a horse's mouth that can turn a great big horse around. It has such power for good or evil. The power of your tongue depends on the power of your position. Think of Adolf Hitler. When he was a corporal in the First World War, the only power his tongue had was the power of a corporal. So, he could push privates around and he did, but he couldn't push nations around. But as he came to power, his tongue got more power. As he rose in position, his tongue became more powerful. At first this was not all for bad. For instance, it was that tongue that ordered the first Volkswagen car. It was that tongue that ordered the first motorways to be built in Europe. We still drive on motorways in Volkswagens and we never think of the man whose tongue made those possible. But his tongue gained greater power for evil too, until his tongue would plunge Europe into disaster and cause suffering throughout the world and cause the deaths of thirty million people. It depends on your position.

Jeremiah is saying, "I'm but a youth." Yes, he was. If he had spoken just as a youth then he would have had no power whatsoever. His words would have fallen on deaf ears—on nothing. But when God puts his words in your mouth, that will not just give you a fluency, an ability to speak, an eloquence—that will give you power. God would use his words spoken through Jeremiah, setting him over nations. God is letting Jeremiah know that those words of God have power in them—to pluck up, to destroy, to break down, to build, to plant. Jeremiah will have power in his mouth. He will be the most powerful man in the world—a teenager.

Notice that the power would be more destructive than constructive. If you look into your Bible you find that there are four destructive things to two constructive ones. To pluck up, break down, destroy, and overthrow are destructive; to build and to plant are constructive.

Remember that God is so powerful that he just has to say, "Let there be," and there is. It was with his word that he created the world, and it is with his word that one day he will destroy the world in fire. He can do both. He can break a man's life; he can make a man's life. He can pull a man down from the top of society. He can lift a man up from the bottom. His word can do both. Jeremiah, a teenager with God's words on his lips, could smash kingdoms and build them up; he could change the atlas and write history with his words.

Notice which comes first. God has to destroy before he can construct. Let me give you two examples. I was talking to a gardener and he had been very busy. He had got a barrel full of couch grass, weeds and dandelions from one square yard of soil. He had pulled all that out, working for hours to pluck up, and then he was going to burn them and destroy them. Why? Because he wanted to plant something beautiful there.

A few days later, I walked along and paused to watch something that was happening in town. I don't know why it is so fascinating to see buildings pulled down, but there were cranes with their great weights smashing into brick walls, and things tumbling down in a great heap of rubble. Why the demolition? It was so that they might build something new there.

God's Word has to smash before it can heal. It has to humble before it can exalt. It has to clear the site before it can build. How can God build a new life in your life when there is so much rubbish there already? How can he plant beautiful fruit of the Spirit in your life if there are ugly things already growing there? Christ talked about sowing seed among the weeds and thorns and thistles. You will have to get those out if the seed is to grow.

So, God's Word is destructive as well as constructive. It has to break before it makes. It has to get rid of other things before it can produce something new. Jeremiah was given this double-edged weapon of God's Word. Jeremiah would have to break down a lot and pluck a lot up and overthrow a lot and destroy a lot before God would build and plant. But notice that there is a little gleam of hope there that God intends to build and plant.

Well, that is the note of predestination. God has freewill and he is free to choose any one of us to go anywhere, to say anything, to do anything. The only choices we have are to rebel or submit; we have no other. He is God and he made us for himself.

Now the second note, more briefly, is prediction or divine omniscience. Though it follows verses four to ten, it is obviously on another occasion and it is equally obviously in the middle of the night, though Jeremiah is awake. Now for the first time God is going to teach him some lessons in prophecy and he will put Jeremiah in the kindergarten where you can learn simply. Now in a kindergarten, if you are going to teach little children things, here are three ways in which you may teach (among others).

Firstly, use pictures. If you go into any kindergarten or Sunday School you will see the walls plastered with pictures. Pictures are good for beginners. Secondly, use rhyming words: cat, mat, sat, and all the rest of it. You will find that here God uses rhyming words in Jeremiah's kindergarten lesson. Thirdly, if you are going to teach children you have got to start with things with which they are familiar, things that they see every day, so that you can draw lessons from them. So, you have "show and tell" time and they bring all kinds of things from home and show you. You use that task to teach them something new. I am not trying to teach teachers their job, I am drawing out what God does here. He is a great teacher.

So, Jeremiah's first lesson consisted of two pictures—of things he had seen many times before and was thoroughly familiar with, but now a lesson is drawn from them and with rather clever rhyming words that are going to bring out the real lesson that God wants. The first is a budding rod, an almond tree. I am sure you have seen an almond tree and I guess you know it is the first tree to blossom in the spring. The blossom comes long before the leaves and so it is the first sign that nature is waking up again after a long winter. It is exciting to see the pink and white blossom come out—a real tonic. In the Middle East it is therefore called the "Waker tree", so they say, "Look, the waker tree is blossoming, spring is waking up." God said, "Jeremiah what do you see?" Well, he said, "I see an almond tree." Maybe he was looking out of the window of his bedroom and saw an almond tree outside, and he saw the blossom coming. With a very skilful play on words, by just changing one letter, God changed the word from "waker" to "waking": Jeremiah, I'm waking up; I'm stirring; I'm moving.

Here was an object lesson which Jeremiah would never forget: that God was alert, that God was stirring himself, that God knew what was going on, that he was watching, and that he was going to act now. Something was going to happen— that almond tree had looked dead for months through the winter. For seventy years there had been no prophet. For seventy years Judah had heard no word from God. They had gone through a cold winter spiritually. God is now letting them know that the winter is over, something is happening. After all, it is the same God in nature and in history, so you can draw the parallel often, as Jesus did. Consider the lilies and you learn something. Consider the almond tree. God is waking up and there is springtime, life, stirring.

But there is just one little note in this. Jeremiah saw a rod. It means a branch of the right size and shape for applying corporal punishment, as we might talk about a switch or a birch. There is already a slightly threatening note in the picture, that it is a rod, not just a branch; that God is waking up but he is waking up in the form of a whip, a rod. That must have made Jeremiah think twice.

The second picture changes from the outdoor to the indoor and maybe Jeremiah in the one-room home in which he would have lived was now looking not out of the window but over to the fireplace where there were the dying embers of the fire of the day before, and sitting on the embers was a big boiling pot, which would have seemed like a cauldron, precariously balanced on the burning charcoal. He seemed to see that the water was bubbling and boiling—steam was coming up.

Suddenly the whole thing lurched as maybe a piece of charcoal burnt away underneath, and it spilled. In a home of those days that was a terrifying thing to happen. You know how careful we are today with safety in the kitchen. It is the most dangerous place. But any missionary in any more primitive society will tell you, indeed any nurse will tell you that you get hundreds of people coming with scalds, burns, and if a little child is in the way of that cauldron it can be fatal. That is what Jeremiah saw, and immediately with his young heart he felt terrified and he reacted strongly; a boiling cauldron tipping over towards the south. What do you see, Jeremiah? I see a cauldron and it is tipping over from the north and there is scalding water coming straight at us. God says, "Now I will tell you what this means. I've told you I'm waking up but I'm pulling from the north enemies of Judah; they are going to boil over into your country. They represent my hot anger with your people."

Who were these dangerous people who were likely to

come? We know from history who they were. Away up north of the Black Sea there was a group of tribes called the Scythians, and suddenly they were on the rampage. Their relatives were the Goths and the Vandals. Isn't it interesting that one of those names has come right through to today — vandals; vandalism? The Vandals were stirring up in the north and they were laying waste to countries. They were invading their neighbours and burning towns down. They were raping women, they were destroying everything they could, just for enjoyment, for the sake of destroying.

That is why we speak of vandals still to this day. Jeremiah would know about those Vandals, but he would say, "Oh, but they are north of the Black Sea." They were beginning to spread further south and beginning to frighten the Middle East because they were such vandals. God says, "It's tipping over you." The fact is that those Vandals got as far south as Judah, even to Egypt, and God said, "The cauldron's boiling over and it's me who's allowing them to come." If you think God is not a God of war you will have to think again. God says, "I am bringing those Vandals upon you," as I firmly believe the increase in violence and vandalism in this country is God's doing. Sometimes he has to bring such things to bring us up with a jerk.

We say, "Oh, it couldn't happen here. This is peaceful England." Don't you believe it. You mark my words, violence is going to spread in this land. Vandalism is going to increase. God said to Jeremiah, "I'm calling them. I bring them." Why? There are three answers. One, because they have forsaken their God; two, because they have gone after other gods; three, because they now worship the work of their own hands. Do you think none of those three apply to Britain today?

It would seem to be an appropriate indictment of our nation. "You have forsaken me after all I have done for you as a nation." You know what he had done for Israel. Do you realise what he has done for this land? Do you realise that our hospitals and schools were begun by God's people? Do you realise that most of our social welfare was inspired by God through his people? God has done so much for our green and pleasant land. But, as with Israel, we have forsaken him. Less than two percent of the people of this country really know and love God today.

Less than five percent go to church at Christmas and Easter, and even then they have to be drawn by a special nativity play or such like. You have forsaken your God.... That is not all. It would be bad enough if people had just left him but they have turned to other gods. Consider the growth of interest in other religions. British people are sold on yoga, Zen Buddhism, and I don't know what else. British people are taking part in occult and black magic, all kinds of religion, all kinds of superstition, reading horoscopes. As if that were not enough, in reality people are worshipping themselves, because they are worshipping what they make. People are saying: I'm god; I can do this; I can make this; we can get ourselves out of our own mess.

I was debating humanism with a university professor. He gave a much more brilliant talk than I could give, very compelling, very convincing, but his final sentence was, "I believe that man can solve his own problems, and if he can't, then God help us." The whole lecture theatre burst into laughter and applause, and he had given me my text to carry on! But, you see, he was simply stating what most of our politicians believe. They must believe themselves capable of getting us out of the mess we are in. Worshipping the work of our own hands, whether it be our scientific works, our works of art, our works of politics, whatever our works may be, goes with believing that we can solve it all—and we do indeed worship the work of our own hands. That is why God brings vandalism—because people needed to get back to him.

Now by this stage Jeremiah listening must have been in quite a state. Dismay was on his face and his jaw must have dropped—this was what he was to tell to the nations. God noticed the look on his face and said, "Now Jeremiah don't you be dismayed." That tells me what he was looking like. Jeremiah was to go and tell others. If he felt a little uncertain when the call came, how do you think he felt now that he knew what he had to say? He must have felt exactly like the little boy Samuel during the night. He too had a call from God so real that he thought it was Eli in the next room. He said, "Alright Lord, here am I. Speak, your servant hears." Now this is where we always stop in our sermons, in our readings. We don't go on to read, but the next thing is: "Samuel you've got to go and tell the nation and tell Eli; you've got to tell them these terrible things." When Samuel woke up in the morning, he couldn't bring himself to tell Eli what he had been told. It was so terrible, and Eli said, "Now come on Samuel. You've got to tell me what the Lord told you. You've got to tell me," and the boy had to get it out.

Now, having received this in the night, Jeremiah gets up in the morning and God says, "Now get dressed and go and tell them."

"Tell them this?" You know, it's nice being a messenger of good news, but to take bad news to people—who likes to do that? To take bad news to people who won't believe it or don't want it, to people who hate you for telling them what's true—that is even worse.

So, we come to the third and last note—protection, divine omnipresence. "Jeremiah, if you are dismayed over this, I will dismay you in front of them. The very thing you fear will come to pass. You'll be a fool."

Here is a profound thing, if we are afraid of people, God

will make us fools in front of them. Jesus said, "Whoever is ashamed of me, I'll be ashamed of him." God can be ashamed of people, and if he is ashamed of people he will leave them to be a fool, to be a disgrace, to look like a clown in the eyes of the world, and those who go dismayed will be dismayed by God. In this way, God seeks to pull Jeremiah together firmly, in a tough way, to get his morale together, like every army trainer has got to be tough. God is saying: now pull yourself together Jeremiah; don't look so dismayed; you'll look a fool; I'll make you a fool in front of them if you're dismayed; don't you fear them, you fear me.

Then, more tenderly, God says, "I can make you a fortress." Jeremiah must choose. He will either be a fool or a fortress, and God could make him both or either. If you are ashamed, embarrassed, afraid or dismayed, he will make you a fool in front of them. But if you will go and tell them what God has told you, if you will go where he sends you, and without fear will tell them the truth, then he will make you like a fortified city with iron pillars and bronze walls. Now notice the honesty of God. He didn't say, "I will keep you out of trouble," he said: I will protect you in it. They will attack you; the princes will be against you; the priests will be against you; even your own family will be against you; don't worry, you will have walls of bronze around you because I will be with you.

One plus God is always a majority, "I am with you"—he offers protection. Jeremiah had to learn that God can be ashamed of his servants. He also had to learn that God will be alongside his servants to deliver them. He will either disgrace us in other people's eyes, if we do not do what he tells us, or he will deliver us if we do. The fact is, God kept his word even though Jeremiah was put in prison, even though his life was threatened, even though he was thrown into pits, even though he was pushed around. The fact is that when the nation was taken off in chains, Jeremiah was left free. God kept his word to Jeremiah: "I will deliver you. You will never be made to look a fool." The fact is that Jeremiah comes down to us today, not as a fool but a fortress; as a great hero.

Are you thinking, "Well that's all very interesting, I've learned a few things by the way but what has this got to do with me? Thank God he didn't call me to be a prophet." Did he not? Way back in the earliest pages of the Old Testament, somebody came to Moses and said, "Moses, there are two people at the other side of the camp prophesying but you're the official prophet." Moses said, "I don't mind those two prophesying. I wish that all God's people were prophets." That wish of Moses was taken up centuries later by a prophet called Joel who said, "It will come to pass in the last days, says God, that I will pour out my Spirit on all flesh". Regardless of age, sex or class, they will prophesy. In the New Testament, Peter stood up and said that this was that. God can speak through his people. Paul was later to write to the people of God at Corinth, "I would that you all spoke in tongues and even more that you all prophesied." I would that God had our mouths—I wish we would all give them to him. Even tongues, that would be a step forward because then he would have your mouth, but it doesn't help anybody else. It edifies you, but it is in a language that others don't understand. So, even more, I want you to go on so that you become the mouthpiece of God, so that you can speak the Word of God to people in their own language and thus become a mouthpiece for God.

You may have heard me teach on the priesthood of all believers, but I also believe in the *prophethood* of all believers. God now does not want a people like Israel in which only forty were prophets. He wants a new people, his church, in which all the Lord's people are prophets, and he has my mouth and your mouth, so that at any time if he tells you to go somewhere and to say something, he can use you. Therefore, Jeremiah's call is most relevant. You must not with human impetuosity rush off and think you have God's word when you haven't, but when God unmistakably tells you, "I want you to go and say..." then you have no choice except to rebel or submit. We are all called to be prophets. We shall be made fools in the sight of the world unless we grasp firmly that God predestined us to such a ministry—that God predicts what will happen, that God protects those who go out in his name and are faithful.

READ JEREMIAH 2:1–3:5

We come now to Jeremiah's very first sermon. As you read it, imagine a young man in his late teens preaching for the very first time, not inside a church or a temple to a sympathetic congregation but in the streets to a very unsympathetic crowd who did not want to know. What a way to begin! Something of the power of God's Word as it must have come from that young man comes through the very reading of this passage, and as we study it more deeply God will speak to us because this is his Word not just to ancient Israel but to modern Britain. Just over two hundred and fifty years ago in this country an Anglican clergyman was forbidden by bishop after bishop to preach in his diocese. He finally arrived in the diocese of Bristol and the bishop of Bristol said to him, "Enthusiasm is a very horrid thing sir, a very horrid thing." Enthusiasm was the eighteenth-century word for emotionalism.

So, the bishop would have no emotion in his diocese. The clergyman, The Reverend John Wesley, did not know what to do, so he sought the Lord and the Lord told him to go and preach in the streets of Bristol. He had never preached outside an ecclesiastical building. His soul was horrified. He thought it was indecent, undignified, not worshipful to stand up in a dirty street with the miners' dirty faces looking at him and preach the pure Word of God. But he said in his diary, "At four in the afternoon, I submitted to be more vile, and proclaimed in the highways the glad tidings of salvation, speaking from a little eminence in a ground adjoining the city, to about 3,000 people ...," — in the Bristol streets; that was the beginning of the revival of the eighteenth century.

Just over two thousand five hundred years ago, the young man Jeremiah was called of God to preach. Unlike John Wesley he had had no theological training, no experience of preaching to sympathetic congregations within church buildings. When Jeremiah was in his late teens, God said to him, "Jeremiah, I've called you, now go and preach, and you will have to do it in the streets. Just get out and preach. Whether you get a congregation or not, just get out and preach." Jeremiah went out to preach this, his first sermon. Its theme was a pretty stark one. There are only one or two little rays of hope here.

Jeremiah was a doom and gloom man, no question about that, and increasingly people who are doom and gloom men are going to be unpopular. There is now a wave of reaction against this. Lord Hailsham, being interviewed by a journalist, was asked what he thought of Britain now. The journalist quoted to him something he had said many years earlier about Britain, the glory of her future, and strength of character, etc. The journalist said, "Would you stand by those words now?"

He said, "No, I would not, we are now living in the city of destruction." The interviewer said, "I regard that as hyperbole, exaggeration."

Lord Hailsham replied, "That is what they said to Noah."

Jeremiah was called to be a doom and gloom prophet, not because this was a hopeless situation but because the only way through it was to help people to realise the reality of what was going on. That involved a pessimistic message, and this is almost a tirade. It is certainly an indictment, but it is an indictment by God. God says, "I will contend with you" — which is the legal term for "I am the prosecution and

I put you in the dock"—and I contend against you and I will contend against your children and your children's children. I will contend with you until you realise the truth, until you can see what is happening to your nation clearly.

So that is what made Jeremiah go out and speak as the prosecution. The whole sermon was full of questions asked by God of the people, that they might answer. Here are some of them: What wrong did your fathers find in me that they went far from me? Has a nation anywhere changed its gods as you have done? Is Israel a slave [or a born slave]? Then why have you become a prey to other nations? Have you not brought this upon yourself when you forsook God, who led you in the way? What do you gain by going to Egypt? What do you gain by getting into a common market with Assyria? What do you gain? How have you become degenerate and become a wild vine? How can you say, "I am not defiled"? Why do you complain against me? Where are your gods that you made for yourself?

Have I been a wilderness to Israel or a land of thick darkness? Why then do my people say, "We are free, we will come no more to thee." You have played the harlot with many lovers, would you return to me? Question, question, question —this is very direct preaching. It is asking fundamental questions of the people. Then, also, God, through Jeremiah, quotes the people's answers. Here are some of the sorts of things they were saying to him.

You say, "I will not serve." You say, "I am not defiled." You say, "It is hopeless." You say, "We are free." You say, "I am innocent." You say, "I have not sinned." You say, you say, you say—and in the contrast between the questions which God poses, demanding an answer, and his quotations from their lips, you have got the feel of a tremendous dialogue, of God saying: Why have you done this to me? Is the fault in me? Can you point to anything in me that has deserved this? Have I broken any promise I made to you? Have I done anything that should make you talk like this? Do you get the urgent feel? This is not just a polite sermon—"My text is blah, blah, blah. Amen." This is a direct encounter between God and men, through his servant.

First of all, he talks of a holy honeymoon. That is where God starts—with nostalgia.

It was God who thought of marriage. Indeed, he thought of it because it would help us to understand him, so he said, "Let us make man in our own image." So, he made man in his own image, male and female he made them. There is something very profound in the relationship between a man and a woman that should be a picture for us always of the relationship between God and his people. It is in the Old Testament—Israel is always regarded as the bride of God. In the New Testament, the Church is the same. From heaven he came and sought her to be his holy bride. The sexual relationship is a perfect picture of the spiritual one—that is why this metaphor runs right through the Bible, and why the Song of Songs is in the middle of the Bible, a song which began as an erotic love song between a young boy and a young girl but has become a lovely expression of our love for the Lord.

So, the two are very close, and God not only thought of marriage but he thought of honeymoons. When he wanted to marry this nation, this people Israel, he made sure that they got a honeymoon with him away from everywhere else—in a land not sown, where they would not be distracted with a lot of agriculture or industry; he took them out into a land where he could have her to himself and she could have him to herself and they could be alone for their honeymoon. But then they got into the Promised Land and they had to get down to digging the fields and many distractions came. It is as though God were saying: Can't you remember the honeymoon? Don't you remember how devoted you were to me, how devoted I was to you? You had no one else. You loved me so much in those days you were willing to go with me into a desert, a land not sown where there was nothing for you but me. You were willing to go anywhere with me in those days. Now you won't even cross the street. Do you get a glimpse of God's heart here? Do you get the feel of the frustration? God says, "You were really devoted," and the word he uses there is translated as "devoted" from the Hebrew word *hesed,* which means utter loyalty or true love or troth. It is a word that is still used in marriage services meaning not just I love you but I am loyal to you—that was the kind of devotion.

You followed me wherever I led you when the pillar of fire moved by night or the pillar of cloud by day. You followed me into a land not sown. You would have gone anywhere for me. You didn't ask, "What do I get out of this?" You didn't ask if it was going to be a pleasant land. You just went with me into the wilderness, and because of that you were very precious to me and I protected you and anybody who dared to touch you I really let them have it; I was jealous for you. You were the first fruits of my harvest and anybody who tried to eat you I dealt with them. Now what does it mean—the first fruits of my harvest?

Here we touch on the deepest point of all, because this was God's great purpose when he made the world, when he put people in it: he simply wanted a big family of children who would love him and love each other—that was his harvest. That is why he planted the earth in space; that is why he planted people on the earth. That is why he took the dust of the earth and made Adam—that is why he did it. So, the first fruits of his harvest, the first bit of the human race he really got to himself, was this little nation of slaves.

It was the first fruits, the beginning of a family of every

tribe and kindred and tongue. This was his first family and: I brought you out and you loved me and for the first time in history I had a family, the first fruits of my harvest on earth. Now you have forsaken me.

Now all this opens up God's heart and helps us to see things from his point of view. Often we are so self-centred that we think primarily that if we get away from God we are going to suffer and we think of what might go wrong in our life. But think of it from God's point of view. What does he lose when you are away from him? That is the way to look at it. So, God talks about this holy honeymoon that they had. He is saying something profound about Israel which is true of the world, and that is we are not a rising people, we are a fallen people. The title of Darwin's book *The Ascent of Man* is the exact opposite of man. The Bible talks of man descending, and if you claim to me that man has descended from the apes, if you mean by that that he is morally lower than the apes, I agree with you. We are not a rising race whether it is what Charles Darwin or anyone else says, whoever says we are on the up and up and up, and we are getting better and better, is totally contradicting the Bible. We are fallen; we have come down from something ideal—all of us have; the whole human race has. In the Garden of Eden there was perfect fellowship with God, perfect conditions for man's happiness—the perfect environment, everything was very good. We have fallen from that, we have not risen from our origins; we have fallen from them. Israel, too, has not risen over the years; she has fallen from her origins, from the honeymoon with God in the wilderness.

That is the first note that has been struck: remember the height from which you have fallen. In the next section (vv. 4–13), God accuses them of bad business. I think this would appeal to the Jewish hearers. The key phrase is "no profit" — you have done a bad deal. Jeremiah taught: You once were on a holy honeymoon, now you are in a bad business and you are trading in something good for something far poorer. You are trading in a living spring for broken cisterns. Have you ever heard of this happening anywhere in the world: a nation trading in a God who helped them for gods who couldn't help them? Well, I am afraid we have heard of it because Britain is doing it this very moment and it is bad business. There is no profit in it, far from it. There is a loss in your account, but let us see how he works this out. He says, first of all: you have become distracted from me. You see, when they were in the wilderness there were no other distractions. There were no amusements, there was no agriculture and no industry. They got their bread direct from the Lord. They went out each day with baskets and collected what came straight from heaven. They got their water from the rock in the same way. They got everything straight from God. There was nothing else and so they were not distracted. God says, "I brought you through a land where no man dwells," and it is true. In 1967, the Egyptian army perished in just three days for lack of food and water. Consider how God brought two and a half million people through that area and kept them, and in him they found all their needs met. So that was the profit to them from following God. All their needs were met and God kept his word and brought them through.

So, they came into a new land where there was cultivated countryside, and they were now distracted with agriculture. They came into a land of sophisticated society. There were now entertainments and things that could fill their time. They came into a land of perverted practices, which appealed immediately to the lower side of their nature, things they had not seen in the wilderness. Above all, they came into a land of rotten religion, of which we will say more later, and they were distracted. Suddenly, there were too many things to look at, too many things to do. So they stopped saying,

"Where is the Lord?" The people, the priests, the princes, the prophets, the rulers and the politicians forgot to say, "Where is the Lord?" Do you know, the only thing you need to do to get away from God is to forget? You don't need to do anything terribly bad. You just need to be distracted. You just need to have so many things to do that you never ask, "Where is the Lord in all this?"

Therefore, their food came to them less directly from him and so they thought more of the secondary resource from which it came. Just as nowadays there are many children who never even dream that milk comes from cows. They just think of it as coming from the supermarket and not coming from the cow. We think more of the supermarket than we do of the God who gave the food in it, because it comes in a second-hand way. It is like those South Sea islanders who used to worship the moon, and had you asked them why they did so they would have said, "Well it's like this: the sun only shines in the daytime when it's light. The moon shines at night when it's dark"—and they had no idea that the light of the moon comes from the sun, Is that a picture of what's happening? You entered this land and you got distracted. No longer did your bread come down from heaven, it grew up in the earth, and you got distracted. So, we have become distracted with our bank when it is God who gives us the money. We have become distracted with our supermarket when it is God who gives the bread. We are so far removed now from the direct source of our livelihood that we are so much more distracted by the intermediate sources and we just never stop to say, "Where is God in all this? Where is the Lord?" The result is therefore that when you are distracted you are defrauded. That happens in business—if someone is going to con you, he has to distract you. Have you noticed? If he is selling you a second-hand car he won't show you the rusty bits. He will say, "Get in and feel the seat," and he distracts you so that he can defraud you.

God is saying: you have been so distracted you have been defrauded. Take your water supply, he says, and this is a marvellous example. Now a water supply in Israel is all-important to life. Water is the fundamental source of life because the hills are limestone and the water goes straight through them. Therefore, water is a key issue: irrigation, storing water. Now happy are you if on your land you have a living spring that never runs dry. There is such a one on Mount Carmel which I have seen — a spring that has never in all the centuries ever run dry. It was the one Elijah used, and he was able to use it after three and a half years of drought. Think of a spring on your land where you can go and draw water all the time, and the more you take out, the more comes back, and it is still there, a living spring.

The alternative is to hollow out a cistern — to dig a hole in the rock, line it with clay, and store water, and you see many such pits in Israel. Of course, you have to fill it, and when you take water out it doesn't fill up again itself. You have to get more to put in, and there is one serious drawback with a cistern there: it is an earthquake area and there are tremors, and therefore most cisterns very quickly develop hairline cracks. There is a slight movement on the earth, the cistern is leaking, and your water is going out all the time. So you have got to keep filling it up, and it is a race to keep it full.

Jeremiah is saying: "Look what you've traded. You've traded in God, a living spring constantly supplying your need, always welling up so that the more you draw from him the more there is to draw, and you've traded him in for broken cisterns that you have made yourself that you have got to fill up, that leak like anything and go stagnant. That is bad business. I contend with you and your children until you realise it. Have you made a profit on this deal? "

God is saying not only that it is a sinful thing to have done, it is a silly thing to have done. It is a surprising thing to have done. You read the early history of the human race—there isn't a case of a nation that switches gods, especially when it is from the real God to a god who is not real.

To sum it up, Jeremiah says, "You've left God and gone after worthless things and therefore become worthless. You've gone after bubbles and you've become hollow"—that is the meaning of the Hebrew. If you go for unreal things, you become an unreal person. If you pin your hopes on hollow things—broken cisterns, just bubbles, vanity, emptiness—you become an empty, worthless, hollow, vain person yourself. I don't think I need to labour this point because you can see it happening all around you—people turning away from God as a living spring who could supply all their needs and go on supplying them, and putting their hope in their bank balance—that is a bit of a broken cistern, isn't it? It is leaking like mad.

Putting their hopes in their possessions, they have to keep renewing them and buying more, putting their hopes in some worldly pleasure, and you have to keep putting more into it to get anything out of it, and so we go on. It is a broken cistern and not a reliable source of meeting your need. It is a bad business. Says God: "My people, you see, have committed two evils. The other nations are guilty of having idols but they are not guilty of having turned from the truth to idols. My people have done two bad things: they have turned from me and they have turned to the other things that the other nations already had."

Do you know what the word "worship" means? It means "worthship". We are saying: "God, you really are worth worshipping. You are worth coming to. This is good business, to turn from these broken cisterns to a living spring."

Now let us look at the third note. This comes even closer to home. Jeremiah is saying: You have become a national non-entity. I don't know whether to laugh or cry when I watch the Last Night of the Proms. Have you ever seen a greater farce, a greater spoof, a greater send-up of patriotism than those flags waving, and the singing: "Land of hope and glory ... Britons never, never, never shall be slaves." It is such a farce because it belongs to an era when we were somebody. Those songs came out of a day when God gave us stewardship of a large part of the world but now it is as hollow as a broken cistern. That is what happened to Israel. They had been a nation to be reckoned with, a power in the Middle East. They had been a key power under David. They had reached the heights of peace and prosperity and power, but look at what happened to them next. They were a national nonentity. They were slaves. They were being pushed around by other nations, and God says through Jeremiah, "Were you bought as a slave?"—or the other way to become a slave: "Were you born to a slave?" You were either bought or you were born into slavery. God says through Jeremiah, "Why is it you are being pushed around. Why are you becoming prey to the nations? Why do they despise you now?" Some years ago, the Africans coined the following phrase about Britain: "a toothless lion". You don't respect a toothless lion—no longer to be reckoned with, second-rate, other people's property to be pushed around.

Now here is a vivid picture. He says, "You've been in the lion's mouth." If you go to the Assyrian room in the British Museum in London, you will see the stone monuments which show the lion of Assyria. This was the mighty symbol of this mighty nation. Assyria had already devastated ten tribes of Israel. Ninety per cent of their land was now lying waste and empty.

Interestingly enough, it was now being inhabited by real lions because, now that there were no people to keep them down, they were over-breeding in the Jordan jungle, coming up into the former country of Israel and, literally, if you went through that country you came face-to-face with real lions—not just Assyrians pretending to be lions. So, Jeremiah points out that ninety per cent of the country has been in the lion's mouth. His message means: now that you are out of the lion's mouth you are just climbing on the tiger's back. That is not his phrase, it is mine. He means: you are now trying to make friends with the powers that are trying to devastate you, and you think that's where your security lies. It is an extraordinary situation, but what strange things happen in alliances between the nations.

So, Jeremiah says, "You have never asked why. Have you not brought this upon yourself?" That is the answer and he says: it's no use going to Assyria and Egypt, they won't help you out. It is not enough for a Prime Minister or anyone else to be seen in church and read the lesson. What we need are people who will apply the Word of God to their politics, to the questions they ask of a situation, and the solutions they seek, and what Jeremiah is accusing these people of is ignoring principle and simply living by expediency; of never asking the deeper question "Why?" and only asking the shallow question "How?" If you don't let God lead you as a nation, then other nations will sooner or later lead you.

The picture changes from a bride, from a businessman, from a slave, to a lover. The picture changes and has strong sexual overtones. The reason for this is not just what I wrote earlier. The reason is that the rotten religion of Israel was deified sex. It was a fertility cult. "Nature is beautiful, nudity is natural"—this was the kind of thinking in the rotten religion of Canaan. When they came in they were not only distracted by these things, they became part of them. So, these overtones are due to the fact they had committed a double prostitution with God and with people, for the two things went together, and worship became an orgy.

So here are some very blunt things. I hope they won't offend some sensitive spirits but Jeremiah doesn't mind using very earthy pictures to try and show them what is happening. He first of all takes a picture from the plant world and he says, "I sowed you as a choice vine." The word he uses refers to a vine which is a beautiful, quality red grape used for the best wine. What came up? Wild vines, weeds. What do you do when weeds come up? You pull them out of the land, don't you? You dig them up. No point in leaving them there, they will pollute the land further. "What's gone wrong?" asks God. "You've become degenerate. It is not just how you behave, there is something inside you that has gone wrong. You have degenerated in nature—a choice vine has become a wild one." How did that happen? You have not only become degenerate, you have become defiled. Here the cruellest picture he uses comes in. He says, "You are like a young she-camel in season or a wild ass in heat."

Now let me bring that home. We used to have a lovely little dog. She was normally well-behaved, obedient, cooperative and friendly. Indeed, for most of the year she preferred us to other dogs and came when we called, telling them to go away and snapping at them. But at certain times of the year there was a total change in that picture. She behaved as if she was not our dog. She was at the door wanting to get out. She would go into the garden just as soon as she thought we were not watching—how she got out we didn't know, she was off and we would find her with a lot of other dogs. She was in season.

God was saying: you seem to have got into a sinful season; you are like a young she-camel. You seem to have driven away from me and suddenly you are not my children any more. You are running after anyone. You are like a she-ass sniffing the wind for the scent of a male. He doesn't have to come looking for you, you go running, looking for him.

It is a vivid picture and a very telling one. That is why, at the end of this little section, Israel says, "It's hopeless, we can't help it. We've loved too many people. There's an urge, we've just got to go—hopeless." It is a vivid picture of those who have got away from God and have become so caught up in other things. It may seem incredible to you that they should take a pure religion of God and mix it with others. That is what they were doing. They still kept up a formal acknowledgement of God. They still used his name for official occasions. They still had their "Westminster Abbey" ceremonies in the Temple. But they had mixed all this in with it.

How can you possibly mix Christianity with other religions? We do it, so how can we blame them? Every time a Christmas tree appears in a church at Christmas we have incorporated the symbolism of a pagan festival right into something that is Christian, for the Christmas tree with lights goes back to the fertility cults of early Europe and the nature rites that worship nature and the returning of spring and the ending of the shortest day with the returning light—the lights and the evergreen trees are the symbol of spring. It is purely nature worship but it comes in.

The Bible never tells us in the New Testament to have a harvest festival, but how we love harvest festivals. Now these are comparatively innocent mixtures but we soon bring a mixture in. That is what they did, only their nature worship was a little more degraded than the kind of nature worship we tend to bring in. So, we can understand how it happened. That doesn't excuse it, doesn't explain it, but God says, "Why? What's gone wrong with you that you must go for these things?"

Now for note number five. There is only one end to such things: a time of big trouble is coming, Jeremiah taught. Why? Because this is a moral universe. It is not based on chance but on justice, and therefore trouble comes to this kind of thing. No one ever gets away with anything. There is a day of reckoning. Now the word "crisis" in the Greek language is the same as the word for "judgment", and therefore whenever we say there is a crisis we mean there is a judgment. Crises are judgment. Now God says, when that crisis comes, you are going to be disgraced and deserted; disgraced in the same embarrassed way as a professional thief when he is caught by the police just leaving the house with a bag of loot over his shoulder.

If ever you have seen that happen, you know how embarrassed the thief looks. There is really no way out of that situation. There is no way to retain your dignity when you are caught in that situation. You know you have nothing to say for yourself, and that is why most of them just go silent. There is nothing you can say if you are caught red-handed. As a thief is shamed, so the princes, the priests, the prophets, the politicians of Israel will all be ashamed. They will have nothing to say in the time of trouble.

More than that, they will be deserted because then they will say, "Save us, save us, save us," and God almost laughs in irony and says, "You've got as many gods as you have cities. Where are they?" And here comes a profound principle, which applies not only to nations but to individuals—the test of the reality of your religion is: will it help you when the time of trouble comes? It is all right when you're affluent, when you are comfortable and you can afford to play around and dabble in all kinds of faiths. But the real test of faith comes when the time of trouble comes—will that religion help you?

Let me apply it individually: when tragedy invades your family, will your faith help you at that time? Faith in your own gods will not help you. They will not come to save you, but faith in the real God will save you. What about the trouble of death, for it is a time of real trouble which none of us looks forward to. (By this I mean here death in itself, not what lies beyond.) None of us looks forward to this time of trouble. We hope it will be an easy time for us. Will your religion help you at that time? Will your God see you through? When things are going well you might dabble with a Ouija board or play around with any religion you like, but when you come to die, will your god save you? The biggest time of trouble that will come to every man and woman is the day when he or she stands before God in the Day of Judgment. For it is appointed to everyone to die — and after that, there follows the judgment. Will his or her gods help at that time? The answer is that they will be deserted unless they have the one true God, for there is no other.

So, Israel is heading for a time of trouble. Will false "gods" see them through that trouble? The answer is no. You will be embarrassed like a thief caught red-handed. You will look so silly. You've said to a tree, "You're my father." You've said to a lump of rock, "You gave me birth." What will they do for you when you are in a time of trouble? Will the tree bend down and pick you up? Will the stone bend over and sustain you? Never. It is clever preaching; it is irony and it hurts.

We are reminded of the incredible inconsistency of human thinking: when we are in trouble we can always see that God is to blame; we can never see that we are at fault. Isn't it extraordinary? When we get into a real jam we complain against God. "Why did God allow the Second World War?" —so many people said that at the time. "Why does God do it? Why isn't he doing something? Why, why, why"—complaining against God.

The implication is that if you blame God for the troubles that come, then you have got to say honestly, "That's because I believe I am innocent. I have not sinned. I have done nothing to deserve this."

I recall a television interview following an earthquake. A man sitting in the ruins was asked, "Why do you think this happened?" He replied, "It was the will of Allah"—which is the proper answer for a Muslim, for the word Muslim means, "surrendered one"; "Islam" means "submission". They are fatalist in their religion. The interviewer said then, "Why do you think God decided to do this to your village?" The man answered, "Because of the sinners here." Now what is your reaction to that conversation? Do you have a worldly reaction, or the reaction that Jesus Christ had to a conversation like that? The worldly reaction is, "I can't accept that because those people were innocent. They were as innocent as we were. Therefore, they didn't deserve it." That worldly reaction is how fallen intellect thinks. We are basically innocent people, none of us deserves such tragedy, therefore they were as innocent as we are—therefore it was wrong to say God did it. That was not the reaction of our Lord Jesus. He was asked about a disaster, a collapsed skyscraper that killed a number of people, and they asked him, "Were these greater sinners than anybody else because they had this tragedy?"

Do you know what his reaction was? "You are all guilty and you all deserve it and unless you repent you will all likewise perish." Now isn't that a different reaction? The unbeliever's reaction is, "We're all innocent so the people didn't deserve it." Christ's reaction is, "The people were guilty and did deserve it and so do you. That disaster should be a reminder to you that you need to get right with God in case disaster strikes you."

What a different reaction! You see, inherently we are so big-headed that we think we are innocent and we have never done anything to deserve tragedy.

The most extraordinary case of that I came across was a man aged ninety-six, in hospital, and I went to visit him.

He said, "I don't know what I've done to deserve this. I've always lived a good, clean, upright life."

"Have you never been ill all your life?" I asked.

"Never."

"You've never been in hospital?"

"Never. I don't know what I've done to deserve this."

All innocence at ninety-six. First trip to hospital and he was out again, fit, in ten days, but he thought that ten days in hospital was most unjust of God.

Now that was an extreme case but he was simply saying what comes naturally to fallen nature. We complain against God and say, "God, why have you done this?" and God says, "I've told you why I've done it, and all you do is kill my prophets. You don't want to know."

"Why have you done this, Lord? I'm innocent. I've not sinned."

He said, "Look at you. The blood of innocent people is on you. You trot about Egypt and Assyria; you pay no attention to me. I'm your husband and you say, 'I have not sinned. I'm innocent.'"

We can think like this. Can a bride forget her wedding dress? Yet you have forgotten me, days without number. You complain against me. You dare to blame me for disasters. You are not innocent. If you run to Egypt you will come back with your head in your hands, nursing your bruises and hiding your shame.

It is an important reminder to us that unfortunately sin affects our intellect as well as our moral life. It affects our thinking so that we can't think straight and we think everybody is innocent and doesn't deserve any disaster. When disaster comes we blame God for it. We just can't think straight.

We come to the final note in this sermon: from a loving bride, Israel has become a hardened heart, living a dissolute life. The extraordinary thing is that her feelings are so desensitised that, unashamedly, when trouble comes she comes trotting back to God expecting him to receive her—that is the incredible thing. So God says, "Listen, even at the human level if a wife runs off and plays the harlot and has many lovers, does she think she can just walk back in to a partnership? Does she think the husband can just have her back?" This is what Hosea said to the ten tribes in the north, and now Jeremiah has to say it to the two tribes in the south.

Do you honestly think you can just walk back in as if nothing has happened? Here now comes a very extraordinary thing. He says: "You've come to me because I stopped the rain. You now realise that all this fertility cult doesn't control the rain. All this nature worship doesn't control the rain and I stopped the rain—now you come crawling back to me. Do you realise that your real security lies with me, and that your real hope lies with me, and you come crawling back to me?" He says, "You call me father and friend when you are my divorced wife."

Now I find that so remarkably real a picture—but get the feel of it. Here is a wife who has run off and played around with so many people that she is divorced. Then she comes back with a sort of smiley approach, grinning on her face and saying, "You're not really angry with me, are you? You see, I just look on you as a kind of fatherly friend. Let's keep it platonic. Can I come back and have you as a father and friend? I'm not really happy to have you as a husband, you see, because that is a bit of an exclusive relationship, isn't it? I've really got rather fond of a lot of people but can't we just be friends? Can't you be a father to me?" Can you imagine that happening in real life? Well, it does. So, you get him, and her having sampled other wives, saying to the press: "We're just good friends again." The delusion!

"So," says Jeremiah, "You come crawling back to God

because the rain has stopped. You come crawling back for the national day of prayer and you say "father", "friend", but God says, "I am your husband, your holy husband in holy matrimony. Do you think you can come back and just have me as a friend?" You see, this is true to our human nature. Wouldn't we much rather have God as a father and a friend rather than have him in holy matrimony? Then we can play around with other things. But God is saying: "The only relationship I will have with you is an exclusive one." Keep thee only unto her so long as you both shall live—that is what it has got to be. You can't have God as father and friend unless you have him as husband in holy matrimony forever and exclusively together—what a message!

So, having begun the sermon with a honeymoon, he now says: you come back as holy wife or not at all. There is no in-between. Why? Because God says in the last sentence of this sermon, "I'm sick of hearing what you say and having to watch what you do. Your words and deeds don't match. I hear what you speak. I hear your prayers but I know you just go out and do the opposite." "This people worship me with their lips," God says through Isaiah, "but their heart is far from me."

It is a bit depressing, isn't it? It is a depressing sermon. The big question that may be left in your mind by Jeremiah's first sermon is this: did he hope that they would come back, or did he think the situation was too far gone? Was he a pessimist or an optimist?

Well, there are just one or two gleams of hope but Jeremiah knew that they could not come back as they were and that they could not change. The leopard can't change its spots any more than an Ethiopian can change his skin. So, in a sense he had no hope. He knew that God wanted them back. He knew that God loved them still, but no real hope comes through this sermon that they will respond to his sermon.

Now I will tell you why: because God knew that it would need more than a Jeremiah to do the trick. God knew that he would have to send his only Son Jesus to bring a new covenant—not an old one, but a new one.

This Jeremiah realised later, and in chapter 31 we will look at that: a new covenant that will be sealed in his blood, the blood of the new covenant. Jeremiah later realised that God would have to do something totally new and would have to change the leopard and give a new nature and make a new covenant. Hallelujah! What Jeremiah would never have been able to do Jesus has come and done and there is a new bride for the Lord. There is a new harvest, a new family, and there are new children who love him. There is a holy matrimony again. God loves his people.

What a sermon—and that was Jeremiah's first sermon as a young man in the streets of Jerusalem. Did they listen? Did he get more than two or three curious people listening? I do not know. The important thing is that the Word of God has to be preached, and when it is preached the Holy Spirit of God can move—but if God has spoken, who can be silent?

The Assyrians came, in a huge curve, down into Israel, and they conquered ten out of the twelve tribes. God not only let them do it and stood by watching, he had actually brought them—because of what had been going on in the cities of the north.

Jeremiah, living as he did in Anathoth, looked to the north and saw that God still yearned for the people of the invaded land, and that he wanted to bring them back from exile and again to have a family for himself.

In the first half of the passage we are studying there was a note of hope: "I will bring them back and they will live in this land in unity with me and with shepherds after my own heart." But did you notice, then, that suddenly the atmosphere changed and there was only doom and disaster, and it finished with a terrible murder? Some people have asked of this passage: which is the real Jeremiah? Which is the true Word of God? Hope or disaster? If you study your Bible very carefully you realise that in the first half of this reading he was speaking to the north, "Israel", which was the name for the ten tribes who had been taken away, and in the second half he is speaking to Judah. The theme is in 3:11—faithless Israel has shown herself less guilty than false Judah. In other words, the faithless north is less guilty than the false south and we have got to ask why. Then we shall get the message for today.

Now there are two keywords throughout this first half on Israel. First, the word "faithless" occurs seven times. Then the word "return" occurs eight times. This is the summary of the message to the north: you have been faithless, but return; come back, all is forgiven. You have suffered enough; you have lost enough; you have been punished enough. My anger is abated. I am angry with you no more. But to the south the message is worse: You are not only faithless like your sister in the north, you have been *false* and therefore you must go. That, too, came true in history.

We will look at the first half of the reading, from 3:6—4:2. Once again, when Archbishop Ussher of Ireland put the chapter numbers in, he put the figure four just two verses too early. The division comes, he finishes speaking to Israel at the end of 4:2, and then he speaks to Judah thereafter. So, let us look at what he says to Israel. Chapter three could have come at the beginning of v. 6 and we would have had the right division.

Here is the word for the people in the north, and all through this section there are family terms used—sisters, spouse, sons, father, husband—and in the use of these terms you have got the heart of God's purpose for mankind. When God created the world, and when he chose Israel as one of those nations, why did he do it? The answer is very simple: God wanted a family. You misunderstand the whole Bible unless you start with this single thought—*that it is all about God trying to have a family*. God had one Son and loved him so much that he wanted more sons, many sons. So, he made a planet and he put people on it, and he wanted a family who would be sisters, sons, a faithful wife to God as though he were her husband, but he didn't get it.

So, having not got it from the nations of the world, he chose one little nation, and his message to them was: Look, the rest won't be my family; you be my family and then you can teach them how to become sons and daughters. I will put you in a lovely land and you can call me "my Father" and I will be a Father to you, I'll be a husband to you; I'll be everything to you, but let us just be family. I am afraid it went wrong even with the Jews.

We look now at the family from three points of view: first as two sisters, second as a wife, and third as two sons. I know it is all getting mixed up but the Bible doesn't mind mixing metaphors. It is all family. The first viewpoint is asking Judah to look at her sister, Israel, and see what her sister did. The second viewpoint is God looking at the whole of them, Israel and Judah, as a wife. The third is the viewpoint looking up, from the point of view of Israel having been punished, coming back as prodigal sons to a father and saying, "I've sinned in your sight."

So we look at the first. Now Luke 15 is a parable of two brothers, but here we look at two sisters—the parable of the prodigal sister and the elder sister. Only there is something different and rather twisted. Once upon a time there were two sisters, their names were Judah and Israel. Israel went off into a far country and devoured her substance with riotous living, played the harlot on every high place and under every green tree. The elder sister (Judah) stayed home, and the elder sister looked at the younger sister who was in the far country, and the elder sister said, "I'm going too." The father said to the elder sister, "Are you going to the far country also?" The elder sister said, "Oh no, I wouldn't dream of doing such a thing," but her heart had already gone.

Now do you get the parable? This is the message of the parable of the two sisters: faithless Israel went, and you, Judah, pretended to stay at home, and you came to the Temple but your heart had already gone with them. Therefore, you are guiltier than your sister. She was quite open and honest about it. She went and she played the fool and she was faithless; my wife—and she went. You pretended not to go, but your heart had gone. Worse than that, your sister went without any warning before her, but you have seen what happened to her. I divorced her, I cut her out of the relationship and now she doesn't belong to me. You have seen that and therefore you are guiltier than your sister.

Do you understand the greater guilt now? God counts those as much greater in guilt who have wanted to do things that others have actually done, and who have also had a warning when they have seen what has happened to those others who have done them and still do it—that is the guilt of Judah. So, the two sisters are both guilty but, of the two, the one who stayed at home is more guilty than the one who has gone.

The second family relationship is of a husband and wife. We now look at Israel not as a sister of Judah but as a wife of Yahweh, who pleads with her: Come home, all is forgiven; only acknowledge your guilt, only admit you have been faithless and you can come home and live with me. I have ceased to be angry with you. You have been punished enough. You have lost your land; you have gone into a labour camp in distant Assyria. Just admit it. I ask for nothing else than that you admit it. Now here is the father and the prodigal again: I've sinned against heaven; bring the fatted calf; come home.

Look what God will do for them when they come. If they come home he will give them good leaders, shepherds after his own heart. He will be so real to them that they won't need any symbol of his presence. They won't need an ark of the covenant. Nobody will even ask for an ark of the covenant. Isn't it wonderful when God is so real to you that you don't need a church building to remind you of his presence? You don't need any symbols, you have got him.

They would have that, and nobody would even want to build a sacred ark when they came back. Not only that, but he said: I will make you a nation that will influence the world

... I will bring you back to live with your sister—Judah and Israel will come together again ... I will give you your land back again. Only come home, Israel.

Then comes this very poignant passage (3:19)—is there anything that could touch your heart so deeply? God is baring his thoughts. He says, "I thought how I would set you among my sons and give you a pleasant land, a heritage most beauteous of all nations. I thought you would call me 'My Father,' and would not turn from following me."

When God looked down on earth and said, "Let us make man in our own image," he saw Adam and said, "That's good, that's very good", and he thought Adam would call him "my Father". Do you get that feel of God's heart, the frustration of God in this passage? "But surely, as a faithless wife leaves her husband, so you have been faithless to me."

The third picture in this section on Israel I would call "remorseful sons". The prophet even tries to help them to come home by giving them the words to say. You know, one of the most difficult things after you have fallen out with someone and become estranged from them is that you want to get back to them but you don't know what to say. Have you ever had this problem? You don't know what words to use. God, in his mercy, through Jeremiah tells them exactly the words to use. Isn't that lovely? Some people say that you have got to use your own words for them to mean anything to you, but that is not true. You can mean something even when using someone else's words, otherwise every time we sing a hymn and every time we say the Lord's Prayer would be sheer hypocrisy. It can be hypocrisy but we need the words to help us to know what to say, and that is why we are so glad that people have written hymns. It helps us to say what we want to say to God and to mean it. God gives the words to say, through Jeremiah. Just come back and say this: "Behold, we come to you, for you are the Lord our God.

Truly the hills are a delusion—the orgies on the mountains. From our youth the shameful thing has devoured all for which our fathers laboured"—there are the words.

The word which God is giving us to say today could be: we are losing all that our fathers laboured for in this country, and it is our fault; the things we have run after have been a delusion; we thought that more and more money would bring us the things we needed, and happiness—and they are a delusion. They have let us down; they simply frittered away the qualities of life in this land. Rebellious sons, remorseful sons, come back. But God gives a warning at the beginning of chapter 4. If Israel returns, they have got to mean business. There is to be no pretence, no half-heartedness like that of Judah.

It is to the Lord they must return—not just to the land, but to God. You know, going back to *church* is not returning. Going back to religious observance would not do anything for this land. In World War II every church in Britain was packed with people praying for the war to end—that was not returning, because as soon as the war was over the churches emptied again.

They must leave the far country behind and leave the abominations behind. They are to come back and live lives of truth, justice and uprightness. That is the cry to Israel, "Come home. Here is what to say. Here is what is waiting for you. You have been faithless, but my anger is over."

But now we turn in the second half to the little south that is left: Jerusalem, the tribe of Judah around it, and the little tribe of Benjamin, just the capital and the immediately surrounding countryside. Those who have a sentimental view of God won't be able to take this next bit. By a *sentimental* view of God, I mean a view of him like an old grandfather sitting up on a cloud, smiling down, only wanting to help us, never getting cross with his children, indulging us, patting us on the head and saying, "Well, boys will be boys. My, you're just like all the others." The great advantage in being a grandparent is that you never have to discipline the children—you can indulge them. That is why some children love to go and stay with grandparents, because they have such a good time. When ours were little we used to regularly take about three weeks to get them back into shape after they had been indulged and spoiled by their grandparents. God is not a grandfather—he is a Father who can be angry. If you think God can never be angry then, frankly, you will never fear God; you will never be afraid of his anger. But now, to Judah, the message is: "Yahweh's anger". It is hot; it is burning. If you are afraid of human beings who get angry, what do you think it is like to face an angry God—the wrath of God? Some people have never realised this. They have never considered that God is like a raging fire. As Jeremiah says here, "Lest my wrath go forth like fire and burn with none to quench it." I didn't see *The Towering Inferno*, the film of a skyscraper burning, and the terror that it causes, but that is nothing compared to facing an angry God. Your reaction to your house being on fire would begin to give you the feeling that people would have facing an angry God. Jeremiah says they must do something quickly or that is what they are going to face.

He says two things in two vivid pictures. The first picture is "plough up your fallow ground". What does that mean? It means that God can't get into your life because it is choked with so many things. It is choked with thorns; it is choked, as Jesus said, "with the thorns of riches". It is choked with the business of making a living, it is choked with too many interests. But there is a little bit in your life that is lying fallow, that is not being ploughed or used. It is hardened because people have trodden over it. But break it up, get the plough into that part of your life which is not being cultivated because you are too choked with other interests. It is a marvellous text. Get that part of your life that has got out of shape—if you stop exercising part of your body it will begin to atrophy and will begin to lose its powers. If you neglect part of your soul then the same thing happens. Get that fallow ground broken up so that God's Word may enter in and be received as seed.

The other picture is even more direct: "Circumcise your hearts"—a word the Jews would understand particularly well. Stop cutting off bits of your body but start cutting out those things in your heart that are symbols of an unregenerate nature. Cut it out and break up the fallow ground and get back to the Lord lest his anger come. Now we know from the rest of this chapter that it did not work. They did not listen. The fallow ground remained fallow, their hearts remained uncircumcised. Nothing was cut out, and the result was that God's anger came.

The rest of this chapter I hardly need to deal with in detail. It is a dreadful picture of a lion coming and devouring their land. If you want to see that lion, go to the British Museum— you can see it there. You can see the Bas-relief stones of Assyria, the great lion coming. The lion was their symbol and the lion came and gobbled up little Judah and Jerusalem. Jerusalem was besieged, princes and priests were amazed and prophets were appalled. It was so unexpected. Much as when, in the 1930s, we didn't think there was going to be another war. People like Churchill were voices crying in a wilderness. Only in the last few months before that war did we feverishly try to get ready and suddenly we were in it, in a second world war in a lifetime. We were appalled; we were astonished at the speed of the events that drew us into that war. We were plunged into something almost without realising, and that is the feel of this chapter.

Jeremiah can't understand it either. He is perplexed; he

starts arguing with God. He says, "God I don't understand it. You were promising a good future for us and now you're letting this happen. Have you deceived us?" Even Jeremiah was thrown off balance as he saw what was going to happen. He saw it in a series of pictures. He saw the lion coming out of his lair. He saw the hot wind from the desert which would neither winnow nor refresh—the hot, burning wind that drives dust before it and burns the grass up until there is none. So, we get this dreadful picture of the anger of God showing. The most important verse is 4:18: "Your ways and your doings have brought this upon you. This is your doom and it is bitter; it has reached your very heart."

Winston Churchill not only warned us in the 1930s that war was on its way and was proved right, he also led us through that war, but at the end of the war he wrote the history of the war, and Volume 5 was entitled, "How the Great Democracies Triumphed and Were Thus Able to Resume the Follies which Had So Nearly Cost Them Their Lives." What an indictment! Looking back over the decades which followed, was he not right?

We have looked at Yahweh's anger; we have seen the threat of Judah's annihilation; now, in vv. 19–31, we look at Jeremiah's anguish. There is a vivid description of his feelings: "My anguish, my anguish, I writhe in pain. The wars of my heart. My heart is beating wildly." You have got the sense that here is a man who is so involved in his country that everything is caught up, including his emotions: "For I hear the sound of the trumpet, the alarm of war, disaster upon disaster." Then he says something about his people in Judah, in the southeast. He says, "They are skilled in doing evil but how to do good they know not." In bad things they are professionals; in good things they are amateurs. Do you think that has anything to say to us? It is a tragic fact that every child has to be taught to tell the truth, but never has to be taught to tell lies. It is a fact that a child has to be taught to be obedient; it never has to be taught to be disobedient. It is a fact that we have to teach every child to consider other people; you never have to teach a child to look after itself. This is our human nature.

Now Jeremiah has a vision, and it is a horrible picture. He looks on his beloved land and it has returned to the state in which it was before the creative hand of God got on it. Verse 23 is exactly the same phrase as occurs in Genesis 1:2: "and the whole earth was waste and void". He looks at the land and God has, as it were, taken his beloved land of Judah and he has wiped out everything that has happened since creation. He has put it back in its original state, as if the potter has taken the clay and just put it back as a lump because the vase has not been shaped rightly.

It is as if God says: I'm fed up. I haven't got anything out of my creation; all the love and care, making the dry land, making the hills and the clouds, separating the waters, all that has been wasted—I've got no family. Back to waste and void, and it was dark. Darkness was on the face of the waters and so the sky has gone black and Jeremiah sees in the vision that the land of Judah has gone all the way back to the beginning, all the way back to that dark, empty mass that it was before God shaped his lovely land. What a vision! The mountains are shaking; the men have gone; the birds have flown; the fields are bare; the cities are ruined; the sky is black. Judah has not repented, so neither has God. In v. 28 God says, "I have not relented nor will I turn back." There is one last thing in the picture: what about Jerusalem? The land of Judah has gone back, what is Jerusalem doing? Isaiah has an extraordinary vision of his city, Jerusalem, as a lady painting herself up, putting on a nice dress, and jewellery, putting eye shadow on to make her eyes look big and beautiful. She is simpering before her enemies; she is trying to give them love and trying to save her life as other women have done during invasions. In this, Jeremiah sees that the city, instead of looking to God in her extremity, is going to try and make love to the invader. But it won't work.

In the final bit of the picture, this painted woman is writhing in agony. She is having a miscarriage. All her plans are miscarrying and she is dying. Jeremiah says, "Did you not realise your lovers despise you? They seek your life, not your love." Jerusalem dies, shouting, "Woe is me, I am fainting before my murderers."

So, there is hope for the north, but Judah had been worse than faithless, she had been false. That is something God could not accept. His people had pretended to put things right and had not done so

Here is part of a prophecy delivered in England on 9th July, 1975.

Whereas once my hands were around your country in protection, now are my hands changed. They are above and pointing in judgment for I am opening the way for the workers of iniquity to come. I give them liberty to damage and harass your land because you have rejected my protection. There are among the peoples of your country those who with skilful words and with the touch from the pit are bringing about those things that shall cause chaos and bloodshed. For the blood of your own countrymen and countrywomen shall stain your streets, even these streets, when you are given over to these tyrants who shall then come fully into view. My beloved people, I tell you of things that are to come, that you might hear my voice and that you might respond. I wanted to make your land a demonstration to the world of that which is good, that which came from a country that owned and honoured my law. But, alas, it has become a demonstration for the enemy of that which comes when every polluted thing is not only permitted but made legal by the leaders of your country. I will judge them and I will judge them heavily. I will cast them down and I will put [in] such rulers that shall bring this country to the very edge of complete destruction. Yet my ears are still open to hear any cry that might arise to me from my people.

READ JEREMIAH 5–6

There are two very remarkable things about the nation of Israel which the world finds difficult to understand. The first is their suffering and the second is their survival. This nation has suffered more than any other nation on earth and this nation has survived better than any other nation on earth. The reason is very simple: they are the people of God. Their suffering is a perfect demonstration of the justice of God and their survival is a perfect demonstration of the mercy of God. For God is the God of truth, when he makes a promise he keeps it, when he threatens to punish those who disobey he does precisely that. If he calls a nation they will survive.

Therefore, Israel is a perfect example to all the other nations of the world of the secret of history. I think again of that man Karl Marx sitting in the round reading room of the British Museum—reading, studying, thinking with a brilliant intellect. He was trying to find the laws of history which would explain why nations came and went, which would explain the struggle of the human race and he came up with his answer; it is called dialectical materialism. It is an answer that is not true because Karl Marx, Jew though he was, rejected from his analysis and his thinking the God of the Jews and the Jews of God.

The result was that he missed the meaning of history. Though at one point in the twentieth century a quarter of the world's population was living under his theory, nevertheless it does not explain history. He missed that the real clue to the laws of history is not dialectical materialism but divine morality. If he had only studied his own God and the history of his own people as a Jew, he would have understood why peoples come and go and why the atlas changes and why nations and empires wax and wane.

It is only when you read a prophet like Jeremiah, who also looked at history but looked at the God of Israel and the Israel of God and understood why things happened as they did, that you understand how history operates and why empires rise and fall. There is a process; a very simple, logical process clearly discernible in history—most clearly in Israel—as if God wanted us to look to that nation supremely to understand how the rest of us are to live and how the rest of our history is to operate.

When you first read through Jeremiah 5–6 it may seem to you like a jumble, almost like a tirade of separate prophecies, jumping from one subject to another. In a sense it is—these prophecies were not all given at the same time. This is a compilation of words that burst from Jeremiah's lips time after time, and someone collected them and put them together; a man called Baruch wrote them down so we have got them in a kind of systematic form.

They burst spontaneously from Jeremiah. Yet you can analyse them. Usually I analyse them in the order in which they occur. I am not going to do that here but I am going to look at the analysis of history which emerges from these two chapters—the explanation as to why nations come and go. It can all be said in just three simple, logical laws of history, or one law with three stages. The laws of cause and effect apply rigidly in this setting. Stage number one is *spiritual decline*. That is the inevitable cause of stage two: *moral decadence*. That is the inevitable cause of stage three: *national destruction*. That is the lesson written over history, but supremely and most clearly written over the nation of Israel. For every single detail threatened in these two chapters you have read came true to the absolute letter.

You can go to that same British Museum where Karl Marx wrote *Das Kapital* and you can see the evidence in stone of these very things. Go and see the Lachish stone if you want to see the fulfilment. It happened—these are God's laws of history, they cannot be broken, they can only be illustrated. It is true that these are the negative laws. In her earlier years, Israel illustrated the positive laws: that the nation that seeks God will be blessed and will have ample harvests.

Let us now turn to those three spiritual laws. Law number one is that when a nation goes into spiritual decline and ceases to be afraid of God, she will become far more afraid of other things: unemployment, violence, economic problems. Lack of fear of God is the root problem which causes all other troubles. This is the root problem of our nation, though it is not as clearly seen as it was in the nation of Israel, which was that much closer to God. That is why they suffered more than others—because their privileges were greater than others and they had a closer relationship than we as a nation have. Nevertheless, the same law applies.

How did this spiritual decline happen in their nation? First of all, it happened because the people generally forsook God and tried other religions—their people rebelled. They had a long history of knowing the true God and of hearing the truth about God, but they became crazy to try new religions—anything for kicks, and that is precisely what our nation has done. We have had the Christian faith for nearly two thousand years but now any religion other than Christianity seems to be of interest and attraction.

On the morning BBC radio, you can listen to talks on Buddhism, meditation; anything you might like to name. We are now being labelled a pluralistic society and we have to face the facts, that is true. Anybody can worship any god they would like. If we ever were a Christian country, which

I doubt, there is certainly no doubt that we are no longer a Christian country. We are a pluralistic society in which even those brought up in church and Sunday school will try any religion at all, from astrology through black magic to anything that can be imported from the East or the Far East or anywhere else, and if we can invent a few religions, so much the better. Our imagination knows no bounds whatever in trying anything but the truth. Now that is what happened in Israel. They had forsaken the true God for a god call Baal, and it was a foul fertility cult. Baal means "husband" and sexual orgies were a part of every act of worship.

We were once in Jersey where we found a little road near the hotel labelled "Rue de Baal"—the very word. Some of our company thought they would walk up that road. You know what they found just up the road? They found a brand-new top security prison with barbed wire. There is a parable there, and what a parable! The "Rue de Baal" looked like a road that led to a nice place but it led to prison. This is what they found in Israel. The road of Baal looked nice, it looked enjoyable, it looked like a road of free love, but in fact, it became a road of lust instead. They found themselves imprisoned, trapped. They had forsaken God and tried other things that looked more interesting.

But what were the religious leaders doing to let this happen? The sad part is that when Jeremiah looked at the religious leaders he found that they had not stopped the rot because the priests were only interested in carrying on the public services and carrying on the offerings. The tragedy is that this land of Israel still called itself "The Land of God" and still thought that they were a godly country. The priests had no idea that it just made God sick, even the religion, even the offerings, even the sacrifices. The most expensive incense and perfume offered to God stank in God's nostrils—of course it did. If you give someone a present and you don't love that person, doesn't that present become an offence? Of course it does—you can't substitute presents for love. Oh yes, a man may try to when he feels a bit guilty, going out and buying his wife some flowers, but what she wants is a right relationship with him. Then the flowers will be acceptable, but the flowers are an offence if they are an excuse, an attempt to get around the real situation.

It was not only the priests who were going through all the formal rigmarole. Here we come to the saddest part of all. The prophets were the preachers of the day. A very few used to speak the truth, but the people didn't want to hear it. They scoffed. They said: We don't believe anything will happen; nothing will happen to us, no evil will come; we are not going to listen to Jeremiah; we are not going to listen to doom and gloom. Things will pan out all right, they always have done in the past. They scorned; they heard, but they did not hear. They saw, but they did not see. Their problem was not ignorance but stubbornness. They knew the truth but they didn't expect it.

The tragedy is that most of the prophets would not preach the truth because they didn't want to be called "windbags". That's what they called any prophet who spoke the truth. But most of the prophets told the people what they wanted to hear, and this is the biggest pressure on a preacher. It is the biggest pressure on a man of God who wants to speak the truth. People want comfort, they want soothing, they want nice things said. Prophets and priest had "healed the wound of my people lightly" and said, "Peace, peace, when there was no peace" (see 6:13f.) You can't heal a wound by pretending it isn't there. You don't really help people by saying that things are all really nice and smooth.

An archbishop appeals to the enormous number of good people in this land inside and outside the church. Do you think that is really an appeal that gets through to the real problem? Is it not the enormous number of bad people inside and outside the church that is the real problem? Are we not all part of the affluent, indulgent mess? That is the question. Are the prophets of doom speaking the truth?

Where you have false prophets preaching peace and comfort where there is none, and priests going through the rigmarole as a kind of religious aspect of society, and a people who are trying anything they are interested in, you have the first factor in the moral process of the breakdown of a nation, which is damaged from the inside long before it is destroyed from the outside.

Jeremiah is teaching that the real root of the tragedy is that the people are no longer afraid of God. To illustrate the fact that you should fear God, let me mention one thing on which your very life depends: water. Have you ever realised how delicate is the balance of water on planet Earth? In space exploration we have probed and taken photographs, and what have we been looking for? Water, because without water there's no life. This little planet of ours has water. Jeremiah is telling us what a delicate balance it is in. Do you realise that it is God who sets the bounds of the ocean? (See 5:20ff.) Look at the photographs of Earth taken by astronauts and you can hardly see any land; almost the whole planet is water. The size of the ocean—nine miles deep and thousands of miles across. What an expanse of water! Do you know that if the Antarctic ice cap melted, the oceans would rise two hundred feet and that would wipe out almost every major city in the world? Does that not make you afraid of God? The only thing that God would need to do would be to say, "Ice, melt," and most of London would disappear beneath the waves. Don't you fear God?

Then think of the control: millions upon millions of tons of water are lifted out of the ocean and dropped on the land to keep us alive, yet it is dropped in tiny drops so that it is not a threat. Millions of tons of water are transferred by God and he sends the rain from heaven. One year, in an English town where we were living there were just two and a half inches of rain in forty-eight hours, and our High Street was five feet under water! Think of the balance, think of God in control. "Don't you fear God?" says Jeremiah. Do we fear God? God turns the tap on and off.

Do you not fear God? We are so afraid of what man is doing to the environment, what man is polluting the oceans with, that we don't ask about God. What about God in all this? He would only need to upset that balance by a tiny fraction and we would be finished. He gives us our harvest, he gives us the rain, he keeps the oceans where they are. No, we're more afraid of pollution by man than the control by God. We have ceased to think of God as being in control of it so we are not afraid any more. Now when a nation fears unemployment and inflation and violence more than it fears God, it has taken the first step down this slippery slope.

Now what is the second step? It follows inevitably. The second step is moral decadence, for belief affects behaviour; creed affects conduct. If one generation says, "Why be married in church?" the next generation will say, "Why be married?" If one generation says, "Why bother with God," the next will say, "Why bother to be good?" If one generation says, "Why bother to worship?" the next will say, "Why bother to work?" It is inevitable, it is a process. You can't halt that process—it goes on. Once the spiritual climate change has taken place, the moral decadence follows.

We have some wonderful impressions in Jeremiah chapter 5 of his first visit to the big city; what he saw when he left the village in which he had been brought up. From that little hamlet, imagine Jeremiah coming to London for the first time. The country boy comes to town—what are his first impressions? His first impression was of guile; he probably lost a bit of money very quickly through a crooked dealer trying to sell him something on the streets. As he walked around he realised that people were no longer honest or fair, that each of them was out to trick his neighbour. This country lad thought he probably got duped by a number of traders, and he began to say, "Is there any honest dealer here? Any truthful man whose word you can trust?" Because the whole of commerce depends on trust; it depends on the fact that your word is as good as your bond. Commerce and business depend on good faith. Wherever Jeremiah went, he found guile. He found that ordinary people just were not to be trusted any more.

An Indian student came to England after being converted through a missionary's work in India. The missionary was worried about what the student's impression of London would be—Christian England. The student looked forward to visiting Britain, but when he came back to India the missionary asked, "How did you get along?"

He replied, "Marvellous! In the first morning in London I saw three miracles."

"What did you see?"

"Well," he said, "I saw three miracles on a bus. Somebody had to get off the bus before the conductor could come downstairs; the conductor was upstairs. Somebody getting off gave the money for the fare to somebody sitting there—miracle number one. Then, when the conductor came down after the passenger had got off the bus, the other passenger gave the conductor the money—miracle number two. When the conductor received the money, he didn't put it into his pocket, he put it into his bag and he issued a ticket for it—miracle number three." But that happened in 1920. Would he see three miracles today?

Jeremiah noticed how things were in the city. He thought, "Well, these are just ordinary folk; they're poor, they're ignorant," and they were in those days. He saw that the people were uneducated and didn't know any better, but it was the leaders he would go and see. He went to the top, those in government. Surely they would know the way of the Lord. But Jeremiah found that they were as unprincipled as the ordinary people in the street, and that their private lives would bear no more examination than the crooked traders he met.

Unprincipled government was one of the things that Jeremiah saw. In the capital city there were men of political expediency. Then he moved on, and found uncharitable greed right through society, from the bottom to the top. He saw such greed that they were able to gain immorally —there was bribery and corruption. If you know anything about business today, you know that it is almost impossible in some spheres of business to run a business at all if you are honest. It used to be possible to say that honesty is the best policy— but that depends on an honest society, so it is becoming more and more difficult.

Jeremiah uses a picture of a fowler. A poacher is setting his traps to catch people, knowing that he is not getting gain the honest way but trapping other people. Who suffers in that kind of a society? It is the people who can't defend themselves, the orphans and the needy. In a society that has become a jungle, where it is every man for himself, it is the helpless who suffer, the people at the bottom who go further down while everybody else is scrambling further up. Isn't this relevant?

The worst thing of all is that they cannot even blush. God has given us an ability to blush. Have you ever thanked God for the ability to do so? No, we don't usually thank God for that because it is an embarrassment to us. We don't like to be seen blushing but isn't it a gift of God and isn't it a sign that you have gone so far away from God that you can no longer blush? You see, moral decadence reaches a point where people are no longer ashamed, no longer embarrassed, no longer blushing.

There is a third stage of this moral process. This is not dialectical materialism, which does not explain what happens, this is *divine morality* which does. The third stage is this: when religious and moral values have gone, then society loses its stability and collapses. It collapses from inside long before anybody from outside attacks. The real rot has set in. Read *The History of the Decline and Fall of the Roman Empire* by Edward Gibbon (1737-1794) for a marvellous example, but if you want a much clearer example read the life and times of Israel—it is all there.

God says in vivid picture language, "The lion, the wolf and the leopard are coming. It's a jungle now." He says, "It's like a vineyard and a grape gatherer going through it to see if he's missed one grape to pick the last little thing off you and leave you stripped and bare." He said, "It's like a forest fire and the words of my prophet Jeremiah will become burning words, which will be like a spark to kindling wood and burn you up"—vivid pictures.

But there are three examples of specific punishment mentioned here. Number one: God's first punishment for them was *failed crops*. It was the first way he tried to get through to them and show them what they were really like. So poor crops came and the rains didn't come. Food was scarce and expensive and the poor and the needy had to struggle the most. "Your iniquities have turned the rains away." The irony of it all was that they had worshiped Baal because he was the fertility god who it was supposed would give them fertility of the land as well as in their relationships. God was teaching them: It's not Baal, it's me and your crops have failed.

The second warning he gave to Israel was that of *a fearful conflict*. In this case he used not nature, but human beings. He said, "I'm bringing a fearful foe from the north, cruel, relentless." We now know who that was: Babylon. They were cruel and relentless. Can you imagine what it was like to be occupied by a people whose language you could not speak? You can't plead for mercy, they don't know what you're saying and you don't know what they are saying. You can't talk to them, you can't negotiate with them. They do not speak to you; they are strangers, they are foreigners. A people whose language they did not understand would take their lands and their wives.

In fact, there is a vivid picture here of Jerusalem as a helpless, beautiful girl. In ancient warfare there was no person in a more desperate or vulnerable position than a beautiful girl in a country that had been invaded. The invading army regarded her as something rather than someone—spoils of war. Oh Jerusalem, you are like a helpless maiden, beautiful and delicate and doomed.

The final punishment of God, which would burst on children and adolescents, married adults and the elderly would be this: as you have chosen foreign gods from other lands rather than the God of your own land, I will send you to those lands. You have already gone there in heart and you will be deported and there will be a forced captivity of Israel for seventy years. That happened. You see, the third stage of this process is that you are no longer aware of danger.

Have you noticed the three steps? Spiritual decline—you are no longer afraid of deity; moral decadence—you are no longer ashamed of disgrace; finally, national destruction— you are no longer aware of danger. One of the most tragic things in this passage is where the people say, "He will do nothing. Punishment is incompatible with a God of love; no evil will come to us." Oh, this is being said even within the churches of our land. Clergy no longer believe in a God who punishes. An archbishop said, "Let us live out our faith that God reigns and cares." This nation needs to hear about a God who punishes as well. That is the God we are not hearing about; only a God who cares. But he is a God who cares about truth as well as people, who cares about justice as well as joy. God does care very deeply about all these things, even when it happens to them, "Even in those days," says the Lord, your people will say, "Why has the Lord God our God done all these things? Why?" just as people said in World War II, which was needed to bring us to our senses, and which did. People used to say: "We were all together in the war. We faced a common enemy, we fought together, we were on our toes. We had far less goods maybe but we had far more grit." But when it comes they say, "Why did God allow this to happen? Why did God send a war, why?" It is incredible stupidity and stubbornness that can be so unaware of the dangers of living sinful lives in the presence of a holy God.

There is optimism in these two chapters. One of the little rays of hope is this: God says, "I will not make a full end." Twice he says it. "I'll punish the nation, I'll take them away, but I will not make a full end." That is one ray of hope and there is one other that comes to me so forcibly: every person counts. Humanly speaking, that is a silly thing to say, because don't we all feel helpless as individuals? Each of us is one little person out of millions. How can I change the situation? There is a frustration. Well now, you couldn't if you were only one or two or even a handful, a minority. I know that Abraham Lincoln said that even five per cent of the population can change public opinion. I believe that to be true but I can only find 1.5% who are real Christians in our land. Therefore, the first task, if we are going to change public opinion, our first immediate target, is to treble the number of committed Christians. When we have done that we shall see the beginning of the change in public opinion, but not until then. But I am still not hopeless, for this reason. At the beginning of Jeremiah chapter 5 it says, "Jeremiah, go through Jerusalem, search the squares, see if you can find one upright man that I may pardon her." Now does that hit you? You would have expected to read: "Find me one upright man that I may pardon him." No, God wants to pardon and he will spare a nation for the sake of one upright man in a city. That is what happened to Sodom—Sodom was pretty degraded. Just to look at its nightclubs would have convinced you that that city was ready for destruction, and Abraham pleaded with God, "If there are fifty righteous men in the city, just fifty out of the whole city, would you destroy it?" God says, "Would I destroy it? Do you think I would, the Judge of all the earth?" Forty? Ten? Five? Abraham knew that God would spare a city for the sake of a few godly men in it—that is when minorities count. God is not asking for the whole nation to turn, he is too much of a realist. But he says, "Just find me one man in that city that I may pardon her."

The tragedy is that Jeremiah went through the city and God says, "You're like an assayer of silver. In all this dross, you are trying to find some sterling silver." Jeremiah went through and he came back and he said, "I can't find any, it's all dross." We would call it fool's gold.

In the Lake District in Cumbria there is fool's gold. You can really be fooled by it though it is only iron. Try refining it, melting it down to see if you get any gold and you get none. That is what happened to Jeremiah when he went through that city – sifting it, refining it with his word. As the fire of his word burnt through that city, did he get sterling silver? No. There's a wonderful pun here, a play on words. It is a pun that can be done in English too. In English the word "refuse" (meaning to decline) and the word "refuse" (meaning rubbish) are the same word – as they are in Hebrew.

This is what Jeremiah says: "It's all refuse silver because they have refused God and therefore God has refused them." If you refuse God you become refuse—fool's silver. But that need not happen to Britain. Part of Jeremiah's prophecy is a call from God for just some people in the towns and cities of this land to mean business with God. "Find me one man that I may pardon her...." We are not helpless. We are not trapped. We are not unable to change the situation. It depends on whether there can be some godly men and women who respond to God.

How? My last word is this: there is one verse I haven't mentioned yet: "Go back to the ancient paths." Go back to the old ways, they are tried and true. Don't mind people calling you old-fashioned. Go back to the old ways and you will find rest for your souls. Now the old ways for Israel were to get back to the covenant of the wilderness period when they had their honeymoon with God. The old way for us is him who is the way: Jesus. Go back to the ancient way—"I am the way", and you will find rest for your souls.

READ JEREMIAH 7:1–8:3

(See also 2 Chronicles 34)

Jeremiah was the same age as Josiah in Jerusalem at a time
of revival. Many people would have said, "We've turned the
corner." It was a great big festival; the crowds had gathered
in the capital and they had responded to the call of the head
of the people of God.

This message is about offering God a lot of religious
activity but not doing what he tells us—and every one of us
needs that message. There were two young men in Judah
in the year 620 BC who were desperately concerned about
the condition of their nation. They were both, by this time,
in their early twenties, possibly even early thirties; they
were in their prime and they both wanted to do something
about the state of the nation. The difference was that one
of those young men had the power to impose reform, and
this he proceeded to do. From his throne, he changed the
face of the nation. The other young man had his own voice
and the power of God's Spirit. We are going to study the
contrast between how Josiah tried to put the situation right,
how much he achieved, and how much he failed to do. We
are going to see that history vindicates Jeremiah as the one
who understood most deeply the real need of the human
heart. A call to reform is not enough.

The facts are to be found in 2 Chronicles 34. Josiah was
a good boy. At the age of sixteen he underwent a religious
conversion. From then on, he wanted to be like his ancestor
King David, and to know God as well as David knew him,

and to be a man—a king—after God's own heart. So he began to put things right. He noticed that the building of the Temple of God was shabby and neglected. Therefore, the first thing he thought should be done would be to bring the place of worship to the same condition as his own palace and the people's homes. He began a renovation scheme, collecting the money and starting the work.

You notice an intriguing little thing—they had discovered "music while you work" 2,600 years ago. The people had a mind to do it and they loved to do it. You see, that doesn't challenge your life. You can wield a paintbrush without a change of heart; you can get on with the singing without a change of heart. You can do such things without repenting, and you can believe that you are doing them for God and that you are really doing something that pleases him, so they got on with it. Then, as they cleaned out the cupboards and they turned out all the rubbish that had accumulated in that Temple, they found an old scroll. It is a tragic comment that it was covered in cobwebs and had not been used in years. They had had worship without scripture for too long. There are still people who don't want too much of the Bible in worship—"Let's just worship..." but the Word must be at the heart of all true worship, and if people don't gather to hear the Word, they can't worship properly. They had been going through the services but they had not been going through the scripture.

Hilkiah discovered it and gave it to the king, who read it, and he shook. He realised that God wants far more than a spring clean of his sanctuary—that he demanded much deeper things than that. So, he tried to put the law into practice. After all, he was king; he could pass the laws. He could order the whole nation to put itself right. He could try to make people good and so he tried very hard. He began to destroy the foul idols that had sprung up outside most villages and towns in his country. He really made them eat dirt. He ground those idols to powder and scattered it on the bones of the priests and prophets who had led the people astray. He did everything he could to bring the message home, but he was doing it as king. It was part of an established religion; it was by order of law. This was to be the religion of his country from now on. You don't change the situation that way.

If you want to have this confirmed, read English history. See how, time and time again, the government, or the King or Queen of this land, has tried to impose religion, tried to make people good by Act of Parliament, tried to change the face of England by law; it can't be done that way, however sincerely it may be attempted. Religion cannot be imposed by the state.

I remember having an interview with a minister of state for education in connection with a commission report that we were producing. I remember asking him, "What is your considered opinion of the effects of having compulsory religious education in schools since 1944?" His reply was: "Negligible." I agreed with him and he told me that his own two teenage children, a daughter and a son, had both recently found the Lord and been converted. He said, "They did it in spite of all the religion they had at school. They did it because they went to a group of people who were on fire for God."

You can't make people good, you can't do it from the top; you can't impose religion in the heart. You can spring clean a house of worship. You can pass a law forbidding certain things and they won't be done outwardly. But God looks at the heart of people and asks, "Do they still want to do it or do it in secret?" That's the important question and so Josiah did his best. He had the biggest Passover they had ever had. He piled up the carcasses of sacrificed animals sacrificed by the thousand, as if God is the kind of God who likes a bigger pile of sacrifice more than a smaller pile. You see the thinking? He ordered it all and he set a good example and he was a good king. Because he was good and because he meant it sincerely God said, "I will not bring disaster while you live." But this dear king was killed in battle at the place called Megiddo; a battle of Armageddon came and the Egyptians killed Josiah.

You notice what God says: "Because your motives are sincere in this, because you're seeking me, I'll hold this off until you've gone, but I can see perfectly well that this is imposed on the people. It is not their desire; it's yours, Josiah. So I will only keep you from this; I can't keep them." Reform that is imposed is not the answer. Reformation is no substitute for repentance. If you study Church history, that lesson is written large upon the pages.

What did Jeremiah think about all this? It is one of the puzzles that scholars have debated. You see, the interesting thing is that although Josiah and Jeremiah were literally contemporaries—they were born in the same year—and though they lived within a few miles of each other, and though they were both tremendously concerned about the nation, in all the story of Josiah's reform, Jeremiah isn't mentioned once. Have you noticed that? In the account of Jeremiah and in all his prophecy, Josiah is not mentioned once. Here were these two (and only two) working for the redemption of the nation at the same time and they seem to have had nothing to do with each other.

Jeremiah came in for a lot of criticism because he didn't join in the popular protests, and the popular movement, and the popular reform which the king had initiated. But Jeremiah held off and said in his prophecy that it was too little, too late. The amazing thing is that Josiah got the support. The people came from all over the place.

Now this is the difference between Josiah and Jeremiah.

This is why Jeremiah was sent by God, from Anathoth, to go and live in Jerusalem and to preach at the gate of the Temple, to catch the crowds coming in, for there had been a return to worship and the crowds were following the king. It had become popular again to go to worship. Jeremiah stood at the gate of the Temple and he said, "God has told me to tell you something." The message that he gave comes through loud and clear: ritual is no substitute for righteousness; offerings are no substitute for obedience. Sacrifices are no substitute for submission. A popular religious reform is no substitute for repentance of the heart—that is the message he gave, a lonely, solitary, heroic figure standing at the gate of the Temple.

Why did he say this? Nobody listened to him. They said, "You're a doom and gloom man. Why don't you encourage people? After all, they're getting religious. You should be encouraging this movement." But Jeremiah said what he did for two reasons. First, he took a deeper view of the situation. He took a heart view—an inside view, not an outside view. The other thing is that he took a longer view. It was not the response of a moment, a nine-day wonder. He took the longer view, and in this passage he saw that the present was related to the past and the distant past, and related to the future and the distant future—that you can't just have a momentary response.

Today is yesterday's tomorrow and today is tomorrow's yesterday. Yesterday, today and tomorrow are part of a process. You can't isolate today and just say, "We've got a response today." It's what the people did yesterday and what will happen to them tomorrow. He takes a longer view. When you take the longer view, you see a short-term response in a true perspective. You ask, "How lasting is it? How deep has it gone?"

Let us look at the three things that Jeremiah says here.

He looks at the present, then he looks at the past, then he looks at the future. First of all, in the present, he draws their attention to the Temple of Jerusalem. Well he hardly needed to do that; it had been magnificently renovated. I want you to realise how grand, how superb it was. You could take thirteen English cathedrals and put them inside the Temple of the Lord at Jerusalem, yet Jerusalem was then a little town. Jeremiah stood at the gate and said, "You say, 'The Temple of the Lord, the Temple of the Lord, the Temple of the Lord' – and God will destroy this Temple." That was his message, just when they had renovated it, and that hurt. What is he saying? He's saying that the very thing they were so proud about, the very thing that they had trusted in for their security, had become superstition; it had become a fetish, a charm, a talisman. It was rather like thinking that as long as you live below a cathedral you are safe. Indeed, this is one of the snags of living in a cathedral city. Somehow, seeing that above everything else makes you feel a little too secure.

Jeremiah was teaching the people that they were putting their trust in something that they could not trust. A building is what people make it. A building is what people are like inside it. So, Jeremiah looked at that beautiful building and the people in it, and he delivered God's word of prophecy. It was a den of robbers. Now that is a very carefully chosen phrase. It doesn't mean that rotten things were going on inside it. Robbers don't commit crimes in the den—it is where they hide in between, where they go to be nice. It is where there is honour among thieves. It is where they behave themselves but it is an escape because they don't behave like that as soon as they get out of it. That is the key meaning in the expression "a den of robbers"—not that if you go into it, you will be robbed, but that everybody behaves nicely here. There is honour among thieves there; they behave themselves there, but they use it simply as a retreat. If you watch them when they go out, it is quite different. The message concerns their pride: don't think that because it is the house of God he won't destroy it. The Lord says, "Go now to my place that was in Shiloh." That was the first shrine of Israel, in the Holy Land and it was next door to Anathoth, where Jeremiah lived as a boy. He had seen the ruin of Shiloh. It is one of the few places that tourists never visit today. There is nothing to see; there are just a few old stones at Shiloh. I remember going on the bus, north of Jerusalem, and seeing a signpost which said, "Shiloh". I thought, "Well, I wonder what there is to see up there?" But no guide takes you there now, yet it had been the holy place. God said: "...see what I did to it for the wickedness of my people Israel."

Here comes a most extraordinary thing. As Jeremiah spoke about this beautiful, magnificent house of God thronged with worshippers, God said to Jeremiah, "Now don't you start praying for them." It is astonishing, isn't it? Because as he talked, he must have begun to feel, "Oh God, can't I intercede for them, can't I pray for them?" God says no. It had gone too far. The situation was hopeless.

Do you know there are few more terrible things in the Bible than when we are told not to pray for someone because the situation is too hopeless? This can happen. It is not just in the Old Testament. Read 1 John 5 and you will find there some teaching on how to intercede for those who are sinning. Right in the middle it says, "And there is a sin unto death. I don't tell you to pray for them." When God says, "Don't pray," that really is the end. That then was the present. It was clear that no matter how many carcasses were piled up in the Temple, no matter how big the congregation, they were all still crazy, mixed-up people.

Now we are taken back to look at the past to find the origins of all this—back to the wilderness in Sinai. Do you think God said to the people of Israel in Sinai, when he brought them out of Egypt, "Now the most important thing for you to do is to pile up sacrifices for me; the most important thing I want from you is worship, good services, big congregations, and a nice building in which to worship"? Did the Lord command offerings and sacrifices as the first thing? No.

The book of Deuteronomy, which is almost certainly what Josiah had discovered in the Temple, puts the emphasis not on sacrifice but on obedience; it puts the emphasis on there being one God, one altar and one people of God. So, the prophecy recalls the hearers back to their origins. Offerings and sacrifices are quite a secondary matter compared with obedience and submission. At least seven other prophets had already proclaimed this.

The prophet Samuel declared: Has the Lord as much pleasure in your burnt offerings and sacrifices as in your obedience? Obedience is far better than sacrifice. Or take Psalm 50: I don't need your sacrifices of flesh and blood. What I want from you is true thanks. I want your promises fulfilled; I want you to trust in me in your times of trouble so I can rescue you and you can give me glory.

Here is Psalm 51: You aren't interested in offerings burned before you on the altar. It is a broken spirit you want—remorseful and penitent.

I turn to Isaiah and find this message: I am sick of your sacrifices; don't bring me any more of them. I don't want your fat rams. I don't want to see the blood from your offerings. Who wants your sacrifices when you have no sorrow for your sins? The incense you bring me is a stench in my nostrils. Your holy celebrations of the new moon, and your Sabbaths, and your special days for fasting, even your most pious meetings are frauds. I want nothing more to do with them. I hate them all; I can't stand the sight of them .... Wash yourself; be clean. Let me no longer see you doing all these wicked things. Leave your evil ways. Learn to do good, and to be fair, and to help the poor, and the fatherless, and the widows.

Or Hosea: I don't want your sacrifices, I want your love. I don't want your offerings, I want you to know me.

Or Amos: I hate your show and your pretence, your hypocrisy of honouring me with your religious feasts and solemn assemblies. I will not accept your burnt offerings and thank offerings. I will not look at your offerings of peace. Away with your hymns of praise; they are mere noise to my ears. I will not listen to your music no matter how lovely it is. I want to see a mighty flood of justice, a torrent of doing good.

Micah: Shall we bow before the Lord with offerings of yearling calves? Oh no, for if you offered him thousands of rams and ten thousands of rivers of olive oil, would that please him? Would he be satisfied? If you sacrificed your oldest child, would that make him glad? Then would he forgive your sins? Of course not; no, he has told you what he wants. This is all it is: to be fair, and just, and merciful, and to walk humbly with your God.

Do you see the difference between Josiah and Jeremiah? For Josiah it was: the more sacrifices we can have, the bigger the congregation, the nicer the building, God is pleased. Jeremiah came along and said: no, they live a lie.

We look into the future now, and here you need a little geography. The city of Jerusalem has been moulded by God. It was on a rising hill, leading up to the great Temple at the top, with the little houses of the people rising on the hill, and the Temple above. At the bottom of the hill there is a valley so deep that it is in shade. It was the Valley of Topheth, which means "fireplace", because they tipped all their rubbish down there and burnt it down there in the darkness. Until modern times you could see piles of rubbish burning in that valley and the smoke rising out of it; the worms ate the bits of food and the fire was not put out. Even when the Temple had been renovated, down in that valley some people, where they thought they could not be seen, had erected a high place and they were burning babies to Moloch, a pagan god. You can't see the bottom of that valley from the Temple or even the city of Zion. Way down there, out of sight, they were burning babies. Of course, human life was cheaper in those days. Most babies didn't survive the first year of their life anyway. So what was another baby? There were more where that came from—that was the kind of attitude. So they burned sons and daughters to Moloch and God looked down and said: I'm going to make that a valley of bloodshed. There will come a day when even the bones of your princes, your priests and your prophets will be dug up and thrown in the valley. Animals will come and eat human remains.

You know, there is a desecration of the human body. It is a right instinct that we reverence a corpse. I know it is no longer the person; I know it is just the outside of them, but it has been a person or part of a person. A body is not just a lump of chemicals. It should be reverently buried and treated reverently. When you want to desecrate, when you want to say they are not human, well then you desecrate the body, even after a person is dead. God says: your bones will lie bleached under the sun, and the moon, and the stars that you've worshipped. That Valley of Hinnom will become a terrible place.

This is all a bit grim. I know there are some people who have the feeling when one preaches like this, "Well, this is all Old Testament stuff. Can't we have a bit of New Testament joy and comfort?" May I finish by saying that Jesus himself was nearer to Jeremiah in outlook than to any other prophet. Everything in this passage of Jeremiah comes out in the teaching of Jesus. You can't set the Old Testament against the New like that, as if they have different Gods, though some people have tried.

Consider the Temple of the Lord. What did Jesus do to that Temple? It was being rebuilt and renovated in Jesus' day and crowds were coming to it. It was going to be even more magnificent. Its size, its stones weighing up to a hundred tons, were being put in place under Herod the Great's orders. This Temple was rising again more magnificent than ever. Jesus came into it with a whip and said, "You've made my house a den of robbers," and he is using the exact words. What does he mean? He is saying: you are using it as a place to escape to. Religion is a cloak. God can see what is going on in people's hearts. That whole emphasis that to obey is better than to sacrifice—didn't Jesus constantly teach it? Didn't he say, "You make null and void the Word of God through the traditions of men"? Didn't he also say, "This people honours me with their lips, but their hearts are far from me"? Didn't he make the same emphasis?

In the shortest parable ever, did he not make this point? He said, "There was a man who had two sons. He told them, 'Go and work in my vineyard.' One said, 'No,' but later he changed his mind and went. The other said, 'Yes,' and changed his mind and didn't go. Which of the two did his father's will?" Isn't he saying there that obedience is what the Lord is after—not offering, but obedience? After all, he was to finish the sacrificial system himself totally by offering himself as the one, perfect, full, sufficient sacrifice for the sins of the whole world. No animals have ever been needed ever since, but what he did come to get was obedience.

When it comes to the Valley of Gehenna (or the Valley of Hinnom or the Valley of Topheth), Jesus spoke about it whenever he talked about hell. And it was Jesus who gave us the doctrine of hell. Jeremiah didn't; none of the Old Testament prophets did, none of the apostles did. The only

109

person who really speaks of hell in the whole of the Bible is Jesus. He said, "If you want to know what hell is like, it's the Valley of Gehenna; it's the Valley of Hinnom, where the fire is not quenched and the worm dies not." It was the valley of which Jeremiah spoke—so near to the city of God and yet so far.

When Jesus died, that took place on a hill above the Temple, looking down on the Temple. On the same day, the same twenty-four hours, when Jesus died as a sacrifice to end all animal sacrifice, as the one true offering which ends all offerings, as he died up there, another man, one of his own disciples, died down in the Valley of Hinnom. He was a man from Judah and his name was Judas. He tried to hang himself on one of the overhanging trees and the rope broke and he fell to the ground. His bowels gushed out and he lay there. They called it the Field of Blood. Being one of his own disciples, who had been involved for three years in all the religious side, that was where he finished. That is where the Valley of Hinnom is last mentioned in the Bible. What Jeremiah had talked about six hundred years previously, finishes as the Field of Blood. Jeremiah had said that the Valley of Hinnom will be renamed "the Field of Bloodshed", and it was—the Valley of Bloodshed.

Everyone who reads this passage will finish up with Jesus or with Judas. There is no "in between"—you finish up with Jesus or with Judas. If you try to reform your life, you will finish up with Judas, for that is where Judas finished—in the Valley of Hinnom. But if we really repent and realise that God isn't interested in services of worship unless they are the expression of a life of obedience, then we finish up with Jesus and with Jeremiah.

READ JEREMIAH 8:4–9:26

When I realised that God wanted me to teach on the book of Jeremiah I had a bit of a personal crisis because I guessed at some of the reactions there would be. Early in the series of talks, those who simply go to church to have a bit of a cheer-up were already saying, "Isn't it depressing to go to church on Sunday morning?"

The truth is depressing because God has to humble before he can exalt. He has to show us ourselves before we can see him. If we really study Jeremiah and really live it, and really speak it out boldly, we shall be unpopular. I need no commentary on the book apart from my daily newspaper.

The key passage in this study is, "Let not the wise man glory in his wisdom, let not the mighty man glory in his might; let not the rich man glory in his riches, but let him who glories glory in this, that he understands and knows me...." (see 9:23f.) The great division in this country is not between those who believe in God and those who don't, but between those who believe in one kind of God and those who believe in another. That is a far more important question to us—not whether we believe in God but what kind of a God we do or do not believe in. If I can perhaps oversimplify, I believe the great battle in religious circles in this country is between a sentimental view of God and a scriptural view of God. Most people in this country may believe in God. But when you ask them what kind of a God they believe in, it is so utterly different from the God of the Bible, even in so-called Christian England.

Let me tell you what I mean. You never get to know a

person until you listen to what he says and let him speak for himself. And nearly four thousand times in this book there occurs a single phrase, which occurs fifteen times in this passage. Did you notice it? "Thus says the Lord" – and the only view of God that is the true view is that it is God who has spoken here. Either we do or don't believe in the scriptural God who has talked to us about himself and revealed his heart, how he thinks, how he feels, what his reaction is to situations; only if we believe in that God are we in touch with reality. But we may believe in a God we have constructed in our own image, and I am afraid there is such a gulf between us and God that if you do that kind of thing you get to a very false God. Let me pinpoint one thing that came out in the passage which you may not have noticed. A sentimental view of God is of a God who would never hurt a fly. It is of a God who would never punish someone. It is of a God who cares very deeply and loves very deeply, but would never kill a man. That is a sentimental view of God and is the one which the majority of people who believe in God in this country hold. But five times God says, "I will poison you." A scriptural view of God is of a God who will poison people. Now that is where the sentimental view of God and the scriptural view of God just cannot meet, and you have to ask yourself, "What kind of a God do I believe in?" A God who would never kill anybody or a God who would put poison in people's drink and kill them?

Now why would God poison someone? What sort of a God is it who would poison people? (See 8:14, 8:17, 9:15). The very word is used, "I will give them poison to drink and it will kill them." Why would God kill with poison?

Well there has been a lot of discussion in recent years about the situation in which someone is suffering so severely that somebody else who loves them so much will poison them to put them out of their suffering. Indeed, there have been some critical legal cases recently about this. There is a discussion going on in medical circles, and wider than that even, as to whether you should put someone out of their misery and give them a pill to stop them suffering. You see, already we are within this area of killing to stop someone suffering. That is what some of the parents have said in court when they have strangled their baby, and they have been getting lighter and lighter sentences for doing this and, in some cases, suspended sentences or nothing at all. They are doing it because they can't bear to see their children suffering. But I want you to try and understand that God feels the same way about his children sinning. He would rather they were dead than doing what they are doing, and you can't understand the heavenly Father's heart until you have got right into this; until you have seen that he can't even bear to look at iniquity. To him the thought of his children going on sinning forever is so offensive that he made the law that if you sin you die, because he would rather see his children dead than sinning perpetually, and that is the truth.

So, while there are some people who would rather kill someone than see them go on suffering, God is the kind of God who would rather kill someone than see them going on sinning indefinitely. That is what comes out in this chapter. Here is a God who has got to the point where he feels it so keenly that he says: I have got to poison you. I just can't stand it anymore seeing you go on doing this. It is perhaps a comment on our state of heart and mind that we can understand somebody doing this to their child to stop the child going on suffering. We can't understand it of a Father who would do it to stop his child sinning.

Pastor Richard Wurmbrand understood this. He and a fellow Christian pastor were in a communist prison cell, and every day his fellow pastor was taken to the torture chamber and subjected to indescribable indignities, cruelties and pain to make him deny the faith. Day after day he held out and remained true to Jesus. But one day they flung him back into the cell half-dead and he said to Richard Wurmbrand, "Richard, I can't take any more, and tomorrow I'm going to deny Christ. I just can't face it again; they've broken me." That night Richard couldn't get to sleep and he lay awake worried about his brother going to sin tomorrow morning. He finally found that in his weakness this thought came into his mind. He thought, "If I killed him tonight he would get to heaven without this denial of Christ on his soul," and he stole over to the other bunk and he put his hands around this man's throat as he slept and was going to squeeze the life out of him and kill him to stop him sinning. At that moment, the man opened his eyes and said, "What are you doing?" Richard said, "Well, I was going to kill you; I couldn't bear the thought of you sinning tomorrow and denying Christ." You know, that fact that Richard was prepared to do this for his fellow pastor saved that pastor from denying Christ. He went through the next day without denial, and the next, and the next, until about ten days later he died in the torture, but he didn't deny Christ.

Richard had got to the point where he would rather kill a man than have him go on sinning. Now that was a little touch of the holiness of God getting into Richard Wurmbrand's soul, and we are nowhere near that holiness so we don't feel this. We would feel it about somebody suffering appallingly. I think most of us have had times when we would have wished to put someone out of their suffering. But you have got to be very near to God, and you have got to understand and know God terribly well to understand that that is how God feels about sinning, and that he would kill a person to stop sin going on spoiling his universe, and that he would give poison to drink.

Five times in chapters 8 and 9 the scriptural God, not the

sentimental one, the holy God and Father of our Lord Jesus Christ, said, "I must give you poison to drink. This has got to stop; I can't bear it in my world, in my holy land, in my holy city, it just can't go on any more." Now does that tell you what I mean by the sentimental and the scriptural God? The things I have just said would horrify most people in this country who believe in God. They say, "I just can't believe it—you must be sick, you must be mad to preach a God like that." But there it is in God's Word and either "thus says the Lord" is true or it's not, either he said that about himself or he didn't, there are no two ways about it. It fortunately doesn't matter in the slightest whether you believe what David Pawson says or believes or not, but it does matter what you say about "thus says the Lord" here. Is this God speaking? Is this the kind of God who really exists?

Well now, in the rest of this chapter I want to look at this passage and draw your attention to the fact that the situation is being viewed from three points of view. From God's point of view, then from Jeremiah's point of view (and he has very different feelings to God), and then from the people's point of view. They have different feelings. You can look at the same situation, and God has one kind of feeling, the prophet has another and the people have a third. You can tell where people are from the kind of reactions they have to the same situation. I believe that God has a different attitude to the situation in our country from that of most of us. I think he takes it ten times more seriously than any of us does.

Many years ago, I read out a prophecy given in London, in which God took the situation desperately seriously, and promised that he would take the brakes off the evil powers in this country until London's streets ran with the blood of innocent people. After that prophecy was given, we had bomb after bomb, and it had all been predicted by God — that is how seriously God takes the situation. That is why

115

I think we can't play around, we have to go much deeper until people realise that those bombs are the direct result of God saying, "It's got to stop." Until we open our newspapers and see God's hand in the headlines, we haven't got deep enough into the situation.

Now let us look first from God's point of view as he looks down. You know, you do get a different viewpoint when you are a bit higher up. You look down and see the little streets. When you get in an aeroplane, you look down and you see tiny little people like ants, and then little cars like ants, and you see it so small, and you think: my, those people think their problems are big, but aren't they tiny? Have you had that feeling? Well come up now with me to the highest heavens, and sit with God looking down on the whole mess. How does he feel about it? What does he think about it? How does he react?

He would say that the only part of nature that isn't natural is human nature. That is how he reacts. He observes how human beings behave contrary to their natural instincts. In many ways, people are sensible, but in religious realms, how utterly foolish and stupid they are. That is how God sees it, and it comes out at the beginning of the passage. Here are some normal things. What happens when a child falls down? Instinctively, they pick themselves up. Isn't that what you do when you fall down? Instinctively you pick yourself up. Why do you not do it spiritually? It's the natural thing to do. "When a man falls, does he not pick himself up?" says God. Or when a man gets off his route, when he strays, does he not try to find his way back?

You are going on holiday in your car, you are following the map, and you get onto a wrong road – what do you do? Instinctively, you say let's find the right road, let's get back onto it, and immediately you do something about it and get back on it. Why do you not do it spiritually? It is the instinctive and natural thing to do. Nature does what God tells it to do. Consider the way the birds migrate. The swallow knows when to head for Africa and when to head back. It has a homing instinct, and it follows that. I used to keep pigeons and it was fascinating to let them loose and see them circle three times, get a bearing, and then head straight for home. They head straight for the place they came from. Why don't people do that? We came from God, why don't we head for him? Why don't we let our instinct take over? There is a religious instinct. It is natural for man to be godly. It is natural for man when he is in a jam to call out to God. It is as much a part of us as the bird's homing instinct. So, God could say: The stork knows how to go, and the swallow knows, and the turtledove knows – but look at those people; they fall, they don't pick themselves up; they stray from the right path; they don't immediately say, "Let's get right back to the right path."

They come from God and they should be coming home to him and their heart is filled with instinct given by him to find him. Do they follow that instinct? They will follow anything else but. They will listen to anything but the Bible. They will study any religion but Christianity, they will go anywhere rather than try to get back onto the right track.

The only part of nature that doesn't behave naturally is human nature. People have to go against their natural inclinations to be ungodly. Now is that not true? How religious people can get into a difficult situation! Nothing makes a man religious like knowing he is going to die. It is amazing how a crisis puts us immediately in a religious frame of mind.

"You've made us for yourself," said St. Augustine. "Our hearts can find no rest until they find their rest in you." But is that what people are trying to do? Are people crowding into churches to say, "I must find God, I must get home to

God, I must have this instinct for God satisfied, I must find him at all costs"? Do they say that? No. So in physical ways we behave instinctively. In spiritual ways we do precisely the opposite. So, God looks down at this unnatural folly.

The worst part of it is, of course, that they think they do know the laws of God when they don't – because they have their Bible. From 8:8 onwards the prophet is teaching this: you may have a Bible but your preachers can make it say what they like. To me, the tragedy of our land is not so much that people don't have the Bible, as that, of the bits of it they do have, they have such a distorted understanding. I could take the Bible and prove anything I like from it. You can mishandle the Word of God, as Peter says. You can twist the scriptures until they mean the opposite of what they say. This is the tragedy – that men profess to read this book and to preach it, but they can twist it until it cuts out that scriptural God, until there is no God left who would poison people rather than have them go on sinning, until you are left with a mushy, sentimental grandfather sort of figure, whom you don't fear.

A letter in a local newspaper once criticised me for saying that the Archbishop should teach us to fear God more than we fear unemployment, violence or inflation. The letter said, "But Jesus came to deliver us from all our fears. There should be no fear in Christians." I don't read my New Testament like that. I read Peter's letter, "Fear God and honour the king." "The fear of the Lord is the beginning of wisdom" is what God says in my Bible. The correspondent said that Jesus comes to cast out all fear. What did Jesus say? He said, "Fear not those who can kill the body, but rather fear him who can destroy body and soul in hell. Fear him." There is a godly fear, which belongs to a scriptural God, and we can't get around this. If you get pally with the Deity and lose your reverence and your awe, it is not the scriptural

God you have found, it is the sentimental God. Oh yes, I know perfect love casts out fear. Praise God when perfect love fills this world and fills my whole being, then I won't need any more fear of God. But I know perfectly well that my love is not yet perfect and I need to fear God for those things that need to be perfected. We have the law, but you don't fear God. You heal the wound of my people lightly. You say, "It'll be alright if we all have just one big effort."

The tragedy of God's disappointment is in 8:13. "When I would gather them," says the LORD, "there are no grapes on the vine and no figs on the fig tree, even the leaves are withered, and what I gave them has passed away from them."

There was a devastating cartoon in *Punch Magazine* which showed a mother sitting at a table crying with her head down on the table, and a father looking very troubled, with his arm around her. Through the window you could see a policeman leading away their teenage son. Behind the couple there was a television set on a table. Between the TV and the table was the family Bible, lifting the screen to the right height. The family Bible had cobwebs round the edge. Underneath was this title: "The real culprits". You know *Punch Magazine* can have truth in it, God's truth, and it was there.

God says, "Even the things I gave them have gone." We can say this too – that God gave so much to this land, hoping to get a profit from it. He gave talents to us, hoping to get interest when he came again from the far country and said, "What have you done with what I gave you?" He gave so much to this country and he hoped to get so much back. He came and there were no grapes on the vine, no figs on the fig tree, and even the leaves had gone. Everything he had given had passed away. Everything he showered it with had been dissipated and spent. We have been living on spiritual capital for so long in this country that it has gone, it is not there, we can't spend it any more. All the two thousand years of Christian history – we have frittered it away and God won't even get that back because it has gone. So, looking at it all from God's point of view, how silly it all looks and how profitless. How disappointed God is.

Now let us look at things from Jeremiah's point of view. He was caught between God and the people because he was one of the people. He had intense sympathy with them, he felt for them deeply. But because he had been called of God he was caught by God. He did not want to preach what he preached, he didn't like doing so, but he was trapped between God and the people. Therefore, he became increasingly unhappy and it became a greater and greater burden of agony to him. In fact, he begins to say, "The wound of my people is my wound, the wound of my heart. It's hurting me, this." It did and it is of course a mark of a true prophet that it is hurting him as much as anybody else to whom he speaks. The frustration and helplessness came out in tears. Jeremiah says, "I just feel sick." Decades ago, I felt sick when I opened my newspaper one day and read that a bomb had killed a research professor devoted to saving children's lives. He had been blasted to bits by someone who hadn't even got any complaint against him. I said then to my congregation: this is not going to stop; this is going to go on until the streets of our cities are unsafe places for us. Jeremiah says, "Oh, I could just weep." For one thing, the people are so sure that God is still with them. They say, "Isn't the King in Zion? Isn't God on our side?" They just don't realise he is not – not any more. He is so sad because to worship idols doesn't make any sense. Why have they done it? It hasn't helped them. He is sad because time is slipping away. He says, "The harvest is over. The summer has ended and they are not saved." Now that means there had been a bad harvest that God had sent.

"Is there no balm in Gilead?" Have you heard that phrase? What a quotable quote! Gilead lay over the Jordan. It was a beautiful land. It grew balsam, which was made into ointment and medicine, and balsam is a healer. Jeremiah, from the highlands of Judea, looks across the deep Jordan Valley and there's beautiful Gilead, and he says, "Is there no medicine over there for here? Is there no doctor over there who could come and do something for us?" This is what people are saying today: "Is there no one in the world who can help us? Is there no cure anywhere on earth? Can't we get some cure?" But the answer is that there isn't any.

This was how Jeremiah felt: "I've wept too much." The thing that got him most was the loss of integrity in speech in his society, because integrity in speech and word is crucial to a society that is based on credit. You see, the whole of our commercial world is based on credit. We have many thousands of bankruptcies a year. Creditors are finding that they don't get their money. People who said they would pay up don't, and commerce collapses when credit goes. Lack of integrity makes commerce collapse, and when you can't trust the man who says, "I'll deliver it by next Thursday," then you are in difficulties. We are long past the day when an Englishman's word was his bond, as binding to him as any written legal document. One can only advise businessmen (even Christian businessmen) to be careful. In fact, Jeremiah says "Every brother is a supplanter." Now you won't get the pun in that. There's a very clever pun in the Hebrew. He is saying, "Every Israeli is a Jacob." For the word supplanter in Hebrew is *yahab*, Jacob. You will understand if you know the story of Jacob. You will know that Jacob was a deceiver; that he pretended that he was his brother Esau and he got the birthright and he deceived and he really got on. People would say, "My, he's clever."

At a staff meeting once we watched a missionary film from Guinea, which showed how a Canadian missionary went to a tribe for whom the highest virtue was treachery and for whom the highest virtue was to play a dirty trick on someone else to betray them. The tribe would befriend someone and bring them home and make friends with them, and give them meals, and be nice and kind and smiling to them, and then one day just slice their head off and eat their brains. This was considered clever. When the missionary first told the story of the Cross they were thrilled. They said, "What a hero Judas is. He got away with it and he got money for it. Marvellous! What a fool Jesus was, but Judas...." Judas became a folk hero in the tribe. This may seem incredible, but I tell you that in commercial life you can have the same kind of jungle in which it is clever to do the dirty on someone else, to strike a hard bargain, to have got away with something. That is all it is, treachery.

This is Jeremiah's viewpoint. He gets to the point where he says, "I just wish I could get right away." Just buy a little cottage in the country and just get right away from all the people. Have you had that desire? It's not necessarily God's way for you. Listen: "Oh that I had in the desert a wayfarer's lodging place that I might leave my people and go away from them" – just leave it all, get out of it all. More and more people are trying to do that. You can't buy a cottage in the country now because more and more people want a little hiding hole to get away from it all – to get out. Jeremiah just wished he had a little country cottage. But God said, "You stay right where you are." Here is part of a poem by William Cowper the hymn writer:

> Oh for a lodge in some vast wilderness,
>   Some boundless contiguity of shade,
> Where rumour of oppression and deceit,
>   Of unsuccessful or successful war,
> Might never reach me more! My ear is pained,
>   My soul is sick with every day's report
> Of wrong and outrage with which earth is filled.

Does that strike an answering chord in your heart? It does mine.

So we come to the final viewpoint of Judah. Disaster is certain to come; it is not if but when. The cattle will go, the birds will go, the beasts will go, the jackals will come. All that will be left will be a bitter taste – the wormwood and the gall. Now, if you believe that disaster is coming, how do you best behave in the meanwhile? If you believe that things are really going to come to the brink of destruction, how do you prepare for it? There are two things you can do: one is to live it up while you can; the other is to sober up. Jeremiah speaks to the women of Jerusalem and the men, and he tells them not live it up but to be sober, because when the crisis comes, the people who will cope with it are those who are sober before it comes. Those who live it up will have nothing. He deals first with the women, telling them to open their mouths, and the men to shut them, which is intriguing.

The extraordinary thing is that just before a society collapses women's fashions go crazy. I am absolutely serious about this. Society, in trying to have their last fling before disaster comes, goes crazy. In Jerusalem, Jeremiah says what they began to wear. Bright, vivid scarlet was the favourite fashion colour that spring. Golden ornaments were extremely popular, and the cosmetic fashion in the last days of Jerusalem was eye shadow – painting the eyes. This is described in an earlier chapter. "What do you mean that you dress in scarlet, that you deck yourself with ornaments of gold, that you enlarge your eyes with paint? In vain you beautify yourself." You see, Jeremiah isn't quite so out of date, is he? He's saying: you women, instead of preparing for more sober times you're living it up – all these cosmetics, the gold ornaments, you are going crazy, having a last fling. Why don't you start trying to be sober? Why don't you live more quietly? Why don't you teach your children, your daughters, how to sing dirges, because they are going to need to sing them. In other words, why don't you prepare for what is coming? You will then not have such a big shock, as the other people. That was exceedingly practical.

What about the men? Even though Judah was going downhill so rapidly, the men were still boasting that they were clever, powerful and rich. Speaking as a man, I know that those are the three basic ambitions of men. Very few achieve all three in their lifetime, most people manage to get a bit of one. We love to say, "I'm a successful man," and when you say of someone, "He's been successful", you always mean one of those three things in ordinary conversation. When somebody says to you they have been successful, ask them what they mean by that. It is either that they have cultivated their intellect and got a string of degrees after their name, or that they have got a position of power in which they give authoritative orders to others, or that they have become very rich. The thing that will stand you in good stead then is not that you are wealthy, powerful or clever, but that you know God and understand him.

So let not those men brag about these things, even in their own heart to themselves. But let them say, "I'm prepared for the crunch because I know God and I understand him. Therefore, I understand that my ambitions should be: justice, righteousness, to be fair, to be upright, to be a man of integrity. Then I will be able to cope."

You have a picture of the whole society going downhill. God's message is: sober up, the lot of you, and prepare to be much more serious and get to know me. You see, the Jew was proud of just two things: one, that he was circumcised; and, two, that he was successful in one of the three areas I have mentioned. God would say: Jews, you may be circumcised in body, so are the Egyptians, so are the other Semitic peoples around you, but are you circumcised in heart? What does that mean? You are circumcised in heart when you have had ambition for power and wealth cut from your heart, and when your heart wants to know God.

On a very positive note. I believe the most urgent thing is this: *you* can get ready for the crunch. The way you get ready is to get to know God. Until you know him, and share his serious outlook, and understand how he feels, and how he thinks, and how he reacts to the whole mess, then you will not be ready for it when it comes, and not be able to see others through, to carry them through. But if you know him, you will not be among those running away to some little place in the wilderness to escape it all. You will be where God needs you, firm and strong, and saying, "I know God." When the people really are in a position to say, "We want to know him too," you will be ready to tell them.

Christians, of all people, should not be running away and creating little holes for themselves where they can be safe. Christians should be getting to know God. There is a progression of thought in this. In 8:7, you don't know the Maker's instructions, you don't know the ordinance of the Lord. In 9:3, you don't know the Lord. In 9:6 you refuse to know the Lord, even though he's talking to you. But in 9:24 you understand and know the Lord. How do you know the Lord? Let me be very practical. You cannot get to know a person unless you give time to that person—there is no shortcut. The only men and women I have met who know the Lord are those who have spent time with him. I would never get to know you unless I spent time with you. You would never get to know me unless you spent time with me. That is the first thing. Spending time to know the Lord is the first requirement.

The second thing is this: if, in the time you spend with him, you do all the talking, you will not get to know him. He will get to know you, but you will not get to know him. You only get to know a person by listening and there are people who just don't know how to listen to God. So let me be practical about that, too. I believe that the most urgent thing today is that people should spend more time in the Bible. Ten verses a day may, you think, keep the devil away, but it won't help you to know the Lord. I suggest as an immediate practical step that you resolve to read three chapters a day and five on Sunday. You will be through the Bible once a year then, and you will have listened to everything God said just once in the year. This is so that you don't just read it through, but you think about it and go on thinking. Now I realise I am at an advantage here. People say, "How do you prepare your sermons?" I had to go to college students and answer that very question. I had to say, "Well, I read the passage and I think, and I read the passage and I think, and I read the passage and I think, and I read the passage and I think. Each time I think a thought it goes down on paper. Then I go back and read it again, think again, write it down again, until I feel: God, I understand what you're saying. I know how you're feeling about this; I know your reaction, I understand you, and I can see how you feel about Britain today. I feel I'm just beginning to know you.

That can be an immediate practical outcome of this study. At the end of another twelve months, I want you to be able to boast — not that you have made enough money to see you through, not that you've got a position that will keep you and your family secure, not that you have passed your degree, though all of these things may be part of God's will. I want you to be able to say, "I really know the scriptural God. I really feel as he feels. I really understand why he is so upset about what's going on. I'm beginning to share a horror of sin that would make me rather poison someone than let them go on doing it. I begin to understand." Let me hasten to add that only God himself can take that decision.

Only God could do it fairly and justly and righteously. But if God is acting, then we need to understand, we need to listen, not to all the letters in the papers, not even to all the preachers, for they say so many different things. We need to get to the point where we know what God is doing, and what God is feeling about our country, and then we will be with him. It is not a case, as Israel thought, of being able to say "God is on our side." It is a case of saying *we* shall then be on *his* side. Even though we are lonely, misunderstood, isolated, criticised, persecuted — we will stand with God and we will know him and the crunch will come.

I tell you that when the crisis really does hit, people in this country will then look around for those who know God. They will look around for those who are still living alongside them and have not run away.

READ JEREMIAH 10:1–12:6

There are many parallels between our day and Jeremiah's. Now we are going to be looking much more at the man than his message. It is going to be a rather different study to those we have had so far, for he is one of those who was willing to let us see inside his own heart – in that way to become vulnerable and to be misunderstood. The passage is composed of four sections, quite distinct from each other, and they alternate. The first and the third sections are Jeremiah as a preacher in public. The second and the fourth sections are Jeremiah in private, praying.

There is such a contrast between Jeremiah in public and Jeremiah in private that we are going to have to ask some very big questions. Was he a hypocrite? Was he an actor? Was he two-faced? In public when he was preaching he was dogmatic, very sure of himself. In private when he prayed he was full of doubts and very unsure of himself. In public he was very forthright, in private he was very fearful. In public he was a tough man, in private he was a very tender man. In public he was victorious, but in private he was vulnerable. Was he living a double life? Were these two Jeremiahs? How do they tie together?

I think we shall understand this a little better if we put together sections one and three of our reading and study his public preaching and then study sections two and four together, and look at his private praying and try and understand the man who lay behind the message. For the contrast is so stark that people have raised this question about him. But when you get to know other preachers you find that the same thing applies. If you were to listen to their private prayers you would get a very different impression from that gained from listening to their public preaching. Why is there this duality? Can we understand it?

We look first at the two public sermons recorded for us in chapters 10 and 11. The theme of both public sermons is the same: Yahweh's sovereignty—the power, the glory, the might, the majesty of God in heaven, Creator of the universe. But there's another theme that comes through—this God who is the Creator has made a covenant, with a particular nation on earth. It is because they have gone against this double relationship with God that the Jews, more than any other nation, have suffered so deeply. Other nations have denied the Creator, but Israel denied the covenant God as well as the God who created them.

The nations of the world deny a single relationship but Israel denies the double relationship. So Jeremiah preached two sermons on two different occasions. One is on this: you are denying God as Creator when you make these idols. The other sermon: you are denying the God who entered into a covenant with you, a marriage with you. You are his special people and to deny your Creator is one sin, and a terrible thing to do. It is even worse to deny the Creator who became your own special God and married himself to you in a covenant.

I was visiting a school and trying to answer some of the pupils' questions. One was this: did God make man or does man make god? That is a profound question and my answer was both. God made man but as soon as man rejects the God who made him then he must make a god for himself. There is what Huxley called a god-shaped blank in the human soul and you have got to fill it or you feel so empty. This god-shaped blank you can fill with many things. Every thing that you try to fill it with is an idol in the biblical definition of idolatry.

You see, when we think of this word "idol" we tend to think of ugly little lumps of stone and wood. That is not the only idol that you can make. Your idol is anything that fills the god-shaped blank in your soul. We will think in a moment of the kinds of idols that people use today to fill that blank, but the fact is that God made us so like himself that if we don't accept that and relate to him we feel hollow — life is meaningless and purposeless, and we have to fill it in with something so we make the gods that we like.

In those days it was almost pathetic what they used to fill that blank. One of the things they used was astrology — horoscopes. That is still around in modern times. One day I walked down the Champs-Élysées in Paris and saw a queue of well-dressed French men and women standing outside a shop in which there was a computer that could print out a large sheet and they were queuing up to pay for a horoscope for a month. The brilliance of modern technology was being used to promote this idolatry. They were paying that because they were looking to that to fill the god-shaped blank. Jeremiah warned: Don't try to read your fate and future in the stars, don't get interested in that. Don't be curious about it. It is just a pack of lies. Don't be frightened by its predictions. They can't do you any harm. They can't do you any good. It is fraud. Yet there are many more people in Britain who read their horoscopes than read their Bible every day. So, idols are not out of date.

At this point Jeremiah has a scathing satire on idols. He particularly thinks of the wooden ones they made. He almost makes them laugh at it to see how silly it is: you cut a tree down and then you try and dress it up so it doesn't look like a tree. You have to nail it in place or else it might fall down. This is the god who is going to help you! He is supposed to keep you up, and you have to carry him around because he can't walk!

The fact is that whatever other thing you put in that god-shaped blank, whatever idol you look to, to see you through, that idol is something you will have to carry. It is not something that can carry you, because you made it and therefore it is less than yourself. Anything I make is less than I am. Therefore, to look to something I have made to help me is ridiculous, illogical, unreasonable, and yet we do it. A man builds up his business and he looks to that business to see him through, but he made the business. It is less than he is and he is looking to this business as if it were greater than he is, and it isn't. Whether you make money or make love or make whatever, it is something you make and therefore it is not something that can make you.

Jeremiah makes four contrasts between the idols of his day and the true God. These are four questions we can ask about our modern idols too. The first question: is your god weak or strong? An idol is weak. You have to nail it up. It can't walk, it doesn't breathe, it can't move, it can't talk, it can't communicate with you, it can't respond to you, it can't relate to you—it is weak.

In a beautiful phrase he says, "Your god stands there like a helpless scarecrow in a garden of cucumbers." Can you imagine anything more laughable than looking at a scarecrow in a garden of cucumbers and saying, "This is my god, may I introduce you? Fall down and worship. Take your shoes off, get down before it. It's great." What bitter irony, what satire. Jeremiah is laughing it out of court. But God is great. He is the King of the nations—that is his title. He is not weak, he is strong. Is your god weak or strong?

You know, even the idol of "churchianity" you will have to carry — it will not carry you. Religion, unless it is the religion of the living God, will always be something you carry. As I have travelled around the world and looked at other religions and studied them, I have noticed that in every case people are having to carry their religion. It doesn't carry them. It is one of the things that gives the whole show away. Even religion is an idol. A church building can be an idol that you look to for help. I tell you, if you do, you will have to carry it. It will not carry you. Only the living, great God is strong enough to walk and to talk and to carry you and to be other than a scarecrow in a cucumber field.

Second question: is your god dead or alive? That is a relevant question. Here is a young man and his god is his motorbike. Every Sunday he worships it and polishes it and bows down before it and does obeisance to it and looks at it and stands back and adores it. It is dead — a lump of dead metal. Yet it can have the place in that young man's heart that only the Lord should have. He is filling the god-shaped blank with speed and power instead of with God, but it is a dead god.

You cut a tree down, says Jeremiah, and you may cover it with gold and silver, and you may get your best tailor to make a suit of clothes for it, but it is dead, it doesn't breathe. In that phrase you have almost got the death of all idols. It doesn't breathe. So as one commentator has said, "When you lean your weary head against its breast there is no heaving response."

But ours is the living God, before whom the world trembles. A God who is so alive that he can be angry, and when he is angry you fear and you tremble. The whole world will tremble before our God because he is alive. He is not a dead thing up there, he is alive and therefore he is responding to the situation. He can respond with love and compassion. He can respond with anger — but he is alive, he is not dead.

Question number three: is your god perishable or enduring? "How long will it last?" asks Jeremiah. Any god you have made for yourself will perish before you perish, when you perish, or when the earth perishes. But he says that your gods are perishable, and I care not what other thing or person a man puts in the god-shaped blank of his soul, what has been put there, if it is not God, will perish. One of the biggest questions you can ask yourself is this: this thing or this person to whom I have looked, to whom my life is dedicated, this god of mine, will this god be with me after I die? Or will it perish when I do? Will it cease to help me when I die? Is your god perishable or enduring?

God was always there and he made everything that is. He flung the stars into space. He stretched the heavens like a great curtain. The question "Who made God" is a nonsensical question, but I still get asked it. It is as silly as asking, "Can you make a square circle?" because the very word "God" by implication, by definition, means the one who was always there before everything else was, and who made it all.

Which is your God? Is it a god who has been made or is it the God who makes? The funny thing is that if man will not accept the God who makes him, then he does make a god. But the true, Creator God always was there and always will be. Now that we have seen pictures of other planets, doesn't it give you a sense that God has been looking at those rocks on the surface of those places from the day he flung them into orbit? He knows what the surface of every planet looks like, and so this is the God who doesn't perish.

Final question: "Is your god worthless or precious?" asks Jeremiah. "Our God is our inheritance, our portion," he says, "How much is your god worth?" The very word "inheritance" means that I have got so much to look forward to. He is my portion, he is my share, he is what I want, he is my inheritance, he is what I am looking forward to. Oh, how precious he is! "But your god," says Jeremiah, "how worthless." How much is your god worth?

Do you know the meaning of the word "worship"? Originally it had two more letters in it and was "worthship". This is to give yourself to the person or thing that is worth most to you. When we are in church on Sunday morning, if anybody comes in and joins us, let us say to them clearly, "We are here because God is worth more to us than anything or anyone else, and we are declaring his 'worthship'." But what are your other gods really worth? I tell you they will all be devalued and come to nothing. The God of Israel is my portion and my inheritance.

Let us consider those modern idols. The extraordinary thing is that in Britain today the cycle of sin is so reversed that in fact the very idols of Jeremiah's day are now appearing again. I have mentioned astrology, and it is rife – but there are other things too.

The worship of Baal was deified sex and the idols referred to were huge, ugly phallic symbols, exactly the sort of thing that has appeared on the modern stage, now made of fibreglass. A nine-foot high phallic symbol was the scenery for a Shakespeare play. So we are not as modern as we thought, not so far removed from idolatry. We are not so far from Jeremiah's situation.

But Jeremiah says: your gods are as many as your cities. The fact is that *we* have added many other gods; there are many other idols. A man may have as his idol his own family, and that may come absolutely first even though he goes to church. You can tell just by looking at his house that is what his god is. That is what he looks to, to provide him with peace, security, comfort and everything that he wants. For another, it is his car. You can see by looking at his car. Or it is may be a business. There are idols that fill this god-shaped blank, things that people live for and look to, to see them through. It is very sad because many of these things may be quite legitimate in their place, but that is never first place.

I think of Abraham who was tempted to dote on his only son by Sarah. He could become his god so easily, so God said, "Take Isaac whom you love and kill him" – and when Abraham was about to do that, God stopped him.

Jeremiah spoke of businessmen who take root and their business grows, their profits multiply, and they are rich. They say, "Thank God" but in their hearts they give no credit to God. Applying this to our own times, they don't say, "God, I'm in church because I know that without you my business would collapse. I know that without you I could never have got where I've got." No, they say, "Thank God," but in their heart they think: "I'm pretty astute you know. I've played the markets well." Well, that is a pretty strong, forthright sermon. Let us move quickly on to the second sermon.

Jeremiah's message is not only: you have copied other nations and gone after idols. You filled the god-shaped blank with other than the living true God, King of the nations, Creator of the earth who flung the stars into space. It is also this: you Jews have done something even worse — it is bad enough for godless people to do this. It is bad enough for the nations of the world to behave this way. But what have you done? You have had a covenant with him, you have been married to God. You weren't just created by him, you were loved by him, and brought into a covenant. He is referring to Mount Sinai.

In 11:1-17, Jeremiah is recorded as saying four things which are four steps. The first paragraph: you lost interest in the covenant; you just ignored it. Step number two: you became disobedient. Even when you knew what the covenant said, you didn't do it. Step number three: you became dissolute and you ran after other gods and your moral standards went. Step number four: disowned — when you tried to get back to God you found he wouldn't listen to you.

Now that's a very simple four-point sermon and I want

to give it to you in the form of an analogy. A covenant is a marriage. So, let me trace those four steps in a marriage. Here they are. Step number one: when the wife stops paying attention to her husband and doesn't notice what his feelings are. That is the first step of the breaking of the marriage. (I am using the example this way round, for the wife, because Israel to Yahweh was a wife to her husband).

Step number two: when the wife starts living her own life even though she is still under the same roof as her husband. Not doing what he wanted her to do, not going out with him when he wants them to go out together, but just saying, "No, I've planned this for tonight." The marriage is still not broken but a deeper stage of breaking has been reached. Stage number three: when she finds another man more interesting than her own man and begins to play around with other men. The marriage has broken at this point. Stage number four, she comes back reeking of perfume and says, "Hello darling," to the husband and is surprised that he is cool and that he doesn't want her back. Now that is like Jeremiah's sermon: Israel, that's what you did to God. At first you just didn't pay him much attention, you didn't heed the covenant. Then you began to live your own life, you didn't obey the covenant. Then you went after other gods. You know, the intriguing thing is that the word "Baal" means "my husband", so it is a very relevant illustration.

Then comes the main point of this sermon and it is devastating. Jeremiah says this: "What right has my beloved in my house?" Because when they felt the national emergency, when they needed God, they poured back into the temple to pray and they came back with perfume from Sheba for God and they offered sacrifices, and God says, "What right has my beloved in my house?" Now the bitterness of that comes through in the word "beloved". Did you notice that? My beloved, she ignored me, she lived her own life, she went after other men, and now she comes back. It is the agony of God's heart coming through in that. What right has she in my house when she has done this? God looks at Israel and says, "What right has she to come into my temple?" He says, "Jeremiah, don't weep for her. Don't pray for her. Don't plead for her. Don't make it worse for me than it is. My beloved comes running back with perfume and wants to love me, and look what she has been doing. What right has she to be in my house?" It is a powerful sermon.

I draw from it this one lesson: that God feels even more keenly the agony of knowing someone who has been his, who has had a godly background, who knows him, and who then drifts after other gods and then comes back as if they can just walk in and say, "God, here I am again. I'm yours." You see, God judges by the opportunities we have had. That is why he was more severe with Israel than any other nation. The other nations hadn't got the covenant. They simply rebelled against the Creator, but Israel rebelled against a covenant God. No wonder that Jesus said, "Woe unto you Capernaum!" Capernaum is a beautiful little fishing village on the edge of the Sea of Galilee. Seventy miles to the south is the Dead Sea, and in the bottom of that Dead Sea somewhere under its waves lie the cities of Sodom and Gomorrah. Yet Jesus said, "Woe unto you Capernaum! It'll be better for Sodom and Gomorrah in the Day of Judgment than for you." Why? "Because you've had me in your town, Sodom never had. If the mighty works that had been done in you were done in Sodom and Gomorrah they would have repented but you have had the bigger chance."

It is a sobering thought that those of us who have been brought up in a Christian country, who have heard the gospel, who have had it taught to us in school, those of us who know the truth about God, will be dealt with much more strictly than people in remote tribal areas who never heard. The covenant people are judged more severely than those who are simply the created people.

So much for Jeremiah's public ministry. It is powerful, forthright and strong. Yet when you go into his private prayer life you find a very different Jeremiah, full of questions and doubts and fears, who is hesitant, and broken from time to time. For we have come in this section to the first of what have been called the confessions of Jeremiah, in which he showed how he felt inside about all this — not nearly so sure of himself, his emotions torn in two between his people and his God. From time to time he found himself on the side of his people and against his God, so deeply did he feel.

From one point of view, I hope that there are times when you feel the same. I hope there are times when your heart rebels against the fact that some physical relatives are probably going to be in hell. I hope your heart takes their side against God sometimes, because that will show that you still have a heart. God was patient with Jeremiah when he took the same line. Now Jeremiah was torn in emotions by this fact. On the one hand, he had a deep empathy with his people. He loved them, he wept for them, he prayed for them, and he felt for them. On the other hand, he had such an estrangement from them that they plotted to kill him. This is the tension and no human being likes this. To love people so much that you cannot bear the thought of their being judged by God, and yet knowing that all the time they judge you — that is hard. So, Jeremiah reveals his heart.

We consider first his empathy with his people. In 10:17-25 he feels keenly the disaster, the invasion, that is coming. So keenly does he feel it that in the first person singular he describes a situation that he will never have. He says, "My children are gone." Now, he was forbidden to marry, he never had children because he never had a wife, but so deeply could he feel for his countrymen and women that he could almost feel the invasion already happening. He could feel the moment when they picked up their bags to make the long trek to Babylon, when they said goodbye to their children for the last time, when they closed that front door knowing they would never see their own home again, when they pulled that tent up knowing they would never pitch it again in their own land. He is saying: "Desperate is my wound, my grief is great, my sickness is incurable. My home is gone, my children have been taken away. I will never see them again. There's no one left to help me rebuild my home." It pours out. He feels it so deeply that already he is living in the sorrow of it. You know, a man can only preach in a dogmatic and forthright way and denounce people as strongly as he did in public if in private he feels as deeply as this for what they are to go through. If he can weep for them and if he can really feel the horror of it, that is his empathy.

Out of that empathy with his people comes a prayer: "Lord, I know I'm weak. I know it's not in a man to plan his life. I know it's not in us to live the life you want us to live. I know we're weak, but Lord, please don't be too angry with us. Don't blot us out altogether. Lord, couldn't you just have some of your anger for the nations that are attacking us? Lord, just don't be too angry with us, please. Don't blot us out, don't wipe us out altogether." It comes at the end of chapter 10. "O Lord, I know it is not within the power of man to map his life and plan his course. So correct me Lord, but please don't be angry with me or I'll die." He's feeling the judgment of God and pleading that it be not too severe—that is his empathy. So, he accepts that judgment itself is right. He says we must bear it, but somehow you get a picture of a people picking up their bundles to be taken away. When I read this phrase, my mind went back to a newsreel film of the Jews being loaded onto trains in Germany. Have you seen those newsreel films? Have you seen how they passed, weeping — just picked up their little feeble bundles and got on the train, knowing they would never see their families and homes again? I am sure that in many of their hearts they were saying, "Lord, couldn't you just be angry with the people who are doing this to us?" Jeremiah reveals his torn heart: "Lord, I know the judgment is correct. I know that we've not planned our course right. I know that you have a right to be angry. We must bear our punishment, but Lord, please don't make it too much." It is very human. A man who in public can say, "The judgment of God will wipe you out," in private says, "Lord, please don't." Have you got a sense of the tension?

Finally, let us look at his estrangement from his people. He felt so close to them, but they did not feel close to him. It came to him as a frightful shock about the people of his own village, Anathoth. You can still see the little town — the Arab town of Anata — about three and a half miles north and east of Jerusalem. The people of his own village Anata/Anathoth were actually plotting his death. He never dreamt that their dark looks at him, their whispers when he was around — meant this is what they were doing until God told him one day. Jeremiah, they hate your guts; Jeremiah, they are going to kill you.

Jeremiah realised that a man's foes shall be those of his own household. The incredible thing is the men of Anathoth said, "Let's kill Jeremiah and we'll blot out his name. We'll forget his name. He's let us down and we don't want one of our relatives speaking like this, so let's blot out his name." The men of Anathoth — their only claim to fame is that they tried to kill Jeremiah. But for Jeremiah, they would never be thought or spoken of. I am talking of the men of Anathoth. Why? Because Jeremiah is famous. Because Jeremiah's name is known throughout the world and it has been known by millions. This young boy of worldwide fame, and the men of Anathoth are only remembered because of him.

So, Jeremiah says, "I feel like a lamb before the slaughterer — deal with them." God says, "It's all right, I will. Vengeance is mine, I will repay." You know, if you are suffering any persecution at all — and you may have friends or relatives who despise you — let me remind you, God will put that right. He will deal with them.

In fact, if you realise that God will deal with them, it will make you a little tenderer towards them. Do you realise that if anyone laughs at a Christian because he is a Christian, God will punish him for that? You don't need to worry. Jeremiah says, "God, will you deal with them?" God's answer is: Look, I have already decided to deal with them. Their sons and daughters will perish and starve. Don't you worry about that, Jeremiah. Leave your enemies to me, you get on with the job. So Jeremiah did.

But he not only had to cope with conflict without, but also with fears within. The last thing we look at here is perhaps the deepest. Jeremiah was afflicted with intellectual doubts. Even while he preached without any trace of doubt whatever, he had deep doubts in his own mind. The doubts were these, and it is a very, very old problem: Lord, you tell me that the wicked will be punished, and look at them — they are making money, their businesses prosper; they are fat and sleek. It doesn't tie up. Lord, the facts around me don't fit my faith.

This is one of the biggest questions that a man of God has to cope with and it appears all the way through the Bible. You find it in Psalm 73 and right through the book of Job. What happens when the facts don't fit in with your faith? Jeremiah did the right thing — he didn't preach about his doubts. I love the true story of the lady who went to her minister and said, "I wish you would preach on some of your convictions — I've got enough doubts of my own without coming to church to listen to yours."

Jeremiah coped with fighting without. But fears within? He found that much more difficult. He said, "God, why do the wicked prosper? Here I am preaching this and you just seem to leave them to get on and make money. They don't listen, they don't respond. They are comfortable, happy, secure. Why, God? I don't understand it. Why?" You see, Jeremiah is being shaken by the facts of society. He says, "How long, God? How long is this land to put up with this? How long are you going to delay your punishment? I've said you're going to punish them, but how long before you come and do it? They're just laughing at you because you're not doing anything. How long, Lord? Why?" Here is a man with terrific doubt, whose faith is tottering. I thank God for an honest Bible, don't you? I thank God for a Bible that says men of the calibre of Jeremiah struggled with doubts in private and had to ask God "Why? How long?"

Jeremiah's question was, "Why do they prosper?" But God's question back meant: "How will you preach if you are shaken by these facts? Don't be shaken by what you see. Believe in me and go on speaking. You have got bigger battles ahead, and I gave you these smaller battles so that you were ready for the bigger ones." God is being both tough and tender. He is lifting Jeremiah up, boosting his morale. Jeremiah, now stand on your feet, be a man; don't let these things shake you because there is a bigger battle ahead. God doesn't always answer our doubts. You say, "God, why? Why are you doing this?" God doesn't always say, but he says, "Look, don't let it shake you, go on fighting." God says, "Jeremiah, your own family are going to attack you. How will you cope with that? I know your villages have. I know the men of Anathoth have. But Jeremiah, your own brothers and sisters are going to do it. How will you cope then? Jeremiah, pull yourself together. You shouldn't be asking me questions. I should be asking you questions."

That is how Job was dealt with. Job brought his doubts to God and Job said, "God, why? Why am I suffering? Why are you letting these things happen to me?" Do you know how God answered those questions? He said, "Job, were you there when the foundations of the earth were laid? Do you know where the snow comes from? Do you know where the wind comes from? Do you know how nature works?" He just battered poor old Job into the ground with questions until Job got the answer to his questions.

Do you know what the answer was? God knows he is God, which isn't very odd. That is the answer. It has got to be sorted out in prayer when you are afflicted with doubts. You can go to a Christian and ask questions. They can try to answer them. The best thing you can do is to take your doubts to God and let God ask you questions. Jeremiah would have to trust God who was not going to answer all his questions, he was going to put him back in the battle — and a fiercer, stronger battle — to fight.

So, we have come to the answer to our question. Why is it that in private Jeremiah was so shaken, so unsure, so full of doubt, yet in public he preached so dogmatically, so strongly? Why in public could he say, "God will punish you," and in private could he say, "When are you going to, Lord, and why don't you get on with it?" The answer is very simple. He is not a hypocrite, not an actor, not two-faced. In public, the words of God were on his lips and in private the words of man were on his lips. In public, he spoke from God to men; in private, he spoke from man to God. If you think that is weakness, if you think that is a contradiction, let me take you to the very person whose death we remember in broken bread and poured out wine. There is Jesus himself, the Son of God—in public, listen to his courage. In public, listen to him speak. Listen to him call the Pharisees whited sepulchres. Listen to him defy Herod and say, "Go and tell that fox." Listen to what he says: "No-one takes it [*my life*] from me, but I lay it down of my own accord. I have power to lay it down, and I have power to take it again.... This charge I have received from my Father."

Brave words, strong words, courageous words in public, but now come with me into private prayer, into the garden of Gethsemane, where with drops of blood on his brow he says, "Father, please take this cup away. I can't cope with it. Please take it away. Nevertheless, not my will...." Come with me later, after just a few hours on the cross. Here he is saying, "Why?" Private prayer again, "My God, my God, why have you forsaken me?" And there is no answer from heaven — no answer at all — and God doesn't answer.

Even Jesus himself had this strange dual experience—in public he spoke so strongly, gave the Word of God to men. But in his private prayer he is speaking to the Father, saying, "Why?" So, we do not regard it as a sign of weakness that Jeremiah had this experience. If you are to be a man or woman of God you must be bold, you must speak the truth, whatever it costs, but in private you can take your questions to God. You can take your doubts to God. You can take the uncertainties, the torn emotions. You can admit to him, "God, there are times when I feel that if my relatives are not going to be in heaven I don't want to be in heaven either." You be honest with God. God will not answer your questions. He won't deal with all the doubts. He will say, "I'm God and I know what I am doing. Now get back into the front line. You go right on speaking for me."

These two chapters alternate between prose and poetry in
the Hebrew. In the poetic passages there is speaking from
the heart. The primary thing you need to ask is, "What is he
feeling at this point? What's the emotion of the passage?"
Though there will be mental content, he bursts into poetry
when his heart is being deeply touched. That is one of the
reasons for having poetry and God is a poet – when he
speaks, and he is speaking here, he can speak in poetry. When
something is coming right from the heart, that is when we
tend to burst into song or to write poems.

On the other hand, prose is more ordinary and down to
earth. Therefore, when the Word of God changes to prose
we have to ask: What is the head saying, and how does my
head respond to what is being said? So, when you read the
poetic parts of prophecy, feel them in your heart – get the
gut feel of what Jeremiah is saying. Ask the Lord to give
you the right emotional response to his Word. But when you
turn to prose, then, as it were, turn your head on and think
hard and ask what he is saying. He is not there appealing
to your heart but to your head. He wants you to think more
clearly about something. Now that is a little key that might
help unlock the meaning in these chapters.

The first thing I do when I am trying to get into a passage
is to read it and read it until one word hits me and really
comes out of the passage. Now I don't know if when you
read this you got the keyword. In fact, in the first of the two

chapters there were two keywords. "They have made my pleasant portion a desolate wilderness. They have made it desolate; desolate it mourns to me. The whole land is made desolate but no man lays it out." Did you get the keyword in that little verse? If you write in your Bible, take a pen and put a line under that verse. You have got one of the themes that is coming out. The *desolation* is coming through; he is feeling it; he is writing a poem about it. There is nothing so heart-rending as to see a place desolate that once was alive and prospering and full of people. Have you been back to a house where you lived as a child and seen it pulled down and there is just a rubbish dump where it was? It gets to you, doesn't it?

What would you think or feel if a whole land had prospered, had been flowing with milk and honey, full of kids playing in the streets, but now you saw it empty, deserted, with the people gone and houses ruined? You might write a poem about it. The desolation would get into your heart. You are beginning to get the feel of this by studying the words.

But there is another word that is even more important than the word *desolate* because it goes all the way through 12:7-17: "I have forsaken my house, I have abandoned my heritage. My heritage has become to me like a lion in the forest. Is my heritage to me like a speckled bird of prey? Thus says the Lord concerning all my evil neighbours who touch the heritage which I have given to my people Israel to inherit. I will bring them again, each to his heritage and each to his land."

Did you get the word? I am trying to help you tackle a difficult passage – go through it until words begin to make an impact. "Heritage" – it is a beautiful word. Here it is applied to a plot of land. You may or may not be in a position to understand this. If you have had a plot of land in the family for years and it has been passed down from father to son, to grandson to great-grandson, it may be only a little plot of land, but it is your heritage. You have lived on it all your life and you have farmed it and dug it; you have loved it and looked after it, and as far back as you can trace it has been in your family. It is your heritage and it belongs to you. Yet here it is being taken away. It is dreadful being the generation that loses a heritage of land. Of course, most of us don't have that experience so we don't get the feel of it, but I have met farmers who have had the experience. Smallholders, maybe with thirty acres somewhere, and they inherited it way down in the family. Now they have got to let it go – they can't keep it going. They have got to say goodbye to their heritage and it has been their land and this generation is losing it.

Are you beginning to get the feel of this? Because this is in poetry, not only because Jeremiah is feeling it, but because God himself is feeling it. Do you realise that God, who made the universe, who flung the stars into space, put this earth in orbit, said of all that world there is a little bit that's mine especially – my Holy Land. He set his heart on that little bit of land. He made the whole world, but once you have been to Israel you see why God regards that as something special. It is the most amazing little bit of land. It is about the size of Wales and it has everything in it from flat desert to snow-capped mountains; from deep valleys to high hills; from lush green pastures to deep ravines. It has everything within about fifty miles. It is the most perfect little gem of land. It has the lowest point on the earth's surface. It is a beautiful land – apart from its history, apart from its people, it is special in its own right. It is at the junction of three continents. It is a key little land and this was God's heritage, his special little land, his Holy Land. It was the land in which the worst things that have ever taken place on the face of the earth happened.

If you want to know why God ordered the Israelites to

destroy the cities in that land, you read about what we have discovered regarding the social life of a place like Jericho. It was a foul city, riddled with disease, absolutely riddled with sin, vice, and crime. It was not even safe to marry any of its people. No wonder God said, "Go in and get rid of those cities. They have got to be cauterised; they've got to be blotted out. I want that land for myself." It's the land in which Sodom and Gomorrah were situated. It's the land of the Canaanite paganism which lies behind all this prophecy.

God says, "I want that land. It's mine; it's my heritage. I made it and I made it for myself. So, Israel, go in and get it for me. Go in and get it back, it's mine. I want you to be stewards of it. I want you to look after it for me forever. I want to give you that land forever." So he started by calling an old man, Abraham, who was living in a very civilised town with central heating and running water in the bedrooms – Ur of the Chaldees. He said, "Get out of there and live in a tent and get to a land – it's mine. When you get there, keep it for me." But, alas, as you know, they drifted down to Egypt to try to find food. So God said to the Jews in Egypt, "Look, I'll take you back to that land, will you look after it for me? Will you make it mine; it's my heritage." He brought them forty years through the wilderness and he brought them in, and he said, "Wipe out Jericho, wipe out Ai, wipe out these cities. Have nothing to do with them, don't marry people in them. They are diseased, they are dirty, get rid of them, get my land clean; it is to be a holy land," and he brought them in. He gave them kings and he protected them against the Philistines and the Midianites and all the others that would take them from that land, and there God had his land, his heritage. It was to remain in the family now forever. That was God's desire: that's my land and it is to stay in my family.

Then, of course, we know that the very things that people had been doing in that land before God brought the Hebrews in began to permeate back. They did not blot them all out; they did not keep away from them in marriage. Bit by bit, it all filtered back in until the very people of God whom he brought in to keep this land in the family had taken it out of God's hands again. So now comes this cry from God's heart: "I have forsaken my house, I have abandoned my heritage. I have given the beloved of my soul into the hands of her enemies. I've had to do it. I've had to let go of this land again and my heritage has gone out of the family yet again, and I've had to let my people go and I love my people but now I hate them." You know, there is no relationship so terrible as when love is turned to hate. Love and hate are very close together. I have sometimes found myself wondering if you can hate someone you haven't loved. It seems as if hate is love gone sour, doesn't it?

Sometimes it is said about a man and a wife, or two friends, or even two children, that they have a love/hate relationship. Do you know what that means? Love and hate are the opposites and yet they are two sides of the same deep commitment to people. Somehow when love is refused and love is abused is when love quickly turns to hate. Only those who have loved deeply can know what it means to hate. God says, "My beloved, I hate her." No wonder Jeremiah puts this into poetry. I am not exaggerating the language there. In 12:7, "the beloved of my soul"; the end of v. 8, "I hate her", and God's love has turned to hate. He gave the Jews this land to keep in the family, to keep it holy, and he hates them for what they have done.

So it is a profound poem, full of picture language. God says, "You've become like a lion in the forest to me. I don't want to come near you", and, "You're like a bird with beautiful, coloured plumage being attacked by birds of prey" – vivid pictures. He also says, "I see shepherds coming in and pulling up your vines." Let me try to convey to you the emotion of that.

A vine takes time to grow and a lot of care, and it is a long, slow business. If you go to Hampton Court you will see a vine that has been growing there for about three hundred years. When you have got a vine trained, growing and bearing grapes, it is the fruit of years building up to that. But a shepherd isn't interested in vines, he just wants some grass. So he pulls up the work of years and rips up the vineyard and he lets his goats loose in the place. Sheep wander where those vines grow. Imagine if that were your vineyard and you saw those beautiful trees that you trained for so long uprooted. Well this is how he is feeling here: "Shepherds are pulling down my vineyard." That is what it is saying. All of us have a heritage, but it can be lost so quickly. It may have taken centuries to build up and develop but it can go like that; it can go so quickly—that is the tragedy of it. It happened to Israel and it can happen to any other nation. You see, we have got a precious heritage. If you are from overseas, I am not being nationalistic but patriotic, which I think is warranted by the Bible.

We have a great national heritage in Britain, built up over many centuries. We haven't been invaded and occupied in this land for over nine hundred years. During that time, we have been able to build up a parliamentary system, a legal system and many things which are the envy of other nations. We have had Christianity pervading our society for nearly two thousand years, and the salt of the earth has prevented us from going crazy in all kinds of directions. This is a great national heritage but it can be lost in a moment and it can go in a decade or two, and that is precisely what is happening at the moment.

There is a lot that we inherit that we didn't deserve to inherit in this beautiful little land. It was meant to be a holy land as every land was meant to be. But a national heritage can be lost, and love can turn to hate. and the God who gives us these heritages can take them away again so quickly. Once he has decided to take them away, nothing we can do can stop it. John Stuart Mill said in 1867: "Bad men need nothing more to compass their ends, than that good men should look on and do nothing."

Now before you jump to the conclusion that I am trying to force the Bible on to Britain – that I am trying to force what happened to Israel into our situation, let me just give you one thing that Paul himself said on the hill in Athens when he was preaching at the centre of the greatest civilisation the world had ever seen. Preaching at the heart of Greek culture, this is what Paul said in the open air on Mars Hill: "God made from one every nation on the earth." That is a revolutionary statement. It means there can never be a superior or an inferior race. God made from one every nation on the face of the earth having determined allotted periods and the boundaries of their habitation, that they should seek God in the hope that they might feel after him and find him.

Now there is a whole philosophy of history in one sentence – let's look at it. Why did God do this? Why does he give a nation time and space in his universe? The answer is that they might seek after him and find him. If they do not, then the allotted period comes to an end and the allotted space is given up. That is the biblical philosophy of history and therefore God has given Britain her space in history and her allotted period that Britain might seek after God and find him. He has given America her place in history and her time and her space that she might seek after God and find him. He has given Russia and China their allotted span and their space that they may seek after him and find him. But the one thing that hits me when I buy an atlas is that it is out of date as soon as I have bought it. Do you get that feeling? I think I will go into the atlas business! Every political map has to be redrawn as soon as it is printed. We have a globe which lights up from the inside. When you keep the light off you see the physical map of the world, and the mountains and the rivers. You know, that will always be in date because God made it that way. That is just the way it is. Switch on the light and then it changes, and instead of brown and green you see pinks and blues – sharp, straight lines instead of nice natural ones. You look at that and you realise it is out of date. This line is now here and this country is now divided in two, and so it goes on.

It isn't chance and it isn't man, it's God who does this. He gives each nation the chance to seek him and find him. What he did to Israel, he does to every other nation. You can't fight against God, and when God has said the time has come for this nation to end its allotted period, its time span, its claim to territorial space, then nothing you can do can stop it.

Now comes a more startling thing under this title "heritage". In the last few verses of chapter 12 we turn from poetry to prose and Jeremiah speaks about other nations than his own. We tend to talk of other nations and sing of our own. We speak of our own in poetry. I don't know if any Englishman wrote poems about anyone else's "green and pleasant land", only our own. But we talk about their green land, or whatever. In fact, Jeremiah is true to himself and he turns from poetry to prose because he is going to speak about other nations and their heritage. Well that is very human and very understandable. But what he's saying is this: not only will a national heritage be removed from those who have it, God can give it to others if they learn the lesson from the one from whom it has been taken. Now he thinks of other nations round about; Syria, Moab, Ammon and other nations had taken their share in grabbing what they could from Israel's weakness. They were grabbing what they could from Israel as she went downhill and God says through

Jeremiah: let these nations around about remember this: I can pluck them up as easily as I plucked Israel up. Let them remember this: that if they will learn from Israel's downfall and turn to Israel's God, then I will plant them and give them their heritage. You see, Jeremiah when he was called at the age of seventeen, was told, "You are to be my prophet to the nations of the world, my ambassador at large." He was not just called to be a prophet to Israel. He is now fulfilling this wider task even if he does it in prose and his heart is not in it – and it isn't. Nevertheless, he is saying to the nations around: Look at fallen Israel, learn the lesson. It was you who taught Israel these pagan customs; if you learn godly customs from her downfall then you can be planted where she was plucked up.

It must have been very hard for Jeremiah to say this. We shall come in a few chapters to the point where Jeremiah was thrown into prison as a traitor because he said such things.

Imagine it being said:"France, learn from Britain, and if you become godly you can have Britain" – how would that sound in British ears? No wonder they didn't like Jeremiah and put him in prison. But remember that God could give the heritage of one to another. He can pluck nations up and he can plant them, and we can learn from the downfall of nations and get right with God. We need to think that one through. God rearranges the map and he can give land. It all is his. Britain is not ours; it is not *our* land – that is national pride. It is a heritage; we inherited it.

If you go to the Royal Exchange in London, look at what is engraved above that place where so much money and property has changed hands: "The earth is the Lord's and the fullness thereof." But do we really believe that now? The people who put it there believed it and they wanted everybody in the city to know that it all belongs absolutely to

God and it is only ours by inheritance. It belongs absolutely
to God. So as far as national heritage goes, it can be taken
away from us, it can be given to others. God wants our hearts
and our heads to be with him, to be feeling and thinking as
he does. That is why there is one little phrase in 12:11 that
gets Jeremiah deeply: "No man lays it to heart". God has the
last word, but let not anybody think that God does it without
hurting himself, it's God's heart that is bleeding here.

Now we come to the second part of our study: the root
problem with nationalism. Did you get the key word in
chapter 13? Let me give you one or two verses so that the
word begins to stand out: "Thus says the Lord, Even so will
I spoil the pride of Judah and the great pride of Jerusalem."
A few verses later: "Here in Gibeon, be not proud for the
Lord has spoken." A few verses later: "But if you will not
listen my soul will weep in secret for your pride." Did you
get that word? Pride. You see, this is where national heritages
go wrong; this is where the picture goes sour. It is where
we become proud of national heritage in the wrong way,
as if we had done it; as if we had the right to it as if God
hadn't done it, and that is when the whole thing goes rotten.
Instead of being so grateful to God for the national heritage,
we become proud of it. God is a jealous God and he will
not share his glory with another. If there is one sin deadlier
than any other, it is the sin of pride. Whether it be pride in
an individual, a community or a nation, human pride is an
offensive thing to God and it stinks – it is rotten to him. A
beautiful national heritage begins to go wrong when human
pride takes over and natural pride and haughtiness are linked
with a national heritage.

Jeremiah was told to do a rather odd thing at this point. If
one were to put it in strictly modern language, he was told
to take a pair of underpants and wear them and not wash
them for a very long period. Then, when they were long past

needing washing, he was to take them to muddy water, dip them in, bury them under a stone and leave them for some further months, then dig them up, bring them back and show them publicly — a strange thing to do. It is in prose and you can't get very poetic about this—it is an appeal to the head, not the heart. It is trying to bring home truth with a visual aid, and even more than a visual aid because when the prophets did this sort of thing it was more than just to illustrate what they said, it was to accomplish what they said. It is an acted parable. It is more than a parable, it is an acted word of God, and God's Word achieves what it states. So, in fact, he was actually accomplishing what was happening through doing this.

It is remarkable, isn't it? Jeremiah did this and his message was: you are as rotten as these underpants. It is a vivid thing. You were fresh, close, clean, clinging to me, as close to me as you could get. Now look at you. But he goes a little further after picturing a traveller in the mountains overtaken by darkness, and through this he would be teaching that pride goes before a fall. The darkness will come, the twilight will catch you out among the precipices and you will go over. He says to the king and the queen mother (this would be King Jehoiachin, who was only eighteen at the time when Jeremiah said it) better come off that throne. Leave the pomp and pageantry; leave it behind because there is no people to reign over now. It is now only pomp and pageantry, no longer real or justified. The pride of nations is gone. The people are inebriated; they are drunk. The priests are drunk, the prophets are drunk, the people are drunk; they are confused, and they are attacking each other. They don't quite know what is wrong. They are just not aware of reality. They are bemused. Then he seems to get down to the bottom of their pride and he says, "I will lift your skirts above your face." We don't know if that's applied to a man or a woman because both wore skirts of a kind, and still do in the Middle East. We know this: that the greatest indignity to which a man could be subject was the exposure of his private parts and this was the punishment for all those who were unfaithful. It was particularly the punishment for unfaithful wives. I have seen Arabs doing this to an unfaithful wife in the Arabian Desert. Here's God saying, "I will bring you right down until you've no dignity left, till your pride is gone; it's so rotten. This national pride of yours; get off your throne. I'll lift your skirts above your face; let the world see your ravished limbs." That's literally what it says here in the Hebrew. Down, down — why? You see, so often our pride is in our clothes and that for which our clothes stand; it is the outside, the front we show. It is hiding the real self from others and when we want pomp and pageantry, we dress up in ermine and scarlet and we put it all on—on the outside.

But do you remember the story, "The Emperor's New Clothes"? God says: Look at what you really are; let's get down to skin level and deeper. Then comes this little gem of a verse. Forget the clothes; forget the pomp and pageantry, let us look at nature as it is. Let's lift the skirt and what do we see? We see skin, we see spots—that is the real person. The leopard, it is his skin; the Ethiopian, it is his skin — it is what he is. No matter what you cover that up with, your skin is part of you. The Ethiopian's skin is the kind of golden tan that many long for when on holiday. Can the Ethiopian change his skin? Can the leopard change his spots? Then you can get rid of this pride. If they can do that, you can get rid of pride. You who are accustomed to doing evil, you could do good, you could change your life. You could reform yourself, you could become a good man even though you have done evil all along.

You and I know—and Jeremiah knows, and God knows —that we can no more become good than the leopard can change his spots or the Ethiopian his skin. It is not pomp and pageantry and the tradition of national heritage, it is what we are by nature that counts, and by nature we have done evil. I am not free to say: "From now on I'm going to be a good man. I am never going to do anything wrong again. I'm never going to sin again, I am going to change myself." I would then soon be embarrassed to meet you. Why? Well, first because every wrong thing I have done has become part of me, part of my nature; it has become as much me as my skin; like the leopard's spots.

So, an act can reap a habit, a habit will reap a character, a character will reap a destiny—that is an inevitable process of human nature. This means that I am not free to wipe out the past as if it had not been done; no matter what clothes I wear, it is part of me. Worse than that, the Bible makes it quite clear that I was born this way and that I was born in sin and that my very nature is sinful. It is always easier for me to lie than to speak the truth. It is always easier for me to be dishonest than honest, to protect myself. You only have to teach a child to be good; you never have to teach a child to be evil; we are leopards and we can't get rid of the spots. No wonder the chapter finishes with a cry.

I am not going to finish on that kind of a note. If I did, then it would just depress you no end and leave you in a very sad state. I want to give you the whole Word of God. I tell you this: the God who made the leopard can remove its spots and the God who made the Ethiopian can change his skin, for the Creator is needed, not a reformation from within. A man can no more make himself good than a leopard can change his spots, but the God who created that man can make a new creation of that man, can change the leopard, can change the Ethiopian. That is the glorious gospel of Jesus Christ — that if any man is in Jesus he is a new creation – a new man, a new heart. Not a clean-up of the old one but a new creation.

Only God himself can do that and that is the only hope for a nation once its heritage has started disappearing.

It is pride that will not admit the real situation. But there is hope that when pride has been dashed and humbled, and when a nation has come down to the bottom, men and women will look up into the face of God and say, "God, forgive us and remake us. God, I can't cleanse myself; cleanse me. God, I can't remove my spots, so God, remove them. You are a God who has created me; you are a God that can re-create me" — that is the gospel.

Jeremiah of course could not have understood fully what I just told you; he lived the wrong side of Jesus. He knew that something radical would have to happen. He knew that God would surely do something some day that would stop this endless round of nations inheriting so much and then, through pride, wasting it away. He knew that there was something God could do but he didn't have too clear a picture. We shall see in chapter 31 that he could see God would have to make a new covenant; that he would have to write his laws not on tablets of stone but on the heart. He could see that there would have to be an almighty big forgiveness on God's part to get this thing going. He could see this in the distance, but you and I live the right side of Jesus Christ and have seen men and women changed; we have seen new lives, the spots changed and the nature changed.

I found myself thinking again of two people I met in Berlin. I shook hands with an Auca Indian straight from the savage jungle, unable to use a knife and fork, who had never seen a toilet in his life. I looked into the face of a man who used to kill and eat, and I looked into the face of a man who I would gladly trust a baby with. It happened not through a long process of civilisation, it happened because a brave woman whose husband had been killed by that man went to him with the love of Christ and offered him new life and a change.

The other man was in New Zealand. He was worth millions by the age of forty which achieved his ambition — the most ruthless, hard man, and I could see he had been that way. They said that the softest part of him was his teeth, and woe betide anyone who crossed the path of this ruthless property developer. He had ground people into nothing, he had wrecked his home, his children hated him, he was becoming an alcoholic, his wife was on the point of leaving him, and God stepped into his life and he became like a little child. I walked with him around the decadent luxury yacht as we sailed around a little Island in the Pacific Ocean, and he talked to me of love. He pulled a letter out of his own pocket from his son who had run away from home because he couldn't stand his dad. When he became a Christian, this multi-millionaire who had been tough as nails wrote to his own son and said, "Sorry, son" — a word he had never used. His son wrote back and he said, "Dad, I'm sorry and I've become a Christian too." The father said, "That is worth more to me than all my millions. No money could buy that."

Can the Ethiopian change his skin? Can a hard, ruthless millionaire become a gentle, loving man? Can a savage Indian from the jungle, who loves the taste of human blood, become like a child? Yes, he can. Until we have swallowed our pride and admitted that we can't be good and that all our national pride and all our personal pride is the real problem, God can't do the miracle. As soon as you swallow your pride, then God says: "Here's the heritage. Here's the inheritance. I make you my son and heir and you will inherit the earth!" The heritage is given back. God takes the inheritance of this nation and of that and that and that, and he gives it to those who swallow their pride and say, "Lord, change me."

READ JEREMIAH 14–15

People who don't read and study the Old Testament usually come to an unbalanced view of God because God is the God of the whole Bible, Old and New Testaments. If we pick and choose in the Bible, we are virtually making God in our own image or at least in the image that we want him to be. You see, the God of the Jews and the God and Father of our Lord Jesus Christ is the same God. The only Bible Jesus had was the Old Testament. Yet for many centuries people have set the Old Testament against the New and drawn a contrast between "two gods". This heresy is at least thirteen hundred years old. Centuries ago there was a man called Marcion who claimed to be a Christian. He said the God of the Old Testament and the God of Jesus are two different gods. Therefore, he proposed that Christians should stop reading and studying the Old Testament. Very significantly, only a few years passed before he began to advise Christians to cut out parts of the New Testament too, because he found that the Old Testament God appeared in the New Testament also. For example, he began by cutting out the book of Revelation and he worked backward through the Epistles and then he found that even in the Gospels the God that he didn't like was still there in certain passages. All of which underlines that you cannot say the God of the Old Testament is like this and the God of Jesus is like that. The God and Father of our Lord Jesus Christ is the God who brought the Jews out of Egypt and is the God of Jeremiah, because Jesus was a Jew as well as the Son of God. That is why we are studying

Jeremiah. However, having said that, there are differences of emphasis between the Old and New Testament; they are complementary, not contradictory. But the Old Testament certainly lays a heavier emphasis on the justice of God whereas the New Testament places more emphasis on his mercy. The Old Testament places more emphasis on the law; the New Testament on the gospel and on pardon.

The reason why there is different emphasis is this: the Bible tells you which part of God's character you need to understand first. If you try to help people to understand his mercy before you have conveyed to them his justice; if you try to preach to people about pardon before you have talked about punishment; if you try to preach the gospel before you have talked about the law, then you will finish up with a sentimental, romantic, soft view of God which will result in people never taking sin seriously, like the dying German Heinrich Heine saying, "God will forgive me; that's his trade." That was the word of a man who had never been taught the Old Testament and who simply thought of God as an indulgent grandfather who would always have us in heaven, no matter what. Now that is not the God and Father of our Lord Jesus.

When we read Jeremiah chapters 14–15, we come across something about God which at first sight will hurt and hit us. We come against this simple truth – that God can get tired of forgiving people, that he can come to the end of his patience. There can come a point at which, even though people confess their sins, God will not listen to that prayer and forgive them. We will ask how that lines up with the story of the prodigal son in Luke 15 – the teaching of Jesus that the heavenly Father wants to give, and with the emphasis of the New Testament on the grace of God longing to pardon. Somehow we have to tie these together because it is the same God.

In Jeremiah 14 and 15, the people cry, "We've sinned, we confess we've sinned against you. We're full of wickedness and iniquities!" God says, "Take these people away, I'm tired of them; I'm tired of listening. I am just not going to answer that prayer." We need to ask, "When does God reach the end of his patience?" When does God get to the point where he says, "No more prayers, I am finished; no more from now on, no more confession from now on." It is from this moment too late to ask for forgiveness. We shall find that Jesus taught of exactly this kind of a God.

I will give you one example now, so that you can be thinking about it. Do you remember the parable of the ten virgins? There came a point when the door was shut, and even though the five came and prayed and pleaded to be let in afterwards, they were told, "It's too late. The door of opportunity is closed." You find that Jesus taught this same truth. The patience of God will not last forever. He reaches the point where he says, "I've had enough. I've closed the door. I've closed my ears even to a prayer of confession," but we have got to look into it more deeply.

Now these two chapters are concerned with Jeremiah's prayer life, not with his preaching life. We have noted that there was a great contrast between Jeremiah when he preached and Jeremiah when he prayed. The contrast we saw was that Jeremiah, when he preached, was bold, dogmatic, definite and sure of himself. But when he prayed he was very unsure of himself. When he talked to men he was strong and clear; when he talked to God he was just the opposite.

Now in these two chapters we are going to see another great contrast between Jeremiah the preacher and Jeremiah the pray-er and we are going to have to learn something for ourselves from this. The contrast now is this: when Jeremiah preached, he stood firmly on God's side, over against men. But when he prayed, he stood firmly on man's side over against God. God had to deal with this inconsistency and we shall see how God dealt with it.

Jeremiah felt for people so deeply that he began to say things to God that really should never have been said. I'll give you a very down-to-earth kind of example. When disaster strikes, we tend to take the side of men rather than God. When tragic events happen, we have to face the fact in those situations, if we really believe what we preach when things are going well, that some who die are not ready to meet God. But we tend instinctively to take the side of the deceased and say, "Surely, surely God will have mercy on them and take them to glory." We should not give any false assurance that is in contradiction to what we really believe. When disaster comes, your human sympathies so easily go straight to those who suffered, and you pray from their angle and think from their angle, and want to say, "God, why did you do it? Why did you allow it?" We will find that disasters of drought and famine and war came to Israel and that Jeremiah, in his prayer life, took the people's side, time and time again.

He confessed their sins, but he kept saying, "Why, God, are you behaving like a stranger to us; a stranger passing in the night? Why are you smiting us?" Indeed, at one point he starts telling God, "God you're like a dried-up brook. You help us sometimes and other times when we come to you, you are not there." He is saying all kinds of things that should never be said to God, because Jeremiah's sympathies are with the people and he is being torn.

We are going to learn a deep lesson from this because in the troubles that are coming on our nation our sympathies are going to be very much with the people who are going to suffer: people on low incomes; people who are unemployed. Our sympathies are going to go more and more that way unless we learn the lesson Jeremiah had to learn, and learn to stand firmly on God's side even when we pray. It is easy enough to do that when we preach but not so easy to do it when we pray.

There are two cycles of prayer, if you like, that follow an identical pattern. They probably happen within a few months or a year or two of each other. Jeremiah told somebody what happened in his prayer life so they could write it down – probably that scribe called Baruch who wrote most of Jeremiah down for us. He has shared with us these two cycles of prayer in which he argued with God. Each time God had the last word, as he usually does. This is recorded for us so that we can learn.

The first cycle is 14:1-16, and then the second cycle which follows in identical outline goes through to the end of chapter 15, so Jeremiah went through the whole business twice. He got the message at the end of the second time. Such is the patience of God with his servants that he sometimes has to take us right through the same lesson twice before we begin to get the message.

Let us look at the first cycle, 14:1-16. The first step is a description of Judah's problem, which at this time was drought. In the Middle East that is serious because they live on limestone hills which are porous and the rain goes straight through; therefore, they were dependent on a continual supply of rain. This only came if the wind came from the west and drew the moisture from the Mediterranean and dropped it when it hit the rising slopes of the Judean hills. So, they either had hot, dry weather or cooler, wet weather. They had had no cooler, wet weather all summer. The grass was brown and dry and the earth was cracked. It is a vivid description of drought. The animals are standing, panting. Mother deer are forsaking their young because they cannot produce the milk. There isn't enough moisture in their desiccated bodies. It is hitting rich as well as poor. The nobles send their servants right around the country to well after well. You see, in a time of shortage the rich can do something about it and so the rich are employing servants to travel miles to bring back a bucketful, but even they can't find it. The poor may be travelling around themselves with an empty bucket. It is a vivid picture and you can feel the situation.

We have rarely ever experienced such drought ourselves. But if you went to some hot, dry countries today, you would see it. We don't know what drought is in this country, living in a temperate zone with prevailing south-westerlies that bring from the Atlantic the moisture that makes Ireland the "Emerald Isle" and makes England a "green and pleasant land".

Jeremiah realises that this is not just a natural event but a supernatural event. He knows Deuteronomy and that comes out again and again. In Deuteronomy God says, "I am bringing you to a land flowing with milk and honey, but if you do not look after that land properly, if you do not obey me then I will stop the rain." Jeremiah also knew about Elijah, one of his predecessors who had stopped the rain for three and a half years by prayer alone. They had suffered drought and now Jeremiah realises that God is saying something to his people. What is he saying? The answer is very simple: "You have forsaken the fountain of living water so you cannot have any fresh rain water."

Now comes Jeremiah's prayer. It is a prayer addressed to God in the first personal plural "we", but whose prayer is it? It is on Jeremiah's lips – had the people told him what to say, had he listened to other people's prayers in the Temple, or was he trying to pray for and on behalf of the people? I think that is the real answer. Jeremiah, in saying "We have sinned", is trying desperately to express what he feels God needs to hear from the nation. He is identifying with the nation, interceding for the nation, and so he is saying, even if they are not saying it: we have sinned, Lord, I understand what you are doing. So, it is a prayer of confession, yet he is so mixed up in his prayer that even though he is saying, "We have sinned against you. We are full of iniquity and wickedness," he then says, "But why, Lord, are you treating us like this?" This is such a typical human prayer. We admit we deserve disaster and then say "Lord, why have you sent it?" We are still not seeing things clearly from God's point of view. We admit we have done wrong and yet feel somehow we are really nice people underneath: "Lord, we don't really deserve it so why have you done it?" Do you get the inconsistency of a very human prayer? So, he says: "God, I'm puzzled by your attitude, you seem like a stranger just spending the night and passing on. You don't seem like our God and yet you are the hope of Israel, you're the Saviour of Israel," (notice those titles), "Why aren't you helping us through? I don't understand it one bit. But Lord, I beg you, don't desert us now."

That is a very human prayer. It was a prayer that on the face of it should have got through to God, but it didn't. It was a prayer of confession but God didn't forgive. It was a prayer for help, but God didn't come to help. It was a prayer challenging God to live up to his titles of hope and Saviour, yet God did not live up to them and that is the problem that Jeremiah had with Yahweh's answer. He did answer the prayer but not with the answer that Jeremiah wanted. His answer was no.

That is not the problem of unanswered prayer—I'm afraid that the problem of answered prayer when it isn't the answer you want is even greater than the problem of unanswered prayer. It is one thing for heaven to be silent – that is the problem of unanswered prayer, but when heaven says no, then that is an even bigger problem— the problem of answered prayer.

In fact, God goes on to speak of Israel as if he is a stranger passing in the night, as if they don't belong to him. He doesn't say "You...," he says, "Get this people out of my sight." This people, them — do you notice that? Not "You, my people".

God is saying that his decision is already made. This people love to run away when things are going well. They only run back when things are going badly. Where does their heart really lie? You see, when things are going well you find out if your heart really loves God. Many people will run to God when things go badly, and that doesn't prove one little thing. When disaster comes, many think about God who normally never do so. But when the immediate trauma has worn off a year later, will they still be thinking about God? When things have got smooth again, when they are comfortable again, will they wander away from God then, or will they stay with God? That is the real issue.

God is saying: I am fed up with people who only run to me in trouble. I know perfectly well that when things are alright they love to wander away; they make no attempt to live right and they place no restraints on themselves. The message is: Jeremiah, I am not listening any more because they love to be away from me and that's the real truth; it is no use saying "they admit their faults"; it is no use saying "they are in trouble". I know that. But I also know that their hearts are still away from me and you are only praying because this drought has come, and as soon as I give the rain, they will run away again. God is just not going to put up with it any longer.

It is a severe word and in fact he says, "The punishment is already decided. My people are going to suffer from war and famine and disease." Or to put it in one word: *death*. The wages of sin is death, and every cemetery and crematorium is a reminder of that stark fact. God says, "I've decided to punish them. It is too late for you to pray, Jeremiah, stop praying."

Jeremiah makes one final attempt to persuade God to change his mind. "But don't you see, Lord, that really their behaviour can be excused because they have had false prophets who told them that disaster wouldn't come. They have had so many preachers who have gone around the country saying it's alright, God will bless you. God will bring peace one day. God will put it all right. He is not that kind of a God who would finally close the door." Jeremiah is saying: can't you excuse them? God says, "Jeremiah, I know those preachers. They tell lies concocted out of their own hearts and they will suffer war, famine, and disease along with their congregations." In other words, God won't excuse congregations because of the false preaching. False preachers would suffer with their congregations. That is tough talk.

Poor Jeremiah is feeling beaten into the ground because he feels he just can't win. Have you ever felt like that in prayer — that you are just beating against a heaven that will not listen and isn't open to entreaty; that can't be argued with, can't be pleaded with? Jeremiah certainly had, and although preachers there would suffer a fate worse than death, what is that in God's sight? A fate worse than death in God's sight is not only to die, but to have no one to bury you — the ultimate indignity, the ultimate horror of a human being's corpse left in the streets for the animals. It is tough talk so Jeremiah retreats from that one.

The next cycle is from 14:17 to the end of chapter 15 — almost identical to the first cycle but much more detailed. I want you to remember we are dealing with fact not fiction. All of these things happened. Those bodies were left in the streets for the animals; it all came true. So, we are learning from history, and those who will not learn from history are condemned to relive it. Now Judah's problem is deeper. From the drought has come famine, from the famine have come disease and weakness, and from disease and weakness has come war, because the enemies around Israel, when they saw how weak she was, began to attack her. The Egyptian troops attacked. Nebuchadnezzar sent raiding parties against her.

It was a whole cycle: the drought led to shortages of food, bringing weakness, until they were a prey to other nations to attack and couldn't even fight. Therefore, Jeremiah came back again to God to pray for the people, to intercede. His sympathies were now even deeper, because he said: as I go into the fields, I see bodies lying; the raiders have attacked, the terrorists have been in and they have just laid the bodies; if I go into the streets I see rotting corpses from disease and famine; wherever I go, the whole situation is breaking down – the worst thing about it all is there are still plenty of priests and prophets plying their trade around the country and doing a good trade, still telling people that things are going to be all right, still giving hope where there is no hope and speaking of things they have no knowledge about. As we see, Jeremiah feels the burden even more deeply and he is going to learn the lesson this time, so we will go in even more deeply with him.

He goes back to God and prays again, and the prayer is almost word for word what he prayed several months earlier. The prayer is: "Lord, we've sinned. We have knowledge and we confess our sins. Lord, you are the hope." There it comes again: "You are the hope of Israel. Lord, you have saved us in the past, you are our Saviour. Lord, you made a covenant with us. Lord, your name, your reputation, your glory, Lord!" Then comes the same note again: "Why are you smiting us? You are not just a stranger, you're now a smiter — why?" Same prayer, almost identical, and he is trying a second time to pray for his people and to intercede for them and get God to change his mind, but God does not. Back comes the same reply from God: "This people, them ..." Do you notice it? Mind you, it is a longer reply this time, and halfway through God says "you" for just two verses (vv. 5 and 6). Then, as if he realised that his relationship had got the better of him, he immediately goes back to "them". God is finding it difficult to say "them", for this is his covenant people. He is finding it very difficult to write them off. But he starts by saying, "Get this people out of my sight, get them away." Jeremiah says, "Where to?" He says, "To death, to famine, to pestilence, get them away; get them out of my sight."

Then comes this extraordinary phrase at the end of v. 6 where God says, "I am weary of relenting" or, as another version has it, "I am tired of always giving you another chance." Now I tell you that God's patience is much greater than man's. It goes a long way; much further than man's. God is slow to anger but that doesn't mean he never gets to it. God is slow to lose his patience but that doesn't mean he never loses it. We dare not tread on God's patience as if he is going to be patient forever. There comes a point when even God gets tired of giving people another chance. That is the truth we have got to grasp. It is a vital truth because most people in this country who believe in God do not believe the truth about him. The way they behave shows they don't believe this. The way they think about life after death shows that they believe that there will be an infinite number of second chances. Even after death—if there is life after death—then God will always let us in to heaven some day. And hell gets changed into the doctrine of purgatory. But it is the stark truth that there comes a point when God says, "I am sick of giving you another chance."

I have used this illustration before, but it brings it home. Imagine you are walking on Brighton Pier and you see someone drowning in the water, and you jump in and save them at risk to your own life, then you pump them dry and bring them around and they say, "Thank you so much, you saved my life." Then they turn right around and walk off the end of the pier and shout, "Save me, save me!" So you pull them out again and bring them around and they say, "Thank you so much, you saved me!" And they walk right off the end of the pier again. How many times are they going to go on doing that before you walk away? How many times would you go on jumping in? Have you ever asked yourself that kind of a question? You may have had this problem with your own children or close relatives. How many times do you give them another chance before you say, "It's no use, you have exhausted me now. I cannot give you another chance." Well, praise God, he gives us more than man would, but nevertheless, there comes a point where he says, "I am not going to come in and save you again; the door is shut. You may shout 'Save me!' but I cannot hear; I just won't listen."

So God says, "Get these people out of my sight. I am tired of them." He says to Jeremiah something that was a bit humbling for Jeremiah: "Jeremiah, even if Moses prayed, even if Samuel prayed, I wouldn't listen." That is as much as to say, "Jeremiah, there are even greater men than you who could pray." You know, both Moses and Samuel prayed successfully for the forgiveness of their nation. Moses prayed on four separate occasions as they wandered through the wilderness. When the people of Israel went away from God and worshipped a golden calf or grumbled against God, Moses used to go and pray to God and say, "God, please change your mind. Please let them off." Moses' prayer was very human, like Jeremiah's; he was putting himself with the people. But with Moses every one of those four times God changed his mind, it says that God heard the prayer and "repented".

Samuel when he saw what his nation was doing – pleaded twice with God to change his mind. It says in 2 Samuel that

God changed his mind; now Jeremiah does the same things and God says, "No, Jeremiah, even if Moses or Samuel prayed, I wouldn't listen now." Of course, both Moses and Samuel had got the people's repentance first, which was the difference. Jeremiah had not got that yet.

I will tell you why God wouldn't hear now. It was because there was an exact date when God had decided to shut the door, and he told Jeremiah here when that date had been, when his patience had run out. It had happened before Jeremiah was born. That is one of the hardest facts to face here. God says: I made a decision not to listen to any more prayer, not to change my mind regarding the punishment of Judah, during the reign of Manasseh.

Manasseh was king of Judah just before Jeremiah was born, and God says, "Your life is too late." Can you imagine the agony of being called to be a preacher in an era of "too late"? In fact, that was Jeremiah's position. Then why on earth did God tell him to preach if it was too late, if God had shut the door? I'll tell you why: because God had shut the door to the nation but not to the individual. That is why Jeremiah had to go on preaching. In a sense, I am being driven more and more to the view, though I am not quite there yet, that God has shut the door on Britain, but I will go on preaching because he has not shut the door on individuals.

He was not shutting the door on Jeremiah, for example. But he said, "In the reign of Manasseh I made up my mind." What happened during the reign of Manasseh? He was the son of a very good king called Hezekiah. Hezekiah destroyed the pagan religion of Judah and got people back to God, but then he had a son who didn't follow in his father's footsteps. Manasseh came, and do you know what he introduced? He introduced astrology, star worship, into the very temple of God. He introduced spiritism, he introduced wizards and mediums into Judah. He introduced human sacrifice so that babies were being offered to pagan gods, and he shed innocent blood through the streets of Jerusalem. He was ruthless. If anybody opposed him, they were dead.

So, the whole pagan religion came in and the Word of God says in 2 Kings that Manasseh seduced the people of Judah to do more evil in God's sight than the nations whom God had cast out before Israel. In other words, the Holy Land became less holy than it was before the Jews got into it, and that's saying something. It was during the reign of Manasseh that God said that nobody could pray for the nation any more. He would listen to the individual, but the nation was finished.

It happened before Jeremiah was born, so Jeremiah tried one more protest. He was always trying, wasn't he? Jeremiah comes out now with a prayer that is the deepest part of our reading. Oh, it's very human. He started out by talking to his own mother. He said, "Mum, why did you ever have me? I wish I had never been born." Do you understand that cry? It is a hard cry. "I am disliked; I am hated on every side. It's not as if I put anybody into financial embarrassment. I am not a creditor trying to foreclose when dealing with a debtor that won't pay up, why do they hate me? God, you know I've prayed for them, why do you hate me? Why do you let them hate me? Everybody is against me, God; you're against me, the people are against me. I just feel all alone."

In fact, in that final protest, Jeremiah says, "I sit alone." You know, most people of God go through this kind of a depression. Elijah did. "I, even I only, am left." Have you ever felt that you were the only one and you felt all alone? Jeremiah is reaching a crisis point and God has to see him through his crisis or his ministry will be finished. If God doesn't bring him through this one, there will be no more preaching from Jeremiah. For he is at rock bottom, he wishes he had never been born. He feels the loneliness of being hated.

He says, "Lord, the only thing I enjoy is studying your Word. I eat it; I devour it; it delights my heart." He is saying: I don't enjoy parties any more, I don't sit among those who make merry at feasts, I sit alone.... God, I thought you were going to be springing living waters springing up within me, instead I find you're a dried-up brook. When Jeremiah felt most alone, he felt far away from God. Lord, what's the matter? It's a heart cry—a lonely, anxious man who feels that he has somehow been deserted by people and by God because he tried to preach.

So, God speaks to him and he doesn't speak tenderly, he speaks very firmly. He says, "Jeremiah, get back on my side. Return to me and I'll restore you." The rest of what God says is almost a word-for-word repetition of the call Jeremiah received that you read about in chapter 1, years earlier when he was seventeen: you can then be my mouthpiece; you can be my spokesman; you will be like a fortress of bronze. They will attack you but I'll protect you and I'll deliver you from these ruthless men. But Jeremiah, do you not see what's gone wrong? You have got into this depression; you have got into this state because you got onto their side. That is why you are feeling that neither they nor I are with you. You've got all mixed up; your sympathies have gone astray. Jeremiah, get back on my side.

You know, that is our problem: because I am human my sympathies will lie with those who are also human. But if you just consider for a moment what God had done with these people and with this land: bringing them in, driving out the people before them, giving them a land flowing with milk and honey, giving them everything they could ask for; giving them a king, prosperity, and peace! They just threw it back in his face and went down and down until his Holy Land was less holy than it had been before God began. Can you not spare sympathy for God, Jeremiah? Can you not feel for him? You see, if what happened to God happened to a human being, your sympathy would be with him, wouldn't it? "Jeremiah, get back on my side."

We conclude this study with two pieces of advice. The first concerns you if you have not yet found forgiveness for your sins. I want to say as solemnly as I can: don't trade on God's patience. You see, when you turn to the New Testament you find that God has already appointed a day beyond which it will be too late: The Day of Judgment. For you personally there may be a day before that when it will be too late. The Bible is quite clear that the minute you die, God closes the door to repentance and forgiveness. There is a great gulf fixed beyond that, but that day can happen in a person's life even before they die. They can push God so far that, as he says in the first Epistle of John, "Don't pray for that man, he is sinning to death." In other words, his sin is too serious to pray for. Therefore, I beg you, don't trade on the forgiveness of God. Don't think that the door will always be open, that you have plenty of time, that you can get on with all the more immediate things and then some day when you feel like it you can become a Christian. You cannot treat God that way. God alone decides the day when it is too late for you. How important it is *today* if you hear his voice, to harden not your hearts. Today is the day of salvation; not tomorrow—today. That is the first thing and I can't force you or press you. I just tremble for those who come along to a service and have been interested and listened, but have presumed on God's patience and who will, like the five foolish virgins, knock at a door one day and say, "Let me in." Then God will say, "No. The door is shut, the bridegroom came."

The other thing I want to say is to Christians, and that is: make sure that your sympathies are with God when you pray. It is the most difficult thing in the world when you are praying for someone who is desperately sick, your instinctive

178

sympathies are to pray that they may be made well. But just try to get on God's side and say, "God, what are you doing in this situation? What do you want to achieve in this situation?" Your sympathies change. You look at the whole situation from a different point of view.

The prayer that is going to be most effective and will not lead us into the questions of "why, why, why", the prayer that will keep us firm and strong even when we sit alone, is the prayer that is in sympathy with God. Look at the situation from his point of view and therefore, pray that his will may be done on earth as it is in heaven.

This was a crisis for Jeremiah. His sympathies for human suffering had run away with him in his prayer life and he was finding himself praying against God instead of praying with God, and asking God, "Why?" But I am very happy to tell you that he came through this crisis. He returned to God's side and he became strong. From then on, though the battle became fiercer—he was to be thrown in prison, he was to be threatened with his life—Jeremiah stood because he was now back on God's side and he could preach and pray from the same side. How desperately he needed to get through this crisis, because in the very next verse, God is going to say, "Jeremiah, you must not marry, you must not have children, you must go on alone with me."

But he came through it and he heard again the call that he had heard at seventeen, and he responded to it and he was restored, fortified, and he went on preaching and faced a whole nation alone. God kept his word, for when the whole nation was destroyed, Jeremiah was still around. He was delivered from the hands of all the ruthless men. He was protected, and he and God made a majority.

READ JEREMIAH 16–17

Very often, the prophets in the Old Testament not only brought a new word from the Lord but used old words – especially the prophets who had been brought up in a pious background. Jeremiah, if you remember, had been brought up in a godly home and therefore he knew the scriptures. Psalm 1 is almost word for word that little bit about the blessed man and the cursed man: the blessed man, like a tree planted by the water; the cursed man stunted and soon destroyed.

In a sense, Jeremiah posed this question in his preaching: what kind of a society do you want? He was always presenting people with alternatives, and that is the way the Bible presents the big questions of life to us. That is why Jesus presents us with the broad way that leads to destruction and the narrow way that leads to life; the house built on sand, the house built on rock; the wise virgins and the foolish virgins; the wheat and the tares. Almost every part of our Lord's teaching presented people with alternatives and said: choose. The great prophets of the Old Testament did the same. Moses would say: I have set before you life and death; choose, which way do you really want?

In this passage Jeremiah presents us with alternatives: good news or bad news. And he says: choose. He presents these alternatives at three levels. First, the national level: what kind of a future do you want your nation to have? Secondly, the individual level: what kind of a person do you really want to be—a stunted shrub in a desert or a fruitful tree by a river? Thirdly, the social level: what kind of a society do you want—a society that spends seven days a week in commerce trying to make money, or a society that can switch off and give time to God? These are the three alternatives that he is going to present to us and we will go through them.

Let us look first at the national level and the alternatives he presents. Most of it is bad news and then suddenly the good news comes and he presents the possibilities for the future for those who look to God. The keyword, occurring sixteen times in this first section, the whole of chapter sixteen and the first four verses of chapter seventeen is the word "land". The reason is that a nation must have land. This is in the very nature of things – that if we are to have national identity and independence, we need land of which we can say, "That is our national heritage." To be ourselves, to have identity, to have independence, we need territory; we need a place to call our own. That is how some people have found their identity in private life. You may have a little house, a garden, a piece of land and it is yours, and it gives you your identity, your security.

Right through this first section the key question is: will the nation have land? We need to remember that every bit of land on the whole of this planet earth is only held leasehold, and that the lease can be cancelled at any time. There is nothing binding about any leasehold on land. We play around with freehold and leasehold documents, but they are not the real situation. The real situation is that, "The earth is the Lord's and the fullness thereof." On Mars Hill, Paul said, "It is God who allots land to nations." We may think we are drawing the atlas, but it is God who does so. He allots a nation its own identity in time and space and says: you can have this land provided you do not forget me.

I have a fascinating atlas of world history. You can turn the pages and you don't turn between different countries but stay with the same countries from age to age. You see the borders move and the colours constantly changing, and you are reading the story of God's allocation of land. Any nation that honours the light they have received from him will have its land in security, and any nation that does not honour the light received from him will find that its land will shrink and ultimately go—that is the lesson of history.

It is fascinating that you can get great historians who can draw profound lessons from studying history, but who cannot see this simple lesson, and it is written large. You will find that as soon as a nation's morals began to go down, their territory began to shrink. God gave it to another, who may at first sight have seemed unworthy of that land, but God was giving another people the chance to look after that land for him. If they did not, theirs too would shrink. This is supremely true about Israel because, of all the territory on earth, God settled on that little area the size of Wales, which includes such variety within it, from snow-capped mountains to deserts, from lush plains, flowing with milk and honey, through valleys to hills. It has got everything, that little land, even including the deepest point on the earth's surface, and of that little land God said: now I want that land to be holy; that is my special plot, to whom shall I give that plot to look after? I'll give it to those slaves in Egypt who haven't got any land of their own. Surely, out of gratitude for their freedom, they will look after this little plot of land. He gave it to them and he said, "I give it to you to look after for me. The day you forget me, that day the land will shrink."

You study the atlas of the Old Testament and see how under King David, a man after God's own heart, that land was more extensive than it had ever been and was filled with peace and prosperity. Its borders were further out than at any other time, but as soon as David died, those borders began to shrink. Soon there was civil war and the ten northern tribes started seeking independence and it shrank until there was just a little bit left. Now God, through Jeremiah, says: I'm going to take that little bit from you too; you are just not fit to have the territory you have had.

I looked at that atlas — not many years ago, I looked just a generation back. The colour that was most predominant right through was red, which represented the British Empire. God gave us, in trust, a great deal of territory and it stretched from Canada to Australia to New Zealand, to many parts of Africa and to the Middle East. Everywhere you looked, the map was red. Who would have believed that within thirty years God would have taken that territory from us?

God says: if you are not fit to look after what I give you, I will take it back. He said it to Judah through Jeremiah. Jeremiah was living in a very shrunken land. It was just composed of two little tribes in the south, just the environs of Jerusalem and stretching down to the Negev in the south. That was all they had left of what had been the great kingdom of Israel under King David. So, Jeremiah presents them with the alternatives for the future. But first I must begin with a very personal thing which God said to Jeremiah. He said, "Jeremiah, the time has come when I command you to live without a family." Jeremiah by this time was in his late twenties. It would have been natural and normal for him to be married by that time. Reading between the lines, it may be that Jeremiah had fallen in love, and with the lonely ministry that God had given him, how much comfort he could have received from the right wife, to whom he could go back and share the frustrations and burdens of his ministry. But God said: Jeremiah, it is not to be for you—no wife, no children. I don't want you to get involved in this society. The time has come when it is so far gone that you must keep out of it. You must be in it to preach, but don't get involved emotionally. Don't fall in love; don't have kids because, Jeremiah, the women and children are going to die in this land and I don't want you to go through that. I don't want you to have that and to see your kids lying in the streets dead, unburied. Jeremiah, I want you to keep out of your people's social life now. Don't go to funeral wakes because, in fact, there's coming a day when even a funeral wake will not be held. There won't be a meal and a comforting drink after the funeral. Keep out of their feasts and merry-making because laughter is going to stop. Jeremiah, keep out of social life. I don't want you to get involved socially at all.

There come periods and times when the situation is so serious that people think twice about bringing children into the world, even about marriage. Jesus said something like this. He talked about those who were eunuchs because they couldn't help it and those who were eunuchs because they chose to be for the kingdom's sake. Paul says something about this in 1 Corinthians 7. Paul talks about when real pressures come on a Christian society — it will be easier for the unmarried than the married. Because if there is one thing harder than suffering yourself, it is seeing your wife and kids suffer. There are situations in our world now where it is advisable for Christians not to become socially involved where the pressures are too great—stern language. "Now Jeremiah, go and tell them this: I'm going to take this land from you, and ... tell them it's because your fathers left me and you are worse than your fathers." That is interesting because it implies that it is something that has happened over a few generations. The word "fathers" implies perhaps two or three generations. There is something very profound about the third and fourth generations; moral factors take that time to work out, both negatively and positively. A good man can influence his great-grandchildren, but not much more than that. A bad man can influence his great-grandchildren, but not much more. Yes, the sins of the fathers are visited on the children to the third and fourth generations. I have seen that happen again and again. We can't live with only ourselves in mind; the life I live is going to affect up to, and including, my great-grandchildren. Moral influence goes down through the generations and not just out to our contemporaries. So, God says, "Your fathers left me and you are worse so the land's going," and that is precisely what happened.

If you study the figures of churchgoing in this country, do you know when the first great slump came? Just before the First World War. Many men went to war with an inadequate understanding of God, which alas had been given to them by liberal preachers during the first ten years of the twentieth century. They went with an inadequate view of God and they came back without any view of God and said, "We've seen and done things in the trenches that just don't line up with what we heard in church," and the result was a great dive in churchgoing. We have now had three generations away from God and churchgoing sliding down, and every denomination in this country reporting declining figures ever since the First World War. There is a slight bump up during the wars, when we panic, but as soon as a war is over it is back down to the minority. God says, "Your fathers left me and you are worse."

One of the amazing facts of our situation is that there are young people coming to Christ today for whom Christianity is a totally new experience. They are coming fresh. If they go back in their family history, they will find their grandfather and great-grandfather were Christians, but they have been so long without faith that they are coming back to it new and fresh. That is why the young people are sometimes so much keener than some of us older ones who were brought up in that minority that doggedly kept the church doors open. A new generation, a new discovery. Praise God, that is going to affect their great-grandchildren. Hallelujah for that, but we have been through this ice age spiritually in this land,

and God says, "You don't deserve to have territory when you're like this." We lost God as a nation. We still crown the monarch in Westminster Abbey, but that is not keeping God; that is putting the religious face on it. We lost God and so we lost land. I am not an imperialist and I am not justifying imperialism — let me make that quite clear. I am saying that we had that land and, therefore, we must have had it by God's permission, but we forfeited and lost it.

God would hurl them into another land where they would serve other gods, for he would show them no favour. It is a very sad part of the book. But now for the good news. There are two remarkable predictions in this section which burst through like a stream of sunlight through a thundercloud. Suddenly, there is another possibility for the future. Possibility number one was that the nation could be rebuilt and that one day God could bring back the people to their homeland. Did you notice that? The whole topic of conversation was that God was bringing his people home. Now this is peculiarly true of Israel. They were seventy years away and God brought them back home after that period. Alas, it is true that they had still not learned their lesson. When God gave them his greatest gift of his only Son, his Son wept because they would lose the land again for many centuries until the time of the Gentiles was fulfilled. The result was they were away from it for another two thousand years. That is a very long time to be away from home. But they never forgot it, and every year the Jew away from home would greet his fellow Jew at Passover time with, "Next year in Jerusalem." The hope was kept alive for two thousand years that God would bring his people back and re-establish them in the land and build them up again. He did it after seventy years and he is doing it again after two thousand years, but this is the hope in God that you can have: that he can restore a people, can revive a people, can bring them back home and build them up again.

The other half of the hope is even more wonderful. Jeremiah is saying: Lord, my refuge, not only can you bring this nation back to its own land and re-establish it as an independent nation, but also I see other nations dropping their religions and gathering around us to learn that you alone are God. In other words, Jeremiah has the vision and hope for his nation not only that they will get back home but that they will become again an international influence for good.

That is what Britain was, make no mistake about it. Yes, there were abuses; yes, there was the gunboat diplomacy, but wherever the colonisers went, missionaries went. The great era of our exporting the gospel was during that imperial era. Though there were businessmen who went to grab and exploit, there went missionaries to give and to die. They took that faith and they were an international influence. This country, until recently, did more than any other to give the gospel to the world and to send men, money and medicine wherever people would receive them.

So, Jeremiah sees Israel back in its land again and the nations gathering. Instead of seeing the Jews scattered among the Gentiles, he sees the Gentiles gathered around the Jews. He can see a future for his nation influencing people for God, and there is a ray of hope. He is asking: which is to be our future, a shrinking territory that will some day disappear until no longer is the name 'Israel' on the map, or a future where you are established in your land and where other nations will come and say: You have the truth; your God is the God of power and might; your God is God alone. Will you tell us about him?

Let us move on now to the individual level. Jeremiah, like most prophets, has a zoom lens. He zooms in from the nation to the individual because a nation is made up of individuals; this man and that man and this woman and that woman and you. So now he presents you with the alternatives: what kind of life do you really want to live?

The section changes to beautiful poetry. It is very close to Psalm 1 and it is full of pictures. When Jeremiah gets poetic and picturesque I find I enjoy him even more. The truth comes in a way that touches the heart. He presents two pictures: the curse of human weakness and the blessing of divine strength; and you can live two kinds of lives.

You have got to go to the Middle East to understand, but he pictures a stunted shrub, probably the terebinth, a dwarf juniper that struggles to survive in the middle of a desert. He particularly says, "Salt encrusted desert." You need to go to the shores of the Dead Sea to see that. There, where it is so barren and dead, you just get little stunted shrubs struggling to survive – a bad season and they are gone. Now he says that is the life of the man who trusts in man, whether he is putting his trust in himself or other people: stunted, dwarfed. He does not say he is nothing or that he achieves nothing. He does. He grows up quite a bit, but in God's sight it is so stunted. When drought comes, when the bad, dry period comes, it shrivels. It doesn't produce any fruit; it is there. It has grown a little; it has grown crooked. There is nothing much about it. It is no use to anybody. You never pick those shrubs for anything. Then he pictures a beautiful green bay tree standing by a river, roots going deep down into the water so that even in a drought it stays green and the fruit comes. A bay tree is so luxuriant in its foliage that in a drought people say, "Have you been down to the river? Look at those trees." The hot, scorching sirocco wind from the desert won't touch that tree.

These two pictures are of the man who trusts in man and the man who trusts in God. The man who trusts in man, when the crisis comes, withers, he can't cope with it. The man who trusts in God simply carries on. He has deep roots; he is refreshed. He has a source of life deep down and he just goes on. Believe me, when crisis comes, this sorts out those who carry on. I am old enough to have seen the Depression in Jarrow and I saw what happened to men's self-respect—out of work, marching to London in their cloth caps. But I knew some Christians among those men and they were like trees planted by the river—they did not lose their self-respect. They did not come to despair even though times were tough; they were planted by the river. Which kind of person do you want to be in the years that come? For, believe me, it is going to come. Do you want to be a stunted shrub that withers when the hot wind blows and the resources dry up, or do you want to be a tree planted by the waters? The stunted shrub will have two problems. He will have problems with his motives and with his money, and Jeremiah speaks about both. The Hebrew is, "The reins of the heart." That's a very clever word, "the reins" — the reins that turn the horse, the reins of the heart. In modern language we use the word "motives" — that which steers us. Jeremiah says the man who trusts in man is a man who will have mixed motives; the heart is deceitful. We don't even know why we do certain things. The man who understands his own motives is a brilliant man.

We do things and we don't know why we are doing them because our motives are mixed up. The heart is deceived; it is corrupt, and when God judges us, he searches the heart and looks at the motives. He does not look at what we did; he looks at why we did it. How mixed up your motives can get in a crisis. Why are you doing this? You say, "Well, I'm doing it for the good of my family. I'm doing it for this; I'm doing it for that", and you don't really know why you are doing it. You may be doing it in a desperate panic to save yourself; out of greed; to make sure you don't go down while others do. It is awfully difficult, and your motives get mixed up. God says that he will search the heart and search your motives.

The other thing that is the problem is money. There is a vivid picture here. Jeremiah says a rich man is like a partridge. There is a proverb about the partridge in the Middle East: that the partridge, when it finds some eggs, sits on them and hatches other birds' eggs. I do not know if that is a true characteristic of it or not, but they used to believe it in Old Testament times. Jeremiah says a rich man is like a partridge that has found some eggs and is sitting on them. But as soon as they hatch, they are off and he has lost it.

Jeremiah says the rich man will be left a poor fool without anything. A fool in the Bible is not someone who is mentally deficient but someone who is morally deficient. That is very important. Jesus said you must never call anybody a mentally deficient fool. But morally deficient — he was constantly calling people fools. A rich man who built up his business — "You fool." Blessed is the man who puts his trust in God, for he has got a sanctuary, and his sanctuary is his throne set in the heavens from the beginning. A sanctuary is a place you can run to when you are in trouble. A sanctuary is a place where you can hide.

At Durham Cathedral there is a great big ring knocker on the west door, and any criminal who was in trouble could run there and could hold on to it and he had got sanctuary. Westminster Abbey used to be the same. Most churches in this country were the same and there was a phrase in old English called "taking Westminster", which meant getting into the sanctuary. It was a real cave of Adullam of criminals, and cutthroats, and I don't know what else. But it is interesting that "sanctuary", which means, "holy place", means also "hiding place". Do you find that interesting? Surely that would be the very last place to hide if you were a sinner, yet the churches of this land were sanctuaries for the criminal. The last place you would run to hide if you were doing wrong would be the throne, from which judgment comes, the representative of justice in every court of law. Here is Jeremiah saying that the man who puts his trust in God has got a sanctuary; it is a throne set on high. He has got a place to hide; it is a holy place that he can go to. He has a refuge and he can hide in that. Which kind of man do you want to be? The man who has hedged himself against inflation, who is a stunted shrub in a desert, who will finish up a poor old fool, or the man whose tree is planted by the water, who has a river of living water underneath, who has got a sanctuary to run to and a place to hide?

Jeremiah says, "Lord, I'm coming to you. You're my refuge, you're my hope." That is one of Jeremiah's favourite titles of God: "the hope of Israel". "Oh Lord, hope of Israel, I'm coming to you. Heal me; save me. Protect me; deliver me and even avenge me." Jeremiah was having a pretty tough time. People were saying all kinds of things about him. They were laughing at him. They were saying that he is such a doom preacher but it's not happening. Where is the word of the Lord? Why doesn't it happen, Jeremiah? You're threatening us with all these things, but actually it's not too bad. We're surviving; it's all right." Jeremiah had to run to his sanctuary, run to the throne, and say, "God, will you deal with them?" Jeremiah prayed a prayer that has puzzled many people. Psalm 139 is a beautiful psalm:

O Lord you've searched me and known me. When I stand up, when I sit down, you know. You know every word on my tongue, even before I utter it. If I ascend into heaven, you're there. If I make my bed in Sheol, you're there. If I take the wings of the morning and dwell in the uttermost parts of the sea, you're there. Oh, how precious are your thoughts about me, Lord. When I wake up in the morning, you're still thinking about me.

It is a lovely psalm and then suddenly the Psalmist says, "Don't I hate those who hate you? Don't I hate them with perfect hatred?" Here Jeremiah does the same thing and suddenly he is praying, "Lord, bring double destruction on them." Now Jeremiah is in a very tricky position here, praying. When you pray on God's side rather than man's, you can hate God's enemies with perfect hatred. It is not vengeance; you are on God's side, praying. The so-called imprecatory psalms, which have been a puzzle to many young Christians, the psalms that pray for vengeance on the enemies, are very godly psalms. They are saying, first: God, I'm not going to take vengeance; vengeance belongs to you; you take it — and that is a right thing to say. Secondly, they are recognising that God has enemies who hate him. It is taking God's side rather than man's side in that situation. But if you pray this kind of prayer, "Lord, really deal with my enemies because they are your enemies," then the danger is that vengeance can come in, and you can really get your own back through the prayer. So, Jeremiah says this: "Lord, I don't want the people crushed by terrible calamity. The plan was yours, not mine. It is your message I've given them, not my own. I don't want them doomed." There is a man who has had to be absolutely honest. Do I preach hell because I enjoy dangling people over the pit or do I preach it because God's told me to preach it? That is a question every preacher has to ask himself. Does he enjoy doom? No, but nevertheless he says, "Destroy them. Lord, you're my sanctuary. They're attacking me because they're attacking you. It's your word, not mine. I don't enjoy telling them doom is coming, but Lord, they're blaming me. So Lord, I'm running into your sanctuary; you deal with them" — and that is a thoroughly moral prayer to pray.

Finally, let me rush on to the social level. There are certain fundamental features of Jewish social life. One is kosher food and one of the main features of Jewish social life is the Sabbath, their day of rest (Friday 6 p.m. to Saturday 6 p.m.). The good Jew should do no unnecessary work for himself on that day. God gave the Jew the Sabbath, not because God wanted to restrict his activities. As Jesus said, "The Sabbath was made for man, not man for the Sabbath." It was a gift of God, and God knows that man is not just an animal. As soon as you believe that man is only an animal, he doesn't need the Sabbath because no animal needs a Sabbath. Our dog doesn't need a Sabbath, though it gets one and it knows when Sunday comes around! Man is made in the image of God. He has more in common with the angels than with the animals. Therefore, he needs to be lifted above his work of getting food. He needs to shut off from just staying alive, to remember that man shall not live by bread alone.

So, once a week, one day in seven, they stop their work and God is saying: now you be a man; you are not just an animal scraping around this earth for bread, you are a man and you live by my words. It is not just what goes into your mouth that makes you live; it is what comes out of mine that makes you live. So they turned off for one day every seven days, and God was able to speak and remind them that they were human beings made in the image of God. Therefore, they needed to behave like he did, not as the animals did. When God had finished his work of Creation he rested, and so do we. They had this lovely gift. Now God says, "Jeremiah, do you see what's happened? Go into the gates. Go to the gate where the king comes in; go to the gate where the citizens come in. See what happens." And from Friday night at 6 p.m. to Saturday night at 6 p.m. they were rushing through with bags and boxes, loads, and burdens, to the market place, just to make more money. Now I know that it was a time of inflation. I know they were hard up. Read between the lines and you can see they had inflation and they would have been saying: we need money to live; we've got to keep our families going so we must do more work. So that was what they were doing, just keeping going, desperately trying to provide perhaps for their families. God said, "Jeremiah, tell them that if they go on doing this, I will burn those gates with fire, and even the palace. They will lose their royal family, they will lose their security because that lies in me." I tell you the solemn truth: those gates and that palace were burned down just a few years after this was said. But here is the choice: Jeremiah, tell them.

There is more good news than bad news in this final section. "Jeremiah, tell them that if they give me the time they should, they will still see people carrying things in through the gates, but they will be burnt offerings and sacrifices and incense, and they will be a grateful people instead of a greedy people." There will be people coming, full of thankfulness to God. They will come in with things for God.

Now here is the question: which kind of a society do we really want? A society that is intent on getting more from people, or a society that is intent on giving more to God? That is the choice and it is a very clear one. Let me make this quite clear: I do not believe that Christians are under the Sabbath law, or that Sunday is a legalistic Sabbath which we must observe. Therefore, I am not in sympathy with the Lord's Day Observance Society and its main thrust, though I believe their motives are right. They have seen what is true – that a nation that has no time for God will suffer – but you don't improve the situation by seeking to impose observance of a Sabbath. You did in Jeremiah's day because they were breaking a law under which they lived. But can I put it a different way? We may not be under the law of the Sabbath, we are free, and if one man wants to treat one day differently from the others, let him. If another Christian wants to treat all days alike, as every day is the Lord's Day, let him. There is no principle involved here. "Let no man judge you in respect of Sabbaths," said Paul. The fulfilment of the legal Sabbath is that we should every day cease from our own works and rest in his. So, if you want to know when my Sabbath is, my answer should be as a believer on the basis of Hebrews 4, "My Sabbath is Sunday, Monday, Tuesday, Wednesday, Thursday, Friday, Saturday" — that is a good deal better than one.

But having said that, just as Christians are not under the tithe law (to give a tenth of their income), shall people who have more reason to be grateful to God give less than the Jew? That is the question, and therefore I think a Christian would gladly give at least one day in seven to shut off the things that can so make us like animals, scratching a living, and turn us again into human beings reflecting the glory of God as in a mirror, and being transformed day by day into the same glory and becoming truly human. So, though a Christian is not under any law to give one day in seven, I think he will at least want to do that so that he may live not by bread alone, not by Sunday joint alone, but by every word that proceeds from the mouth of God.

Be willing to spend time listening to God's word and worshipping him. It is when we get to the way of thinking that an hour is enough, and a couple of hours on Sunday — that really is the limit. But we have lost something then. I notice that where God is moving in this country, where the Spirit is really bringing God's people back to life, services of worship are getting longer and longer. You go around the country and see. I used to go to some other countries and would find elderly people sitting for five and a half hours. I find people worshipping God and just wanting to go on and on, to be really human—they get so little chance. It makes me embarrassed and ashamed. Jews were under the law of one-tenth of their money and they were under the law of one-seventh of their time. We are not under law; we are under grace. We are free, but if, in our freedom, we tear home from the church service to grab the phone and just tie up that bit of business from the previous day, no wonder God says, "You haven't time for me." You need to give God time — to read the Bible for yourself. Frankly, that is often the most rewarding time of our communion with God. The key to this passage is this: what kind of a person are you going to be?

READ JEREMIAH 18–19

We are now going to wrestle with the question of predestination, so our minds are going to be stretched. The great problem is how to reconcile God's free will with man's free will, because you cannot have two parties both with absolute free will in the same situation. Two people getting married cannot have absolute free will again. They are now involved in a relationship in which neither party is as free as they were. Just to balance that up, so that you don't think I'm being cynical, somebody commiserated with me on the night before I was married in saying, "Well, your last night of freedom." I replied, "No, tomorrow I will be free to be married." There are different kinds of freedom, and the freedom that one has with one's wife is the freedom of relative free will, and the freedom to be limited by each other and to enjoy the freedom together as a unit that was not possible before.

I am going to say that God's free will is not absolute but relative, and men's free will is not absolute but relative, because God and men are in relationship with each other and that limits the freedom of both parties. It is, however, still of God's grace that he has thus limited himself, for the day he created man, God limited his own free will. However, that does not put God and men on an equal footing. God may not have total free will now, but he does have the final word in any situation. The picture of predestination and free will, which the Bible uses again and again—Isaiah uses it, Zechariah uses it, Jeremiah uses it, and that's the passage we're looking at, Paul uses it — is the picture of a potter with clay. This picture helps us as much as any other to understand the problem of predestination and free will, and what control God has over us, and what control he does not have over us.

Now to those of us who have little experience of pottery or clay, we will almost certainly misinterpret this picture. There was a time when I did not truly understand this single sentence: "Behold, like the clay in the potter's hand, so are you in my hand." Now the first reaction you have to that is that man has no free will at all, that man is simply a lump of flexible material and God can do with that lump whatever he wishes — and that he decides to do this or that or the other. Everything is under the potter's control and he has absolute free will over the clay. I read commentary after commentary in which the commentator said that this is a picture of God's absolute control over man. But I do not believe that is the message of Jeremiah 18–19. The message of Jeremiah here is this: the clay is in control of the situation — the clay, not the potter. If the first impression on you was that the potter was in control of the situation, then I want you to think again. The whole message is that the potter is limited by the clay and that is really the profound lesson we are going to learn about God's free will and man's free will here.

Chapter 18 is about clay in a soft condition when it can be moulded in different ways. Chapter 19 is about clay after it has hardened, when you only have two choices. One is to keep it and the other is to break it. But in chapter 18 you have the earliest stage of the clay when you don't break it. In fact, you can't break a lump of clay—you can mould it, you can tear it. You can't break it – it is soft, pliable. But in chapter 19 it has become hard, and there Jeremiah breaks the vessel. It is a very delicate balance we have got to strike. I want to go step by step, so that you are with me all the way. Then you will understand that God has relative free will and man has relative free will, but God has more relative free will than man has—that is the message of the chapter.

Let us start with chapter 18. Clay is very much part of our lives. Most of us live in houses made of clay ultimately. Clay is very plentiful. The London Basin of clay is full of it. Our houses may have clay tiles — we owe a very great deal for the gift of clay. Have you noticed that there are hardly ever two bricks the same? Have you noticed that the clay produces entirely different coloured bricks and tiles, because clay varies enormously? You have got to have the right clay for the right kind of brick. If you want a hard engineering brick for foundations, you need to go to a certain place for a certain kind of clay. If you want a decorative, sand-faced, handmade brick, then you go to another brickfield and another sort of clay. There is an infinite variety of clay, and if you know anything about bricks you know that. Likewise, when you are making vessels of clay, and I daresay you will have had a clay vessel on your breakfast table this morning, you will know that clay varies so much that some clay is alright for thick mugs — about three-eighths of an inch thick, glazed. But if you want really fine china and a beautiful vessel, then you will have to go down to Cornwall and you can find there that deposit of the most fine, beautiful china clay. You see, you cannot do what you like with clay. It is the clay that determines what you can do with it. You cannot say, "I'm going to make this shape of vessel and any lump of clay will do." You need to have the right kind of clay; the potter is limited by the clay all the time. The architect of a new church centre was a Mr Potter, and I remember the day when he brought different samples of brick for us to see, made of various kinds of clay. Which clay was suitable for what we wanted to do in the building? It was quite a decision to make. Any old clay would not do, for clay produces different appearances, different weathering and different textures.

"Jeremiah, go down to the potter's house. I want to speak to you. I want you to learn a lesson about me and Israel." Jeremiah trotted down the street and came to the potter's house, and he saw the potter trying to make a clay vessel. He took a lump of clay — and it is a vivid description. It says, "He was working with his wheels." I'm afraid the Revised Standard Version says "wheel", which is wrong. It is wheels, plural, and that means there were two wheels on a spindle, and the spindle was upright. The top wheel was for the potter's hands to work the vessel on and the bottom wheel was for his feet. His feet would be turning the bottom wheel while his hands shaped the pot on the top wheel. So you see how accurate the Bible is. It is we who don't know anything about it who say "wheel" instead of "wheels". That is how we can get misunderstandings in an English translation.

So the potter was working at his wheels—his feet going and his hands going. Jeremiah watched; he took a lump of clay and he tried to make it into a certain kind of pot. It didn't work out and the fault was not the fault of the potter, it was the fault of the clay. That clay was not right for that vessel. It wouldn't work, it wouldn't run, and it wouldn't shape. Maybe it had grit in it; maybe it wasn't soft enough or fine enough; maybe it wouldn't stand that kind of shape. That is the situation—the clay was wrong. So the potter put it into a lump again and made a totally different kind of vessel with it. Now this is the key to the whole chapter. He did not start again and manage to produce what he originally intended. What he originally intended had to be cancelled. The vessel he wanted to make could not be made, so he made a totally different kind of vessel. That does not come out in the Living Bible. It comes out partially in the Revised Standard Version, even more in the Hebrew. He reworked the clay into another vessel. I am going to put this very crudely, but I want to get this across to you so it is in terms you can understand, because most of us really have little experience of potteries. Instead of a vase, he made a chamber pot—that is what was happening here. The clay was too rough to make a delicate, beautiful object. It must therefore be made into a vessel that would be useful, that he could sell, that would do something fairly ordinary, maybe even be used to contain dirt. It is this message which we shall see as taken up by Paul in 2 Timothy 2, that in houses there are many clay vessels, some for noble use and some for ignoble use— and it is the same picture. If the lump of clay will not be shaped beautifully and finely, and withstand the contours of a beautiful flask, then it has got to be made into a pot that will at least do something useful for the potter and for the person who buys it. Now that is the picture, and it is a very sad picture. It means the potter's original will was not fulfilled, and he had to change his plans and think up something else to do with that lump of clay because it was not responding.

Now are you beginning to get the message? Now we understand the word that came. Jeremiah watched the method of the potter, and then he got the message. The message was this: O Israel, are you not in my hands as the clay is in the potter's hands? Israel, I wanted to make you a vessel of my grace and mercy among the nations. I wanted you to hold my love for the nations. I wanted you to be a beautiful thing. I have tried to mould you and you will not be moulded, you will not conform, you will not respond to my hands. The vessel is spoiling in my hands, and it's not my fault, it's yours. The clay is not responding, and therefore, Israel, listen carefully. If I decide to make a nation the vessel of my good grace, and if I plan good for that nation, and I plan blessings for that nation, and that nation does not respond and will not listen and rebels, then I will make you a vessel to hold evil before the nations. I will still use you—you will demonstrate some part of me. If you will not hold my mercy, then you must hold my judgment, but you're going to hold me. I'm going to use you for one purpose or the other.

Similarly, God says: Tell Israel, if I shape evil for a nation, and decide that I will make that nation a vessel of my wrath, and that nation turns and listens to me and amends their ways, then I will repent.

This is God speaking, "I will repent" — and you know that "repent" means change your mind. I will change my mind. I will devise another plan. Now here is a God, he is not a God who makes decrees and says: that shall be that and you're just a lump of plastic and I will make you, I will force you into my role. But here is a God who says: I will make one plan for you, and if you respond to that, then we can carry out the plan; if you do not respond, then I will devise another plan, and I will still use you, but in an entirely different way.

You can't refuse to be used by God. You can choose whether you are used as a vessel of his wrath or of his mercy, and it is the clay that decides. God makes his original plan and we can refuse that original plan — God can make other plans and make you a different kind of vessel. Now that is predestination as it is taught here. It is not an arbitrary potter, making any lump of clay into anything he chooses. It is a potter saying: I'd like to do this with you, but if you don't respond, I will decide to do that. He is a potter who can still make you into something, but it will not be what he originally intended.

Now I want to apply that very personally. There may well be people reading this who are not now what God planned them to be in their life. There is nothing fatalistic about God's plans. There are people for whom God had a dream and a vision, and he wanted to shape them in a certain way; he wanted to use them in a certain way, and they did not respond. Maybe they kept to themselves the best years of their life, and they did what the Israelites here say: "We will follow our own plans." You have kept that plan. Has that defeated God? No, it hasn't. He can change his plans. He can make you into another kind of vessel. It will not be as beautiful a one as it was originally meant to be, but he will still use you. Sometimes he changes plans and uses you still for a good purpose, though it is not the best. But he can still use you for good. It is glorious that some people who have wasted their lives, then come to God late in life, and God can make something of them. He cannot make what he originally intended. The plan has had to be changed, but when they amend their ways and come to him, he can make something of them for good. But if a man spends his whole life refusing to be mouldable, refusing to be malleable clay in God's hands, then ultimately God will make him a vessel of wrath.

There is no cannot in God

Everyone reading this will one day be a vessel holding something of God. You will either be a vessel of his mercy or a vessel of his wrath but your life will demonstrate God's mercy or his justice. You are a lump of clay, but he will use you for some purpose, for he is the potter. The tragedy is that many, many people, whom he wanted to be vessels of grace, holding his mercy, holding the treasure of the glory of Christ in an earthen vessel, cannot do that because they were not responsive to his hands when he sought to shape them.

That is the message. It is a pretty stark message but hidden in it is a wonderful offer. The offer is to Israel: "Behold," says God. Do you see what he's saying? He is saying: In years gone by I called you Israel because I had a beautiful plan for you; you were going to be the most beautiful people on earth; you were going to be in a land flowing with milk and honey. You were going to have my blessing poured into you. You were going to be full of grace. You were going to be such a lovely vessel but now I am shaping you for evil. I

What about His remnant?

have changed my plans. I have repented — I have changed
my mind. I am now going to demonstrate before the world
my justice, my judgment, and you are going to be an ugly,
dirty vessel holding my wrath. But tell them, Jeremiah: if
they will amend their ways, if they will return, I will change
my mind again. God is saying as clearly as he can: clay, if
you change your mind, I may change mine. Will you respond
to my moulding and become a beautiful thing? There is an
appeal here, and it is never too late. I care not how many
years you have wasted, how many years you have been out
of God's plan, how many years you have followed your own
plans and not allowed him to mould your life. If you amend
your ways and return, he can change his mind, and he can
make you into something useful. He cannot give you back
the years you lost, but he can make you into something very
useful for the years to come.

What was their response? We turn from the potters to
what I have called the plotters, for that is what they became.
Jeremiah 18:12 is their response to God and v. 18 is their
response to Jeremiah's call — and their response is a very
sad one. In v. 12: "We will follow our own plans, thank you."
How utterly foolish people are to say that! This is where God
has more relative free will than man, because God, while
he has limited himself by making us clay, and making us
breathe, and giving us minds of our own, has not given us
the absolute free will to follow our own plans. No man can
say that; no man can say, "God, I will not have your plan
for my life. I will have my own." You cannot say that for the
simple reason that clay cannot mould itself. In fact, the only
thing that I know that clay can do is to settle down. That is
precisely what most people do who follow their own plans.
Have you noticed? They settle down to something or other
sooner or later. They finish up, settle down in a retirement
house on the south coast; settle down like clay. You can't

[handwritten margin note: THEN THEY ARE NOT THE ELECT]

mould your life yourself. You may think you can, but you can't. "We will follow our own plans, thank you God. We're not interested in being clay in your hands. We don't want anyone shaping us. We don't want anyone telling us what to do. We will follow our own plans." How foolish! —God cries out from his heart. Have you ever heard anything like this? Have you ever heard people say this kind of thing? Well, I'm afraid we have, but in Israel's situation it is even starker. "It's like the snow disappearing from the highest mountains," says God. It's like the mountain streams ceasing to flow. It's so unnatural — it is as if the sky turned pink and the trees turned to stone.

Yet people do this and Israel did it. They forgot their God. Do you notice what God says? "As soon as you forgot me you got off the highway and you got into byways." That is a vivid description. As soon as a man says, "I will follow my own plans," he turns into a cul-de-sac without realising it. He gets off the road that leads to life. It may be a very nice cul-de-sac. It may be a beautiful one, but he gets to a dead end. It's a byway. You get off the road when you say, "I will follow my own plans, thank you." God says: If you do that, you will see my back and not my face.

I think there is no more terrible thing that could happen to a man than to have God turn his back on him, because you can't talk to someone's back. It is something awful when you are talking to someone and they turn their back. God says, "I'll turn my back on a man who says, 'I'm going to follow my own plans.'" So, Jeremiah told them the answer of God to their answer. Now comes their answer to Jeremiah: "Let's plot against Jeremiah too, for the law shall not perish from the priests, nor counsel from the wise." They mean this: We are perfectly happy with our own religious leaders; who's this Jeremiah? He thinks he is going to put all our priests and prophets out of a job — who does he think he is, telling us what to do? He has no authority. We've got priests, we've got prophets, and we've got leaders — we don't need any others; away with him. And they began to plot to get rid of him.

It was this that made Jeremiah realise that the clay had absolutely refused to be moulded, and he changed his prayer. I don't know what you think about this prayer now. Just remember that for years, probably for about fifteen years already, Jeremiah had spent his private prayer life pleading with God to forgive the people of Judah, and to turn wrath away from them and make them a beautiful vessel. He had pleaded and pleaded. Now he realises the clay cannot be made into that kind of a vessel. Out comes a very honest prayer. He has now switched over to God's side, from having been rebuked by God for being too sympathetic with man's side. He has stepped right over, and now he prays an awful prayer. He says: Father, you know I've prayed for forgiveness for them. Now I pray forgive them not. He prays all kinds of horrible things on them: "Deliver up their children to famine; let their wives become childless and widowed; may their men meet death by disease; may their young people be slain in battle." It is a terrible prayer, but Jeremiah is being wrung in the depths of his heart with the agony of clay saying, "No, God, I'm not going your way at all". So he prays this dreadful prayer.

I do not want to say any more about that prayer except that it is a very honest prayer. He is on God's side and that is why he is praying as he does. He is not praying out of personal revenge. He is not praying to get his own back. He is realising the situation as it really is—the nation has gone too far. The enemies of his have gone too far ever to be made into that beautiful vessel. He is saying: Lord, make them into the other kind of vessel — demonstrate your wrath through them; demonstrate your judgment through them.

This same theme is taken up in the New Testament. Lest you think I am explaining a doctrine that is only in the Old Testament, read Romans 9:14-24. Do you understand that passage now? It is not saying that God is arbitrary, and it is not saying: I'll pick him to be a vessel of mercy, and him to be a vessel of wrath. No. The simple fact is that no lump of clay walking the earth today has been fit to become a vessel of mercy. We have all refused God's plans. There was only one lump of clay that ever responded perfectly to the potter, and his name is Jesus. The rest of us have rebelled and said, "We'll go our own way," so we are all fit to be made into ugly vessels of wrath. Therefore, if God decides to have mercy on some, that is his prerogative; that is his free will. But notice it says there that he has had much patience with the vessels of wrath. He has tried. *GOD HARDENED Pharaoh's HEART*

Consider the outstanding example of this, Pharaoh. Pharaoh was keeping the children of Israel under his iron grip, killing the little baby boys in Egypt. God sent Moses to Pharaoh and said, "Let my people go." If Pharaoh had said at that moment, "Yes, I will," history might have been different. But it says that Pharaoh hardened his heart. The clay was that much less flexible. So, God said a second time, "Let my people go," and a second time Pharaoh hardened his heart and the clay became tougher. God tried seven times, and that is the perfect number; seven times God had patience with that vessel of wrath, and tried to make him into something beautiful. Seven times Pharaoh hardened his heart. Three more times God said to him, "Let my people go," but on the last three times it does not say Pharaoh hardened his heart, it says "God hardened Pharaoh's heart". It is as if, indeed it is the case that God, by the seventh time, said: Pharaoh, you will not respond. You are hardening, and so, before you are totally hard, I am going to shape you into a vessel of wrath; I am going to smash you and your army — and God did that.

EXODUS 7:3

209 *GOD WITHELD HIS GRACE*

It was not that God sort of picked names out of a hat like the FA Cup draw. He didn't just pick a ball out and read "Moses", and pick another one out and read "Pharaoh" — "Pharaoh, vessel of wrath; Moses, vessel of mercy". He had great patience and he worked hard with Pharaoh, but Pharaoh's clay got harder and harder, and before it got too hard to make anything, God produced a vessel of wrath, and hardened him in the shape he had chosen.

You see, it is not absolute predestination by decree that no one can do anything about. That is when predestination is used as an excuse for not responding to God.

People say, "Well, if God has chosen some to go to heaven and some to go to hell, there is nothing I can do about it." This is the first stanza of "Holy Willie's Prayer", a satire by Robbie Burns:

> O Thou, who in the heavens does dwell,
> Who, as it pleases best Thysel',
> Sends ane to heaven an' ten to hell,
> A' for Thy glory,
> And no for ony gude or ill
> They've done afore Thee!

That is blasphemy, a libel on God! It is as if God is an arbitrary picker and chooser of men. God has had patience with vessels of wrath. He has tried to make people into something else, but if they don't respond, then he makes them into a vessel that will demonstrate his anger and hold his wrath. You therefore choose, not God. You choose to respond to God. You choose to be moulded. You choose to be pliable in his hands. "Are you not in my hands as clay in the potter's hands, O Israel? You won't respond, you won't be moulded." I can pray: "If I have so messed things up that I have missed your original will, then Lord, will you think again and will you bring me another plan for my life?" To me this is lovely, because it means that if I have missed God's will, and if I have made a mistake, the situation is not totally lost. I can come back and say, "Lord, there's still something you can do with me." I think vividly of a man who came to Christ when he was seventy-two. He was an invalid; he had a lot of things wrong with him. He could never come to church because he couldn't go more than ten yards from a toilet. He was housebound and his life was wrecked. But he came to Christ and the Lord healed him, body, mind and spirit, in one fell swoop. He was baptised at seventy-two, and after his baptism he was weeping. I said, "Whatever's the matter? You should be full of joy!" He said, "Well, when I think of all those wasted years...." We had to assure him that God could make another vessel. Not the one he could have made when the man was twenty, but God could make another vessel, and he did. I think he lived about seven years, and for those seven years he was a beautiful vessel of mercy.

God doesn't harden people until they have hardened towards him. God wants to make every lump of clay into a beautiful thing. But now we must turn to the other side of our study. Supposing the clay has got too hard to be moulded. You see, you have only a limited amount of time once you have started working with a lump of clay. Whether we have seventy or eighty years, it is not long and it goes more and more quickly. God has only a limited amount of time to work in. The clay is malleable and there is something quite profound in the fact that the moment you die, your clay goes hard. My clay is very flexible at the moment, so soft and mouldable. My very body is a symbol of the fact that while I am living, I am mouldable. Things can change, but the moment I die my body will begin to stiffen, until it is a hard lump in this mortal clay. Having hardened, it will then disintegrate.

That is the meaning of chapter 19. "Jeremiah, go back to the potter, and this time buy a jar that's hard, that's fixed...." Now which of the jars do you think he bought? I have the feeling, indeed the Hebrew implies it, that he didn't buy a beautiful vase but one of those ugly things, one of those ignoble vessels. It is described here not as a vessel, but as an earthen flask, a word which means a chamber pot or something like that – "Go and buy one of those vessels that might have been a beautiful thing, but the clay just wasn't up to it. Get one of those, and take it out to the Potsherd Gate, to the Valley of Topheth."

I wish I could take you to Israel. You have almost got to be there to see this. I would love to show you Jerusalem on its hill, the hill of Zion. It has a ring of hills around it, shaped like a horseshoe. Then if you know the tongue in the middle of the horseshoe, the horse's foot, that's the hill of Zion pointing down, and the temple at the top of it, and the city of Jerusalem below it. That sort of crevice, that deep horseshoe-shaped valley, between the bit in the middle and the shoe outside — if you can imagine that valley, the deepest part of it in the bottom part of the horseshoe, so deep that there are parts of it that never see the light of day, it is a deep ravine called the Valley of Topheth. Then a man called Hinnom bought it, or his son, and it was called the Valley of the Son of Hinnom. It was the obvious place to put the rubbish, and that is what was put out there.

On the Hinnom Valley side there was a gate, and it was called the Gate of the Potsherd, and the reason for that was twofold. Down in the bottom of the valley there was a clay deposit, and a potter owned it. It was the Potter's Field, and in through the Potsherd Gate came the clay to be made into jars inside, and to be sold. Out through the Potsherd Gate went the jars that people were finished with, that had got chipped or cracked and were leaking. They were taken out of the Potsherd Gate and smashed outside. The ground was littered with broken clay pieces.

You find this outside every ancient city in the Near East. I remember walking around outside Beth-Shean seeing a great area of broken pottery. There was Philistine glass there. Beautiful pottery, two and three thousand years old, just lying there for the taking. Just piles of broken pottery, thrown out. "Jeremiah, go to the Potsherd Gate and carry that old pot that you have bought. Tell them what is going to happen to that valley." That valley had already had certain things happen to it. Not only was it a rubbish dump, but because it was hidden and dark, all kinds of things began to happen in its shadows. That is where people at first had gone to build little altars and burn incense to the stars of heaven. That is the valley where people had gone and built a bonfire and thrown live babies on the bonfire to Moloch and the stars of heaven. God said, "Jeremiah, tell them that valley will be known as the Valley of Slaughter." Do you know when Jesus came preaching the good news he constantly used this valley in his teaching? By the time Jesus came, the name "Hinnom" had changed to "Henna", and it was called the Valley of Gehenna. Jesus constantly said, "It's better for you to enter into life maimed, than having all your faculties to be cast into Gehenna." In our English Bibles it is translated "hell", but just as the earthly Jerusalem provided a picture of heaven, the Valley of Hinnom, the Valley of Gehenna, was always the picture of hell. Jesus said, "That's where you'll finish up, in that valley."

When Jesus died on the cross of Calvary, he was up at the top of the horseshoe. He was up on the hill at the other end. At the same time, just a few hours before, one of his own followers died in the Potter's Field at the bottom of Gehenna, and he hanged himself. The rope snapped and his body dropped into the valley, his bowels gushed out, and he finished up there a smashed vessel, a broken flask. Jesus died at the top, and Judas died at the bottom, in this very valley, and Jeremiah is saying, "It will be the Valley of Slaughter." Do you remember that the very money that Judas had got to betray his Lord, he threw back in their faces and they went out and bought the potter's field at the bottom of that valley?

How the centuries roll away! There are over five hundred years between the events we are speaking of — between Jeremiah and Judas — but this valley was there all that time. It stood there as the place to which the useless, hardened clay goes to be smashed. It says of Judas, that when he went and hanged himself in the Potter's Field in that valley, the field of blood, *Akeldama*: "He went to his own place." What an epitaph!

"Jeremiah, go to that valley. Take that pot and smash it, and say to this nation...." Notice the words, "you have stiffened your necks, refusing to hear my word, therefore I will break you." The tragedy is that a human being — made of clay, out of the dust of the earth, breathed into by God so he's a living soul — can so harden himself and so stiffen his neck that God one day has no choice but to say, "Go to your own place. I shall smash you in the Valley of Gehenna."

Here are solemn words, which place before every one of us this supreme choice: either I respond to God's loving potter's hands as early in my life as possible, so that his original design for my life might be fulfilled, or if I have refused that, then as soon as possible I put my life totally in his hands so that he may still make some vessel. Or every time I hear his Word, I become more critical and harder, more resistant, until one day God says, "You've stiffened too much. There is only one thing I can do with this lump of clay, and that is put you beyond mending." God says through Jeremiah, "I will break this people as one breaks a potter's vessel, so that it can never be mended."

To me, hell is the place where people can never be mended. So, while we are still mouldable and while we are still soft clay, we are to respond. Then we can hold the glory in earthen vessels. Poor vessels though we are, we can nevertheless hold this treasure in earthen vessels. Or listen to Paul: "In a great house there are not only vessels of gold and silver, but also of wood and earthenware, and some for noble use and some for ignoble. If anyone purifies himself from what is ignoble," notice *himself*, "then he will be a vessel for noble use, consecrated and useful to the master of the house, ready for any good work."

It is the clay that decides. The potter is not an arbitrary dictator. The potter can mould; the potter will have the last word. The potter will use every lump of clay in one way or another, and the potter will decide to smash those that go hard. So, the potter has a lot of free will, but by making clay he has put himself in the position where he will have to change his plans according to the clay's response—and I believe that to be a profound insight into the doctrine of predestination and free will.

READ JEREMIAH 20–21:10

This passage is part of a series which must have come from Jeremiah's private diary, in which he was honest enough to record his depressions. We are studying a passage in which Jeremiah touched rock bottom and we are going to see how God dealt with him when he did, and how God lifted him from his depression. I hope you won't find it depressing. I hope you will find it helpful and hopeful that other people have got as low as this, that some of God's greatest servants have got as low as this, and that God caught them at the bottom and held them.

If I were asked to give a title to these two chapters I would simply say, "Jeremiah hits rock bottom." I am so glad the Bible is an honest book and shows both the elation and the depression of some of the greatest men of God. It doesn't hesitate to let us know that Elijah wanted to commit suicide, that King David felt the same way, that Jeremiah got to this point. It is comforting to us to know that the greatest servants of God have felt like this from time to time. Jeremiah must have been willing for us to know that. Even, the holy of holies, the Lord Jesus himself, Son of God, came to the point where he cried out, "My God, my God, why...?" The trouble with many of us today is that we will not let other people know when we are going through it. We bury it. We become introverted, we keep it in. We are the last people to cope with it. We need to share, we need to get it out. Jeremiah wrote it down and a man called Baruch later put it together with

217

the rest of his prophecies. But I want you also to realise that God wanted us to know. God didn't mind us knowing that people like Jeremiah said the most awful things to him. What a wonderful God we have, who is willing to let us know that he has been so criticised and so complained against unjustly.

Here is Jeremiah and he is going to say: God, you've deceived me; you fooled me; you've been having me on — it's not me who's joking. It's you, Yahweh.... You've led me into this trap. You never warn me, you've just led me on; you've used me. God wanted us to know that that had been said, and God doesn't defend himself against the charge. Isn't he patient with us? God would much rather you accused him unjustly to his face than that you didn't talk to him. He would much rather you would throw it in his face and say, "God, why? Why was I born at all?" than have you run away into a little corner and say it to yourself until you have got yourself in a real state. Much better to get it out. God can take it, otherwise he wouldn't have put it in his book.

Before we look at the actual depression and try to analyse how Jeremiah got into this state, and why he said what he did, and try and understand his heart, it is worth noting that it is sandwiched between two narratives. It is in poetry and it is between two sections of prose. As I have already mentioned, the poetry in Jeremiah comes from the heart and the prose is from the head. I think we need to look at the sandwich, take it whole and chew it up and digest it, and then we will get the feel of it.

Let us look at what led up to his depression, let us look at what followed it, and then we will see it in perspective. The trouble with depression is that when you are in it you can only see the depression. You can't think about what went on before and you can't think about what might happen afterwards. You are locked into the present moment, into the existential experience of depression. But we can see the whole thing so let us look first at chapter 20 and what immediately preceded the depression.

Let me just remind you that the last thing we saw Jeremiah do was to take a clay jar and smash it into pieces outside the Potsherd Gate, and then from there he walked into the temple, which was a short distance away, and in front of the large worshipping crowd he shouted, "God says, 'I will break you as my servant broke that jar because you've stiffened your necks against my word.'" Not the kind of preaching calculated to comfort a congregation, not the kind of thing that would just enable them to go on worshipping and singing their psalms as they had been doing, with everything in dignified peace. Jeremiah appeared in the temple as a disturber of the peace. What happened next came directly from that, because the temple had two main officials: the high priest in charge of the service and the chief "bouncer". He was not called that in Hebrew, he was called the chief officer, but in fact that is what the name meant. He was second in power to the high priest and his job was to get rid of disruptive people.

So, the high priest went on with the worship and the chief officer threw people out who were destroying the peace of the service. He had a job to do but he did it wrongly here. His name was Pashhur. Little did he dream that his action that day would make him infamous. It shows that a little action can be terribly important from the point of view of eternity. He saw Jeremiah purely as a disturber of the peace, not as a preacher nor as a prophet, but as someone likely to cause upset, as someone likely to lower morale. Therefore, he decided on a short, sharp lesson, and without trial he flogged Jeremiah, which was the first time anybody had laid a finger on him. He had had many things said to him before. This was the first time he had actually suffered physical violence. He was flogged, and it really would have meant flogging – until his back was probably torn in ribbons and bleeding. Then he was taken out of the north side of the city and he was put in the stocks. Now stocks to us are just two beams with hollows in for the feet and a form to sit on—that was not what stocks meant then. It was a scaffolding so shaped that when the human being was put in it he was distorted in a crooked way until his muscles were so cramped that he was totally in agony. It was, of course, also a humiliating punishment because people would come up and laugh at this person so crooked and so cramped and they would probably throw things at him. For twenty-four hours Jeremiah suffered that.

That is what brought on the depression, as we shall see in a moment. Jeremiah was the sort of sensitive, poetic person who could not take ridicule — extremely sensitive inside. He was bold when he preached, but inside he had a very soft heart. He was what the Israelis today would call a "sabra", which is the fruit of the cactus, very prickly and tough on the outside, but very sweet and soft on the inside. When he was put in that silly position, flogged, humiliated, laughed at, things thrown at him, Jeremiah couldn't cope with that, and he was depressed.

I want you to notice that his depression came out of persecution for his faith—that is rather important. We must be a little careful before we apply scriptures to our own depression if we got our depression through self-pity or through something other than persecution. This passage is primarily to comfort those who are having a tough time because they belong to the Lord. I know that some who read this now are having a tough time because they are Christians. There are some times when you can't take it and there are times when you just get depressed and say, "It's not worth it. What's the use? The Lord has trapped me in this situation." You are going to get a great deal of comfort from this.

So Pashhur flogged him, put him in the stocks and released

him the next morning, thinking that Jeremiah would be thoroughly subdued, humbled, and wouldn't give any bother again. As soon as he got him out of the stocks Jeremiah really gave him an earful. Jeremiah with great boldness, having been flogged, having been in the stocks, having been humiliated, far from cringing before this man, gave two names to him which were very frightening.

First, he gave the man a nickname, which he would never live down. He called him "Terror on every side". That stuck to Pashhur for the rest of his life. It has been a name that has been used down through history, especially in an age that knew its Bible better. Jeremiah gave him this nickname in the name of the Lord for two reasons. First, Pashhur's treatment of him showed that he was going to be a terror to many other people. This is the kind of unjust treatment without trial that belongs to a tyranny. The second reason was that terror would one day rebound on Pashhur. He who had made others frightened would one day see his own family taken away as slaves to a foreign land. Pashhur would go too, and be in terror. He would die there in a foreign land and be buried there. It was pretty bold of Jeremiah to give him such a nickname. The other name he gave him was this, and it's the first time he had ever used the word. For many years, Jeremiah had said that there was going to come from the north an enemy to wipe out this little land, but he had never named that enemy. He had never given any indication as to who it might be. He just talked in vague, threatening terms. Now to Pashhur, for the first time, he names the enemy who was going to come—Babylon. "Babylon is going to produce terror in your heart." I wonder if you realise what that means. I can give you a little bit of a history lesson now and a geography lesson—it won't really give you the main feel of the word "Babylon", but let me just try. There is the Fertile Crescent, as it is called, in the Middle East. It is a great curve of green surrounded by mountains and desert. The green is composed of the Tigris and Euphrates rivers, curving up the side and then down through the Holy Land to the Nile Delta and the Nile River. If you trace it on a map it is a beautiful curve. Israel is about two-thirds the way around, between the Nile and the Tigris and Euphrates.

It is green, not because it has a big river, but because the rain from the Mediterranean comes. Along the Mediterranean it drops on the Judean hills, so they are right in the middle of that crescent. Anybody who moves around it has to go through this little chosen land. If you live in the middle of a crossroads you will always get run over and that is what was happening to Israel all the time. Therefore, there were only two directions from which enemies could come: from the Nile—south, or from the Tigris and Euphrates —north. At the other end there was a nomadic people called the Chaldeans, in what is now called Iraq. In the middle of their land there was a town called Ur of the Chaldees, and in that town had lived an old man of eighty. To that old man Abraham (or Abram as he was called then), God said, "Get out of there and travel around to a land that I'll show you." That's where Abraham came from and that is when the people of God began. That is when the story of our salvation began.

Centuries later, in the time of Jeremiah, the Chaldeans became strong and they grew. They wanted a capital city so they rebuilt Babel. If you know your Bible you know that Abraham was called in Genesis 12, but in Genesis 11 it describes a tower reaching to heaven in that land of the Chaldeans called Babel. They rebuilt Babylon (Babel; babble, the place where God confused speech) and it became a powerful metropolis of a growing empire that spread out and out and along the Fertile Crescent. By the time of Jeremiah, it was pressing down on Judah and that was the situation. Do you realise now the threat of the name

"Babylon"? God is saying: I will take you back to where you were before I called Abraham; I will take you right back to Genesis 11. I will treat you as if I never called Abraham — I am going to put you back in Babel. Do you realise now the significance of that name? It wasn't just a foreign name that he was sending them back to. He was saying: I wipe my hand off your history. It has just been no use, it has come to nothing. I will put you right back to Babylon, as if Abraham had never lived. Do you get the feel of it now? What would you feel if God said to you, "I'm going to put you right back where you were before I touched your life — before you had heard the gospel of Jesus." Now that was the meaning of the word "Babylon", a dreadful word. Jeremiah was let out of the stocks and said, "I call you terror, and you'll go back to Babel." It was quite a bold thing to say.

Well, so much for Jeremiah's boldness in public but as I have mentioned already, people who are bold in public are not necessarily so in private and before God. When Jeremiah got away from that situation, alone with God, a great black, heavy cloud of depression settled over him as he thought of the humiliation, as he felt again the taunts of the crowd, their laughter, their mockery. He was a very sensitive person. As the depression got hold of him he went down and down, wondering what punishment would come for having said those last things to Pashhur — whether he was even now reporting them to the high priest and to the king — and just what was awaiting him after being so bold. As he got low then he poured out the things that we have seen here. As he limped away, his boldness deserted him. He had a strong reaction to those twenty-four hours. Psychologists have examined this and they have tried to say what they feel is the pattern and the cause of his depression. But I don't think there is much help in analysing him psychologically. He was a human being—I am so glad that the prophets were not vegetables or machines, but people of like passions to ourselves, and they could have this kind of reaction. If you are involved in Christian service, if you are serving the Lord and you run into opposition and you have a reaction like this, then you will make straight for Jeremiah and draw comfort from the fact that he had this reaction and he came through it—but while he was in it he was very low indeed.

We look first, then, at the complaint he makes about God. It is a cry of a very insecure person expressed in very powerful poetry but humiliation had hurt him very deeply. He accuses God of deceiving him: Lord, you've deceived me; you are bigger than I am and you've won — you've trapped me, you've made me a joke; you've made me the laughing stock. That is an intriguing phrase, isn't it? It comes from the stocks: you've trapped me. Now was this true? Jeremiah is saying: Lord, you never told me that I would be in this kind of trouble. Lord, I thought you were going to look after me. I thought you would protect me. I thought you would deliver me. You promised your protection and now it hasn't happened and I've been flogged. Look at my back, Lord. And they laughed at me, Lord. I thought you were going to look after me.

He went on to say: ... and Lord, you know the trouble is you never give me anything nice to say; it's all doom and gloom; every time I open my mouth you put in it a message of death and blackness and dreadful bad news. The people want comforting and they want uplifting, and you're not giving them any ray of hope. You're not giving me anything nice to say to them. Lord, you're even preventing me from refusing to speak ... If I decide not to preach anymore, if I say, Right, that's it. I'm just not going to preach any more, it's just not worth it, you won't let me go through with it.

He said: There is in my bones a fire burning; words flare up and I can't keep them in, and out it comes again. I can't even decide whether to preach or not, you just force me into it, and you give me these dreadful messages to preach. I just can't get out of it....

Now you know it is a little unfair, but when we are depressed we get very unfair. We say things that are exaggerated and that are not strictly true. We accuse other people and, above all, we accuse God of things of which he is not guilty. What was the truth of all this? Well, let us look at some of the points. First, he says, "Whenever I open my mouth it's all doom and gloom." But we have studied Jeremiah and time and again there was a ray of hope — an offer of help; God said, "But I'll bring you back home one day." It wasn't all doom and gloom. I will agree it was ninety per cent doom and gloom, but it wasn't *all*. But when Jeremiah says, "Now God, you promised to protect me and deliver me" —what had God actually promised? This is very important. He had promised this — and you can read about it in chapter 1, or you can read about it in chapter 19 also, because God repeated the call — "Jeremiah, they will attack you and they will fight against you, but they will not win." In other words, God hadn't said: I'll keep you free from all trouble; I'll keep you out of persecution. God had made it quite clear: There's going to be suffering, but they will not have the last word — I will deliver you. Now you cannot be delivered out of something unless you have been in it. That sounds so obvious when I say it that you wonder why Jeremiah hadn't spotted it, but still today people think like this.

Scores of Christians think that God's promises are that he will keep us from having any trouble. His promise is that he will deliver us *out* of troubles, which means that you have got to be in them before he can deliver you out of them. What shall separate us from the love of Christ? Famine, nakedness, peril, sword—no, in all these things we are more than conquerors—*in* them!

"Who are these who are arrayed in white robes, and where did they come from?" the elder asks John in Revelation 7:13–15. "... These are the ones who come out of the great tribulation and washed their robes and made them white in the blood of the Lamb" They were *in* it. Too many Christians today believe that the church will be taken out before the tribulation comes on the world. Don't you believe it. Prepare for tribulation. Jesus said, "In the world you'll have tribulation." You don't get out of these things because you have become a Christian, but I will deliver you. The tribulation won't have the last word, says God. You may go through it, but this thing won't win, "You will be more than conquerors and neither death, nor life, nor angels nor principalities nor powers, nor things present nor things to come, nor height nor depth, nor any other creature, shall be able to separate us from the love of God which is in Christ Jesus."

This is so important. Many Christians want wrapping up in cotton wool, and the kind of protection that will not give them any trouble at all. Jeremiah had misinterpreted God's promises. God said: They'll fight you, they'll attack you, but I will deliver you. They won't have the last word. You will be more than a conqueror — and so he was out of the stocks. Worse was to follow. He would be in prison. He would be on trial for treason. He would be thrown into a pit, but every time God would deliver him — and he did.

The worst thing that people can do to you is kill you. If anybody kills you then God will deliver you. "Fear not those who can kill the body," said Jesus. Jesus himself went to the cross believing that God could deliver, and God did, and on the third day he rose from the dead. God has not promised to keep us out of trouble, he has promised to deliver us from it. That is the promise he made. He didn't deceive Jeremiah at all. He told him clearly: they will be against you, they will hate you, they will attack you; they will fight you but they won't win.

Jeremiah is just so hurt with the humiliation. He's saying: God, you let me down. God, your word is not true. Your promises are not kept. As Jeremiah thought this through he began to realise that he wasn't being fair, that God was on his side, and that God plus Jeremiah is a majority. His spirits began to lift a little and he began to say, "Lord, yes, you are on my side, I know. You'll fight for me, I know. Lord, I put my cause in your hands. Let me see vengeance on my enemies. Let me see you deal with them. But Lord, yes, you're going to."

He tries to lift himself from his depression. Finally, he says, "Sing!" It is an order to himself. He is talking to himself here and he is trying to make himself say "Halleluyah" anyway. See 20:13: "Sing to the Lord; praise the Lord! For he has delivered the life of the needy from the hand of evildoers." He's not saying he *has* delivered me yet. So: come on, sing! And, you know, he can't. When you are in depression, this violent change of mood is characteristic. Great elation followed by a very deep valley almost immediately. So, he says, "Sing to the Lord," and then the very next breath he says, "Cursed...." He goes from singing to cursing just like that. It is understandable. Now he touches the very bottom of his depression. He becomes quite suicidal. Here is the man of God cursing. He dare not curse his mother and father for making love and producing him. That really would be more than he could do. Yet he gets as near as he can to cursing that. It was his mother and father who were responsible for bringing him into the world. But he couldn't do that. So he curses the day he was born. Then he curses the man who spread the news around and actually told his dad, who obviously wasn't around when Jeremiah was born. He may have been out in the fields somewhere. But a man went from the mother's bed to the father and said, "Unto you a son is born." We will come back to that announcement in a moment. Then he finishes with this question: "Why was I born?" One of the characteristics of someone in depression is that they may well curl up in bed and assume the position they were in in their mother's womb, draw their knees up and curl up, wanting to be back in the security of the womb, which we can't remember consciously but which we do remember unconsciously. It was a secure world. We didn't face any of the things that we have come to face in the world outside, and so we curl up. This is what Jeremiah is doing here and I can see him now. I think this must have happened at night or in the early hours of the morning, when depression is worst. I can see him curling up in a pre-natal position and saying, "Why did I come out of the womb? Why didn't someone abort me?" It is an awful thing to say, but that is what he is saying. He finishes up with this question: "Why should a man be born to trouble and shame and sorrow?" Are you thinking of anyone else at this moment? Why should the words be said, "Unto you a son is born," when that son would simply face sorrow and shame? The answer is: God knows what he's doing. He needed a Jeremiah, and he needed another boy called Jesus — for sorrow, for shame. Because only if someone will bear sorrow and shame can God fulfil his purposes in the world.

The answer to Jeremiah's question he had had at his call. Jeremiah asks, "Why was I born to a life of sorrow?" God had said when he called a young man of seventeen, "Jeremiah, I want you to be a spokesman, an ambassador to the nations of the world and tell them about me." You notice it was not a call to be a prophet to Israel. Israel was too far gone, but God wanted Jeremiah to know the sorrow and shame of all that, so that the lesson might be learned by the United States of America, Britain, China, Russia, and every other nation of the world.

Many tell me that we have never had Bible studies that seem so relevant to Britain today. That is why Jeremiah was born to sorrow, that he might be God's spokesman to *all* the nations of the world, and that he might speak to people. It seems as if Jeremiah is coming alive. All over the place I am finding people are turning to this book. Jeremiah is being a spokesman to the nations at this moment. Indeed, a thought came to me (back in 1975) of how I could spread my little exposition of Jeremiah in a new way to many more people — that they might hear. I knew when I gave talks on Jeremiah that thousands more would hear through tapes as they were able to hear Jeremiah himself in those days. This was one way that I could get this word out to the world of today. Jeremiah will speak and is speaking, and that is why he had to go through what he did.

In chapter 21:1-10 we are back to prose. Many years have elapsed between chapters 20 and 21, though it comes next in the book. The book of Jeremiah has not been compiled in chronological order. We have to ask: why did the editor put chapter twenty-one next to chapter twenty? Why did he take something from many years on and put it next to this? It is presented as a sequel, but it was not the immediate sequel. There is a man called Pashhur in chapter 21 who may or may not be the same Pashhur as in chapter 20. If it is the same person then there is a very ironic twist that has taken place. There is a new king on the throne. Instead of Jehoiachin, who was in chapter 20, we now have Zedekiah, the last and the weakest king. The situation now is that Babylon has so expanded that Babylonian troops are surrounding Jerusalem, ringing the city, and Zedekiah the king wonders what to do. He knows they can hold out for quite a long time in siege. He knows they could send a message to Egypt for help. He is in a political situation. He needs desperately to make the right decision or he could lose everything. To whom does the king turn for advice? To the man whom Pashhur put in the stocks — that is the glorious irony of this chapter.

When the king really wanted to know what to do he said, "Pashhur, go and ask Jeremiah." From being a publicly ridiculed figure in the stocks, Jeremiah is now the counsellor of kings, the royal advisor. That is what God can do with a man who is faithful. He may be the laughing stock of the man in the street, but he will speak to kings. God exalts those who have been humbled.

That is what happened to our Lord Jesus, too. They laughed at him on the cross but today he is King of kings and Lord of lords. Zedekiah sent for Jeremiah and then asks him, "Are the Babylonians likely to win or not? Shall we fight or not? Shall we go to Egypt for help or not? Tell me," and Jeremiah gives him a disturbing answer: "... I looked out and saw the Babylonian troops and behind them I could see their general. I could see the one in charge and it was God. Zedekiah, God is directing their troops; we don't stand a chance". It was a hard answer and an honest answer. He said: "I can see them besieging this city until we are eating each other, until pestilence is spread through the city, and I can see us with nothing left." To the answer he added a word of advice: "every man, woman and child who can do so should go out of the city and surrender now to the Babylonians. The only thing I can promise you if you do is that you will keep your life. You will keep nothing else. You will be taken away to a far country but if you surrender now at least you will still live, and while there is life there is hope. If you don't surrender, you will die. I set before you life and death: death if you fight; life if you surrender".

There come such points in human history, as in France in 1940. The point comes where the leaders of a nation have to make the most difficult decision of all, and that is to surrender and choose life, any sort of life, rather than fight and choose death. When I visited Jersey I became very conscious of the awful decision they had to make when the Germans came to the Channel Islands and they decided to surrender and have life, any sort of life, rather than fight and have certain death.

It is a difficult decision and those who make it will be accused of treason. They will be regarded as unpatriotic but it takes a profound patriotism, when that point is reached, to surrender. It takes a profound love of your country to preserve something of it, and it is one of the most difficult decisions a leader can ever make. Now Jeremiah begged Zedekiah to make that decision and surrender. Jeremiah was going to be imprisoned and put on trial for treason for this advice. He was going to be regarded as a traitor to his country; in fact, he was a patriot. He said it out of love for his country but he would be regarded as an enemy, a quisling.

But I will say this for Jeremiah, even though all people should get out and surrender was his advice – Jeremiah didn't take his own advice. He stayed until the end. He could have gone then and saved his life, but he didn't. He was free to go, but he stayed. When the city and the king were taken off to Babylon, Jeremiah was delivered by the Lord and he stayed home. It is a remarkable story. Here is a man who was so depressed that he said, "Why, what can I do? What's the use? I'm getting nowhere, you've trapped me. You've deceived me. I'm not getting anywhere." And a few years later that man is controlling the destiny of his nation. He is speaking to kings. His advice is sought by those at the very top. That is what God can do with a man who may feel it is hopeless and useless — that he can do nothing.

I want you to notice that when Jeremiah was so depressed, God said nothing to him. That is one of the most awful features of deep depression, that we can't hear God speaking.

231

It seems as if he is not there and that he is not concerned. In all of chapter 20 God says absolutely nothing. Was this because God wasn't speaking or because Jeremiah wasn't hearing? I think it may have been a bit of both, but you know, when you accuse God unjustly, he doesn't argue, he doesn't defend himself. He just waits patiently until you can talk rationally. If God had spoken when Jeremiah was in deep depression it would have done no good. God knows when to be silent. Contrary though it may seem to common sense, in fact God did well to leave Jeremiah alone when Jeremiah was saying such things, and not to answer. Somehow, through not speaking God was able to use what I might call the passion of Jeremiah to bring him through and make him the consultant of kings.

Jeremiah had said, "Cursed is the day that the man said, 'Unto you a son is born'" — because he was born to sorrow and shame. You can't help but think of Jesus, can you? "Unto you a son is born", and he was a man of sorrows and acquainted with grief, bearing shame and scoffing. The remarkable thing is that the place where Jeremiah was tortured in the stocks was the very spot where Jesus was put on the cross. It says he was taken out on the north side of the temple and put in the stocks. That is the place that later became Golgotha. Once again, the parallel between Jesus and Jeremiah is so clear.

We think of Jesus on the cross in the same place, weighed down with the humiliation, the shame, the suffering of it all, pressed down in depression, crying out, "My God, my God, why have you forsaken me?" You notice that the Father said nothing at that time. But Jesus came through it and finally said, "Into your hands I commit my spirit", just as Jeremiah came through it and committed his cause to the Lord.

When you are depressed and when you feel, "Why was I born at all?" and when you are going through it, and when you are saying all kinds of unjust things against God, he will not reply. He will not argue with you. He is too great to do that. But as soon as you commit your cause to the Lord, he will bring you through. He will lift you up and he will give you – I promise you this – a greater ministry than you had before. He will give you words to say to people you have never spoken to before, and he will set you high upon a rock.

READ JEREMIAH 21:11–23:8

Royalty in this country does not reign. Indeed, one of the features of our modern societies is that royalty is disappearing and being replaced in country after country by republicanism. Between World War I and World War II, twenty-four crowned heads of Europe fell and disappeared from history. In England we like to have the best of both worlds. We like to think we have kept something even when we have lost it. We have managed to muddle through in typical English compromise and we say we still have a sovereign but she has no sovereignty. The irony of that is supremely illustrated by the State Opening of Parliament once a year, when the Queen, almost as a puppet, reads a speech that has been prepared by the real monarch in this country — the Prime Minister, who is allowed to stand just inside the door to hear it. It is so ridiculous it is almost laughable. But that is the way we have managed to keep a semblance of royalty. In this topsy-turvy world, this whole notion of where the real power lies has become a very difficult issue, especially in the complexity of modern industry. All of which is a preamble to try and help you to realise that when we talk about royalty in Bible days we are talking about kings who really reigned, who had the power — such power that their word was law. In their hands rested, for example, the leadership of the military, and the king would lead his troops into battle. The last English king to do that was George III.

An ancient king was the commander-in-chief and he made the decisions in battle. He was also the head of the courts. His word was law and he had to arbitrate, and ultimately the standard of justice rested on the character of the king, through these and many other ways in which he really had power. Royalty is a hereditary thing and our modern democratic society doesn't like hereditary status or position. That is why royalty is disappearing, but if you are going to have royalty then it must be hereditary, and that is one of the reasons genealogies are so important in the Bible, especially those of the royal line. Anybody in the royal line kept their family tree carefully to prove that they had royal blood in their veins. That is why we talk not about individual queens and kings but about "houses" — the House of Windsor, the House of Judah, the House of Stuart, the House of David. That house — David's — is the most important royal house there has ever been, for it is the royal house from which the babe at Bethlehem was born. The genealogy is complete and it is there in the Word of God. He inherited that position—there is nothing wrong with inheriting a position. The important thing is the attitude of the person who inherits it. If they regard their inherited status purely in terms of privilege for themselves instead of responsibility towards others, then they abuse that inheritance. If you read through the books of Kings you will be startled by the way that God divides kings into two categories and two alone, and there is nothing in between. He either did good in the sight of the Lord or he did evil in the sight of the Lord. You alternate between good kings and bad kings—there are no middling ones in the Bible. The reason why this king is good in the sight of the Lord and that king is bad is that the good king regarded his inherited position in terms of responsibility, service to others. The bad kings regarded it in terms of privilege and status for themselves. It was mixed up with a lot of other things too.

Behind this attitude to other people and to themselves lay their attitude to God. The good king was the one who listened to God and recognised that he was under a King himself.

When Her Majesty the Queen was crowned in Westminster Abbey she was handed a Bible and was told, "This is the royal law." In other words, "This is the law for you. You are under law if you are going to be a good sovereign. Here is the law for kings from the King of kings." That is the setting of this passage. We are discussing what we might refer to as *noblesse oblige* — the obligations of nobility. Those who have inherited the status of royalty have an obligation, a responsibility to serve those over whom they reign. Jeremiah is now for the first time in touch with kings. He now has the privilege of preaching to the royal family. What is he going to say?

Billy Graham had that privilege in St George's, Windsor of preaching before members of the Royal Family. What would he decide to preach upon? He preached on "You must be born again," and the Queen and the Queen Mother afterwards told him, "We know what it is to be born again." There was a Vicar of Sandringham who regularly preached before King George VI and his family, and that King once said to that vicar, "Why is it that, of all the preachers I listen to, your words strike home to my heart the most? Why is it that you preach right into my heart?"

The Vicar said, "I don't know that I want to tell you, your majesty."

He said, "You can tell me. I won't be upset. Tell me."

"Well," he said, "I fix my attention on the humblest servant girl in Sandringham House sitting at the back of the congregation and I preach to the servant."

King George VI, who certainly knew the Lord Jesus, received his words because he saw himself as a servant, and the Word of God struck home.

What would Jeremiah say to the king? Remember that Jeremiah was born in a humble little village called Anathoth about eight miles northeast of Jerusalem, a country lad, and God had thrust him into the big city and made him preach in the streets and smash jars outside the gates and even go into the temple court. Now, in this chapter and the last bit of the previous study, he has the ear of the king. Indeed, the king is now asking him, "The Babylonians are around the gates, around the walls, they're besieging us. Is the city lost?" The king sends two men, Pashhur and Zephaniah, to Jeremiah, to ask him for God's opinion.

This was the first time royalty had ever approached Jeremiah. Indirectly, it is true — they were not yet face-to-face, but Jeremiah had the chance to send a message to the king. He said: "Tell the king three things. First, give him an answer to the question. The answer is: no the city will not survive, for God is fighting for the Babylonians, not us." Then he dared to go further and give him some advice, and his advice was surrender to the enemy as quickly as you can. It is a matter of life and death. You can just snatch your life if you surrender now. He dared to go even further. That second piece of advice was interpreted as treason and would land him in prison, but the third thing was an admonition. Not content with giving an answer to the king's question and advice about what to do about it, he went as far as to admonish the king. It takes holy boldness to do that in a country where the king really reigns and where his word is law. So, Jeremiah said, "Give him this admonition. Zedekiah, you see to justice. You see that the poor and the needy get looked after. You see that there is no innocent blood shed. You see that violence is cut out of the city. Execute justice in the morning." In other words, as soon as you can, as early as you can, as quickly as you can — execute justice and righteousness.

Here we have got the theme for this passage—there are two qualities needed in someone who is going to be a king. Whatever other human qualities they possess or do not possess, whether they are pleasing to look at or not, whether they have engaging attributes of personality or not, the two things that a king must always have are justice and righteousness. Now those are big words—let me put it more simply. A ruler must always be fair and straight. Why was Watergate such a trauma to the American people? The whole nation lost its morale over that and I sensed it when I was over there. They are no longer the people with a superiority complex. Why did they lose their morale? Because their president was not fair or straight; that is what happened.

When the people at the top are not fair or straight then authority loses all respect and you are finished and the nation crumbles. So, Jeremiah dared to say to the king, "You get fair and you get straight. Execute justice in the morning. Look after those who can't defend themselves: the immigrant, the orphan, the widow, the poor, the needy, the people who can't fight in this jungle. You look after them—that's your job as king." This has a strangely modern ring to it, doesn't it? The immigrant; the homeless — these are the people the king should be most concerned about, the people who can't fight, who cannot defend themselves.

Therefore, his message is first of all a message of justice and righteousness. The next thing I noticed as I read through what he said to the king was that there are the keywords "do" and "doings" and I kept underlining them: Do justice and righteousness; do no wrong or violence; your evil doings; the fruit of your doings. It is not enough to issue a manifesto. God is not interested in the politicians' manifestos. He is interested in what they do about those manifestos. It is not enough to say "I stand for truth and righteousness"; it is not enough to hold the sceptre and the orb in the hand. God says,

"What are you doing? What are you doing, Zedekiah?" So — fair and straight doing. What more does God say? He says that he will punish injustice and unrighteousness in the rulers.

His anger will be like a forest fire—and that is a vivid picture. Most of us have never seen a forest fire. If you lived in Canada you would see it. Thousands of acres get destroyed every year through forest fire. They now bomb them with water from the air to try to stop them. A forest fire sweeps ahead and it burns holiday homes and farms. I remember that in our church at Gold Hill there was a family, and one night the mother had a vivid dream of her daughter in Tasmania. She dreamt the daughter was trapped in a forest fire and she painted the scene. I have seen that oil painting of the daughter at the window of a house, and around the house a blazing forest fire. In fact, her daughter was at that moment in that dreadful forest fire not far from Hobart.

God says to the rulers who are not fair and straight: "I am a forest fire." There is no defence against a forest fire. That was the admonition, and Jeremiah had sent it to a king who was weak and crooked, the last king of all Judah, a man called Zedekiah, whose name meant "The Lord is my righteousness." Jeremiah says, "Unless you listen to this word and put it right and get straight, then there is a forest fire on its way."

Having sent that message to the king indirectly, Jeremiah then is told by the Lord: "you go down to the house of the king and tell him yourself the same thing. Don't just be content to send a message indirectly. Go and tell him." Can you imagine a countryman being told to go and visit Buckingham Palace and tell the Queen in person? The equivalent today would be to go to 10 Downing Street and tell the Prime Minister: "You bring justice. You be fair to the immigrant, to those who haven't got a home. There are thousands of them." That is what Jeremiah was told to do, so he went and he said it to the king's face. "Zedekiah, a day will come when people will go past this very city and they'll say, 'What on earth happened? Why is it like this? Why did God allow such a great capital city to fall to pieces? Why did it crumble?'"

They will answer, "Because they left God."

Notice that — not because the king was unjust or unfair, but because they left God and they got away from God. You see, the injustice and the unrighteousness are the symptoms, not the disease. Loss of respect for authority is a symptom, not the disease. Increasing figures of violence and crime are not the disease, they are the symptom. The disease is that we got away from God. The symptoms we know only too well, and our newspapers are crammed with symptoms, but our newspapers never tell us the disease. They just keep on throwing the symptoms at us. They don't diagnose, they only describe. The diagnosis is: When a nation gets away from God, injustice and unrighteousness abound; the poor and the needy are the worst affected and the most exploited.

Now, added to his personal repetition of the message he sent by the two emissaries of the king, Jeremiah went on to warn Zedekiah who was to be the last king of all, and they were within eight years of the fall of the capital when Jeremiah said this. Only eight more years to go and Jerusalem was finished and Zedekiah was gone. It is a last-ditch appeal from Jeremiah. He reinforces the appeal by reminding Zedekiah of the dreadful end of his three predecessors. The last good king of Judah was Josiah. He came to the throne when he was eight and was killed in battle at thirty-nine. Who was Zedekiah followed by? He was followed by the one who should have had it all the time, and the Egyptians decided to put Jehoiakim on the throne provided he paid tax to them, so that was the arrangement. He was a puppet and a little man, and therefore he tried to be big. He said,

"I'm going to build the biggest palace there's ever been," and he built this magnificent house. It had upper storeys. He panelled it with cedar and painted it with vermilion. This potty little king in a tiny little kingdom was trying to be as big as Pharaoh and as big as Nebuchadnezzar. He wanted to say, "I'm a great power." There are few things more pathetic than seeing a shrinking nation trying to kid itself that it is still a great power. He did it with forced labour and heavy taxes. He did it with oppression and injustice, and now we know why the people didn't want him. He was a man who saw his position not to serve the people but to use his power so that they might serve him for nothing. Jeremiah says, "He wouldn't pay his neighbours for what they did," and Jehoiakim built up this magnificent imposing status symbol of a palace, and God said, "Jehoiakim, at your funeral there won't even be any mourners. You'll be dragged through the city gates like a dead donkey and left. You won't even be buried." Of course, a big funeral is the last status symbol you can have. If you have lived in a big house then a big funeral follows. God said, "No, Jehoiakim."

One of the other things that God said to Jehoiakim is, I think, very relevant to us today. He said: "Jehoiakim, when you were prosperous you wouldn't listen to me." This, of course, is the tragedy. In adversity most people will try to get in touch with God; in prosperity they don't. As long as they can build a bigger house for themselves they forget God. As long as they can build up status symbols and are in a position to do so, and can get the wealth however they get it, that's fine and God doesn't get a look in. This is the tragedy: that when we try to contact God in adversity we can't get through because we didn't listen in prosperity. It is like trying to put the anchor down after the storm has begun.

God gave a similar warning to the people of God in the book of Deuteronomy: while you are in the wilderness and you are dependent on me for manna and water in the rock you think of me, but when you get to the land flowing with milk and honey, and when you've got wealth and built for yourselves fine houses, then be careful that you don't forget the Lord your God. It is our tragedy that since the 1960s our very affluence has meant we thought we could do without God. We do not listen to him in prosperity. That is why things have gone wrong later and that is why in adversity we find confusion, and we can't get away from God and we can't get through.

The other thing Jeremiah says to Jehoiakim is this: "Didn't your father live well? He ate and drank, he lived well but he judged the cause of the poor and needy and then it was well. He did justice and righteousness and then it was well." Who is Jehoiakim's father? Josiah. There is nothing wrong with living well provided you live well in every respect. Josiah lived well materially but he lived well morally, and the two went together. Josiah ate and drank well and he practised justice and righteousness well, and then Jeremiah says: "Is this not to know the Lord?" In other words, to know the Lord means to live well. God wants us to live well in every way—that is his intention. When we get to heaven we shall live well. The first thing we will do is have a feast, and there is nothing wrong with eating and drinking. It is a perverted Christianity that thinks austerity and asceticism is what Christ commanded. They criticised Christ himself because he ate well; they called him a glutton and a winebibber, but he did well because he did justice and righteousness. He cared for the poor and the needy. Jehoiakim, your father lived well—it was well with him. He knew the Lord, he lived well. Oh, how much meaning there is in that. But Jehoiakim, you have eyes and heart only for your dishonest gain. So he was finished too.

Jeremiah reminds Zedekiah about Coniah, Jehoiakim's

son. Jehoiakim died, and there is no record of any funeral in the Bible for Jehoiakim. With others it says, "They died and they were laid with their fathers" or, "they were buried" — but not with Jehoiakim. When he died, the next in line was Zedekiah. He inherited the throne, but instead Coniah was chosen. For by this time Babylon had defeated Egypt, and now Babylon was power number one and Jehoiakim had switched sides and he tried to make friends with Babylon.

Let us come to our closing passage. Jeremiah has said to Zedekiah: consider your three predecessors. All of them were useless. Two of them were taken away after only three months: one into Egypt, one into Babylon. The one that had eleven years was a corrupt, ostentatious man, full of oppression. Here is the warning: you cannot get away with bad kingship.

Finally, we have the lovely passage 23:1–8, Jeremiah's final comment on the royal line of his days, and here I want you to notice that in an amazing way Jeremiah puts together two callings: king and shepherd. You don't realise what a shock that is until I tell you that the king was at the very top of the social ladder and the shepherd was someone at the very bottom. The man sent out to look after sheep was the lowest man of all. That's why Jesse said what he did when Samuel was looking for a king among his family. Samuel asked, "Are these all your boys?" He replied, "There's just the lad looking after the sheep, David." But God likes a shepherd for a king. That is why he sent Moses into the wilderness to look after sheep before he made him the leader to bring out his people. God needs shepherd kings. In the ancient world it was an offence for a shepherd to become a king. But someone at the very bottom of the social ladder knows how to be a king at the top and a king at the top should know how to be a shepherd at the bottom. It conveys the sense of a king who is willing to humble himself to serve the sheep; a king who is willing to regard himself at the bottom of the nation of which he is top. It is a remarkable concept, very humbling. That is why Jesus, when he came, saw the crowds as sheep without a shepherd, and they tried to make him king. There was a shepherd's heart there, and shepherds and kings belong together. That is why the birth of the King was announced to shepherds, the people at the bottom of the social scale, first. The shepherds came to see the babe. Can you see God's lovely picture unfolding there?

So, Jeremiah says to Zedekiah that God deals with bad shepherds. If the flock gets scattered instead of gathered, if they are not cared for but are destroyed and scattered, then God will deal with evil shepherds. He will attend to them because they have not attended to the sheep. But he says that one day God is going to bring all the scattered sheep back, the survivors that there are.

In 1947, I was working on a farm in Northumberland and it was a dreadful winter. We were cut off by snow for approximately six weeks. I will never forget what happened the night before the snow came. It was a beautiful, clear night, a beautiful sky, a perfect winter's day, the sort of day on which you just want to be outdoors breathing the pure wine of the air. That afternoon the shepherd on that farm said to the farmer, "We must get all the sheep down near the buildings, down into the meadows from up on the hills." So, we all did overtime that night and brought all the sheep down — perfect weather, but we had a good shepherd and in his bones he knew, and we lost not one sheep. On the next farm they lost hundreds. They were going out digging them out of the drifts. There were helicopters from an airport which was just at the edge of the farm dropping hay on the snow trying to save some. We had a good shepherd who kept the sheep safe, and he knew. But even those who lost most of their sheep, as long as they got a few when the snow went, began to breed and they built up the flock again.

They built a flock. God said, "I'm going to do that with the remnant of my flock — just a remnant. I'm going to bring them back from the countries where they've been scattered. One day I'll bring them back and I'll give them good shepherds who care for the sheep. They'll be safe in their own pasture."

Now comes the climax, like a burst of light. The only mention of the Messiah in the whole book of Jeremiah: "Behold the days are coming when I will raise up for the house of David a righteous Branch [or shoot]."

One Boxing Day our family went for a walk, to Pitch Hill. We walked among the lovely trees on that hill. There, my daughter drew my attention to an unusually shaped oak tree. The trunk almost looked as if it had been stuck together from bits that had been picked off the ground. She was pointing me to this unusual shape, but I looked down at the bottom of it and there I saw something even more unusual. It was not an original oak tree. There was the great wide stump of an oak, a great, round flat bit that had been sliced off with a saw, and it had obviously been cut down many years ago because it was rotting. Here was this great, flat stump that must have been a great oak tree at one stage. The tree that we were looking at was growing from the side of that flat piece. It had come out as just a little shoot and now it was growing to be another great tree and would be as great if not greater than the original. It was just a shoot growing out of the side—that is the meaning of the Hebrew word here, a righteous shoot. The tree will be cut down — and with Zedekiah it was cut down. Three hundred years of a royal house was finished, or so they thought until just over five hundred years later a little shoot came from the root, a little baby lying in a manger who grew up and he was to rule the land as King — wisely, righteously — and Judah would be saved and Israel would dwell secure, and the name of this baby would be "The Lord is our righteousness" — almost the same word as Zedekiah.

If you turn to the New Testament you find that Jesus is to us our wisdom, our righteousness. He is the shoot. "Unto us a child is born, unto us a son is given and the government shall be upon his shoulder. He shall be called wonderful counsellor, mighty God, everlasting Father, the prince of peace, and of the increase of his government there shall be no end." "No end" — that is the bright spark that comes through this dark prophecy to King Zedekiah. Jeremiah finishes with this blaze of hope: Zedekiah, you are going to be cut down, the royal tree of three centuries will be cut down to a stump, but from the stump there will come a new shepherd King and he will reign.

So the prophecy finishes with Jeremiah saying that whereas up to now the people of Israel have always looked back to the Exodus from the south — as the greatest example, the greatest proof of a living God, "as the Lord lives who brought us out of Egypt", from now on they will say, "As the Lord lives who brought us back from Babylon, as the Lord lives who gave us a new king, as the Lord lives who put us back in our land." The final sentence is perhaps the sweetest to any Jewish ears: "and they shall dwell in their own land".

What has all this got to do with you? That is what is needed in a king, but what about me? There is an unresolved contradiction in 23:1–8 that I must finally point you to. It says: "I will give you shepherds to care for you." Then it says: "I will raise up one King" — a righteous reign. Which does God mean? Is he going to bring them back and give them many kings or one? That is the unresolved question and it is another apparent contradiction in scripture, which is only resolved by the most remarkable truth. When Jesus called the twelve disciples — simple, humble men, a clerk, a few fishermen — he said to them, "You will sit on twelve thrones judging the twelve tribes of Israel." If that is not wonderful enough here is something more. Paul writes to the Christians: "If we endure, we shall also reign with him." The book of Revelation four times says that Christ's faithful disciples will reign with him. Therefore, I count it a holy privilege to be preaching to the royal family —princes and princesses who are preparing for a much more important and more permanent reign than the heir to the British throne. You are preparing in this world to reign with Christ, to sit on thrones with Christ (see Revelation 20:4). Do you find that exciting? Do you feel the royal blood in your veins? It is a hereditary position. You inherit it because you are joint heirs with Christ. You inherit a throne. You can wear a crown. What does one have to learn to be a king? To learn to reign over yourself before you can reign over others. To learn to control yourself before you can control others. That is the message of the New Testament to the saints of God. It is necessary for every believer to learn what it takes to be born into a royal family and to inherit a throne.

Remember that Jeremiah came to the heart of the big city from a simple country village life in which people knew each other with all their faults but were really human. The young prophet had been transported into a city in which there was a great deal that was false, unreal and untrue. He went through a series of traumatic shocks but none so great as the shock in this passage of the book. His first shock had been the general level of dishonesty among the shopkeepers and traders and in commerce. He just couldn't get straight change for his money. He couldn't find a shopkeeper who was straight in his dealings and who put the right figure in the till, and that was a shock. He hadn't expected to find that in the city.

His next shock was to find that the political leaders were corrupt, and he said, "How can you blame the people if the politicians are like this?" If those in positions of national leadership are corrupt then you can understand why the ordinary man is just out to get what he can and doesn't mind how he gets it, and that was shock number two. Shock number three came when he went into the temple and looked at the priests, the religious leaders, and he said, "They've turned the house of prayer into a den of thieves."

There was one group of men whom Jeremiah hoped to find intact, a group among whom he hoped to find integrity because he was going to join that group and he was called to be a prophet. He had been called as a seventeen-year-old to be a prophet and he knew perfectly well there were other

249

prophets already in the nation, and that when he went to the big city he would meet lots of prophets, for by this time it had become a profession and there were professional prophets trained in the schools of the prophets. When Jeremiah met the prophets, he was so shattered he said, "My bones shook, my heart broke, I felt like a man who's drunk." I don't know if he had been drunk or knew what it felt like, but he felt he went to pieces because he found that the prophets too were part of the total picture, though not all of them. Thank God as we read through the book of Jeremiah he found that some of them were still men who were true. We will come across them later in the book of Jeremiah, but many of them he found were the opposite. It was not so much what he heard at first as what he saw. In a word, he saw that the prophets were sleeping around with any woman they could get hold of. That is what he found and it shattered him.

Then, when he listened to what they said and claimed to be the word of God, he said: "That's not the message of God. They're making it up, it's coming out of their own imagination. They are dreaming it up." They were telling people what they wanted to hear because that is the way to popularity. In other words, he found out an important truth: when the amateur becomes a professional, he has got to watch what that does to him. It is true of sport, for example. When a sportsman is still an amateur you can be much surer that he is playing the game because he loves it than you can be when he becomes a professional. You begin to wonder: what is he in it for now — the fame, the money? As soon as the prophets of Israel became professionals and went to their seminaries and got churned out as professionals who could lay on a message from God to order, something happened to the men of God who were prophets. The amateurs had become professional — success, status, prosperity; all kinds of opportunities were now open to them that had not been open before. When Jeremiah joined the group that he thought he was being called to join and minister with, he was shattered. We are now going to go into details.

Jeremiah was shocked, firstly, by their loose lives; secondly, by their wishful words. He was shocked, thirdly, by their deceptive dreams; and fourthly, he was shocked by their banished burdens. We deal with the first now—their loose lives. He applied two heavenly equations to their lives, which we have to apply to ours. Here is the first: *wickedness equals ungodliness*. That is not an equation the world will ever make, but it is an equation that God makes. It is a mathematical formula to apply to my life and to yours. Now this is not how the world interprets wickedness, but it is how Jeremiah did. The second, positive, equation which Jeremiah applies is this: right equals might. Now those are the two equations he applied to these prophets. They did not fit and he found them wanting. He says there is adultery right through the prophets—they were running off with other men's wives.

Why does he condemn that? I'm going to ask the question very simply because it is being asked today. What is wrong with adultery? After all, if two people really love each other, why should they not be together? What's wrong with it? God doesn't make a lot of rules which are purely arbitrary. God doesn't say, "Now let's think of everything that people enjoy doing and put a 'thou shalt not' in front of it and really put them on the spot." Do you think God is like that? The God who gave us freely all things to enjoy? That is a libel on God. Many Christians think it is wrong because it is physical and sexual, and they could not be further from the truth, because when God made us he made us physical and he made us sexual—male and female. What is wrong with it? It is *ungodly*. Why is it ungodly? Is that because God hasn't a body and therefore doesn't have sex? Nothing of the kind. When God loves someone, he is loyal to that person to the end. His love is loyal—that is what godly love is like. That is why Jesus, having loved his own, loved them to the end. That is why when a man was told to divorce his wife because she didn't care that much for him and because she went around with other men and because there was nothing in the marriage to hold on to, he said, "Stop. Never speak to me like that about my wife. I love her and I shall love her as long as there is breath in her body." He did and she died a few years later as the result of her sin with his hands spread over her in love. When God loves there is in that love an element which in the Hebrew is called *hesed,* which means loyalty. That is why in a Christian marriage service the vows are about loyalty to that one person for better, for worse, for richer, for poorer. Is this a promise of loyalty or is it just that you are saying, "I have fallen in love, which I may later fall out of"?

If there is one phrase that comes out in the Bible on the lips of God it is "I will". Did you notice 24:5–7? "Thus says the LORD, the God of Israel: 'Like these good figs, so will I regard as good the exiles from Judah, whom I have sent away from this place to the land of the Chaldeans. I will set my eyes upon them for good, and I will bring them back to this land. I will build them up, and not tear them down; I will plant them, and not uproot them. I will give them a heart to know that I am the LORD, and they shall be my people and I will be their God, for they shall return to me with their whole heart.'" Do you see? *I will.*

So, how could prophets speak about God's love if they themselves were not loyal? You understand that the world usually reserves the term "wickedness" for things that are dreadfully perverted or full of vice, things that society generally would say are dreadful. But in fact, the word "wickedness" in the Bible covers anything that is unlike

God. We were made in the image of God to be like him. We can drop into the world's habit of pointing at particular things and saying that they are really wicked. But God says that anything that is not like him is wicked. Gossip within a church can be as disloyal as adultery. It is a question of loyalty, for God is so loyal and that is love — to be loyal. You find that the prophets here are denounced for telling lies and that is also a disloyalty. It is unlike God — when God speaks he tells the truth. Therefore, to tell a lie is to be ungodly and it is wicked.

When you look at things from God's point of view and see this equation — wickedness equals godliness — you can look at yourself and you can look at a church congregation and you can realise that God could put the word "wicked" on even churchgoing people, whereas we tend not to. We tend to say it is those dreadful perverted people out there, they are the wicked people. It would be too easy for us to read this passage and not apply it to ourselves. If in anything I am unlike God then God calls me to leave my wicked ways.

The second equation, which he applies is this: *right* equals might. Now once again this is totally the reverse of the world's attitude. To the world, might equals right and if you are bigger, you are better. That is how Hitler used to think, but many more people think this way. If you have the power of money, that puts you in the right; if you have military power, that puts you in the right, and God's Word comes sharply into that picture and says that the man who really has might is the man who is right. The prophets are told: your might is not right. There is no man so powerful in this world as the man who is right. Unfortunately, modern English has squeezed that phrase right down until it doesn't mean what it meant originally.

When we say "He's right" we mean that in an argument someone in fact proved to have the right answer to a question.

But when the Bible says, "This man is right," it means he is right morally as well as mentally. He is in the right or he is upright or righteous.

We live in a world in which people grasp for other kinds of might or power, and then when they have got that power they think that that gives them the right to do certain things. In the long run, the person who is in the right will be the one who will bring it to pass. It is the difference between people of principle and people of expediency.

I believe in God the Father Almighty, but wherein lies God's power? Does it lie in the fact that he is bigger than I am? Is he like the kind of earthly father who tells his children not to do a thing not because of the moral implications but because he doesn't like them doing it and because he's bigger than they are and he can only say, "Because daddy says so"? Is that the kind of power God wields? No, the kind of power that God wields is the power that is based on right and says you cannot do that because it is wrong. It is not an exaggeration to say society is wicked, because it is not like God. The world will not accept that. They say that this is exaggerating, but in fact it is the simple truth. God's curse is on those who put might first rather than right.

Jeremiah sees a direct connection between human nature and nature. He could see now why there was a shortage of water in the land. To the unbeliever there is no connection between human behaviour and what nature does, so they can never identify a connection between the weather and wickedness, but there is a connection and the connection is God. He controls the weather and he takes notice of wickedness, and therefore there is a connection. I believe that nature and human nature are so interlocked. It is funny but people will believe that when anybody but God says it. If someone says, "You can talk to your geraniums and they respond," it is believed that nature and human nature are interlocked and such stories spread in the media. Yet the Bible has been saying this for years — that the geraniums can suffer from your wickedness. That is the Bible outlook on nature and there is nothing new in it. Jeremiah knew now why the pastures were drying up. He saw the connection. Let me take this a little further. I was talking with someone about earthquakes and the lady felt that we as Christians could and should be reducing the number of earthquakes that are happening in the world. She had moved her house and now lived on the San Andreas fault in California quite deliberately — to pray that the earthquake which all the seismologists are predicting may not happen. There we found common ground and differing ground. I agreed with her entirely that prayer can stop an earthquake. I believe entirely that the earth is bound up with the condition of man living on the earth. But I said I believe also that Jesus said: in the last days there will be more earthquakes as nature herself protests against what man is doing and against the sheer ungodliness of man. So we agreed to differ on this one.

Jeremiah could see why God was not blessing with rain. Why should he send rain? Why should *we* have rain in our condition? Why should we not have drought? Do we deserve rain as a nation? Jesus taught us that earthquakes would be the protest of nature against what man is doing, living on those floating plates of earth. Jeremiah could see that the men responsible for the condition of his society were in a very dangerous position, and that God was doing two things to them: putting them on a slippery path and giving them poisoned water to drink.

Now those are very strong words. A nice little god who simply wants everybody to be happy, healthy, and comfortable? You can pack a cathedral with hundreds of people who want physical health. Wherever people have more of this world's goods, they are more interested in physical health because that is the one threat to them losing their enjoyment and comfort. Yes, we are interested in health and in comfort, but God is dealing with things at a much deeper level and he says, "I will put them in a slippery place. My wrath will come like a whirlwind, like a tempest." It is not all light and love, there is the wrath of God in the darkness as well. If we are going to preach the whole Word of God it has to include love and wrath, light and darkness, rain and drought. It has to include both the truth that he set the bounds of the ocean and the truth that there will be more and more earthquakes. As Jeremiah says, in the last days you will understand this more clearly.

The second thing that disturbed him about the false prophets was the kind of message they brought: wishful words. There are two sources of prophets' words: one is the imagination of the human mind and the other is the intention of the divine mind. Jeremiah said: "You're getting your messages from the imagination of your own minds." The source of their messages was basically their own human nature, and human nature is basically optimistic. "Everything will turn out all right in the end." "This is just a cycle." "There will be an upswing." "Look on the bright side." You can either live by human optimism or by faith in God — you have no other choice except utter despair. I can understand unbelievers trying to convince themselves that things are not as bad as they seem. I can understand them desperately clutching at wishful thinking. I can understand them glad to have someone tell them, "It's going to be all right." I can understand them clutching at straws of hope, whoever gives them. But this is the imagination of the human mind, not the intention of the divine mind. As Jeremiah says, this is vain hope.

The problem with being a professional speaker is that your bread and butter depends on people supporting you, and you are therefore tempted to tell them what is popular and what they want to hear—it is the subtlest pressure and it had come on these prophets. These are vain hopes, said Jeremiah. They were saying to people who would not let God speak to them that everything would be all right. To those who stubbornly followed their own hearts, and in other words, lived exactly as they wanted to, they were saying: no evil will come upon you.

Decades ago, I was talking to a member of a small group that advised the Archbishop of Canterbury on his publicity programme about calling the nation to think again. The question that I believe ought to have been asked is: what sort of a society do you think *God* wants.

The question we have got to ask is not from the imagination of our minds — "what do we think we want?" but: what is the intention of God's mind? What kind of a society does he want us to have? Jeremiah doesn't like their wishful words — vain hopes. Jeremiah says: Don't listen to these men because they have not listened to God. How can a man say what God is saying unless he has used his ears before he has used his mouth? I didn't send the prophets but they run to the people. I didn't charge them but they speak. I didn't put words in their mouths but their mouths jabber away.

We have got to listen first to what God is saying. Jeremiah says here: Behold the storm of the Lord. Wrath has gone forth; a whirling tempest, it will burst upon the head of the wicked. The anger of the Lord will not turn back until he has executed and accomplished the intents of his mind.

I believe God's intention is to teach us a very severe lesson. For we have been the nation that has received as much of God's blessing as any other nation in the world. We have been the nation that has sent the gospel out to more countries than any other nation until America more recently.

We have had all this but we don't have it now.

Next, consider their deceptive dreams. There is an extraordinary statement: God is everywhere so he knows everything. He knows where the message came from. He knows where men get their ideas. You can fool yourself, you can even fool others, but you can never fool God, and if you say that God is saying something, he heard that and he will confirm whether it is true. Five times in this next section (23:23–32), the word "lies" occurs. Where did they get these lies? They said, "I've had a dream." Dreams are a very unsure way of getting the word of God. God can speak through a dream. He spoke to Joseph in dreams in the Old Testament. He spoke to Joseph, the foster parent of Jesus, in dreams. God can speak in dreams but you know as well as I do, and you don't need Freud to tell you this, that many of your dreams at night come not from God but from your subconscious and are an outworking of your own thoughts, your own desires, your own wishes, your own frustrations. That is why a psychiatrist will sometimes say, "Lie there and tell me what you dreamt about last night." It is a clue to the subconscious. If you believe a dream is of God it has to be really tested by the Word of God, by the advice of God's people.

But these prophets were saying, "I've dreamed" – and this is terribly impressive. The pagan prophets of pagan gods used to give their oracles through dreams. The Oracle of Delphi would have dreams. In the ancient world it was a favourite way of imagining that the spirits had spoken. God says: I was there. I fill the heaven and the earth. I was there when you were dreaming and I tell you, you didn't even get this from a dream; you pinched this message from another prophet. I was there when you talked together.

Do you know what these professional prophets were doing? They were going around and saying, "Have you had any good dreams lately?" Some would say that they had a dream and they would share it and then they would all preach it and they had dreamt nothing of the kind. This may be a devastating revelation of what was happening then, but it was happening and God says: they are lying. Let the prophet who has a dream tell the dream but let him who has my Word speak it faithfully — that's what God asks. You can be led astray by deceptive dreams but God's Word is clear and that is what is to be passed on.

When God's Word is passed on rather than a dream, you can tell what is happening by two things. First, you will get burnt and second, you will get broken. Is not my word a fire? Is it not a hammer that breaks the rock in pieces? I'm afraid here is an easy test. If you have listened to God's Word you feel you have been burned or broken. Two were on the road to Emmaus and a third drew near and they didn't recognise him. It was Jesus. There was no New Testament then, so let those who deride the Old Testament note that he took them through the Old Testament. What was the result? "Did not our hearts burn...?" The Word was fire, and fire burns, but the Word of God is also a hammer that breaks. In *Digging up Jerusalem*, the famous archaeologist Kathleen Kenyon, wrote of the old wall of David's city, the Jebusite Wall, dating from before King David. On top of the wall were some huge lumps of rock covering what they wanted to get at. They couldn't think how to get these rocks out. They were in a deep hole and they could get no machinery down the hole to lift the rocks, so the only way was to smash them. They broke sledgehammer after sledgehammer trying to break this rock until finally it was suggested that there was someone who could do the job. He was a tough looking individual. The toughness of his appearance was irrelevant to his efficiency. Introduced to a difficult stone in the overlapping fill, he would look here and there and he would sing a little song.

I am emphatic about my evidence but my Arabic was quite inadequate to catch the words. He then struck the stone a blow at just the right point and it fell apart into fragments that could be carried out of the dump. That remained in my mind as an example of complete expertise. What God wants to get at in your life is overladen with fill — all kinds of things with big stones that get in the way. When God's Word is preached it is as if God sings a little song. Then with the hammer, with one blow, all that has covered what he wants to get at is shattered. That is what God's Word is like. It is not dreams; it is not airy-fairy things. It makes your heart burn within you — burn with shame, burn with excitement, but *burn*. These prophets were not giving that word.

Don't you touch God's Word unless you are prepared to get burned or broken. There is a lovely English pun in the last verse of that section, v. 32. These prophets do not profit these people at all. They may comfort you, they may make you feel safe, but you are no better off, there has been no profit.

Let me now come to the final section of chapter twenty-three, which is entirely based on a Hebrew pun on the word for "burden". That word occurs ten times in a few verses. You see, when men of God become professional they develop professional jargon. It happens in every profession, doesn't it? When men of God become professional they develop a theological jargon and it becomes a kind of technical terminology that covers a multitude of things. In those days, a professional term they had developed was "the burden of the Lord". Whenever they said this, people accepted whatever they said after it. In modern terms it could be: "I feel very burdened to share this with you." Jeremiah says: "God forbids you to use this phrase ever in any connection." It had been so abused and so misused that it no longer meant what it originally meant. People still use this term: "I have a burden for you, brother. I'm burdened to share this with you...."

That is what they were saying then, only it had become such a technical phrase that anybody could say anything. If you didn't like the way a brother prayed in the prayer meeting you went and you said, "The burden of the Lord. I'm burdened brother and I must get this burden off my chest" — and you let him have it, and really it was you saying it. Or you didn't like the way that person dressed: "I have a burden about the way you're dressed in church. I'll be burdened until I've shared it with you." Sometimes when we are saying that, we are getting a burden off our chest but it is not the Lord's burden — it is just that we have been burdened or frustrated with a Christian brother or sister. Here the prophets of the Lord were saying, "The burden of the Lord," and it was nothing of the kind. The word "burden" in Hebrew means two things. It means something that is heavy on you, but it also means something you have got to get rid of. We say, "I've got to get this off my chest" and that is the same kind of language. God says: "Tell these people who keep using the phrase 'the burden of the Lord' that my burden is not what they're saying, but what they are. Tell them, 'The burden of the Lord is you. Stop unburdening all the things you think about other people to them and saying it's the burden of the Lord'. The burden of the Lord is you." That is a challenging word.

God says, "Because you are my burden I am going to cast you off, you and your city. I am going to get rid of this heavy thing on my chest; the heavy thing is not the message you say is my burden. My heavy thing is the messenger and I am going to get you off my back. You will be in everlasting reproach and shame" — including the city, and when one goes to Jerusalem you feel so burdened for that city. It is the city that God threw away. Thankfully, he has not finished with it.

Sometimes when we are tempted to go to someone and

say, "I'm burdened for you and I must get this burden off my chest," God just might be saying to us, "You are my burden. Not what you're going to say, *you* are my burden." Though we have thought about nothing but false prophets right through chapter 23, chapter 24 comes in from the true prophet. Thank God that wherever there are false prophets there are also true prophets, otherwise there wouldn't be false ones. There is no point in counterfeiting something that isn't real. Nobody, as far as I know, is counterfeiting half-crowns at the moment. He would be a fool if he was because there are no half-crowns around. It is a sign there are true prophets speaking if there are false prophets around. There were true prophets and Jeremiah was one of them. Through from chapter 23 to chapter 24 we jump a period of many years, and it is one of the problems in the book of Jeremiah that you go backwards and forwards through the years — you don't know where you are chronologically. Now that is not because God edited this bit badly. The Gospels are in order but this is out of order. God had a purpose in putting two things next door to each other that belonged years apart. Suddenly we jump forward to after the year 597 BC. When all the leaders of the nation had been taken away into exile, Jeremiah's worst predictions had come true, and the royal court, the politicians, even the skilled craftsmen had been taken to Babylon, and we suddenly jump ahead to the years when, already, the cream of the nation has been led off through the desert. Why should God jump the years and put together two things that didn't happen together? It is because God is interested in more than chronology. He wants us to see what a true prophet says as distinct from the false prophet. Through the years ahead we go, and God says, "Jeremiah." Jeremiah is listening and looking to God before he speaks. That is why he was a true prophet. He was prepared to listen and say, "God, what do you want me to say?" He didn't come out with the first dream he had, he didn't tell the people what they wanted to hear. He didn't cry "Peace, peace" when there was no peace. He didn't care what the people thought.

God said, "Jeremiah, what do you see?" Jeremiah had a vision. It was not a dream. You have dreams at night but Jeremiah was awake in broad daylight. A vision in broad daylight is usually much more reliable than a dream at midnight. He saw a vision and he just saw two baskets of figs. One held the first ripe figs — that is, the first crop on the fig tree. They are the sweetest; they are the delicacy — beautiful, tasty, sweet figs, a basketful. Then he saw another basket and the figs in it were mouldy, rotten, and he wouldn't touch them. Both baskets were sitting on the steps of the temple of the Lord as if they were being offered to him. "Jeremiah, do you see?"

"Yes Lord, what does it mean?" He was listening as well as looking.

"Jeremiah, you see those lovely, ripe, sweet figs? They are the people of God away in Babylon, the people who have already been taken away, and they are sweet. I like them. I am going to accept them and I will bring them back into this land. I will plant them. I will build them up." What a lovely positive note here. But why were those people sweet to God? Then he said, "Now look at the basket of rotten figs. Who are they? Those are the people who escaped the exile, who are right here in the land still and who are still comfortable and safe, and I don't like them one bit. Even if they flee to the other superpower [Babylon and Egypt were the two superpowers], even if they change sides and go to Egypt, even there I will follow them and make them a taunt, a joke, contemptibles, and war and famine and disease will decimate their numbers until there are none of them left."

What is the difference? Some would say well, this was

the upper class taken to Babylon; these were the working class—no, that's not the difference. There were skilled craftsmen and unskilled labourers. There are those who still think that God somehow favours one class rather than the other—but no, that is not the difference. The difference is that the exiled ones had been burned and broken by God's Word. They had been chastised. They were willing to be punished and they had been punished. So, God could do something with them. The people whom God can use to plant for the future are those who have been chastised, who have suffered, who have gone through it for him.

Many decades ago, some thousands of us stood at Hyde Park Corner, and there on the back of a lorry were two Russian men in navy blue suits. One of them was just five weeks out of Russia and he was telling us he had spent five years in jail for the Lord. I wanted to run up and jump on that lorry. It would have been a disturbance; it would have been out of order, but I wanted to run up and jump and say, "This man is a better Christian than I am. He's been in exile; he's been through it for his Lord. He's been chastised, he's suffered. He's been burned. He's been broken. He is sweet figs."

We, the thousands sitting there licking ice creams — it had cost us nothing to walk a mile and a half through London. We were not being burned. Because I was leading the singing in our group the police saw a ringleader there and they just closed in and looked at me sideways. My wife said, "They're watching you." They were. What was that compared to what those men had been through? Nothing.

God would say: "Are you a good fig or a bad fig for me? Do you just want to stay in your own land, comfortable, and escape the troubles that are coming or are you willing to accept my word that burns and breaks? Are you willing to go through it? Those are the people whom I can accept and use. Now that is a true word from God, it doesn't mince matters, it doesn't offer easy comfort but it does offer hope. It is not "an old Jeremiah" kind of word, as people say. It is not depressing. It offers hope and joy but it offers shame first. We fix our eyes on Jesus, the pioneer and perfecter of our faith, who for the joy set before him endured the cross, despising its shame (see Hebrews 12:2).

God looked to those in exile and saw a basket of ripe figs — they had been through it, they were sweet, they were refined; they had been through the fire. That is a true prophecy and I believe that we are not the people God wants us to be until we have been chastised of the Lord. Those whom the Lord loves he chastises and if you are never punished by God in this world then you are not a son of God, you are a bastard, says the scripture, not legitimate.

Hebrews 12 says God's Word is like a fire and a hammer. It is not to be played with. It is true and it brings you through the fire, through the brokenness, and then he mends you again, and the burns heal, and he plants you in the land, and he builds you up and he gives you a heart. It is not enough only to be in the land. "They shall return to me, the Lord," he says.

The tragedy of modern Israel is that they have got back to the land but not to the Lord, but the people who are sweet to God are those who come back to the Lord as well as to the land. I must just go one stage further. You see, all this is Old Testament stuff. Let me take it into the New Testament. There are still prophets, but supremely above them all stands *the* prophet. Remember that ever since Moses the Jews had waited for *the* prophet, and when John the Baptist appeared, they said, "Are you the prophet?" He said, "No, I'm not, but there is one coming after me whose shoes I am not worthy to untie." Jesus is the true prophet who, by his words and life, gave the absolute truth, the integrity of God's Word.

Whatever anybody can say about any other man of God and his message or his life, the one true prophet you can look at and say nothing against is the prophet Jesus Christ, the prophet who gave the truth and turned men from their wicked ways. Whether their wickedness was of the kind the world would call wicked or whether it was the kind of wickedness God calls wicked — just being unlike God — the true prophet came into the world and said these things: "In the last days there will be earthquakes and famine and wars and rumours of wars." That is not false comfort, is it?

But he said: "When these things begin to happen, let not your heart be troubled."

"They will drag you before princes and accuse you falsely for my sake, but let not your heart be troubled."

"Lift your heads up. The day of your redemption is drawing near, but beware there will be many false prophets in that day."

One of the marks of the last days is that we shall see many more false prophets giving the people delusive hopes, telling the people "peace" where there is no peace, raising human hopes on false foundations. Pandering to the optimism of human nature, there will be many false prophets and they will culminate in one man who will be *the* false prophet, and that man has yet to appear on the world scene. So, at the end of history people will be faced with only two to choose between: the true prophet Jesus, and the false prophet who will say, "Everything's going to be all right. Everything's fine." In that day the Word of God will burn and break, but out of it will come a people like a basket of sweet figs, and God will say, "I like them." From them I will plant a new people and a new heaven and a new earth and I accept them. Therefore, the question that you and I have to ask is simply this: "Which basket will I be in?"

READ JEREMIAH 25–26

These two chapters of Jeremiah are among the least known in his book. There are few memorable details. The first thing that strikes you very forcibly is that these chapters are back to front. Did you notice that? If you read them carefully you must have noticed that chapter 26 was in the beginning of the reign of Jehoiakim and chapter 25 was four years later, in the fourth year of his reign. Why is that? Well, the Hebrews wrote backwards. They therefore often think backwards and it is a very practical way of thinking. Our western theoretical approach to truth usually thinks forwards.

Let me illustrate it. Here is a medical student who goes to college to learn medicine. He is training to be a doctor and all his training is theory, so he is taught to think forwards. He is told about a certain germ which causes a certain disease which would produce a certain symptom. That is the logical forward progression – cause to effect – and that is theory. But when he becomes a General Practitioner do you think he begins that way? No, he begins with symptoms and he works back to the disease and the cause. Hebrew is a very practical language. It is not so much concerned with theories but with practice, and therefore throughout the Bible, and particularly in Jeremiah, you often have the effect described before the cause, the verdict given before the evidence. We are familiar with this technique in the cinema – it is called "flashback". That is what is happening between chapters 25 and 26. Chapter 25 describes the situation in the fourth year of Jehoiakim, which was an absolutely hopeless situation.

There was by then no reversing of the tragedy that was going to come. Then chapter 26 tells you the cause of the hopelessness by saying that four years previously Jeremiah had given them one last warning after twenty-three years of preaching. They had had their last chance, and because they had refused it in the first year of Jehoiakim, four years later Jeremiah had to say that it was now too late.

In the first year he said there was still time to listen; in the fourth year he said that it was now too late to listen. There comes a point in everyone's life when it is too late to listen to God. God may be wonderfully patient, God may speak to you over twenty-three years. I identified with that. Over twenty-three years God had been saying his word but there comes a point when it is too late. I will never forget a man coming to me once and he said, "You know, during the war in the middle of a battle God spoke to me," and he said, "I promised God that if he brought me back to my wife and kids at the end of the war alive and safe and sound that I would be his man from then on. I came back from the war to my wife and kids but I didn't come back to God. Now, about eighteen years later, is it too late or can I have a second bite at the cherry?"

I replied, "The fact that you've come and asked that shows that God is speaking to you." Ever since, that man has been a lovely servant of the Lord. Can you have a second bite of the cherry? Yes. Thank God he is so patient that he will go on with someone, but there will come a day when he will say that it is too late to listen. It could come before your death and it will most certainly come at your death, when God says, "I can't speak to you anymore." This is the lesson – we are going to have to learn this today, for the one word that goes right through chapters 25–26 is this, and you will find it there if you underline it. I hope you always look for keywords and the keyword in both chapters is listen.

In chapter 25, the word is "Listen" – listen while there is time. In chapter 26, the word is "You have not listened." So, the theme is listening to God. I am going to take the chapters in reverse order, put them back in the normal order of cause and effect, the normal order of the calendar. We will tackle the first year of Jehoiakim, see what went wrong, and then we will understand the very harsh message of chapter 25, but in Hebrew thinking they say, "Look at the verdict first and look at the evidence second."

Even in chapter 26, when Jeremiah is on trial, they give you the verdict first and then the evidence that led up to it. Again, Hebrew thinking, just back to front to us – or is it we who are back to front? They are certainly more practical than we are. In the book of Jeremiah in chapter 26, the year is 609 BC. That doesn't really matter at all. A new king was on the throne and therefore there was the chance of a new start. When you get a new sovereign there is hope that a new direction may be taken. When you get a change of Prime Minister there is hope there is going to be a change of direction. He or she is not set in their ways, they are feeling their way, and so Jeremiah at the beginning of the reign of King Jehoiakim is going to speak and see if the nation will listen. He chose his time and place carefully. In modern terms, he was a master of the media and he knew how to get his message across to the people. The Lord, of course, guided him in this. The Lord led him to the temple during a national festival when the whole nation was gathered together in one place and everybody was talking. In the most public way possible he used the media of his day to get across his message. He took his life in his hands to do so. He must have known this — any man who speaks to a nation that has got away from God and says what God is saying, takes his life in his hands and he is running great risks. Smooth talk will keep the people but the Word of God will not.

Jeremiah was a man of few words but he held back not one word because God said, "You must speak every single word I tell you and you mustn't miss one word out" — because God knows the pressure is on you to leave things out that somebody is not going to like, when you are preaching.

So, Jeremiah told them: Before you entered the land, you received the law of God. That was the way to live, the way to conduct national affairs; the principles of happiness and holiness. Ever since they had got into the land they had prophets sent to remind them to keep it. They could not plead ignorance but only admit disobedience. They were not ignorant, they knew how they ought to have lived. They had not listened to the law and the prophets.

"But," says Jeremiah.... And there is good news, an appeal based on God's mercy. He says, "If..." — and that means the statement is conditional, a prediction that could alter – "If with this new king you will listen, then God will repent." I wonder if you realise that we have in our hands the power to make God repent. Have you ever thought of that? You know we say prayer changes things? Well, it also changes people. But did you ever realise that prayer changes God? It is startling. Moses succeeded in changing God's mind by prayer. Here we have a very definite condition attached. If you will listen — if you will amend your ways and your doings, if you will put things right, then God will repent, and the word "repent" means change his mind, and he will not bring the national disaster upon you that is on its way. Now that is the very simple message. Notice that it was a reminder of the past: you have had the law and the prophets whom God sent to you persistently. Notice it contains a warning for the future to which we will come in a moment as to what the national disaster will be if they don't listen, but he is primarily concerned with the present and their response at that moment. He says, "Look what God has done in the past.

I warn you what he will do in the future," but the present is the moment when you can change the future. You can't change the past but you can change the present and if you can change the present you can alter the future, and that is the glorious freedom in which we live. We are not Muslims. A Muslim says, "Allah wills" — it is all settled and sealed. It is fatalism. I don't believe in a God like that. I believe in a God who says, "If my people... then I will change my mind." That is a co-operative relationship.

It doesn't mean that there is inconsistency in God—he always acts consistently with his character, which is righteousness, which means that if people will not listen, he must punish them. But it means also that if they will listen he can change his mind and not punish them. He has not changed his character one little bit and it is lovely to have a God who never changes in character. It is also lovely to have a God who will change his mind if we repent and so there is an "if" here.

The warning about the future which Jeremiah added is this: if you do not listen, then this house (meaning the temple) and this city will be ruined, desolate. It was like telling a Roman Catholic that Saint Peter's and the Vatican City would be abolished. I want you to get the feel of this. You see, in Jerusalem they looked on this temple and this city as inviolable, sacrosanct. They looked on this temple as the house and city of God and therefore believed they were immovable.

Jeremiah dares to tell them that God would not hesitate to destroy his own house and his own city if they did not listen to him. In other words, the strength of a city does not lie in its religious buildings but in its character. That is what God is saying. The strength, the sign of the presence of God, is not a religious building, nor the fact that God has founded the city, it is the present relationship of the people who live within it

to the God who first started it—that is the message. To the
Jew that was not only treason it was sacrilege to talk about
the house of God and the city of God like that. They were
sheltering under what had become a fetish, a superstition —
that because they had such a big religious "cathedral", if you
like, and the city, they were always all right. God would not
hesitate to destroy a cathedral city. It is the character of the
people in the city that matters. That gives you the feel of it,
doesn't it? That was the trap they had fallen into. The result
was that immediately they planned his death, and in the
rest of the chapter the word "death" occurs eight times and
it is always applied to Jeremiah. They turned what he said
around so much that they thought they had a case for capital
punishment. I want you to notice that it was the priests and
the prophets, the ecclesiastical leaders, the religious people
who did it. Is this beginning to remind you of someone else?
They then tried to get the civic authorities to agree to the
death sentence. Does that too remind you of someone else?
Human nature doesn't change and the religious authorities
were so angry at this threat to their security, this man who
challenged their city, their temple which was their livelihood,
that the priest and the prophets ganged up on him, reported
him to the civic authorities, and they got the princes together
in the court (which was then the gate – the new gate into the
temple which was the main court) with the assistants. The
princes sat and then the priest and prophets said to them
this: "He said in the name of the Lord this temple would be
ruined and this city would be ruined." Now that was not what
Jeremiah had said, was it? He had said, "If," and when they
reported his preaching they didn't leave the "if" in. Have
you ever noticed how twisted it is? They turned what was
a conditional word into an absolute one. They said, "This
man has predicted that certainly this house and city will fall."
He had said nothing of the kind. He said, "If you amend

your ways you can keep it." They didn't put the conditional on it. Do you know why? Because Jeremiah hadn't been prophesying against the temple of the city but against the people in it. They said he had been preaching against the places. They didn't mention that he said anything about the people. Isn't that subtle? Do you remember when they put Jesus on trial? What did they say about him? They said he would pull down their temple in three days, that he was going to attack the place, whereas what Jesus was talking about was people. So, we get all mixed up between holy people and holy places. They twisted his words and they thought they had a good case, so Jeremiah found himself in court. For his own defence Jeremiah was given no lawyer, as Jesus was given no defence. They said the same thing about him: "You have heard from his own lips what he said: He deserves to die."

So, Jeremiah spoke, and when I think that Jeremiah began as a shy, retiring seventeen-year-old boy frightened of other people's faces, I see what a long way he has come in twenty-three years. He is not concerned about his safety any more. Here is a man who will now stand in the court and say, "Do to me what you feel is right and good." He reminds them of two things. He had actually said: amend your ways and your doings because he was prophesying about people not places. Secondly, he reminds them that if they put him to death they will become murderers because he came to them in truth in the name of the Lord. In other words: Do to me what you like but that is what I said and these are the consequences. This is a bold man, isn't it? He is not afraid now to get up in public in front of other people. Here is a man of God who has been made into what God said he would make him into. God said when he called the seventeen-year-old: I'll make you into a fortress; I'll fortify you. Here is the fortress standing facing princes, priests, prophets, people, and saying, "Do to me what you like, but amend your ways and your doings, that's what I said. Don't you dare to become murderers; innocent blood will be on this city if you kill me."

So, the princes gave the verdict: this man has done nothing to deserve death. Does that remind you of something? The religious leaders were saying he said he would destroy the temple and that they had heard it from his own lips, and the civic authorities were saying: this man has done nothing deserving of death. How history repeats itself, and Jeremiah and Jesus went through the same thing with this difference—that Jeremiah was released. Why? Because certain older people had long memories and some elders in the land stood up.

We desperately need older people— "elders" in the land. I don't mean those who've got staid and starchy but those who can remember God's ways. The elders of the land stood up and they said, "Remember" — and there were some there who could remember way back to the days of another prophet called Micah. They could say: remember Micah — he said the same thing, and you know perfectly well that we deserved that and Jerusalem wouldn't be here today if Micah hadn't spoken to us and we hadn't listened, so be careful what you do with this man — remember that God changed his mind and he didn't send the disaster.

They also reminded the people of another thing: that the king at that time, Jehoiakim, had already killed one prophet — Uriah, who had been a colleague of Jeremiah and he had spoken in the name of the Lord. He had heard that the king was going to put him to death and this is where Uriah made the fatal mistake. Jeremiah stood and faced it and said, "Do to me what you like," but this is my message for you. Uriah ran away and he ran to Egypt. King Jehoiakim got an extradition order from Egypt and got him back and slaughtered him and threw him in the Kidron Valley.

So, the elders in the land, with their wisdom, said: what are you going to do? Are you going to make Jeremiah like Micah, listen and put it right and escape the disaster, or are you going to kill him like Uriah? Are you going to allow the people who shout for the death of the prophet to win, or are you going to remember that you wouldn't be alive in Jerusalem today if there hadn't been another prophet who was listened to? That is the evidence they brought.

Jeremiah had spoken, and the elders — particularly one called Ahikam — spoke on his behalf and the last sentence in the chapter tells us that because of this elder, Ahikam, the civic authorities released Jeremiah and the priests and the prophets lost their case and Jeremiah was free to go on preaching.

One final thing before we leave chapter 26: notice how the people shifted sides. The priests, the prophets and the people brought Jesus to the princes and said, "He deserves to die." But after the elders had spoken, it says the princes and the people said, "He has done nothing deserving death." How fickle people are. They switch from one bandwagon to another. How easily they are swayed. How easily a crowd that shouts "Hosanna" one day can a few days later shout, "Crucify". The crowd shifts in this chapter. When it realises the princes are going to release the prisoner, the crowd shifts to release the man with the princes, which raises this question: which way would the crowd go over the next four years? Would they stay with the princes or would they go with the priests and the prophets? The tragedy is that in chapter 25 Jeremiah reveals that their support for him was very short-lived and that they switched and would not listen.

So, we turn to chapter 25, which is the sequel which followed what we have just studied. Four years have passed and the year is now 605 BC. What has happened in those four years? Has there been a turning? Has there been a national reversal? No. Once again on a national occasion, when all the tribes of Judah are gathered together, when all the people are in Jerusalem, Jeremiah comes and he says that there is no "if" — now it has come. Four years earlier he had given a last warning. Now he had only one message. It was not, "Amend your ways." It was now too late to do that. Jeremiah had spoken to them now for twenty-three years and he was going to speak for another seventeen, but here is a change in his message. Right up till now, the first twenty-three years, he always put the word "if" in; it was always conditional. It always gave them a chance to turn around, put things right, but now he says, "The chance is gone," and that is why chapter 25 is such a harsh chapter. It begins with one word and ends with one word: anger. Not Jeremiah's anger, God's anger. Wouldn't it make you angry if you tried to help people, perhaps if you were a doctor and you saw someone dying of a disease and you tried for twenty-three years to offer treatment and they wouldn't accept it, out of sheer stubbornness? So, God was angry.

Now the message of the anger of God is never popular and that is why so few preachers preach on it. But I believe that it is part of God's Word. It is fundamental to the good news of the gospel when in Romans Paul says what the gospel is: everybody who believes may be saved. That is the gospel he preached, and having said, "This is the gospel I preach", what is the next sentence? For the wrath of God is being revealed from heaven.

As Canon Max Warren, a profound thinker said, "The gospel is always bad news before it can be good news." Indeed, he has a chapter in one of his books entitled The Good News of God's Anger. That is an intriguing phrase. Why is God's anger good news? I'll tell you why: because he cares. If he wasn't angry it would mean he didn't care. If he wasn't cross with his children it would mean he didn't love them. That's why it's good news, and so the anger of God, the wrath of God is the theme of Jeremiah's message in chapter 25. But the anger of God is the other side of his love — there is not a contradiction here. They are both part of his character as is his jealousy for those whom he loves.

So, let us look now at the message. Jeremiah explains why God was angry. They had not listened (or inclined their ears), and they had provoked God with the work of their hands. To incline the ear is to say, "Heaven, are you talking? What is God saying in all this?" Look at what they had done with their hands. They had made idols and said: now this is the real thing. This will help us. This is what will get us out of trouble.

In modern times we marvel at science and technology, and think we can save ourselves with our hands. We marvel at modern medicine, but do we think: "What a God to make a brain"? Your reaction to life depends on whether your ear is inclined to God, otherwise you worship the work of your hands and you say, "What we can do will get us out of our mess."

Jeremiah had been warning people, and now the message was: I give you a warning now — from the north will come Nebuchadnezzar my servant. Did that hit you when you read it? A pagan tyrant, God's servant? You have rejected my servants the prophets so you will have my servant Nebuchadnezzar.

Now to let that hit you, let me tell you something that I believe. Do you know when the downfall in this country began? It began towards the end of the nineteenth century and turning into the twentieth century when theologians and ministers in this country began to incline the ear to German scholars who were tearing the Bible into bits. Even as late as 1950, when I studied Theology at Cambridge they were teaching me about German scholars who had split the Bible up. They were called the German higher critics and they were all the rage. What Germany thought first, England thought next, and America thought the day after. Theology was riddled with worship of German scholars, and that began to alter the preaching even before the First World War. In this country people began to denigrate the miracles; the supernatural went out of our religion and liberalism swept in. We listened more to German scholars than to the Word of God, so what did God do? He said, "Right, the Germans will take over," and I believe he allowed them twice in one generation to take over because we had allowed some of them to mislead us about the Word of God.

You may say that is crazy, and there's no connection. You are welcome to that view, but after World War I we said, "Right, we're going to build a world in which there will be no more war." Did we come back to God? You study the figures. The decline in church attendance began around 1910. After World War II, it accelerated even further. It went down and down through the crazy twenties and thirties, so God let that nation come a second time. When Jeremiah said, "Nebuchadnezzar my servant, I will allow him to come and shake you," it would have been like him saying in 1938, "Hitler my servant will come and shake you." Do you get the feel of it now? It is an incredible situation. He said, "He'll take you away and you'll suffer for seventy years in slavery" —that is history written beforehand. How was Jeremiah to know the exile would last that long? It was to last from 605 BC to 536 BC, and Jeremiah gave exactly the period, seventy years. You see, God knows history beforehand. He had decided seventy years was needed to shake them, and off they went.

Now lest you think that makes Nebuchadnezzar a good man — which it doesn't — the prophecy takes two very surprising turns. First, it says: Nebuchadnezzar will then be punished himself and his empire will be brought to ruin. What control God has of history! He can allow Hitler to chastise the Western world and even the whole world, but then Hitler's days are numbered and his Reich collapses. That is what happened to Nebuchadnezzar. Jeremiah said he is my servant for seventy years to bring you all to your senses, to make you realise what has been happening, to drive you to God, and in a sense World War II did. Our churches were packed with people seeking God. There were national days of prayer called for by the government. Did we learn the lesson? How will God chastise us next? That is what one trembles for because war is one of God's normal ways of chastising a nation and bringing it to its senses. It is a desperate thing to do and I believe he does it as a last resort, but I believe we drive him to it. That is Jeremiah's message. We don't like that message, do we? It is not comfortable, but he says: Nevertheless, after Nebuchadnezzar has been used as my servant he too will become a slave and Babylon will become a wasteland. If you saw a picture of Babylon in the twentieth century there wasn't a single person living in it. Even the Arabs wouldn't camp within its walls because they said it was inhabited by jinn, or evil spirits.

Then Jeremiah branches out in the last part of chapter 25. Do you remember when he was called at seventeen? God said to him, "I want you to be a prophet to your own nation and to all the nations of the world." What a thing to say to a seventeen-year-old boy! So now Jeremiah spreads out his prophecy, from verse 15 onwards, to the whole world.

One phrase comes up: all the nations; all the kingdoms; all the inhabitants of the earth; the ends of the earth, the nations, all flesh, nation to nation, the farthest parts of the earth, the end of the earth — and I am reading the same phrase again and again. He had a worldview based on this assumption: if God is forced to punish his own people, he must in fairness also go on to punish everyone else.

That is the meaning of the phrase, "If Jerusalem does not turn to me I will make Jerusalem a curse for all the nations on the earth." It means that if God is forced to judge his own people, out of fairness, that brings everybody else into the judgment. That is why the New Testament says that judgment begins at the house of God. But if it does begin there it can't end there. What shall happen to the others? If the people of God force him to judge them, it hastens judgment for others, and other nations will get caught up in the conflict. In chapter 25 we have a list of other nations south of Judah and north of Judah who will all get drawn into it and who will all suffer, not because they are innocent, or because they are guilty, but because when God starts he has to do the whole lot to be fair. God is saying: if you force me to judge you Judah, then I've got to judge Edom. I've got to judge Egypt. I've got to judge Uz. I've got to judge Syria. I've got to judge Arabia.

Here is a very profound truth and it is given in the form of a vivid picture. God is telling Jeremiah of the cup of the wine of his anger. Jeremiah must take it to Judah, Edom, Egypt and Syria, and they must drink. Judgment has to come. It is a vivid picture. Can you think of someone else again? A cup that must be drunk.... Do you understand where this is leading us? "Father, if it be possible, take this cup from me...." God the Father says: you must drink it, Son. The cup from which Jesus drank was the cup of God's anger against sin. There is no other cup in scripture, metaphorically speaking, than that. Isaiah talks of the cup of the wine of God's anger, Zechariah talks about the cup of God's anger. The book of Revelation (chapter 14) talks about the grapes of wrath and the great winepress of the wrath of God. It is not a symbol of his anger against you, it is a symbol that there was one person who took that cup and drank it so that it need not be drunk by others. But when Jeremiah was alive

Jesus had not yet drunk the cup, so: Jeremiah, take this cup and make them drink it.

You know they had to; it all came true. In the year 605 BC there was a crucial battle on the bank of the Euphrates, between the two great world powers: Babylon and Egypt. In those days that was the west and the east. They met at a place called Carchemish. That battle was one of those hinges of history, turning the course of world events. That battle signalled the end of the power of Egypt. From then on, Babylon swept through Syria, Edom, Ammon, Judah – right through them. Jeremiah's word came true and every one of the nations he mentions had to drink the cup.

The final picture he gives in this chapter is not of a cup that must be drunk, he changes the metaphor to the picture of a lion that has got into the fold among the sheep. In those days, the Jordan Valley had a jungle in it and it was full of lions, and they came up into the hills around Bethlehem at night looking for sheep. Sometimes they jumped into a fold and the shepherd was in there lying with his sheep. The shepherd was lying across the opening, he was the door and the sheep were inside. The lion would jump in, and the lives of both sheep and shepherds were in jeopardy. Jeremiah was saying to all the nations of the world: the Lord is like a lion who is springing into the fold; you rulers of the nations, you shepherds, watch out. You choice rams of the flock, you lords of the flock, your life is in danger. Look again at 25:30:

> The LORD will roar from on high
> and from his holy habitation utter his voice;
> he will roar mightily against his fold,
> and shout, like those who tread the grapes...

Do you see the two pictures being brought together? A lion and a grape treader; the wine of God's anger and the roar of his voice. I want to bring you back to Jesus for a moment, the Jesus who said, "Father ... take this cup from me..." was the Lion of Judah who became the lamb that was slain.

The one person in the world who has authority to give you a cup of the wine of God's anger and make you drink it is Jesus, and one day he will do that to some people. For when it is mentioned in the book of Revelation about treading out the vintage where the grapes of wrath are stored, it is Jesus who is going to come and make the nations drink the cup. But for you he has said that he will drink it if you will believe in him, he will drink it for you. The lion became the lamb, but when he comes back in the book of Revelation he is the lion roaring. He is the lamb that had been slain and he is the lion of the tribe of Judah roaring. Can you put this together? The Bible is a whole and it interprets itself. You don't need any German scholars to tell you this. The lion and the lamb are together in Jesus, and he drank the cup of wine so that we need not drink it.

I finish by saying just three things. Firstly: not "Did you hear?" but, "Did you heed?" is the question. Listening is not just what you do with your ears, it is what you do with your hands afterwards. To listen to God's Word is not just to hear it, it is to heed it and it is to do something about it. It is to be a doer of the Word and not a hearer only. Those who listen to the words of the Lord Jesus divide into two groups: those who build their house on sand—they have heard the Word but they do nothing about it and their house crashes—and those who hear the Word, follow and obey, who listen with an inclined ear and busy hands, and build their house on a rock so that it stands. This runs right through scripture ¬– that listening to God's Word involves inclining the ear and doing something about it.

Therefore, I apply this theme of listening, which has run right through this passage. Forget all the historical details now except for just two things. At the beginning of the reign of the new leader, Jeremiah said: this is your last chance; listen and God will change his mind. Then, four years later, he said: you have not listened and it's too late. Now bearing those two things in mind, let me apply what we have learned in three directions. Number one, this is a call to the nation to listen to God. Don't ask each other what kind of society you want. Don't listen to each other. Listen to God and ask him what kind of society he wants. Sooner or later somebody is going to have to be bold enough to say, "We are in our troubles as a nation because God is angry with us." Whoever does so will not be popular. It will be a prophetic mission. The moment you say, "God is angry with people," you may lose the ear of the people, but I praise God that Jeremiah didn't stop to ask whether he would get the ear of the people. He said, "I've spoken to you in the name of the Lord, it's up to you to listen." He was not troubled about audience figures. He didn't worry. He said: I'm here to speak in the name of the Lord and I'm here to tell you God is angry and if you amend your ways he will change his mind and the disaster will not come. That is what I believe we are waiting for. I believe our desperate need in Britain is not to get into discussion groups and listen to each other but that we should have leaders who listen to God.

Secondly, I believe that this study is a call to the church to listen to God. There are two major channels through which we listen. The first is scripture, and I think the situation in this land would be transformed if every church were preaching solidly scripture. It would mean away with seven-minute talks – it takes time to listen to God's Word – but I believe that it is a call to the church to put the Bible back in its place, and not the Bible as interpreted by the higher critics but the Word of God, and let it speak for itself.

Dr Samuel Chadwick, my spiritual grandfather, said: "I

never defend the Bible. The Bible is like a lion in a cage. I just open the door and let it out." That is what we need in Britain – more preachers who are letting the Bible loose and showing that it is absolutely relevant to our situation.

The other great channel, and they are closely related, is that of the Holy Spirit. We must listen to what the Spirit is saying to the churches today. That will come in a variety of ways. We need to be listening, and God is saying some things to the churches which we don't like to hear. Let me tell you some of the things I think he is saying that we don't like to hear. He is saying: away with one-man ministries and be the body of Christ with many ministers ministering to each other. That is not easy when we have all been used to having one pastor and having him visit us all.

I am going to be even bolder—I believe that the Spirit is saying today: I am not using denominational machinery. There is a new generation of Christians who are not interested in denomination, and I can't break my heart about that. I believe that God is wanting the Body of Christ listening to the scripture and the Spirit. What then is he saying positively? Well, he is saying: get into groups for prayer, where you can minister to one another; get together in a home anywhere – you don't need a church. He is saying: get into structures in which there are elders who shove at the flock. He is saying all kinds of things like this.

We are going to have to learn from what he is saying in his Spirit to Christians in other countries. We British are going to have to be humble enough to say he is speaking more to churches elsewhere than here, and we have got to listen. It is a call to the church: incline your ear and get your hands busy.

Finally, I believe this to be a call to the individual Christian to listen. Do you remember the young boy who lay down in the temple one night? Just before he dropped off to sleep, a voice said, "Samuel, Samuel."

He ran into the next room and Eli the old priest said, "I didn't call you." So he lay down again.

Then a second time, "Samuel, Samuel."

He ran through and said, "I heard you call."

"No, I didn't," said Eli.

A third time it came, "Samuel, Samuel."

He told the old man and the old man said, "Ah, I can see what's happening. The Lord is speaking. Listen." And he did.

I received a letter from a young man who was in a service when I preached about prayer.

"I want to tell you what occurred on Monday night. I had a little time of prayer. I was praying for the Italian disaster and I'd started my prayer with, 'Living Father, we come to you....' [we – and he was by himself]. We come to you as sons. Please comfort those who mourn. I had not got further than this when I heard a voice say, 'Sinner, do you truly love me?' I got up and went to the door and looked to see who was outside since I was on my own.

"Seeing as anybody could have said it, since there was such a noise, I went back to my prayer. Again, I heard the voice say 'Sinner, do you really love me?' I was now slightly startled and I thought I was dreaming. It happened a third time and this time the words were slightly altered, 'I am the Lord, sinner do you truly love me?'

"I then replied, 'Speak to me further.' I felt that a stumbling block had been removed and that God was answering my prayer."

He then joined some other Christians in a prayer meeting. He had always had difficulty praying out loud. He had been to see me about it and I had tried to help him with advice, but he said, "When it came to my turn, the Holy Spirit just brought out a prayer of me, and all because Jesus had signed the petition."

Do you like that? He was listening. "Master, speak, your

servant hears." That's what God is waiting for. He is waiting for it from the church. He may smash all denominations. He may do incredible things with us, but he is saying: will you listen – don't just keep things going for the sake of keeping them going. Then, finally, he speaks to every one of us as an individual by name, and he is waiting for you to say, "Lord, I'm listening, not just with an inclined ear – I am listening with my hands too. I want to be a doer and not just a hearer."

READ JEREMIAH 27–28

A mountain called Masada, with a flat top and sheer sides of nine hundred feet, located on the edge of the Dead Sea, is one of the most spectacular places in Israel. Herod the Great turned it into an impregnable fortress. He was frightened of two enemies. Firstly, the Jews. He always thought of the possibility that the Jews would one day turn against him because he was a descendant of Esau. He built this fortress as a kind of eagle's nest to which he would retire. He was afraid, secondly, of Cleopatra, Queen of Egypt. He thought he could hold out there against her or the Jews, or both. It had a wall around its plateau on the top, with cisterns hollowed out inside to hold one and a half million cubic feet of water, and storehouses to hold enough food for five years. It was a magnificent, three-level summer villa, climbing down the side of the cliff with most beautifully decorated rooms and baths, which you can still see today.

On a tour of Israel we went up Masada to remember the events of the year 73 AD. In 66 AD the Jews had revolted against Rome and tried to get their freedom. They made Masada their headquarters, for by this time Herod was dead, and they took the fortress from the Romans. The Roman army attacked and totally destroyed Jerusalem in AD 70. Just under one thousand men, women and children escaped and ran through the desert, including some priests, and some Essenes. They climbed up the winding snake path which is the only route to the summit on the eastern side, entered Herod's palace, and they said, "Here we're going to stay, and we can hold out against the Romans indefinitely. We have got water and food for five years."

About eighteen months later, a Roman called Flavius marched on Masada. He took the famous tenth legion, the crack troops of the Roman army, and thousands of Jewish slaves. This one rock with less than a thousand people on top, he surrounded with twelve thousand people in eight camps. He built a Roman wall, which was patrolled every few yards so that no one could get down and out, and he settled down for the siege. He realised that it was almost impregnable, that all it needed was a man with heavy stones at the top just to drop them on the heads of any soldier trying to climb up.

So Flavius, with typical Roman thoroughness, ingenuity, and practical know-how, said, "We are going to build a huge ramp. If it takes us years we'll build a ramp from where we are below, right up to the top. Then we will send siege machines up the ramp, and catapults, and we'll invade them through that wall on the west." The ramp was a great pile of stones.

So the slow work began and the ramp got higher and higher, and as the people at the top watched, they knew that their days were numbered. They had enough food and water. The reason why they could not drop stones on the people building the ramp was that the Romans forced the Jewish captives to build it. So the defenders were faced with the awful situation. Should they save themselves by killing even more than their number of their own countrymen? They could not do it.

For eighteen months that ramp got higher and higher, tons and tons of rock and rubble were put on it, until finally they knew that within twenty-four hours it would be complete. Then the leader of that company of men, women and children gathered them all together. His name was Eleazar, and he made a speech:

My loyal followers, long ago we resolved to serve neither the Romans nor anyone else, but only God who alone is the true and righteous Lord of men. Now the time has come that bids us prove our determination by our deeds. At such a time we must not disgrace ourselves. Hitherto we have never submitted to slavery, even when it brought no danger with it. We must not choose slavery now, and with it penalties that will mean the end of everything if we fall alive into the hands of the Romans. For we were the first of all to revolt and shall be the last to break off this struggle. I think it is God who has given us this privilege that we can die nobly and as free men. Unlike others who were unexpectedly defeated, in our case it is evident that daybreak will end our resistance, but we are free to choose an honourable death with our loved ones. This our enemies cannot prevent however earnestly they may pray to take us alive, nor can we defeat them in battle. Let our wives die unabused, our children without knowledge of slavery. After that let us do each other an ungrudging kindness preserving our freedom as a glorious winding sheet. But first let our possessions and the whole fortress go up in flames. It will be a bitter blow to the Romans that I know, to find our persons beyond their reach, and nothing left for them to loot. One thing only, let us spare our store of food. It will bear witness when we are dead to the fact that we perished not through want but because as we resolved at the beginning we chose death rather than slavery. If only we had all died before seeing the sacred city utterly destroyed by enemy hands. The holy sanctuary so impiously uprooted. But since an honourable ambition deluded us into thinking that perhaps we should succeed in avenging her of her enemies, and now all hope has fled abandoning us to our fate, let us at once choose death with honour, and do the kindest thing we can for ourselves, our wives, and children while it is still possible to show ourselves any kindness. After all, we were born to die, we and those we brought into the world. This even the luckiest must face. But outrage, slavery, and the sight of our wives led away to shame with our children, these are not evils to which man is subject by the laws of nature. Men undergo them through their own cowardice if they have a chance to forestall them by death and do not take it. We are very proud of our courage so we revolted from Rome. Now in the final stages they have offered to spare our lives, and we have turned the offer down. Is anyone so blind as to see how furious they will be if they take us alive? Pity the young bodies, the young whose bodies are strong enough to survive prolonged torture. Pity the not so young whose old frames would break under such ill usage. A man will see his wife violently carried off. He will hear the voice of his child crying, "Daddy," when his own hands are fettered. Come, while our hands are free and can hold a sword. Let them do a noble service. Let us die unenslaved by our enemies, and leave this world as free men in company with our wives and children.

When the Romans got to the top the next day and rushed over the ramparts they found total silence. Everywhere there were families laid side by side, their throats slit. The fortress had been burnt to the ground. They had seen the smoke the night before and wondered what it was. The soldiers were awed – there was nothing to loot, no one to seize. Then they found, hiding, a tiny group of people – there were no men, there were either one or two women and between one and three children – the reports varied. From them we got that speech, and Josephus the Roman historian wrote it down.

No wonder that every Israeli soldier joining the Israeli army today is taken to the top of Masada to swear his allegiance. I believe that today if the entire world converged on Israel, the battle would finish on this hill, in the same way as it finished in AD 73, such is their determination that Masada shall not fall again.

That speech is a tremendous appeal to human courage, is it not? The appeal was not cowardice but courage; not slavery but death. You notice that Eleazar said, "I think that God is with us." The one phrase he could not use was "Thus says the Lord", because I tell you the tragedy of Masada is that God was not with them. Those words did not come from God, they came from the flesh; they came from man. They were a message in the flesh. They appeal to the flesh, they appeal to the courage of man.

I read Churchill's speech at the beginning of the war, when France fell: "We shall fight on the beaches. We shall fight on the streets...." You can almost hear the tone: "We shall never surrender." That was the spirit of Masada. This island was going to be a fortress. We would die rather than be in the hands of an invader. Yes, those are human words. On that day Eleazar's speech – and that's all it was – persuaded every man to slit his children's throats first and then his wife's. Then they drew lots to slit each other's throats.

Masada was lost; its site was unknown until the eighteenth century when it was discovered by two Englishmen. They found on the top the sandals and the hair of a girl, and they found the very pottery shards – with the names on – which they used to draw lots as to who would kill the last ten and then who would finally fall on his own sword. Yes it appeals deeply to human flesh does this, but it was not from God. God has never told anyone to commit suicide—*never*. Oh, it may sound heroic, it may sound a great gesture, but God has never told people to do it because suicide is murder. God has told us in his commandments, "Thou shall not murder." He didn't say, "Thou shall not murder other people," he said, "Thou shall not murder," and that includes yourself.

It is worse than murder, it is sacrilege, because every man and woman including yourself is made in the image of God, and to raise a knife against a man or a woman, even if it be yourself, is to raise a knife to destroy the image of God — and so God never told anyone to commit suicide. So when Eleazar said, "I think God is with us," and, "we must choose death rather than slavery, courage rather than cowardice," he was speaking in exactly the opposite way to the prophets of the Old Testament who could not appeal to the flesh and could not appeal to men's highest instincts of courage, for Jeremiah's message in the passage we read was precisely the reverse: "Choose slavery rather than death. Submit to the yoke of Babylon. Why will you die? Go into slavery." So Jeremiah was thought to be a coward and he was accused of cowardice, not courage. Surely human courage is, "We'll stand and fight to the last ditch." But God said, "Thus says the Lord, give in, surrender. Go into slavery because you can do nothing about it, and you are better alive as a slave than dead as a free man." So Jeremiah's message and Eleazar's were totally contradictory. It is Jeremiah's that is the Word of God, and it was Eleazar's that is the word of man. Heroic though their stand was, and though we are deeply stirred by the story, and it has inspired thousands of Israeli soldiers to go into battle determined to see it through, nevertheless the fact is that Jeremiah gave the exact opposite advice.

I will have to give you a bit of history now. The year is 593 BC when chapters 27–28 were written, or spoken first. It is a rapidly changing scene. Let me try and paint it for you. Judah is a declining nation that once had almost an empire but now is just a little nation and it has even lost parts of itself. It is centred around Jerusalem. On the eastern side is a big superpower that is getting bigger, called Babylon. To the west is another big superpower that is beginning to decline—Egypt. North and south of little Judah were some other little nations. To the north of them was the nation of Tyre and the nation of Sidon. You can still see those names on the map. They are on the coast. South of them were three little nations further inland: Ammon, centred on what is now Amman, the capital of Jordan; then, a little lower down, Moab, and then lower still Edom, with its capital at the famous ruined city of Petra down in the Arabah. That was the situation: a string of little nations in the middle, a great big superpower whose military strength was growing almost daily, and gradually capturing more and more from the east, and another big superpower on the west to which they have looked in the past for help but which is beginning to pull out of the situation. Already in 597 BC, four years before these events, Babylon had invaded Judah, taken away the elite, the nobles, the skilled craftsmen, the artisans. They had lost many thousands of their population, all the upper people. They have been left with unskilled people. They have been left with a weak puppet king called Zedekiah, and he is a politician, a man with no principle; a man of expediency. Zedekiah, full of nationalist spirit, is saying, "How can we get out of this situation? How can we stop the threat of this eastern power engulfing us?"

He puts his trust in two things. He says, "Let's make an alliance, all the little nations in the middle. Let us try to make a strong group of nations in the middle. Let us hope that the west power, as it has done previously, will come to our aid when the east attacks." So he sent for ambassadors from Sidon, Tyre, Ammon, Edom, Moab, and they all came to Jerusalem, and held a six-nation conference with a view to an east Mediterranean alliance, and to forming a power bloc in the middle to resist, and to defend each other. With that backward glance at Egypt from which to get their military arms and their money, you can see the situation. It is as up to date as today and it has been happening since history began.

It was into that situation that God said: Jeremiah, you've got to go and speak to them. If they pursue this political policy it is a disaster. The nation will disappear altogether and I have a future for this people. You somehow have got to persuade them to accept the inevitable, that this eastern power is going to come, and country after country is going to fall to the eastern power. You must accept this and live believing that one day God will give you back your freedom.

Now that is a very big step of faith. Human nature says, "No, we're going to fight on the beaches." We've got Egypt at the back of us, surely she'll come to our aid. We can hold off this threat." Jeremiah said: "No you can't, because God is behind the threat."

Now how is he going to get this message across? It called for pretty drastic teaching because Jeremiah had been teaching now for thirty-two years and still he could not get them to listen. How do you get people to listen after all that time? How do you bring it home to them? The answer is that you use a gimmick. Now those who criticise gimmicks are criticising God because God is a God of gimmicks as I read the Bible. He is not above using something pretty spectacular or out of the ordinary to get attention. Isaiah was the first recorded streaker and he streaked through Jerusalem. Why? He said: "Because only in this way can I bring to your attention that you are going to be stripped of everything if you don't get back to God." Now you dismiss that as a gimmick if you wish, but God used it. When the situation is desperate you have to use desperate methods to get your message across. It was God who led Isaiah to do that, as God told Jeremiah here to use a gimmick — to use something that would really make them sit up and take notice. They may say he is an eccentric, they may even say he is a maniac, but he was going to try it.

In my youth there was a man who used to go around English towns dressed as a clown with a great big round white nose, red triangles and a clown's hat and costume. He had a notice on the front of his chest: "I am a fool for Christ's sake." He would dance up the high streets of town with that placard and people laughed at him as a religious maniac until he got past them and then they saw a notice on his back, which said: "Whose fool are you?" That man got a message through to a lot of people.

Arthur Blessitt said, "How am I going to get a message through — to get the gospel through to people right outside the Church?" He got a large wooden cross, fixed a pram wheel on the end and walked around the USA with it. God used that; he honoured that. All right, let those who cry "gimmick" be doing something themselves. As D.L. Moody used to say, "I prefer my way of doing it than your way of not doing it." We can only accuse somebody of being eccentric if we are as keen as they are to get the gospel across and to get the message through.

So Jeremiah was to use a visual aid which would look pretty startling. He got a yoke and put it on. He walked around the streets of Jerusalem and said: God is putting the yoke of Babylon on you and there is nothing you can do about it. The policy for you is to surrender and go into slavery and live, and believe that God will one day get you out. It will be a long time. It won't happen in your lifetime; it will be seventy years, so you won't see it, but your children will, and for the sake of your kids put on that yoke, bend your neck.

Have you ever studied the Bible teaching on necks? How often God said, "You are a stiff-necked people". What did he mean? You won't bend. You won't let me put this on. You've got to bend to get this on. If you are one of these people you can't carry your yoke. You've got to bow, and then you can cope, you can carry a load. A yoke is not meant for a picnic it is meant for work. It is so that you can carry heavy things and carry much more than otherwise you could—and it was a symbol of slavery. Jeremiah kept it on, and to every group he met in that city he gave the same message: you are believing a lie. The political authorities were saying: this is the way out of our trouble — we negotiate, we get into an alliance, we have the other big superpower to supply arms and money, and we are home and dry. We have got our national independence. Not only were the politicians saying this, the tragedy is that the religious leaders of the nation were backing up the politicians and saying this was the way to go.

So Jeremiah had to fight on two fronts. In chapter 27 he is fighting on the political front against the political leaders; in chapter 28 he has a fight with one of the religious leaders who was encouraging this wrong policy. He said, "It's a lie." Jeremiah knew perfectly well what would happen if they followed this policy because God had told him. So he spoke to three groups. He spoke first to the ambassadors from the other five nations: now you go back and tell your masters that this a non-starter. God has given your lands, not just ours but yours, to Babylon. When God gives land there is nothing you can do about it. Why? Here is the key verse, 27:5, "'It is I,' says God, 'who by my great power and my outstretched arm have made the earth with the men and the animals that are on the earth, and I give it to whomever it seems right to me.'" In other words, God made the earth, he populated the earth, and he maps it — he has redrawn it. That is the viewpoint of the Bible; that is the Christian understanding of history. When Paul preached in Athens, the very centre of what had once been a gigantic empire under Alexander the Great, he said (see Acts 17): "God has made from one every nation to dwell on the face of the earth. He has appointed their allotted spans and the boundaries of their habitation." God draws the map and we only make copies of it. Or, as in Psalm 24, "The earth is the Lord's and the fullness thereof" — and he gives it to whoever he decides. You can't fight against God if he is redrawing the boundaries. Notice that he says, "Nebuchadnezzar will have your lands but he will come to an end too. There is a time when I'll deal with Nebuchadnezzar." I believe that God allowed Hitler to have as much as he did but no further. There came a time when God said to Hitler: Now it's your turn. I've used you to chastise a western civilization that was falling apart but now it's your turn.

Nebuchadnezzar was used. God said that Nebuchadnezzar (pagan though he was) was to throw Shadrach, Meshach, and Abednego into a fiery furnace – though he was to erect a gigantic golden image of himself in the plain of Shinar, though he was to build fabulous Babylon and say, "Is not this great Babylon my kingdom, my power, my glory?" His day would come, and it did. His nails grew long, his hair grew long, they turned him out, and he grazed in a field like a wild animal. For months he behaved like a beast until his sanity returned and he said: now I know who's in charge of history; now I know that it's the God most high who orders.

We are getting a big view of God. We might summarise: I am the God who by my power and my outstretched arm made the earth, put men and animals in it, and I give it to whomever I choose. I have given it to Nebuchadnezzar. Put that yoke on. There is no use fighting against it; Go back to those countries of yours and stop thinking of an alliance — it is useless, it will never work.

Then Jeremiah turned from those nations and he turned

to the king of his own nation and the nobles, and he said the same thing to them: You're believing a lie. Why will you die? Why throw your life away? Listen. While there's life there's hope.

In other words, he was pleading for honourable surrender. Then he went to the priests and the people in the temple and he said the same thing to them — "It's a lie." In fact this phrase "It's a lie" occurs four times. "A lie ... don't believe it."

I find the last part of chapter 27 a very sad part because he says to the priests: "You know that four years ago Nebuchadnezzar took your vessels away to Babylon, and the temple had some beautiful cups and things of gold and silver." To me, the tragedy is that the priests were more worried about the loss of the vessels than the loss of their congregation—that is what comes out here. Do you notice it? Jeremiah says: you are listening to this false prophecy that they will come back within two years, don't you believe it; even the pillars of this house will go unless you accept the yoke of Nebuchadnezzar. That came true just six years after Jeremiah said it. There were two huge bronze pillars at the entrance to the holy place, and those were pulled down and carted off to Babylon just six years later. Far from getting their vessels back within two years, even the pillars were going to go. Until God was ready they would stay over there.

Those of us who are called to lead the people in worship and religion can so easily get tied up with things rather than people. I know there are ministers who would rather be without a congregation than without their altar, their robes and the paraphernalia. Look, the Lord is not interested in paraphernalia, he is interested in people. To priests worried about their paraphernalia, Jeremiah would say: it is no use hoping you will get it back. They should have been worried about the people who had been taken away, not the vessels.

Even so, Jeremiah told them it was no use, so six years later even the pillars went. As we read in the passage, the prophet spoke God's word to the people: "Thus says the LORD...."

In all this, I am doing what the New Testament refers to as discerning the signs of the times. It is a job we have to do in our day. We have got to discern the signs of the times because God is working out his purpose. The events are signs. They point to what God is doing and what is happening. Jesus was once pointing out to Pharisees that they were even good at weather forecasting (when the sky is red at night you say it is going to be fair, and when it is red in the morning you say it is going to be stormy) but they could not see what was happening in front of them and discern the signs of the times. But Jeremiah could. He was an accurate predictor.

I come now to something very big and we should remember: that God told us to love him with all our *mind*. We need to think about getting the right relationship between religion and politics. The problem is that there are some people who keep the two so far apart they never interact. That is not unknown among Christians. "Politics is a dirty business, leave it to worldlings; we'll stick with religion." But, you know, if you study the Old and the New Testaments they are full of political statements. The prophets did not see religion and politics as separate. Jeremiah was here making political predictions, giving political advice to the government of his day. He was giving good advice because he, unlike them, had all the factors in mind. We need to say this to our government and our MPs: "You are not considering all the factors because the biggest factor in the situation is what God is doing. If you don't consider that factor you are going to become unstuck in your legislation because his will is a fact in the situation." Religion has something to say about politics. I am not going to drop into the trap of saying that religion is identified with one party in politics, I am saying religion is *related* to politics. We will have to make political statements that will criticise maybe both sides of the house, but we will make political statements. Jeremiah would not separate these two things into watertight compartments. He took heaven's eye view of the political situation and he spoke to it. It has been said that statesmanship is the art of finding out in what direction Almighty God is going and in getting things out of his way. Isn't that great? How few statesmen we have.

We now turn to chapter 28 and, by way of introduction: just as some Christians keep religion and politics too far apart, some Christians get them too close together and religion gets identified with political nationalism. That is when you land in serious trouble the other way. Some Christians keep right out of politics and some go into it and identify Christianity, their faith in God, with one particular national aspiration. History is littered with examples of this. I believe that one of the greatest disasters that ever occurred to the Christian church was when the Roman Emperor Constantine was converted, because the first thing he did was to make Christianity official and the established religion. He identified religion and politics and you could not be a politician without being a Christian in his court from then on, and it was a disaster. Religion and politics got so close that people began to talk about "Christendom" and the "Holy Roman Empire" and all the abuses of the Middle Ages grew out of this fatal identification between church and state.

At a later stage the Reformation made the same mistake. Martin Luther identified church and state in Germany, only he put the state on top of the church. John Calvin made the same mistake in Geneva, only he put the church on top of the state, but in both cases they identified, and not out of any feeling of denominational pride or anything else. The people who stood out at the time of the Reformation for a

300

free church in a free state were the Baptists, and therefore they were persecuted because in every other case church and state were so intimately bound that people could not see a free church and a free state.

I go further. Henry VIII dabbled in religion. You probably know he wrote theological books. He wrote a book attacking Martin Luther and attacking Protestantism, so the Pope gave him the title "Defender of the Faith", which he has passed on to every subsequent sovereign and which our Queen still enjoys. But it is a title given by the Pope for defending the faith against Protestantism, which is one of the anomalies of English history. When Henry VIII could not get his divorce, he promptly said, "I am going to be the Head of the Church in England" and it became Protestant. He signed away and dissolved the monasteries. After he had died, somebody else said that England would be Roman Catholic. It went on and on until Elizabeth I said, "We'll have a settlement. England will be Anglican." Again, all through that period and for many years afterwards, the people who fought for a free church in a free state were persecuted. I ministered in a church in Chalfont St. Peter, and in the early church minute books there are records of the members whose furniture was sold and who were then taken off to prison. Why? Because they fought for a free church in a free state.

I believe that the Bible does not want religion and politics so tied up that a secular head of state is the head of the church, because what happens then is that nationalism and religion get so closely identified that you get into an impossible situation. The prophet cannot speak.

In the time of Jeremiah, the false prophets were supporting nationalism and saying, "God is behind you in your struggle for independence", and they were giving people good "news". Now which are you more likely to believe – the good news or the bad news? The answer is very simply: good news is popular, bad news is not. When the false prophet was saying "Peace", and Jeremiah was saying "War" – when the false prophet was raising hopes of national independence, and Jeremiah was talking of surrender – who was going to be believed? So he had to change from the political leaders to the religious. In fact, instead of tackling the whole lot, God brought him face to face with just one man – a test case – and his name was Hananiah.

Hananiah got up and preached. He came from the same area as Jeremiah and was probably jealous of him. They were both lads together, one in Gibeon, one in Anathoth, which are just north of Jerusalem. Hananiah came to Jerusalem and said, "It's going to be alright. I predict that within two years the exiles will be back from Babylon and Babylon will be finished." That was a pretty risky thing to say. It meant he could only keep his reputation for two years. If you are going to make predictions I would suggest you make them for at least twenty years ahead and then you are safe for twenty years! If you say two years you are really putting your neck in a noose.

Hananiah said, "I do not believe that the yoke will last more than another two years." That was a sarcastic reference to Jeremiah's activities. It was a straight contradiction. Jeremiah's reaction when he met Hananiah was like this: I wish you were right. I really do. I'm not going to be sarcastic, I'm sympathetic. Amen. If the Lord would do that I'd say 'amen' to it. If only that were the truth, I could wish for nothing more for our nation. I'm not wanting to see war. I don't want to see them destroyed. Amen, if the Lord would do that. But I can't help making an observation, and that is, have you ever noticed that all the prophets that were before you and me Hananiah, every one of them prophesied doom, and you are the first to bring good news? That makes me stop and think. This isn't divine revelation it's human reaction. Why is it that every prophet up till now has been sent to warn people of danger and you are apparently the first to be sent to tell them it's alright? God doesn't usually send prophets when things are alright. I don't figure it out at all.

So since he was still wearing the yoke, Hananiah got that wooden yoke and smashed it. He must have been so incensed by what Jeremiah had pointed out that he didn't fit the pattern of prophets. He smashed the wooden yoke. I take my hat off to Jeremiah, who quietly walked away to talk to the Lord about it. If somebody attacks you and really goes for you, the best thing you can do is go and talk with the Lord about it before you open your mouth any further. Jeremiah said, "Lord, what do we do about this guy?" The Lord says, "You go right back to him and tell him this: that you will make a prediction of twelve months, not two years – you will stake your reputation on a prediction that is months not years. You will tell that man that the wooden yoke will be replaced by an iron one that he can't break because you will not be able to break Babylon and I want you to tell him that within the next twelve months he will die."

Jeremiah came back. It doesn't say that he was wearing an iron yoke, he just came to talk about an iron yoke, and he told Hananiah: "God is going to remove you from the face of the earth and I stake my reputation on him doing it within a year." You know it wasn't even a year, it was only two months later Hananiah died. I guess he died of a heart attack because in his heart he must have known that he had not got his message from God, and in his heart he must have known that God was giving his word to Jeremiah. Jeremiah was gloriously vindicated because the book of Deuteronomy says there is one simple test of a prophet and that is: if what he predicts comes true he is a good prophet and if it doesn't he's not.

Here are two great truths in this passage. Truth number

one: his sovereignty. It is God who settles the fate of nations and individuals. It is God who decides how long you live. It is God who decides where you go when you die. It is God who draws the map. It is God who has the final word over human affairs. He is in sovereign control. To hope that our alliances with our neighbours are going to hold a threat back, or to hope that a great western power will come to our aid as she did in the past, I believe is not enough for our situation. The prophetic challenge is: Do you hope in God? Are you seeing in what direction he is going and getting things out of his way? That is statesmanship. I believe that some Christians in this land are better statesmen than those who are professional politicians. They are getting a God's-eye view of the situation. They are seeking his will and his word. The first truth is God's sovereignty.

The second truth is this: our submission. For Jeremiah's yoke had a double meaning when he put it on. That said to others, "The meaning of this yoke is that it is a visual aid for you." One in the eye is worth two in the ear, as I have said many times. It was an object lesson. It stood for the yoke of Babylon on them, which they could not break. So they were to accept it, bend their neck humbly to it, and live. But it stood for one other thing. It stood for the fact that Jeremiah had accepted the yoke of the Lord. Who told him to put it on? In fact Jeremiah said, "I'm willing to be under your yoke, Lord. If you tell me to wear it, I'll wear it."

Now what does that say to me? Well, we have got right to Jesus. Why was Jeremiah wearing the yoke and talking about Babylon? He was saying to his nation that if they will not accept the yoke of the Lord then they must accept the yoke of Babylon. The simple and hard truth is this: everybody has to wear a yoke of some kind. If you refuse the yoke of the Lord, you have got to wear someone else's. There is no such thing as absolute freedom. All people are made to be yoked so that they may carry their burdens and work as they should. So you are made for a yoke. If you don't accept the yoke of the Lord then you will become yoked to somebody else. It is a tragedy for you if you get yoked to somebody who doesn't belong to the Lord – you will find it a very unequal yoke.

But now listen to Jesus. He said to Capernaum, Chorazin, Bethsaida: "Woe to you Chorazin. Woe to you Bethsaida. Woe to you Capernaum, for if the mighty works that had been done in you had been done in Sodom and Gomorrah they would have repented. As it is in the Day of Judgment it will be harder for you than for Sodom and Gomorrah." All you can find of Chorazin, Bethsaida, and Capernaum are some heaps of black basalt rocks. They have gone.

Do you know what Jesus said? He was a true prophet because he was a prophet of doom. He was a prophet who told these cities they were to be destroyed. Don't you tell me that doom is only in the Old Testament. It is right through the teaching of Jesus, but do you know what he said after he condemned those three cities in which he had preached? After he had condemned them to oblivion – and that is where they are today – straight away he said, "Come unto me all you who are heavy laden. Learn of me for I am meek and lowly. Take my yoke upon you." Why? "Because my yoke is easy and my burden is light."

Now have you got the message? You can't be without a yoke. You are going to have to carry a yoke. You are going to have to carry a burden. Everybody does; everybody has burdens. But you either have the yoke of someone else, which is irritating, chafing, uncomfortable, or you listen to a carpenter who was always making things like this and he made them to fit, not to rub. He made them easy so that people could cope and carry their burdens. He said, "Learn of me. Take my yoke." You won't find rest for your bodies.

No Christian finds that. You won't find rest for your mind. You have got to use your mind an awful lot when you are a Christian. But he did say, "And you'll find rest for your souls."

READ JEREMIAH 29–30

In these chapters two major changes take place. The first is that Jeremiah switches from the spoken to the written word. He starts writing letters and books. The second is that he stops being so pessimistic and becomes optimistic, and the doom and gloom give way to a rosy hope for the future. I am sure you sense the change of tone. These two changes are not unrelated. Let me try to explain. Words are very powerful. They are weapons. Words can bring great blessing and they can bring terrible destruction. Many of the world's dictators have known just how powerful words can be. But the written word can be powerful too, and in some situations has advantages over the spoken word. Jeremiah lived before the days of electronic recording but not before the days of writing. We can imagine that had he lived in the days of electronic recording he would have made an audio file for the exiles in Babylon. He needed to send his words a few hundred miles across the desert, so he wrote a letter. Here is the first advantage of the written over the spoken: in those days it could travel further.

There is another advantage of the written word: it can also travel distances in time. If I had no recordings of my messages, every word would be lost, and it would be limited in its effect to what my hearers remember of it afterwards. I don't expect a congregation to remember everything. When I preach a sermon I hope God will say one thing to everyone present at some point and that they will remember that and go away and do something about it. But if something is written it can travel down through the centuries.

In chapter 29 he writes a letter, which travels a great distance through space from Jerusalem to Babylon. In chapter 30 he writes something which will come into its own seventy years later, and will travel down through the decades and will therefore be used later still – and here we are reading the book now, 2400 more years later. So that is the advantage of writing.

As Jeremiah moves from the spoken to the written word and projects his word through space and through time into the future, he is able to turn from the pessimistic message of doom and gloom in the present to the optimistic message of hope in the future. Do you see how they are related? He doesn't leave all of God's anger and wrath behind, because that would be to distort the picture. There are still little glimpses of God's anger. But most of it now is God's compassion, love and kindness, and I am sure you are relieved to get to this.

Here is a little history lesson to give you the setting. Babylon is now a growing empire with satellite countries around it. Nebuchadnezzar's policy with countries that he took in to the kind of overall circle was this: he would remove from the country, as soon as he captured it, all the top layer of society. It would include the political figures and the religious leaders; it even included the skilled craftsmen and smiths so that he left behind a population that could not rise again—a poor people with no leadership. Then he would set over them a puppet king whom he thought he could keep under his control. He wasn't brutal or harsh, at any rate in his early days. He took away that top layer of society to his own country, enhancing it with gifted people, and he gave them relative freedom to build up their own settlements in his empire, within or near his capital. So when Nebuchadnezzar first took Jerusalem, he took away 3,032 people to Babylon – the top layer of society, and skilled artisans – and he left behind some thousands of unskilled, illiterate, poor people. He put in charge of them a man called Zedekiah, whom he rightly discerned was rather weak, whom he could keep there. It was in that situation that Jeremiah said to those who were left behind: you are going to be obliterated. It is almost as if God was going to build up a new nation from the choice Jews who had been taken away. But Jeremiah now writes to those who have already suffered for their sins by being taken away from their homes. Therefore, with them having been chastened and punished, he can now speak to them more tenderly. You do the same with your children. When they have done wrong you punish them, but when they have suffered a bit of punishment, you change and begin to talk to them gently and nicely, restore the relationship and try and get them back to where they were.

God begins to do this, and Jeremiah has to write to Babylon to begin to restore their confidence in God and the relationship between them. So he is going to say to them: now will you seek him with your whole heart? Now will you get back to the Lord? Because if you get back to the Lord you can get back to the land. So seek him with your whole heart and your future is rosy. But he also had to write for a negative reason, because there were self-styled, false prophets appearing, not only in Jerusalem denying Jeremiah's message, but appearing among the exiles in Babylon to say, "It's all right; this empire is going to collapse in a year or two and we'll all be able to go back." Jeremiah said that was not true. They would stay there for seventy years and that gave them a chance to get right with the Lord. So: start seeking him hard, and one day God will bring you back. But the prophets out there in Babylon said, "Rubbish. Don't you listen to Jeremiah." One of them, called Shemaiah, even wrote a letter back to a priest in Jerusalem, declaring that God had told him that he must take over the job of high priest and put the crazy prophet in the stocks. That was the situation. Poor old Jeremiah stands alone in Jerusalem and he stands alone in the eyes of Babylon. He has to fight on two fronts now and speak to two groups of Jews: the group around him and the group away in exile, whom he can only reach by letter.

The letter to the exiles in chapter 29 may simply be divided into three parts: a word of *advice*, a word of *promise*, and a word of *warning*. I want you to take those three words as from God to you. Here is the word of advice: the instinct when you are a subjugated people is to resist and escape. This is what happened to many Frenchmen in the war when the Germans overran France. The human instinct, if you have the courage and the opportunity, is to join a resistance movement. When the Romans were occupying Israel, the instinct of some Jewish people was to become zealots or terrorists. Instinctively, we do not like to be under the control of another nation and want to get out of it. Or sometimes there is a policy of non-violent, passive non-cooperation.

Jeremiah's word of advice from the Lord was: colonise and co-operate. Don't try to escape; don't try to resist. Build houses, live in them; plant gardens, get their produce; have children, have grandchildren. You are going to be there for seventy years and my advice from the Lord is co-operate with Babylon. Pray for it, seek its welfare, because if Babylon is blessed you will be blessed. Your welfare depends on the occupying power, so co-operate.

That is not popular advice to those who have been forcibly put under another power and it never will be. That is one of the reasons the crowd was so disappointed with Jesus, because he would not lead an insurrection. They called for Barabbas, a terrorist, to be released. That is the message the world responds to. But Jeremiah had to say that God's advice was to co-operate because the better Babylon is, the better they would be. Therefore, seek its welfare because therein lies your welfare.

The advice appears in the New Testament as: "Submit to those in authority," and it was said when Nero was the emperor. It would not be popular advice, but Jeremiah had to give the people unpopular advice. Godly men followed that advice—which is why Daniel got so high in the Babylonian government. That is why, later, Esther co-operated with a foreign power, and the Bible is full of such examples.

Verses 5–7 are in poetry: "Build your houses and live in them. Plant your gardens and get their produce. Get wives for your sons and have children. Get wives for your son's sons," and so on. Jeremiah gives them a little poem, doggerel that will be repeated around the streets. You see, as over against the divine wisdom there is the human wish all the time, and the human wish is contrary to divine wisdom. The wisdom of God is foolishness to men and the human rational mind cannot see the wisdom of God. Human wishes and divine wisdom are often poles apart, and human wishes are often fostered by religious leaders who are prepared to tell people what they want to hear.

Jeremiah is saying: you have got dreamers and prophets out there in Babylon who are telling you what you want to hear – they are dreaming dreams of getting back to Jerusalem. Those dreams will not come true for seventy years, so you build your houses and live in them. Don't listen to human wishes even if they come from religious lips, even if they come from people who claim to be speaking the Word of the Lord. It is a lie. So says Jeremiah. Choose between divine wisdom, which I offer you, and human wishes coming from your own prophets. You co-operate; pray for Babylon, and seek its welfare.

Secondly, there is a word of promise. Even though he says, "You're going to be there for seventy years" – and that is a long time, two generations – here is a word of promise: expect to return from Babylon; don't get so deeply rooted there that when the time comes to return you can't uproot and return. Now here is a delicate balance. God is giving them a hope and a future. He has plans for their welfare.

I praise God I live in a "welfare state". It is not a human one, it is a divine one. The kingdom of God is a welfare state and God says he has plans for our welfare. Now you get a lovely divine promise of God's faithfulness. He has made his plans, he will keep his promise, and in this next section, vv. 10–14, five times God says, "I will...." I sometimes want to count up how often God says "I will". He says it many times in these two chapters: I will bring you back; I will restore your fortunes; I will give you a hope; I will give you a future; I will plan your welfare. That is the divine faithfulness, but God then reminds us through Jeremiah that divine faithfulness is often matched by human fickleness. We sing "Great is thy faithfulness" and it is, but we ought also to sing, "Great is our fickleness, O God our Father".

What do I meant by that? I mean that in spite of the fact that God says "I will" we are still half-hearted about it. In spite of the fact that he plans a glorious future for his people we can be half-hearted even in singing hymns about that. Yet if with all our heart we truly seek him, we will find him. That is the heart of the message of the promise here.

If God took your bed away, the roof over your head, your central heating, your car and every comfort, could you still say wholeheartedly "He is all I need"? One of the reasons many people can't find God is they are so half-hearted about it. They have given part of their heart to their career, another part to their family, another part to their home and garden, another part to this, that and the other, and they have only got a bit left for God, only a little bit of their heart for him to occupy, and he can't get in.

Finally, there is a word of warning. Do you notice he says that in Babylon, without a temple, without a priest, without an altar, without a sacrifice, you will be found of me? That is the beginning of the New Testament. It is the beginning of the synagogue, and we are a synagogue in our churches. We have no high altar, we have no priest, we have no sacrifice, and the church building is not a temple. But if we seek him with all our heart we will be found by him. The word of warning is: "Avoid prophecy in Babylon." Jeremiah is wondering how his letter will be received. He knows that false prophets are saying: "Jeremiah's a liar; he's crazy. Put him in the stocks." He knows they are saying, "Babylon will fall in a year or two and we can all go home," and he knows it is not true. He is thinking, so he sends a warning in the letter: "Beware of that man Ahab. Beware of that man Zedekiah. I know them both. I know what they are saying. They are telling you what you want to hear, but it is a lie."

You see, a man of God who is going to speak the Word of God has to do two things. He has to *express the truth* and he has to *expose the lie*, and that is why preaching becomes unpopular. I have had people say to me, "I wish you'd stick to the positive things and keep off the negative. You know, just be positive and say all the things we can say yes to, but don't say no to anything." That is exactly what our world wants.

The world wants a kind of tolerance rather than the truth of antithesis whereby if this is true that is not true. The world wants both to be true and a mixture to be made, but it can't be. If Christianity is right, every other religion in the world is wrong. You can't get over that antithesis. But the world wants to hear us say "All religions are roads leading to the same goal and you take the best bits of each and lump it all together." Then you have got a world religion but it never works.

Truth is always seen against lies. If the word of God is true then things that men say are lies. You have got to say both. The word of God is, "You'll be in Babylon seventy years," and the lie is, "You will be in Babylon two years." The prophet has to expose the lie as well as express the truth. So Jeremiah says, "I tell you, I've been preaching in Jerusalem and you're in Babylon because you didn't listen to what I said. I tell you now that those who are left in Jerusalem will be followed by famine, sword, pestilence, until there is nothing left of them. You see if I am true, if my word is right – don't you go listening to those false prophets of yours, especially that man who says he has been writing letters back here to Jerusalem and saying, 'Get Jeremiah that crazy man in a collar and stocks.'"

Jeremiah says, "I tell you what will happen to Shemaiah. Nebuchadnezzar will throw him into the fire." That was Nebuchadnezzar's way of dealing with those whom he regarded as potential rivals and traitors. That is what was done later with Shadrach, Meshach and Abednego. So Shemaiah – he will be thrown in the fire. That would only anticipate his ultimate end because in fact those who distort God's Word, those who deny it, those who reject it, those who say the opposite, are heading for fire anyway. There is a lake of fire for false prophets. Nebuchadnezzar just brought that a little early. it was in any case what was happening. God says, "I am he who knows." There it is, in v. 23. He *is* the one who knows. No-one else does. Politicians and leaders don't know. He doesn't need any other witnesses; he says, "And I am witness." So God needs no-one but himself to tell the truth. He is the one who knows and he is his own witness, so what more do you need? The Word of God has to be taken on God's Word, if I may put it that way.

I want to apply chapter 29 to you because I am addressing this to exiles, because the simple fact is that the day you became a Christian you became an alien – a citizen of another kingdom. You became a sojourner, a pilgrim passing through. You no longer belong.

Here is a quote from a letter written nearly nineteen hundred years ago, from a Christian to a man called Diognetus who was not impressed with Christianity. It is now known as the epistle to Diognetus:

Christians are not marked out from the rest of mankind by their country, or their speech, or their customs. They dwell in cities both Greek and Barbarian each as his lot is cast following the customs of the region in clothing and food and in the outward things of life generally. Yet they manifest the wonderful and openly paradoxical character of their own state. They inhabit the land of their birth but as temporary residents thereof. They take all their share of responsibilities as citizens and endure all disabilities as aliens. Every foreign land is their native land and every native land is a foreign land. They pass their days upon earth but their citizenship is in heaven.

Therefore a letter to exiles is so appropriate, and the word of advice is: pray while you are in exile. The welfare of your country is *your* welfare as long as you are in it. That is why the New Testament commands us to lift up holy hands and to pray for those set in authority over us. They need to listen to God. We need far more Christians in the House of Commons. Pray that we may get up to the five percent needed to change its character.

Pray for the country you live in. Build your houses and live in them. Plant your gardens and eat their produce. But remember, don't ever get so rooted down that you are not ready to go home. Expect to return to the Promised Land. Never get your roots so deep down in that house that you have built, that garden that you have produced, or in your children or your grandchildren that you can't leave it and go at a moment's notice to be with the Lord.

Beware of the false prophets who say smooth, easy things. "It's alright. Everything will turn out alright. We'll get through it. We've muddled through before – Dunkirk and all that." Don't believe it; don't listen to it. Here we have no abiding city, and I believe God's hand of judgment is on this land, and until he has fulfilled the intents of his mind we can do nothing about it. But we can pray and we can support our government. It may not be the government you voted for at the last election but in its welfare lies your welfare, and if parliamentary democracy breaks down in this country it is you who will suffer if you are in the UK. Jeremiah's letter to the exiles is so appropriate. Do read it.

We move to chapter 30. It is full of such good news that it has been called by Jewish scholars "The book of consolation". We are ready for consolation. We are all interested in healing and unity – we don't like the wounding and the dividing. But where the Word of God is preached, a church will be divided, and then the Spirit will unite it again. This is God's spiritual surgery and it was necessary for us to go through chapters 1–28, which are doom and gloom, which hurt and cut. But we are now into consolation, lifting up – the Spirit healing the wounds.

This chapter can again be divided into three parts. It is good news, a 'gospel', and Jeremiah, though he is dead and gone, yet speaks because he wrote it down in a book. Nineteen times in this one chapter God says, "I will". He said it ten times in chapter 29 but now nineteen times God is marrying himself to our future: "I will...." God is going to *remove their panic*, *remove their pain*, and *remove their privation*. Or in the terms in which it is expressed in this chapter: "Their terrors will be ended; their wounds will be healed, and their fortunes restored".

First of all, *the terror is ended.* Now I noticed something here that made me very excited. You know, the Jews say there is only one God and they cannot accept the Trinity. I don't know how they manage to get around it. God said, "Let us make man in our own image," and look at v. 5. "Thus says the Lord, 'we have heard.'" We – only one God? Well yes there is. But in the Hebrew it is, "Hear O Israel, the Lord our Gods, the Lord is one." We. "Thus says the Lord, 'we have heard a panic, terror, no peace, a time of real distress when men are behaving like a woman having a child, in pain with pale face, sweat on their brow, trying to contain the pain.'" What has gone wrong when men do this? Time of real distress? Yes, Israel has been through more distress than any other nation on earth. "Yet," says the Lord, "he will be saved out of it, and I will break the yoke."

Jeremiah put his yoke on. God can break the chains and break the yoke. Remember how that false prophet Hananiah broke it and said, "Jeremiah; rubbish". So God said, "I'll replace it with an iron one. See what Hananiah can do with that one." But God can break the iron. Iron gates can yield, and brass is broken before God. God says, "I'll take that yoke, I'll take it off, and I'll smash it." Why? In order that they may be free? No, I repeat it because it is repeated here: "I will break your yoke in order that you may serve the Lord."

There is no such thing as freedom in this world. You either serve yourself or someone else or God. There is only one whose service is perfect freedom and it is not yourself. It is the worst kind of slavery to be a slave to yourself and to have the yoke of your own pride and greed bearing you down. But God can break that yoke and he can break also the yoke of Babylon, or the yoke of whatever foreign power. But he does it in order that he may put another yoke on your shoulders and that you may bend that stiff neck of yours to a yoke that is easy and a burden that is light.

That was why God said to Pharaoh, "Let my people go that they may serve me." God only frees you that you may be enslaved to him. That is why Paul called himself a bond slave of the Lord Jesus. He had been a slave to the law, a slave to self, now he was a bond slave to Jesus. The only question that is before mankind is: whose slave are you going to be? There is no point in talking about freedom. Then God says: "All the nations that have troubled you, I will bring to a full end. But you, I will never make a full end of you." On the basis of that, and on the basis of the muddle that the British got into when we had the trusteeship of Palestine and the Jews, I say very simply, the days of the United Kingdom are already numbered because God says, "I'll make a full end of all the nations that cause you trouble."

We have done so, not least by our folly after World War I in making the same promise to both Jew and Arab that they could both have the land. When we got into a mess, the result of that two-faced promise we just got out and left it to the United Nations. I know it cost us lives and I know we tried to be fair – we tried to do what we could – but we made a mess of it as a nation and God has written our doom in that. I am not telling you when it will be but he said, "I will make a full end of all the nations that trouble you. But of you, I will never make a full end." So I make this prediction: that on the last day of human history there will be a nation called Israel, but I don't know what other nations there will be.

"Your terror, your fear" – going through the museum of the Holocaust in Jerusalem in silence, seeing the photographs of old men, naked women, and little children, faces filled with fear, I think of how they have feared. God is saying in this book for the future for them: "None will make you afraid. No more panic, no more panic." That museum in Jerusalem is filled with panic and fear, and there will be no more.

The second thing that will be taken away is all their *pain*. It is a deep pain. Medical language is used now from 30:12 onwards. "Your hurt is incurable, your wound is grievous. There's no medicine for your wound, no healing. Why do you cry out over your hurt? Your health, your wounds". But what is the wound? What is hurting? I don't think it is the physical suffering because they did not have much in the early days in Babylon, they lived in comparative physical comfort. The hurt is that they had lost their land. They were far from home and they could not go back.

God is saying: "Look, your hurt at the human level is incurable because your guilt is great. Your sins are flagrant. Don't you realise that your sickness is due to your sin?" There can be a connection between those two things – not in every case. You can be sick because you are sinning. Body and soul are too intimately bound up for you to be able to do some things with your soul and not suffer in your body, and to do some things to your body and not suffer in your soul. You are one being.

Then God is saying: What is impossible I can do; I'll heal your incurable wounds. You may have wounds in your spirit. Some of them go back to your childhood, some of them go back just a few years, and some may even have been caused this week. When somebody else touches the wounds they hurt, and they limit your Christian service and spoil your freedom in the Lord. You might say the hurts and wounds are incurable – I'm too old; I've had it too long and I'll never get over it – but God says: listen, I will restore health to you, and your wounds I will heal – all the hurts there have been. That is a lovely promise, isn't it? Why will God do this? "Because they have called you an outcast and said, 'it is Zion for whom no one cares.'" You know, that hurts God; that touches him on a very sensitive point, because God cares more than anyone else. For anyone to say he doesn't care for his people really gets God on the raw. God says: "I will heal the incurable wound because I do not want anybody saying about you, 'No one cares for that person.'" I find that very touching. So if you have a wound, take it to the Lord. If you have a hurt, take it to the Lord, because if you keep it somebody could say, "No one cares," and God says, "I care, and so I'm going to remove your pain."

Then, finally: their *privation*. Here we have a lovely picture of stable prosperity. It is thrilling to read about a city rebuilt, a palace in the city, children playing around in the streets, songs, music, dancing, making merry, and everything beautiful—a lovely city to live in, a kind of garden suburb with plenty of playground for the children, and the old folk looking on. Do you catch the vision? It is a lovely picture. Economically, culturally, politically, socially, everything is put right. "I will restore the fortunes of the tents of Jacob." The climax comes at 30:21, "They will be ruled over by someone from among themselves. Yet someone who will be able to approach God." Now that is the kind of ruler we need, isn't it? We need someone we feel is one of us; with whom we can identify. "Their prince shall be one of themselves. Their ruler shall come out of their midst." You know, the Jews have had too many rulers from outside themselves. They have been ruled over by Syria, Egypt, Greece, Rome. Wherever they have been dispersed as exiles they have been ruled over by an alien. Only one English Prime Minister has been Jewish, Benjamin Disraeli. Otherwise the Jews in this country have been ruled over by a Gentile. The Jews in America are ruled over by Gentiles. "You will have a prince, one of yourselves." You know who that is referring to, don't you? The climax comes, "And you will be my people and I will be your God."

It is the best thing about the city. Not that there are children with plenty of playgrounds, not that there are palaces and fine buildings, not that there is peace, prosperity and security, but that at the heart of it God is relating to his people. You notice there is no temple mentioned here. If you have God you can do without a temple. These very words are taken from Jeremiah 30 straight through to the end of the Bible.

Let me now apply chapter 30 to you: one day *you* are going home and there is a city whose streets you cannot imagine for beauty. That city is described in the last two pages of the Bible – Revelation 21 and 22. There is no temple in the city. Why? Because God says, "I will be your God and you will be my people." Same words. That is what makes society stable, peaceful and prosperous. We cannot solve our economic problems with an economic policy. Jesus said, "Seek first the kingdom of God and all these things will look after themselves."

When in the middle of social life there is a relationship between God and the people, then and only then will our other problems get sorted out. I pray that God will raise up Christian politicians who will be skilled at politics but will start from their relationship with God and then work it out politically. Let them work it out in the House of Commons as all of us have to work it out where we work and where we live.

Now comes the shock – and I am afraid it is a shock. Verses 22–24, after this lovely picture of panic removed, pain gone, privations ended and that climax, "You will be my people and I will be your God", we get three verses full of God's wrath and anger. But the Bible is an honest book and what we read here means: before you can have that stable prosperity, there will be stormy prelude. There will be an exhibition of God's wrath and anger such as has never been seen before – a whirling tempest, a storm.

You may not understand it now but in the latter days you will. The book of Revelation is not only the book that describes that New Jerusalem, that beautiful city that we are going to live in, it is also full of God's anger and wrath. Have you noticed that? Because, I am afraid, God must fulfil his anger and wrath before he can bring us to that city. There will be a time of distress, not only for Jacob but for all nations. It is through great tribulation that we enter the Kingdom, and I believe we Christians have to be utterly realistic: the day of wrath has to come before the day of God's glory.

It is true of Israel as a nation. Have you noticed for the first time Jeremiah is no longer calling them "Jerusalem" or "Judah", he is calling them *Jacob*, all through chapter 30. Why? Because Jerusalem and Judah are only part of the nation. The word "Jacob" covers all twelve tribes because he was the father of the twelve. This is saying that this future is for the whole of Israel. People debate as to where the ten lost tribes are. I tell you, God hasn't lost them. So it is the future of Jacob, but Jacob must go through a time of distress and God's wrath before that future. Every time I go to Israel today I come back with my heart breaking, thinking: when will it happen to them? You see, they have come back to the land but not to the Lord and that plea, "If with all your heart you truly seek me" is still not responded to by the tribes of Israel; they are still not turning to him with all their hearts. So there must be a time of distress for Jacob yet he will be saved out of it.

Not only is there a name – Jacob – first used in this chapter, there is another name that is in this chapter. It may not actually be seen in the print but it is there: the name "Jesus". He was not given that name in Jeremiah's day, but what is used is this: "I will break your yoke so that you may serve the Lord and David the king." David the king had already been dead for centuries. The people would understand what that meant. It meant a descendant of the royal line of David. When it talks about a "prince who will come out from among you, one of yourselves, and yet who will approach God" we have got a perfect picture of Jesus. Born in Bethlehem, born in human frame, one of us – even we Gentiles can say that. Very man of very man, the Word became flesh and dwelt among us. That gives us our Prince.

The future of Jew and Gentile are not two futures but one. Their distress is our distress and we are the other sheep that were not of that fold whom Jesus has bought, and there will be one flock, one fold, and one Shepherd. Jew and Gentile together will enter into this glorious future, if with all our hearts we truly seek him.

Half-hearted people make Jesus sick. He would rather they were cold than lukewarm. But wholehearted people not only find God, they are found by God, which is even better because God is looking for them. He came to seek, to save, and you will be found by him and then he has made plans for your welfare. So who is for the welfare state of God? By the grace of God *we* are. We have no abiding city and our citizenship is there. We are aliens here. We will support our kingdom, for in its welfare lies our welfare, but we are not so deeply rooted here that God couldn't call us at a moment's notice to go home.

READ JEREMIAH 31

Jeremiah chapter 31 is a watershed in the book. Everything has been building up to this and everything will flow from it but we are right at the mountain peak. In fact, I think we are probably at the highest peak of the Old Testament and the point where we are nearest to the New Testament. Indeed this chapter is about the New Testament for the word "covenant" and the word "testament" are the same word.

Jeremiah says, "There's going to be a New Testament," and he was saying this four hundred years before it came. He could see that the Old Testament was not working and there was going to be a new one. So this is the nearest he got to the gospel of our Lord Jesus Christ. So we are really going to climb this mountain. It is going to be quite a climb but the view from the top, I guarantee you, will be worth it.

Verse 1, in a sense, is the link between chapters 30 and 31. Since Jeremiah did not bother with chapter headings, but somebody rather naughtily put them in later, see it as the connecting link. It summarises 30 and 31. Look back to 30:22. It says, "And you shall be my people and I will be your God." Now see 31:1, "I will be the God of all the families of Israel and they shall be my people." Now look on to the end of v. 33, "I will be their God and they shall be my people."

Let us begin with this theme – the thread running through: I will be their God; they will be my people. I want to begin by making the simple statement that our God is unique among all the gods that have ever been worshipped because our God is a family God. Now I say four more things to get that point across to you. First, he is a family in himself, there are three of him and he was a family before there was anyone else. He always has been a family God. Second, when he made man he put people in families so that they might be in his image. He is the Father after whom every family on earth is named. They are named after him and every family is a copy of him. That is why the more godless a nation gets, the more its family life breaks up. You get the message. Thirdly, he therefore in a particular way wanted to be the God of the families of Israel. That is what he describes himself as in v. 1, "I will be the God of all the families of Israel," and he wants to be the God of all the families here. But fourthly, consider the thing that he is aiming at in all this. All earthly families come to an end whether they are Jewish, Christian, or not Christian at all – all earthly families are broken up sooner or later by death, so why then has he put us into families only to break them? The answer is: because his ultimate objective is to have one family. So he puts us in families here that we might learn what a family is like, to prepare to be part of his family forever. The ultimate objective is that God should have one family with many sons. The Father so enjoyed having one Son that he wanted more.

So he is the family God, and the object of the whole exercise – the grand theme of scripture – can be summed up in these words, "I will be their God and they will be my people" – we will be one big family together. These very words come up again at the end of the Bible in the book of Revelation. When the new heaven and the new earth are displayed, God says: I will be their God; they shall be my people. That will be the new home for God's single family.

It is remarkable that right through this chapter Jeremiah describes the relationship between God and Israel in family terms: first of all as a lover with a virgin; second as a husband to a wife; and, third, as a father to children. There is a progression of thought there but it is all in family terms. When God first made an approach to Israel he came as a lover to a virgin. Then he married Israel. That is what the word "covenant" means. A marriage is a covenant. You put a ring on as a token of the vow and covenant. The marriage took place on top of a mountain called Sinai in the triangular peninsula of land between Egypt and Israel. He and Israel took vows to each other and Israel broke her vows and broke the marriage. Therefore God also broke it, and it was right that he should. She broke it so he did, and he broke that old marriage up. That is why Jeremiah realised there had to be a new marriage between the same parties, a new start, new basis, new conditions – a new proposal if you like, and that is the theme of this whole chapter.

But then Jeremiah moved so easily from "lover" and "virgin", through husband and wife, to a third family picture, "I am a father to Israel. Ephraim is my son. How long will you be a faithless daughter?" There is the father's heart beating through this chapter. It is when you think of a father's heart that you get nearest to God. If you want to understand how God feels then understand how a father feels. For example, we will come to a very poignant and tender verse where God says, "I feel like a father whose son is so rebellious that the father has had to turn him out of the house," and some parents need to do that. I know Christian parents who have had to do it with rebellious children, and God had to do it with rebellious Israel.

God says: "You know, every time I speak against my child it goes through me like a sword." Have you got the feeling? There is a father who knows he has got to throw the son out, a father who knows he has got to deal with the rebellious nature, and yet everything he says against his own child brings back tender memories of the time when he dandled that child on his knee. This, then, is the family feeling that runs through this chapter. It is God seeking a family, yearning for children who are rebellious and who will not be a family. It is God having had to throw them out of their home. It is God having had to discipline them, but it is God who waits with open arms for the prodigal to come back.

Jeremiah 31 is nearer Luke 15 than any other chapter in the Old Testament. Again and again we will catch echoes of the story of the prodigal son. Here it is a whole prodigal family, sons and daughters, they have gone away into Babylon into captivity, and it is their own silly fault. They did not like their own land because they did not like their own Lord. They were interested in foreign lords; they did not want to accept the God of their parents and so they rebelled. They went to a far country because they had already gone there in heart. They had already accepted foreign gods, so it is as if God said: Well, if that's what you want, go and live in a foreign land but remember I'm always waiting for you to come back. That is the Father's heart.

Here is a little bit of history and geography to set the scene. Let me draw an imaginary picture. At its greatest extent the kingdom of Israel under King David was about the size of Wales or a little larger. There were twelve tribes in different parts of it. For three reigns they were all under one king – Saul, David, Solomon – and those three kings reigned over all twelve tribes. Then, when Solomon died, there was civil war and they split. Ten tribes stayed in the north and, since they were bigger than the little two who stayed in the south, they kept the name "Israel" to themselves. So the two tribes in the south got called "Judah" because the bigger one of the two was Judah and the other one, just north of them, was the tiny little tribe of Benjamin. So they were both called Judah.

If you try and unravel the next few years of history you have got a job on. Read through the second book of Kings or the Chronicles and just try to sort out who was king where – it is almost impossible. You really have to do some hard work to see it. Then the ten northern tribes began to misbehave so badly, and get away from God so much, that he finally sent a big foreign power from the east called Assyria. The ten tribes were taken into captivity in Assyria leaving the two called Judah (Judah and little Benjamin). Here is the interesting thing which I want you to note carefully because it is going to be important later. On the border between the north and the south, immediately north of the border was Ephraim, the tribe of one of the two sons of Joseph. Just south of the border was little Benjamin. The thing that those two held in common was that they were both out of Rachel's womb, therefore very closely related, and one was gone and one had stayed.

Right on the border, or just south of the border, was a place called Ramah (now called Ramallah), which is now the borderline between Jews and Arabs. It is where Rachel was buried, on the border between her two descendants: Ephraim and Benjamin. The present tomb of Rachel outside Bethlehem is not the original tomb. Rachel's tomb today is simply venerated in her memory but it was at Ramah, five miles north of Jerusalem, on the border. So there was Rachel's tomb – and half her children, Ephraim, had gone. Jeremiah was born in the little tribe of Benjamin just below that, in a little village called Anathoth just outside Jerusalem, Jeremiah realised that the rest of her children were going to go too if they went on behaving as they did. He could almost begin to hear Rachel weeping in her grave that her children were no more—are you beginning to get the feel?

That is enough history and enough geography. The key phrase in this chapter is "hope for the future". It occurs at the beginning of v. 17. "There is hope for your future," says the Lord – even though they have been turned out of their home, even though they are rebellious, even though their Father has had to turn his face against them, there is hope for their future. Another keyword in this chapter occurs about seven times: the little word "for". Why is there hope for the future? "For there shall be a day when watchmen will call"; "For I am a father to Israel"; "For your labour shall be rewarded"; "For as often as I speak against him I do remember him still"; "For the Lord has created a new thing on the earth"; "For I will satisfy the weary soul and every languishing soul I will replenish"; "For they shall all know me from the least of them to the greatest of them"; "For I will forgive their iniquity." Those are some pretty good reasons for hope, aren't they? Why do we have a hope for the future? For these reasons: for he is a Father, for he will forgive, for he will do new things, for God is God. That little word "for" – if you underline your Bible and mark it (and I hope you do), then put a little ring around that word "for" wherever it occurs. It unlocks the whole of God's truth to us in this context.

There are three things on which we now need to focus: *a rejoicing remnant*; *a contrasting covenant*; *a permanent place*. The most important one for us at the moment is the middle one. Let us take the first twenty-six verses. A rejoicing remnant – this portion is full of hope. But remember how the Hebrews always thought back to front. Actually, they could say that it is we who think back to front, but in fact the Hebrews talk from effect to cause. They looked at the end before the beginning. They looked at what would ultimately happen and then said what would lead up to it. This is what throws a lot of Westerners in Bible study because we think the other way. We like to see what began it and what resulted, don't we? But I can tell you why the Hebrews thought like this: because God knows the end from the beginning. God always works backwards. He knows where he is going, he knows what he is going to do, and he works backwards from it. He knows the result so he looks at the cause.

Therefore, in this first section of a *rejoicing remnant* their homecoming and their merrymaking is mentioned first. Their departure and their weeping is mentioned second. I hope that won't throw you. I am going to take them in the order of the Bible, but if you find it a bit difficult just reverse them and think of them the other way around. He is going to talk about the merrymaking when they get back and then he will describe the mourning when they had to go.

Now I want you to notice that this is all about Ephraim and Jacob. Jeremiah is still living in the two tribes in the south; they have not gone yet. The ten in the north have gone, including their cousins Ephraim – same descendants of Rachel. So Jeremiah is thinking primarily: what is happening to those ten tribes that have gone? Now you will hear the weirdest and most incredible stories as to what has happened to those ten lost tribes. I will tell you what has happened to them: God knows where they are and he will bring them back. You don't need to worry your head about any complex theories about where they went. The simple fact is that Jeremiah said that God will bring them back to this country, those ten tribes.

"Jacob" is the word used by the prophets from now on. They no longer use "Jerusalem" or "Judah", they now talk of Jacob, meaning all twelve tribes. God will bring all twelve back, and in the book of Revelation you find all twelve there, 144,000 of them, twelve thousand from each tribe. We are thinking about the northern ten tribes from vv.2–22, and from vv. 23–25 there is a little bit about Judah coming back as well, just to keep them in the picture.

Of the northern ten tribes Jeremiah says that one day they are going to come back and what a day that will be – there will be singing, dancing and praising. I want you to notice how all that goes together. There will be prosperity; they will plant vineyards; they will eat of the fruit. There will be wine; there will be oil. Music, dancing, wine, oil, worship, praise – it is all of a piece. You have to go to Israel to get this thing put together. We tend to separate these things out – so much of this and not that – but this is a picture of life in its fullness, from the God who has given us all things freely to enjoy. So here is wine, oil, music, dancing, the lot, in one package deal. One day I'll bring them back. Why? Because I love them with an everlasting love.

Other parents may turn their children out and let them go, but not God. He turns them out and loves them and says, "Therefore, I'm faithful to you. I can't let you go. I can't say goodbye. I can't see ten of my twelve children taken away from home. Know that it is right, know they deserved it, let them go, but I still can't stop loving them. Those who seek me in the wilderness for rest, they will find me. They will find me because I love them."

A mother who once said to me about a rebellious son who left home and never contacted her again, "How much longer should I pray for him? I've prayed for him every day" – I think that had been for twelve years.

I replied, "Mother can you stop?"

She said, "No. I've loved with an everlasting love."

So you can't stop loving your children while there is hope for the future, and the quality of God's love is everlasting. That is the symbol, as you know, of a ring – something that has no end – and that is why we put it on.

Israel is to be the chief of nations. Notice that, not the largest, not the mightiest, but the chief of nations. "You are the apple of my eye," he says, "I'm going to bring you back. I'll bring the blind back, the lame back, the pregnant back. I will bring you all back. I want you here enjoying yourselves. I want you singing, I want you making music,

I want you dancing, I want you enjoying yourselves as my family," and that is God's hope for them—that is the merrymaking. Judah, the two tribes in the south, and Israel, the ten tribes in the north will be together in Jerusalem. They will say, "Come let us go to Zion. Let us get together and praise him."

That is the future merrymaking on their return and it is exactly what happened in Luke 15. When the prodigal came back there was music and dancing. "It is right that we should make merry," says the father. If you criticise music and dancing before the Lord then I say to you it is right that we should make merry if we have got the right things to make merry about. But now let us come to the second part, which is the mourning part at their departure.

When the prodigal set off for the far country, I wonder what his father looked like at the time. It doesn't say. I wonder what his mother felt at the time. It doesn't say; it doesn't even mention the mother. But the Hebrew, thinking backwards to us, forwards to them, goes back from the merrymaking of the future, returning to the mourning that took place at the departure. Here we have one of the most extraordinary things in the Bible. Jeremiah sees something. He sees the children of Rachel being led past her tomb in chains. Now he is seeing not only Ephraim in the north but Judah in the south. He is seeing Ephraim – and Benjamin, his own tribe. They are being led in chains from the tribe of Benjamin and being led north, away over to Babylon now, not to Assyria. Ephraim was being taken to Assyria; now Benjamin is being taken over to Babylon. Forget the historical details if you are confused, but here is a group of men and women in chains and they are being led north away to exile, knowing that they will never see their homeland again in their lifetime.

They are leaving, they are passing the tomb, and suddenly

from within the tomb there comes the sound of a woman sobbing, a woman who has been dead and gone for hundreds of years, and they hear it from the tomb. You discover that Jeremiah wakes up and it is a dream. But in his dream he sees the prisoners going past the tomb and he hears the dead woman in the tomb weeping and sobbing, mourning for her children because now the last of them has gone. A dead mother's heart is broken – a voice in Ramah, Rachel weeping for her children.

It is all in a dream but Jeremiah can see it vividly. God says, "Don't weep Rachel. Dry your tears up. Your travail, your labour, is not in vain." In other words: "You didn't bring these children into the world in vain. It's alright. I'm going to bring them back." The dead woman is told to stop crying because God is going to bring her children back to their country. He can't let them go. He says, "My son, it's my daughter, not just yours, Rachel. It is mine, and I'm going to bring them back. So don't weep for them going."

In fact, God says to Rachel: "It's alright because in the far country they will come to themselves." Isn't that an intriguing phrase? One translation is: "Ephraim in exile in the far country will say, 'Thou has chastened me, and I was chastened like an untrained calf. Bring me back that I may be restored for thou the Lord my God. For after I had turned away I repented, and afterward I was instructed ... smote upon my thigh I was ashamed and I was confounded because I bore the disgrace of my youth.'" The literal translation of the second phrase in v. 19 is this: "and after I was made to know myself I was ashamed and bore the disgrace of my youth."

Children may rebel and then go away. One day they will come to the disgrace of their youth, they will be instructed, they will get to know themselves. Change came when the prodigal son came to himself and said, "I'm going back."

There are prodigal sons and daughters. When they come to themselves, when they realise what fools they have been to leave the Father's home, they will get up and go back; they will be ready for home and God will be ready for them. He will say, "Return, O virgin Israel. As often as I speak against you I remember you. Therefore my heart yearns for you. I will surely have mercy." When a prodigal comes back, the parents run and fling their arms around their necks.

Jeremiah, remember, is asleep, and dreaming all this. He sees the prisoners passing Rachel's tomb – Rachel weeping inside – and he shouts after them in his dream: "Set up signposts as you go and you'll be able to find your way back." That is v. 21. "Set up waymarks for yourselves. Make yourself guideposts. Consider well the highway, the road by which you went, and then you can get back." Literally, he is shouting at them: "Carve some posts and stick them in the ground behind you as you go, signposts pointing home." I say to any young person who is anxious to get away from home: please set up signposts that point home as you go, and you will remember the way back. Then comes this strange verse: "For the Lord has created a new thing on the earth, a woman protects a man." We will return to that.

So far, Jeremiah has been thinking largely of Ephraim his cousin tribe, taken away to Assyria. Now he thinks of Judah and he addresses his own two tribes, I don't know if he says it before they have been taken away or after, though I think it was said before. But he sees that they are going to be taken away too – to Babylon. He is saying: Judah, you are alright too; there is hope for your future too, because God says once more they will use these words in the land of Judah: O holy hill, Jerusalem, Judah will come back, and the farmers will come back, the cities will come back, the wandering shepherds will come back to Judah.

If the shepherds had not come back to Judah there would

have been no birth of Jesus and no visit of the shepherds to Bethlehem when he was born, so it did come true.

Then we come to this lovely v. 25 and hold it as a promise, "For I will satisfy the weary soul and every languishing soul I will replenish." That is for those who are weary of running away, who have gone where they think they can find life and found no rest, no peace. God says: "Come home and rest." Jeremiah woke up and it was all a dream. But it was a dream that would come true—every bit of it. I will now tell you what is meant by the phrase, "The Lord has done a new thing in Israel, a woman protects a man." Some years later, after this very dream, Jeremiah and his fellow Benjamites were put in chains together. Jeremiah was taken prisoner with his fellow tribesmen, the descendants of Rachel, and they were taken by the Babylonians north along that road to exile and Jeremiah was among them. They came to Ramah. They passed Rachel's tomb and, for some inexplicable reason (the reason is not given), the soldier in charge of Jeremiah took his chains off and said, "You can go back home." At Rachel's tomb Jeremiah was set free. He never was taken to exile, though every one else was.

Maybe you don't know your Bible well enough to know this happened, so if you don't believe me, turn to 40:1. The "captain of the guard" was called Nebuzzaredan: He had let him go from Ramah when he took him bound in chains. It is quoted in the Gospels, the epistles – Romans, Hebrews. It is quoted again and again, this very next passage. God sees, and Jeremiah now sees that God had to pluck them up and break them down but that he is now going to plant them again and build them again, and that he is going to have a new marriage ceremony, a new covenant. He is going to put the marriage together on a new basis, with a new proposal. Indeed, if a marriage does break up the only hope of putting it together is a new proposal, a new basis. The old basis clearly was not good enough to hold it together, therefore there must be a new thinking together of what kind of basis it has got to be on this time. Let us look at the new marriage. It will be characterised by promises: "I will...." Indeed, in v. 33 alone, "I will" comes repeatedly: "I will make with the house of Israel after those days a covenant, says the Lord"; "I will put my law within them"; "I will write it upon their hearts"; "I will be their God"; "I will forgive their iniquity"; "I will remember their sin no more." Six times: "I will". That is the word of a marriage. It is not a contract but a covenant.

When God brought his people out of Egypt he made a marriage with them, an old covenant through Moses at Sinai. It was the old marriage. Now that he is going to bring them back from Babylon he will make a new covenant with them – a new covenant because they broke the old one; it didn't work. Not because there was anything wrong with the covenant but there was something terribly wrong with the people. The old marriage was not a sufficiently strong basis, so God is going to make a new one. What kind of a new one does he make?

He says, "I'm going to make this new covenant." There are two features in it that are so important. Number one: individual responsibility. I am no longer going to deal with you in the mass; I am no longer going to deal with you as a nation. I am no longer going to deal with you together even as families. I am no longer going to deal with you as father and son together. I am no longer going to lump you all together and say, "Now you all together obey me or you all together go into exile." I am going to deal with you one by one; I am going to make a new marriage with the house of Judah and Israel but it will be with every single person in it. Each person is responsible for their own sins from now on.

Now this is a revolution. Hitherto, you had become a Jew by being born into a nation, you were circumcised the eighth day, you were in the law, under the law, you were dealt with in your family. If your parent sinned you suffered, your children suffered, and even to the fourth generation. You were all bound together, and when they were taken into exile there were innocent children going to be born into exile who were suffering because of their parents' sins. They would think it was unfair. Now God laid down that the marriage was on this basis: it was the people who ate sour grapes whose own teeth were set on edge.

From now on, individual responsibility is the basis of the marriage. The new covenant is on an individual basis. You are not to be dealt with as families, or as communities, or as nations, but one by one. Christianity is a one by one covenant and that is why we cannot believe in infant baptism because that treats the family as a unit. Do you understand that the new covenant has to have believer's baptism? "Repent and be baptized each one of you for the remission of your sins." Personal responsibility!

Much as I would love to think that God would accept my three children because I and my wife are Christians, I know that in the new covenant it can't be done. It has got to be one by one and baptism is the sign of the new covenant, not the old. Circumcision was the sign of the old so was given to children because they were part of the community. But in the new covenant baptism is given one by one as they repent, believe, and get right with God. That is the first thing in the new covenant. Not my brother, not my sister, Lord, but it is me standing in need. Nobody can do it for you. Even husband and wife can't do it for each other. If your wife is a Christian, husband, you have got to find God or you will be lost. Christian husband, your wife has to find God or she will be lost. Parents, are your children Christians? If they are not, they have to find God or they will be lost. Individual responsibility is a very important principle of the new covenant. You can't blame your parents any more. You can't blame society any more. You can't blame the way you were brought up any more. Each man shall die for his own sins. We live in a society that would love to say, "It's *them* to blame; it is *society* to blame; it is the way I was brought up that is to blame." But God holds every individual responsible for his own actions – nobody else's. We are not living in the old covenant any more, when you can hide in the crowd and be dealt with as a nation.

The second new feature of the new covenant is that it will not only be an individual responsibility to enter it, it will be an *inward* religion and not an outward one. It will no longer depend on externals; it will no longer depend on the things outside you: tablets of stone with the commandments inscribed on them, temples, sacrifices, priests. It will depend on what is happening inside, and that is a big step forward. That inward religion is composed of three "Rs": a *revelation of his purpose within*, writing his law in your heart; a *relationship with his person within* ("They shall all know me from the least to the greatest"), and *remission of his punishment* ("Your sins I will forgive and forget"). Do you see the new covenant?

Until each individual has had his sins forgiven, gets to know God personally, and has God's law written in his heart, he is not in the new covenant even if he comes to church and is in a family where there are Christians. Whether God writes his law upon the wall or on a block of stone, it doesn't change people's hearts. You may write up a rule, "Thou shalt not" – and what happens? I remember a student at Cambridge who wanted to concentrate on swotting for exams so he put up a notice on his door: "Silence. Swotting." Can you guess what the others did? Put a young man in a library full of hundreds of fascinating books, more books than he could ever read in a lifetime, and put in the middle one book on a shelf "Not to be read by anyone under twenty-one," and leave him alone in that library. That is what happens when the law is written outside you. Your heart stays the same and it rebels, "You're not going to tell me what to do. You're not going to make rules and regulations for me...." This is a parent's problem with their children. We have so to bring up our children that we write our laws in their hearts and they want to do it. The trouble is that if you say now, "You've got to be in by ten thirty tonight," if it is only written outside them it doesn't work and relationships are destroyed. But if you can write it in their hearts and they know that they are going to cause anxiety to you if they are not back by ten thirty, and if their heart has the law written in, it is all right, isn't it? God gives you the inward revelation first: I will write my laws on your hearts and you will want to do them.

That will be based on a personal knowledge of God because we need to *know* him. So everybody will know him. It won't just be a few priests and it won't just be a few prophets, but everybody in his people, from the least to the greatest. That is the way God always puts it in scripture. He never says, "From the greatest to the least" – that is how human beings talk. God always says "From the least to the greatest." When Paul was talking to Agrippa he says, "Since the day I saw the heavenly vision I have witnessed to both small and great." Isn't that lovely? That is how God thinks: "From the least to the greatest everyone will know me."

That in turn will be based on something else. You cannot know God personally until you have had your sins forgiven. So once again Hebrew puts it backwards: the law written in your heart based on the knowledge of God personally, based on the forgiveness of sins. We would put it the other way around in our logic so I will put it the other way around: get your sins forgiven, know God personally, and he will write the law in your heart. You see the new covenant? It is an individual responsibility and it is an inward religion, an inward relationship, and that is the new covenant which will put things right.

How did Jeremiah learn of this new covenant? I think I know. He learned it because he had to live it. Shut off from his family, unmarried, scorned by false prophets, opposed by the priests, imprisoned, he probably wrote this chapter while he was in prison. All alone he had to learn that the real relationship with God is not through the community, it is a one to one in the heart. So he could see that what he had had to learn was to stand alone with God with an inward law in his heart telling him he wanted to serve God, knowing God personally and know his sins were forgiven. That is what is needed in the whole nation for every individual within it. So he said: "Behold the days are coming of a new covenant."

The last bit of the covenant is: God will forgive and forget. Which is more wonderful? You will never forgive yourself for what you have done because you can never forget. It is jolly difficult to forgive other people because it is so difficult to forget. But God has a wonderful "forgettery". He has an almighty memory. He can switch his memory off because he is omnipotent. Once he has forgiven a sin he forgets it, and then you can know him and be free to serve him and want to obey his law. That means that one day when you get to God and he looks at you and you say, "Oh God, I remember what I did and I am so sorry about that and sorry I did that," God will just look at us in bewilderment and say, "Did what? I don't remember you doing that." It is a miracle – that God should remember our sins no more.

The final section I can deal with briefly. How long will this new marriage last? The answer is: as long as the universe— that is long enough. As long as the bits of the universe you see are there, so long will the descendants of Israel be there. As long as you can see the sun by day and the moon and stars by night, as long as you can see the oceans – as long as that. If those things go then there will no longer be a nation of Israel. But as long as they are there, a nation called Israel will be there.

Go even further: the things you cannot see. Who can measure the heavens? Well even modern science knows the universe is expanding so fast we cannot get to the end of it. "When you can measure the heavens and when you can explore the heart of the planet Earth then the nation of Israel will cease," says the Lord. Well we are farther off than ever before. No man has been to the centre of the earth in spite of Jules Verne's vivid imagination. No man has been able to measure the universe and so there is still a nation called Israel. That is how long the nation will last. Since every marriage needs home, there will not only be that security as long as the universe – there will be a city.

In an extraordinary prediction Jeremiah says what the extent of the city will be (see vv. 38–40). It will include the valley of Hinnom – that will be cleaned up and be included – but the direction in which it will spread will be West. In Jerusalem they have now passed a law making it a national park, forbidding any further building around the city walls, and turning the valley of Hinnom into a garden, as part of a national park, and Jerusalem will develop to the West. Isn't that extraordinary? Here we are reading words of 2,500 years ago.

I am going to apply it to you now. All this is for the Jews in chapter 31. It is specifically stated for Jacob, for Ephraim in the north, for Judah in the south, for the twelve tribes. So where do we fit in? The answer is: the first part of this chapter and the third part of this chapter, we don't fit in. The return to the land and the rebuilding of the city is for the Jews. I will tell you where we do fit in. We got the new covenant before they did, and that is where we fit in. When the new

covenant came it was given to Jews first and they passed
it on to Gentiles very quickly, and we Gentiles have been
grafted in. Read Romans 9–11. We have been grafted in and
are in the new covenant, enjoying that new relationship with
God. When Jesus died, he made the new covenant possible.

Remember, in a Western order of thinking there are three
steps: forgiveness of sins, knowing God personally, and
writing the law in the heart. The forgiveness of sins and the
forgetting of them came when Jesus shed his blood. The
night before he did so, he said, "This is my blood of the new
covenant". Jesus could see what Jeremiah never did see, that
the new covenant basis was one that Gentiles could perfectly
well fit into, not just Jews. The new covenant's conditions are
not Jewish, and I as a Gentile can enter the new covenant.

Shall I tell you the day that the whole new covenant
was established? Pentecost – when all of them knew God,
when all of them had the law written in their hearts. Read
2 Corinthians 5 and you get the clear statement that in fact
God writes the law in the heart by the Spirit. Then you are
not living by the letter, you are living in the Spirit. The
new covenant began with Calvary and the blood, but it was
completed at Pentecost when the Holy Spirit wrote the law
of God in people's hearts. All 120 of them knew – quite a
mixed bag of men and women, young, old men and women,
they were there at nine o'clock in the morning and the Spirit
was poured out. Peter said: "This is that which has been
spoken of by the prophet Joel, 'I will pour out my Spirit on
all flesh.'" Young men, old men, men, women, maidservants.
It doesn't matter what your class, what your age, what your
sex, you can know God personally and his Spirit can fill
your heart with his knowledge.

Pentecost, the fiftieth day after Passover, was the
celebration of the marriage at Sinai between God and
Israel. God could not have more clearly said that this is

the new marriage; this is the new covenant; this is the new relationship; this is the new basis – I am putting my law within you. But it is a law of liberty, a law of love, the law of the Spirit of God, which sets me free in Christ Jesus. We want to shout "Hallelujah" because of all this. This is the new covenant. If you are not in personal contact with God, and if he is not writing his law in your heart, you do not belong to the new covenant people of God. If you do, if you know that your own personal sins have been forgiven and forgotten, if you are able to say, "I don't need to go to someone who knows God. I can go to him myself – I know him", and if you know that when you face a problem you don't need to look up a book of rules and regulations, you ask him to write his will in your heart and that his Spirit will do so, then you know what Jeremiah was talking about. There was elderly Jeremiah, probably in prison, yet he knew a personal relationship with God. He knew that if only every individual in the nation could have that, the whole nation could be renewed, could live in peace and prosperity, and there could be singing and dancing, wine and oil, and happy faces.

READ JEREMIAH 32–33

These two chapters really do belong together. Let me paint the background for you. One, Jerusalem is shut in; two, Jeremiah is shut in within Jerusalem. Jerusalem is already hemmed in with the Babylonian army. For three years that city is going to be besieged. Food is going to get very short, money is going to inflate, disease is going to be rampant in the dirty streets for they cannot even get rid of their sewage. All the land around the city is gone. All the fields are now under the trampling feet of the Chaldean army from Babylon. Within Jerusalem, Jeremiah has been put into prison and for most of the rest of the book of Jeremiah we see him in a dungeon within the palace, in the court of the guard.

But when God's men are bound, the Word of God is not bound. So many great things have been spoken and written from within prison walls that have gone all around the world. I think of Paul's letter to the Philippians, which came out of jail. He was in chains, "But the Word of God is not bound," he said. I think of people like John Bunyan. Twelve years in prison, but without that we would not have *The Pilgrim's Progress*. I think of that great French lady, Madame Guyon. It was out of her imprisonment that those matchless devotional writings of hers came. I think of Richard Wurmbrand and many others. How much has come out of prison, and Jeremiah is now in prison but here we are 2,500 years later, reading the words that came out of that prison cell. Isn't it exciting?

Now these two chapters are a part of four chapters which

345

have been called "the book of hope". I am afraid most people who don't know the whole of the book of Jeremiah think of him as a man of doom, gloom, pessimism and despair. It is true that much of what he had to say was gloomy because they were in a bad situation, but if his name is used to indicate that a person is a pessimist, Jeremiah is being libelled because he is the man of hope – a prisoner, but a prisoner of hope.

The four chapters 30–33 are full of hope. There is a note of gloom – a note of realism. The city is going to fall as the fields around it have fallen, but the hope shines through. The night is darkest just before the dawn and the darkness of chapters 1–29 is now highlighted by the dawn of a hope that is unmatched: the hope of a new covenant, the hope of Jerusalem becoming a city of praise and joy, giving thanks to the Lord as it was meant to do.

As Jeremiah sat alone in his prison cell he got this inner feeling that his cousin was going to come and try to sell land that no longer belonged to him. In the incident that follows, you have a clear contrast between a man who follows the flesh and a man of faith; how flesh behaves in a crisis and how faith behaves in a crisis. Flesh does a nice little calculation and says, "I've lost my land. The enemy's already occupied it but I still hold the deeds. Could I get some cold hard cash for those, because cash is more valuable than property? I'm going to redeem my property. I'm going to spend it now."

Jeremiah got this sense that his cousin, who was a man of the flesh, would come and try and sell him a useless bit of property because this cousin would rather have cash that he could spend in the last few days in Jerusalem than a property that was already occupied by the enemy. When the cousin actually came to visit him in prison, and carried in his hands the title deeds, Jeremiah knew that God had spoken. Though there was raging inflation and food shortage, Jeremiah spent his money on a field that he would never be able to walk over because he was a man of faith not a man of the flesh, and he invested for the future.

The money might have bought him the desperately needed food he wanted in that prison, because in some Middle East prisons food is not provided. You are dependent on what you can buy or on what your relatives can bring in. So Jeremiah needed what money he had. But according to the land laws of the Bible, if a piece of land was being sold, the relatives of the man who owned it had the first option on the land so that it could be kept in the family. Leviticus 25:25 states the law of property. So you couldn't build up big property development in the Bible days. Property stayed within the family.

The cousin, Hanamel, came to Jeremiah and said, "Would you buy this plot of land? It's a good plot of land; it's really good soil." He thought Jeremiah was dense. Believers are not fools, and Jeremiah was no fool. Jeremiah said, "I'll buy it." Faith is careful, not foolhardy. So he got it all signed, sealed, and delivered legally. He got the two trust deeds buried in a jar and sealed with pitch — that was their equivalent of a safe.

You know how long documents can stay in those conditions – from the discovery of the Dead Sea Scrolls, which had lasted over two thousand years in a jar. Jeremiah took that land because it was an investment in the future and he had faith in the future. The man of the flesh wanted to get cash and spend it at once. The man of faith would buy that land and believe.

In one church where I served there had been a man who died before I got there, a Mr Beason, who owned the local ironmonger's shop. Some forty or fifty years earlier he had said at a church meeting, "I believe we must buy the four houses on this side of the church, the chip shop and the pub, because one day that land will be needed, because God will send revival." Forty years later it was our privilege to build on that land that the man had faith to believe about. It had taken a lot to persuade a church to buy all that property and not use it for forty years, but he was a man not of the flesh but of faith, so he invested in the future. Jeremiah could see ahead, and he knew that one day that plot of land would belong to his family, so he signed and sealed the deed.

A man of flesh can only see the immediate situation and his investment will reflect what he sees. He can only read the financial times; he can only gauge how business is going. He can't see further than that because the flesh can't see very far. Professors of futurology and think tanks come up with opposing forecasts because all they have got to see into the future with is flesh – the resources of the human mind. But men of faith can see further and will behave quite differently, even in their investments in days of crisis.

The second thing I want to mention from chapter 32 is that from redeeming property Jeremiah turns to very realistic prayer. As you first read the prayer that he prayed after he had done this, you get the impression that his faith was very strong. It is a tremendous statement about God's almighty power: "You created the heavens and the earth. You brought Israel out of Egypt. You brought the Babylonian army against Jerusalem. You are almighty, you are all-powerful and you are just. You visit the guilt of the fathers on the children...." It sounds like a tremendous prayer of faith – but when you read between the lines it is not, it is a prayer of doubt. It is a very honest prayer that is battling to hold on to reason because sometimes faith and reason seem to go in opposite directions. Having signed, sealed, and delivered the deeds for that field at Anathoth, Jeremiah had second thoughts. When he was left alone with nothing to eat and no money, he said, "What have I done? ... Hanamel really was right;

I'm a fool." His prayer is desperately trying to persuade himself that it has been right. He says: nothing is too hard for God so God can give me that field one day, but Lord, why did you tell me to buy it? Why did you say that? His faith is questioning and doubting. I praise God for the sheer honesty of the prayers of the Bible. Here is Jeremiah trying to whistle in the dark in that dungeon which must have had no daylight. He got depressed. Yet you told me.... Read between the lines. Jeremiah is battling to keep his reason. Here he is, starving in that dungeon, having spent money on that plot of land.... Lord, I know nothing's too hard for you; I know you created the heavens and the earth; I know you brought Israel out of Egypt; I know you've brought punishment on this city; I know you are in charge of history, but Lord why did you tell me to buy that property? Do you get the feel of it?

Do you ever feel you have been left out on a limb by God? Then I want you to notice that Jeremiah did not share his doubts with Hanamel, nor with the guard or anyone else. He went straight to the Lord with his question. If you are being plagued with questions about some little step of faith you took, if you are wondering whether you did the right thing, do you know the best thing to do about it? Don't talk to anyone else. Go to God and tell him you are a bit shaky, tell him you know nothing is too hard for him – but, Lord, that is a big thing we have taken on. Go to him, the only one who can sort it out, and say to him: "Lord nothing is too hard for you, yet why did you tell us to do that?"

Jeremiah, in an utterly realistic prayer, was saying: Lord I can't see it. Why couldn't he see it? What was he doubting? Some people say he was doubting God's might. I don't think so, because he says, "God, nothing's too hard for you. You made the heavens and the earth. You brought Israel out of Egypt. You can get Jews out of any situation when they are trapped." I think he is questioning God's morality. Let me hasten to explain what I mean. He is saying: God, they don't deserve to have this land back – you visit the guilt of the fathers on the children and they have rebelled against you; they don't deserve it – I don't see how you can do it for them; I don't see how you can remain a just God and give us this land back.

Therefore he brings the question to the Lord. So in vv. 26–44 God repeats all the promises he has made. He confirms that he brought the Babylonians and that he is going to smash the city, and that the people have rebelled and deserve it. God describes all the dreadful things they have done – killing their babies to a pagan god Molech in the valley of Hinnom, which was later to become the valley of Gehenna, the picture of hell. God says, "I've seen on their flat roofs their idols. I've seen them burning incense up there. I've seen it all, Jeremiah, but I am going to marry them again. I am going to make a covenant with them again."

The two key words in a marriage service are "I will." The longest sentence in the English language! God uses it twelve times in the next few verses: "I will gather them"; "I will bring them back"; "I will make them dwell"; "I will be their God; they shall be my people"; "I will give them one heart and one way"; "I will make with them an everlasting covenant"; "I will put the fear of me in their hearts"; "I will rejoice in doing them good"; "I will plant them with all my heart and all my soul." You couldn't have a better marriage service than that. What wonderful words!

God is saying: Jeremiah it's all right; when I say "I will", I mean "I will". When I make a covenant promise and marry my people then I stay with them. It is an everlasting covenant. I will be their God and they will be my people. Jeremiah's heart, which had begun to doubt, leapt again. You can almost sum up the Bible in two phrases: "I Am" says "I will". Let those two little couplets dwell in your mind – they concern who God is and what he does. Jeremiah is told that fields would again be bought and sold. He would be able to dig up that jar. So God repeats his promises. Yes, he will bring evil to them first, but after that he will bring them good – for them and their children.

Applying this message to our situation, the Christian looks forward beyond the future of his own country. He looks forward to a place to which he is going. He so believes in that future that he lays up treasure for himself in heaven with his money. It is true that you can't take it with you, but it is also true that you can send it on in advance. One of the puzzling stories which Jesus told is the parable of the unjust steward in the beginning of Luke 16. Many Christians have said, "I don't understand why Jesus commends a criminal." But if you read the story Jesus commends the criminal because he used his money so that in the future he might have some friends to welcome him. Jesus meant: use your money in the same way, so that one day, when you arrive in heavenly habitations, there will be lots of people to welcome you and say thank you for spending that money – it brought me to the Lord; thank you for investing that in me. That is what Jesus meant by laying up treasure in heaven. Where does your faith lie? Are you a man of the flesh? Are you reading the financial news saying, "Where can I best put my money immediately?" Or are you also a man of faith? Do you have faith in the future of the church? Do you have faith in heaven itself, and are you sending money in advance? My grandfather, who was a minister, whenever he wanted some money would go to people and say, "I've got a great investment for you – investment in the bank of heaven." He once went to the Duke of Devonshire and said it, and he got his investment. But Jesus talks very practically like this. Where your treasure is, there will your heart be also. But likewise, where your heart is, there will your treasure be, and Jeremiah was a man of faith. I will leave you to make the personal application to yourself.

Now let us look very briefly at chapter 33. The last sentence of chapter 32 is the key phrase for chapter 33: "'I will restore their fortunes,' says the LORD." The word "fortunes" here is referring to material prosperity. If there is one thing that the nations are concerned about at the moment it is economic recovery. Chapter 33 is all about economic recovery. God doesn't mean spiritual blessings, he means that he will restore economically. We are going to see in this chapter the rules of economic recovery according to Almighty God. They are very interesting.

God says to Jeremiah: "Just ask me and I'll tell you some secrets about the future. Things that you don't know." What wouldn't people in the stock exchange give to know the exact state of the stock exchange twelve months from now? Here is a tip straight from heaven—that is what the verse means. So Jeremiah is invited to listen to the secrets of economic recovery that he may invest his money wisely as he did in that field at Anathoth. That was a wise investment because God had told him a secret. I believe that if you really want to put your money where it should be, God will give you secrets too. Call upon him. Ask him where you should put it. Ask him to guide your investment. Ask him to handle your affairs. See if he doesn't make known to you things that all the big men in the city would love to know and just don't know. Because, you see, God wants you to be a steward and so he wants to help you with your investment. He wants to guide you. He wants you to put it where it should be. "So call upon me," he says, "and I'll make known to you my secrets." Well now, the secret is: nothing that man can do to defend the situation is of any use. It is only what God does that matters. The mounds that had been put up, trenches that had been dug around Jerusalem to defend it against the onslaught of the enemy – the enemy would just use them as a grave and fill those trenches with dead bodies of Jews. Man cannot defend himself against what is happening. In that city of raging inflation and food shortage God's message means: Jeremiah, the first thing for you to know is that it is what I do that matters, not what man does to defend himself.

But then God says several things. Here is the secret of renewed prosperity (vv. 1–8 and 12–13). Health must come before wealth—that is the first secret. I think most people would agree and they would rather lose their wealth than their health. This begins with common sense. The first thing God says is: I will heal you. He will bring them health. That is the first step to economic recovery, because you can't earn your money unless you are healthy: you are a sick society and you need to be healed.

But now comes the second secret, and this is where the world would not agree with us: spiritual health comes before material wealth. It is not just health before wealth it is spiritual health before material wealth—that is the secret. The world doesn't understand that. The world would agree that health is before wealth, but if we say spiritual health before material wealth the world does not understand.

You see, God goes on to say: Jeremiah, I will heal them by cleansing them from guilt and forgiving their sins and that will lead them to prosperity and security. The message here is that the road to those two things is the road of spiritual health – not just physical health but spiritual health, for society is sick spiritually and that is the root cause. That produces ill health, physically, morally, economically and every other way.

Some years ago, in a time of financial upheaval, somebody was interviewed who was being fully paid to do no work at all. He said, "It's great; it's the dream of everybody. I can do anything I want – marvellous." A man who talks like that is sick. He has lost the image of God because the image of God is of a God who works. "My Father works until now, and now I work," said Jesus.

We are called in the Bible to be workers, "Six days thou shalt labour...." Be like God – work six days a week. It is a sobering thought for those who press for a five and even four-day week. Yes, you need rest, but take the amount of rest that God did: one day a week. So we see one sign of a sick society. The message here is: "I will heal. I'll cleanse your guilt. Let's get the spiritual health right and then material prosperity will flow."

Do you know what will follow from that? There would be resounding praise; the sounds of a happy holy city praising God. You know, in Jerusalem during the siege there was just silence as people looked at the enemy over the walls. Jeremiah is saying that when the prosperity and the security come back, you will hear singing, music, and the voice of the bridegroom and the bride. People will be happy to sing to God and come in gratitude, and give thanks to the Lord – for his steadfast love endures forever. There will be the sounds of joy in the city. Yes we need prosperity and security to sing, to be happy. The Bible is sensible – it faces facts. But it teaches that this is the way to spiritual health, then material prosperity, then a happy city giving thanks to God that God's love has brought it to pass.

Finally, there is one thing lacking. How can God possibly do such a thing? How can he get a nation on the right lines again? The answer is utterly simple. Get the right leader and you are home and dry. So the last part of chapter 33 says that God is going to keep a promise he made, that from the fallen stump, from the cut off stump of the tree of Jesse, from the fallen stump of the royal family there will come a new sprout. Walking in the woods once, I saw such a thing. Somebody had cut an oak tree down. The original trunk was wide, but from one side of the stump there had come a new oak tree which was already about fifteen feet high and becoming a beautiful tree. It was replacing that which had been cut down.

God says, "I will bring a new shoot from the root of David, a righteous king who will deal justly with the people." That is what is needed. If I talk about the opposite it will bring it home to you. The opposite of righteous government is corrupt government. How many lands in this world of ours have corrupt government at this moment? Corrupt in all kinds of ways – but God can put the whole thing straight if there is a righteous man at the top of the nation. So he is going to restore a son of David who will give righteousness to the government, who will straighten out the thing and cut out corruption. Whenever there is a shortage of food and raging inflation, you get a black market, you get corruption, you get all kinds of things, and it was all happening in Jerusalem.

Jeremiah sees in the future a new king of the line of David. This would not only be the right political leader but the right religious leader too. The priesthood of Levi would be restored. Levi was meant to produce priests unto God. What a nation needs to get right is good government and real religion. So this chapter finishes with a vision of new leadership in both areas. It is an exciting vision and God made a promise that David would never lack a man to sit on the throne of Israel, and the Levitical priesthood would never lack a man to offer offerings. Let us pause and look at God's promise: if you can stop the day and the night coming then you can stop this happening. I made a covenant with day and night that day would follow night and day would follow night and it always does. If you could stop that then you can stop me sending David the king back. What a statement. Why does he dare to say it? Because God is Creator as well as Redeemer and therefore he can draw from nature his own arguments. You see the stars. You see the heaven and earth. I have set the earth in space and I have set the heavens in space. If you can reorder the planets then you can stop me sending David and Levi back. What an argument!

They are hoping to land just a tiny bit of scrap metal on Mars. God says: if you can shift Mars out of orbit then you can stop me fulfilling my word. Doesn't our little bit of machinery look puny beside the God who put Mars into orbit? God says: as certainly as day follows night, as certainly as I made my laws for space, the heavenly bodies, and planet Earth, as certainly as that I will bring back David and Levi.

We know and we rejoice that David and Levi came back in one man, and the name was Jesus. Born in royal David's city of the line of David, with the legal right to the throne, and with the physical right to the throne through his mother, came the Son of David, the King, who was yet a priest unto God the Father to offer him his own life. But there is a little bit of a gap between the prediction and the fulfilment here. God says to Jeremiah, "As many as the stars, and as many as the sand on the seashore, will be the descendants of David on the throne, and the priests of Levi." Yet this was fulfilled in one man. There is a gap – how do we close the gap? Very simply: we are the fulfilment, or at least part of the fulfilment. Does that excite you? In Christ we are going to be more than the stars, more than the sand, a multitude that no man can number. No wonder we can lift up our heads. They may lock us in prison, but our hearts are not bound. There are many Christians now who are in prison cells because they dare to believe that they are prisoners of hope. If they had money they would invest it in heaven because their faith is so sure of the future. When the outlook is bad, try looking up. From that prison cell in which all may appear to be so black, in which the flesh says, "It's hopeless; it's all over; disaster is so near; the city is besieged; everything is going to be lost" – in that situation you look up.

In the last book in the Bible, another book that came out of a prison cell, we read that John was in Patmos. He was in prison on an island, banished from his churches, and he looked up and he saw a door opened into heaven and went through it. He came back into his prison cell with hope – a prisoner of hope.

Jeremiah, with all his doubts, put his money in a field because he believed that the fortunes of his nation would be restored by God to the praise of God's name.

READ JEREMIAH 34–35

From chapter 34 onwards we have a series of narratives – events from Jeremiah's life. At first sight it looks as if someone has gone round interviewing his friends and just put in a big bag everything he could pick up about Jeremiah's life and jumbled them all together. There is no chronological order. For example, the events in chapter 35 occurred seventeen years before those recorded in chapter 34.

Those who study Jeremiah expecting to find a straight biography get very confused. The order of events is not chronological but logical. The events are very carefully chosen and edited to highlight themes and topics. As it happens, most of the chapters we have in our divided Bible go in pairs and that is why I am now taking pairs of chapters – because they belong together and are on the same theme.

The theme of chapter 34 is disobedience to God's command. The theme from chapter 35 relating to an earlier time is the theme of obedience to man's command. The lesson we are going to draw is that there is an extraordinary quirk in our human nature which is more ready to obey human custom than divine commandment. So we come under the tyranny of tradition instead of the liberty of truth. We come under the power of precedent instead of the power of the Holy Spirit. It is a weakness in all of us and we are going to see the contrast drawn out in these two chapters, but the theme is that unmentionable four-letter word: *obey*.

There are two stages in forming a relationship with

JEREMIAH

someone. The first is to know about them; to hear about
them, to find out their name, where they live, what they do
and all sorts of details like that. You may hear about things
they have done and said and have some idea about their
character. Then comes the moment when you step into their
life and they step into yours. You not only know that *about*
them, but you know them.

Both stages are essential to knowing God, too. One of the
important reasons for studying events that happened a little
under 2500 years ago is that this is about God and what he
said and how he felt and how he reacted. It is to help you to
know about him – that is the whole purpose of reading the
Bible. That is why it makes you wise to salvation, because
you know about God. But if you don't take the next step
and then step into God's life or have him step into yours,
then you will know more and more *about* God but you will
never get to know him. It is one thing to study about what
happened to Jeremiah, long before Christ came to this Earth.
It is another thing to take what God said to him and apply it
to yourself and say, "God you are the same today, therefore,
what you said to him you are saying to me and I want to be
involved in this thing."

Let us get right into the particular time and place in
which God said these words. The historical background
is important and, although history can be boring, I am so
thrilled that the Bible, alone among all the scriptures around
the world, is a book of history. It is a book which ties God
down to the particular. That has been called the "scandal of
particularity". All other religious books are not tied down
to real life. They are platitudes, clichés and jargon, and they
state philosophical ideals, whereas this book says that, at
such and such a time and such and such a place, God said
and God did – and that is fact. I can take that fact and then
apply it to my situation because I live in a time and place;

I don't want vague generalities, I want something specific that God will say to me now, here – the God who spoke to Jeremiah then. So let us now see what he said.

Sadly, chapter 34 is one of disobedience to God. But let me first paint the scene very quickly. It is the last days of Jerusalem; the very final weeks have come. Jerusalem, that tiny city, just a few acres, is totally surrounded by a gigantic Chaldean army whose capital city is Babylon, hundreds of miles across the desert to the east. Jerusalem is under siege; inflation is rocketing. Food and even water are scarce. The people are hungry, thirsty and poor, though there is a black market and a few are getting rich.

Most of the land is now in enemy hands. Just three cities are left: Jerusalem, Lachish, which was rather bigger – it was about eighteen acres altogether – and a third town, Azahar. It looked as if everything was finished. The people from the country round about, if they could run into the city, got inside the walls, so the place was crowded with all kinds of people. One man walked those streets, talking to the people from the highest places in society to the lowest, talking to the King one day and a slave the next; talking to those who came in from their caravans and tents to escape the Chaldean army and its cruelties.

So in that thronged, crowded, mixed city Jeremiah speaks and listens to people. But as he listens to people he listens to God, and he has a word for each person he speaks to. That is the background. At one point it looked as if Jeremiah's predictions were going to prove false. Jeremiah had said, "The city will fall, the city will be burned, everybody will be taken away to Babylon." He said it again and again. Therefore, he said, by far the best policy is surrender now, make terms – at least you will live, but if you fight it out you will die. He was therefore regarded as a traitor.

Morale was going down because of Jeremiah, and his

name was going down in history as one of those who lower morale by being pessimistic and looking on the gloomy side. "We've got a Jeremiah in our midst," people say, meaning somebody who says, "It's no use fighting, the tide of history is against us."

At one point it looked as if he might be wrong because the Egyptian army, from the west, marched against the Chaldeans. To meet this threat the Chaldeans withdrew their army from Jerusalem and went off to meet the Egyptians. Immediately, people said, "Jeremiah you're wrong. Jeremiah we're free, they've gone."

Jeremiah said, "They'll be back," and within almost a matter of weeks they were back. Something happened during that brief respite which is the subject of chapter 34. During that little lifting of the blockade something showed what was wrong with the whole nation of Israel. It was like a flash of lightning that lit up the corruption and the character of this little nation, and Jeremiah spotted it by the power of the Spirit of God, and that is what we are going to look at.

I have pointed out that Jeremiah was in touch with everyone from the top to the bottom. In the first eight verses or so of chapter 34, Jeremiah speaks to the king and says: "You will be captive, yet you will be free." The very next day he spoke to some slaves, and of them he said, "You were free, but you are now captive." What did he mean by these two statements? Let us look at the first. It was a very strange relationship between Zedekiah and Jeremiah. I want to try to paint it for you because this kind of relationship exists in many places today. Zedekiah was the professional politician who was a man of pure expediency. You could never pin him down to a principle or tell what he was really wanting to do, whereas Jeremiah was a man of principle who always knew exactly where he stood and said it, and people knew what he stood for, whether they liked it or not. Here we have the professional politician whose only principle was to stay in power and you have the powerful preacher whose principle was that there is a difference between right and wrong. Between two men like that there is a strange relationship. Zedekiah would never have been king at all if it had not been for Babylon. When they came the first time and took away all the aristocracy and even the skilled craftsmen, leaving just a handful of poor, illiterate, unskilled people in the city, they took a nobody called Zedekiah and said: you can be king and look after that poor lot for us. So Babylon put him on the throne and therefore he owed his position to Babylon. Yet as soon as he got that position he was scheming how to get free of Babylon's yoke and be the king of an independent nation and not a satellite of the Babylonian empire. He turned to Egypt and played that nation off against Babylon. So this little upstart puppet king, a nobody who had become a somebody, was determined to stay in power and to get more power by playing off the great powers against one another. It is a strangely modern situation.

His attitude toward Jeremiah was a mixed one as it was bound to be because he was a double-minded man anyway. It was a mixture of fear and fascination. He feared Jeremiah because Jeremiah kept saying, "You'll be taken captive Zedekiah, your city will be burned." He feared Jeremiah because he lowered morale. He approved when Jeremiah was put in prison, yet on the other hand he was fascinated by this man of principle. On four separate occasions he said, "Jeremiah will you tell me, really are we going to win or are we going to lose?" On two occasions Zedekiah saved Jeremiah's life.

Between the politician and the preacher, so often there is a kind of fear and a fascination. Preachers are a nuisance to politicians, yet there is a kind of fascination when a man gets up and says, "This is the truth." You can't ignore that, and part of you wants to know if what he says is right. So Zedekiah and Jeremiah met frequently – sometimes in prison, sometimes out of it – and one day Jeremiah realised something quite profound as he looked into Zedekiah's face. He saw fear. He realised that the reason why Zedekiah was holding out desperately against all odds and why he would not surrender, was the fear that, if he surrendered, everybody else in Jerusalem would live but he would die. Jeremiah saw that fear in a flash. He was given the gift of discernment by the Spirit of God and he realised that this was the one thing holding Zedekiah back from surrendering – he knew that in those days when a nation surrendered the people were safe but the king was put to death. That was at the root of his policy.

So Jeremiah said, "Lord, what do I tell this man?"

God said, "Jeremiah, you go and tell him he will be taken captive but he will die in peace. There will be a royal funeral for him away there in Babylon and they will burn incense and they will say, 'Our king is dead so he doesn't need to worry about this.'" Jeremiah went to see the king and he said, "Your fear is groundless; surrender." But Zedekiah did not take any notice and he went on fighting. The result was that Jeremiah's prediction became absolutely true. Zedekiah was not killed, he was taken captive to Babylon and he did die peacefully. But—but because he did not take Jeremiah's advice when it was given, do you know what happened to him? Nebuchadnezzar gouged his eyes out. He lived, but as a blind man – and he died a blind man. So God's word comes true in detail and yet a man is still free to refuse it. The tragedy is that what God says will come true but it will be worse. Whereas if a man accepts his advice it will come true and it will be better. The very next day after seeing the king, Jeremiah was walking through the streets and he met a bunch of slaves: Jews. He said, "Are you slaves?"

"Yes."

"How long have you been slaves?"

One man said, "Ten years."

Another man said, "Fifteen years."

Another man said, "I've been a slave since I was a boy."

Jeremiah said, "Who's your master? Is it a Gentile?"

"No, we have Jewish masters."

Jeremiah made some inquiries. Let me tell you about God's law for slavery because it is not slavery as we know it. I wish we could use a different term for slavery in the Bible because this is what God said: a man can sell himself. Notice that it is a voluntary action. He can sell himself for a limited period if he needs the money. We would call it a contract. He can sell himself for six years only and then in the seventh year he had to be released because there must be no slaves in Israel. So it was a six-year contract and it was a way of settling your debts if you were desperately poor and you hadn't got money. You went to someone and signed a contract for six years, and do you know what they did to show you were under contract? They pierced the lobe of your ear with a bridle. But you knew that in the seventh year you would be a free man again; your debts would have been paid and you could make a fresh start. It was a humane provision of God's law; it was not slavery as we know it.

But because of inflation, more and more people in Jerusalem had been selling themselves, contracting themselves, and the few black marketeers who were making the cash in that situation were amassing slaves. A slave was worth twenty or thirty shekels of silver. That is what Judas sold our Lord for – the price of a slave. Because of the financial pressures, what was happening was that those Jewish masters were not releasing the slaves after six years. They were keeping them on indefinitely. The situation allowed them to exploit slave labour.

Then came that siege, and as it got worse and worse, King Zedekiah for the first time began to think, "I wonder if we've upset God." It is incredible but he began to think that. Prophet after prophet – Isaiah, Micah – all said: It's God who is doing this to you because you are not obeying him. Finally, something clicked in Zedekiah's brain and he thought, "I think God is upset ... what have we done to upset him?" As if he didn't know! He could have asked Jeremiah, and Jeremiah could have given him the whole works. But Zedekiah thought it out himself and said, "I think I know what it is. We haven't been releasing slaves in the seventh year." That was all he could think of.

So Zedekiah called together all the wealthy businessmen, those who had been making a packet in that besieged city, and he said, "Brothers, I think we have been upsetting God. You haven't been releasing your slaves in the seventh year, have you?"

And they said, "No, we haven't."

"Right," he said, "Into the Temple", and there they swore before the Lord God that they would release their slaves, and release them they did. So at least the siege did some good for someone and the slaves were released.

It was only days after that the Egyptian army marched and the Chaldeans were taken away from Jerusalem to meet this new threat, that the siege was lifted and the blockade went. Why didn't Zedekiah learn his lesson? Why didn't he realise that the first little step of obedience toward God was bringing more liberty? I must now tell you what happened as soon as the blockade was lifted. As soon as it was lifted, the masters forced the slaves back into slavery again—it is all there in chapter 34. As soon as the crisis was over they went right back to where they were. They said, "It's fine, it's over now. Crisis over; danger averted; we can go back to our old life."

Herein lies the message of chapter 34. Deathbed repentance, as you know, is tested as the person recovers. All of us can change in a crisis. The real test is whether we remain changed when the crisis is over. This chapter is so true to human nature. When you are under pressure you make resolution after resolution. Look how we fought during the Second World War – look how we fought to make a world fit for heroes to live in. Look how we resolved to end all wars.

It is your nature and it is my nature, and Zedekiah went back, and the masters went back, and the slaves went back into slavery, and Jeremiah came thundering the word of God to Zedekiah: What do you think you are doing? As soon as the crisis is on you'll obey God, and as soon as it's over you'll disobey again. You haven't changed one little bit. Therefore I tell you that my word still stands; the Chaldeans will be back. Back they came.

I think again of a man I went to visit once in the hospital. He was seriously ill. He had been in the forces and he said, "Padre, if I get out of this, if I get back to my wife, I'll be in your church every Sunday." He got better and we didn't see him. About fifteen months later in that very same place, there he was in hospital again with the same trouble, seriously ill. Again he said to me, "If I can just get out of this I am going to live right." Again he got better and we saw no more of him and I have never seen that man since. I wonder if God will ever give him another chance. How true to human nature.

Now what was going wrong? Because the man at the top was a man of expediency, everyone else down the line was a man of expediency. To repent when there is a crisis is expediency. To put it another way, if honesty is the best policy it is not honesty. Honesty is only honesty when it is the worst policy. Do you understand this? It is not what we do under pressure but what we do when we are not under pressure that is the test of what we really are.

JEREMIAH

Chapter 34 reveals this: like sovereign, like people. So Jeremiah told him about the slaves. If the people at the top are people of pure expediency and keep shifting, and their only principle is to stay in power and get more power, then that will filter right the way down. The tragedy is that the people at the bottom get exploited. They become the slaves. That is what is happening to our society. Isn't this relevant? It is like reading the newspapers and it all happened during the siege of Jerusalem nearly four hundred years before Christ.

Jeremiah accuses them of two things: perfidy and perjury. Perfidy is treachery against man; it is to break your promise. He said, "You've set those slaves free. You have promised them their freedom and now you have taken them back again. But worse than that, you have promised them their freedom in the name of God. You took an oath on the name of the Lord and now you are polluting [that's the literal word he uses] the name of God."

There is the social conscience of the prophets. They combined relationships with God and relationships with man in such a way that what you do to your fellow men is polluting the name of God. Those two things belong together – perfidy and perjury are the same sin in God's sight. These are very strong words. He is saying: because of the top you are men of expediency; all the way down you are men of expediency; people changing their policy not according to principles but according to practicality. So we get the politician and the preacher. The politician says to the preacher, "You are impractical." The preacher says to the politician, "You are unprincipled." Somehow we have got to get together the principled and the practice, if you are going to have a healthy nation that God can bless.

Now let me move on quickly to chapter 35. Bear in mind that it was seventeen years earlier, it is a brilliant piece of editing and it was done by a man we shall be meeting later.

He was a stenographer or secretary. He edited this and he did a brilliant job because he goes back in time seventeen years to a different situation, a different reign. But he remembers an event which stands in stark contrast to this later act of disobedience regarding the slaves – this expediency. He goes back to an event when Jeremiah tried to make some total abstainers drink.

It concerns a group of people called Rechabites. Now when I was a boy there was still a a temperance society by that name. The ancient Rechabites were a wandering tribe, and they wandered around the Sinai desert. Incidentally, I am sure that you know the word *gypsy* means Egyptian. That is where they came from, and the Rechabites were very much like wandering gypsies. They travelled around the Sinai Peninsula and they lived in tents. They lived a very simple life; they never grew anything – they had animals. The nearest group today are the Bedouin. If you have ever seen a Bedouin encampment, you have seen the Rechabites. Only their original name was not Rechabite, it was Kenite. Moses married a Kenite girl and so this tribe became related to the people of God. They decided to go along with the people of God and they tagged along forty years through the wilderness, and they decided to go into the Promised Land with the Hebrews. They went in literally with the Jews because that name means someone from the tribe of Judah and they went in with Judah. The difference was that when they went into the Promised Land the Kenites said, "We are going to stay in tents, that is our way of life. We'll move around. You will see us outside the city in the hills. You can live in the cities but we'll stay out in the countryside."

So they literally remained gypsies but they were so much part of the people of God now that they worshipped the God of Israel and for all practical purposes they were a part of the people. They were the strangers within the gates. Now among the Kenites there was born a man called Rechab. He had a son called Jonadab, so they called him Jonadab ben Rechab. That is the man we have to think about for a moment. He was born in a day when the cities were getting more and more and more corrupt. He saw Israel going down and down, morally and spiritually. Finally, he felt he had to do something about it and he led a very strong protest movement with a Jewish friend called Jehu, and together they cleaned up the nation in the time of Ahab, the king who had brought the corruption in. Rechab, or Jonadab ben Rechab, cleaned the nation up for a time.

Jonadab said, "Now we've got to keep it that way, how are we going to do that?" He got his own family together and said: "Now look, I want you to remain as a perpetual reminder of the pure life of the countryside. Therefore, I charge you solemnly: never build a house but go on living in a tent. Never plant a garden, but go on living off the milk of your goats and your camels. Never plant a vineyard, and therefore never touch wine." He had seen that part of the corruption of the city was alcoholism, which was rife, and which, alas, was associated with religious ceremonies, as later the Greek god Bacchus was.

Because of this, in that situation where wine was being so abused, he said, "You remain as total abstainers as a testimony to the others not to abuse wine." He was not advocating total abstinence for everybody, but that providing there was a group of people within the nation who would be total abstainers, that would hold the rest back. It would be a reminder to them of temperance. So he charged his descendants to do this. From that day, not one of his sons, grandsons or great-grandsons, right down the line, would touch wine. They became a byword for that more than anything else – not so much that they lived in tents but that they were total abstainers from alcohol.

Now when Jeremiah was walking through the streets of that besieged city he came across a tent in the street. Inside were some people and he asked them, "Who are you?" They said, "We're Rechabites." He could see that in the heat of that city and given the shortage of water – for Jerusalem was fed by just one spring – they were thirsty. The Lord suddenly told him to do something, an extraordinary thing. He said, "Will you come with me into the Temple?" He took them into the Temple where there were crowds of people gathered for worship, and then he said, "Now you are thirsty aren't you?"

They said, "Yes we are, everybody is."

"Right," he said, "I've got some lovely cool wine here for you. There you are." He poured out lovely cool wine and he handed them each some wine and they said, "We don't drink. Our father Rechab said no drink." Do you know that this was two hundred years after Rechab had said it? For two hundred years father had told son, "Don't drink." Son had told grandson, "Don't drink." Grandson had told great-grandson, "Don't drink." For all these two hundred years they hadn't touched the stuff and now, though they were thirsty and besieged, they would rather die than drink.

Jeremiah went out to the people and told the crowd that he had not been trying to break their vows, their pledge. He wanted them to see what obedience is. Those men had been prepared to obey a man after two hundred years, and the crowd were not prepared to obey a God who was speaking at that time. What a lesson! I hardly need to draw it out. The Rechabites had taken what was a relative law and made it absolute. By that I mean that Rechab gave it in a particular situation to a particular people for a particular purpose. He was not laying down a biblical law, for the Bible nowhere lays total abstinence down as a law for either Jew or Christian. But Rechab was giving a relative law of man and God did not tell them to do it. God did not order Rechab.

It was a human response to a situation and yet it had been obeyed for two hundred years. Jeremiah then tells them: this little group kept this human custom for two hundred years, and you can't even keep a divine commandment from today until tomorrow. Learn the lesson, because human laws like Rechab are relative. Alas, they so easily become absolute, whereas the divine laws are absolute and you make them relative. When God said, "You shall set a man free in the seventh year," that applied to all time. But the people made it relative depending on whether they were going through a crisis or not.

Here is a profound lesson for us. How prone we are to take human customs, which are relative, and make them absolute, and take divine commands, which are absolute, and make them relative. We are keener to obey the human custom than the divine commandment. How very strange it is. Let me give you one or two examples to bring the thing home to you. I believe the majority of babies are christened in this country because it is human custom. Well my parents did it for me and their parents did it for them and after all, you've got to do the right thing for your baby – and isn't that the right thing to do? We must have a christening shawl and a mug, and how much human custom there is in that. I really do believe that the majority of the parents do it by human custom. But what is the divine command? It is: "Repent and be baptized, every one of you, for the forgiveness of your sins." A baby hasn't sins to forgive. "You shall receive the gift of the Holy Spirit, for the promise is to you and your children and to those who afar off, as many as the Lord calls." Pray God he will call your children and that he will call many who are far off.

Take another example. It is amazing what attention is given to human custom at weddings. "We must have this and we must have that. Couldn't do without confetti, couldn't do without a cake, couldn't do without a best man or a bridesmaid, couldn't do without a toast," and so it goes on, and down it goes through the centuries. Most of these things are superstition. I bet most people don't even know why you throw confetti. Do you know why a bridegroom carries his bride over the doorstep? Because the little demons from her old home are running on the ground and they will catch her feet and drag her back. So he lifts her up above the demons and carries her into the home! What is the divine part of the wedding ceremony? "Till death us do part." I wish couples were more concerned to keep those words than to have confetti and a white wedding and all the rest of it.

It happens in churches. There is a Baptist way of doing things and it is only a custom and it has come down from the year dot and so we do it this way. We may be more concerned about our constitution than about the commandments of God. "Where the Spirit of the Lord is, there is liberty." So we have our customs and they bind us more than the divine commandment does. By both contrast and comparison, the message here is: "If worldly people outside the people of God will obey their human customs so faithfully, isn't it incredible when God's people will not obey the divine commands?

So Jeremiah drew a lesson. Let me take the particular issue as an illustration. You see, it is so much easier to do things by custom; you have no decisions to make. It is safer – it leaves you free outside the area of the custom. The Rechabites had not been told anything about living in cities. They had been told to live in tents, so they moved their tents into the city and they had gone right against the spirit of Rechab. But you see, when you have a law outside it there is freedom to do what you like. It is easy to have these guidelines. I tell you, it is ten times easier to sign the pledge and become a total abstainer than every time you find yourself in a situation to say, "God, what do you want me to do in this situation?"

I attended a Sunday school where a dear Sunday school teacher told me again and again he wanted me to sign the pledge and sign the pledge (to abstain from alcohol). There is nothing in the Bible about signing pledges. There is the freedom in the Bible to say I will not drink wine and by doing so cause my brother to stumble. It is a relative not an absolute, and when we start making it a rule for life it is the easy way out – to say, "I don't touch it." No more decisions to make about that, then, for the rest of your life. Christians are free to drink and free not to. That is real freedom because you are free for others. So the more difficult way is for me to say to God not, "Do you want me to make one decision now for the rest of my life?" but, "God, I am listening. Master, speak."

You see, one is a relationship with a book and the other is a relationship with a person. One is a matter of living by regulations and the other is a matter of living by relationship. One is a matter of tradition; the other is a matter of truth. The Rechabites lived by the tradition of total abstinence but it shows how much God values obedience that his message to them was that even though they were obeying a man-made custom, which was not his commandment, he promised that there would always be a Rechabite before him. He must have been thrilled to find some in his city who knew what it felt like to be obedient.

Obedience to divine commandments is a million times better than obedience to human customs. Lord, what do *you* say? We take our lead from Jeremiah who was walking around the streets, calling in at the palace, trying to remove the fears of a king, talking to slaves who are resentful and bitter, meeting a few gypsies in a tent. Every situation he meets he sees with God's eyes. He listens to God, and he speaks for God, and we learn that the most important thing on earth is that God's will shall be done as it is in heaven.

READ JEREMIAH 36 and 45

While I was at Cambridge they built a new library for the University with eighteen miles of bookshelves! Before I left, their shelves were half full. Every book that is published in Britain, as you may know, has to go to Cambridge and Oxford libraries to be kept for reference, and of the making of books there is no end. There is only one book really and it is the Bible. If a man does not read this book he is not wise. He may be very clever, he may be very knowledgeable, but he is not wise. The Bible is the only book there is that makes one wise – in the most important area in your life, namely wise in salvation.

It is a miracle in itself written by forty different authors in at least three different languages over at least fourteen hundred years, and not one of them knew they were writing the Bible, yet here it is. Its theme is the same from beginning to end; it hangs together with a marvellous unity. It is such a straightforward book that a simple child can read it and get something from it. It is such a profound book that the greatest intellect in the world can spend a lifetime studying it and still say at the end: I have not plumbed its depths, I am still in the shallows as far as this book goes. It is a timeless book and it is the most timely book that was ever written. It is more lasting and permanent than anything else you can see. "Heaven and earth will pass away" – but these words will not, for this is the truth of God and God is everlasting and his Word is everlasting. I am so thankful that God speaks.

Idols are dumb, but God is not. Idols cannot talk but God talks. Idols cannot write, but God writes. Now there are times when God speaks without any human aid whatever. He causes the air to vibrate so that words are heard by the human ear. Think of Jesus' baptism in the river Jordan. The heavens shook and people thought it was thundering, but the words came: "You are my beloved son and I am so pleased with you."

There are times when God does his own writing. It was with his own finger that he wrote the Ten Commandments on the tablets of stone in Moses' presence. It was with his own finger that at Belshazzer's feast he wrote on the wall *Mene, Mene, Tekel u-Pharsin*. So God can talk and write without human help, but praise God that the way he wants to work usually is with human co-operation, to use co-workers to be his mouth to speak and his hand to write. That is how we got our Bible because there were men who were willing to see that it got written down, and the Bible is the record of hundreds of years of God's conversations with men.

Isaiah wrote down what he said, and so did Amos. Others' words were also taken down and written up by the schools of the prophets, and here we have the results. Do you realise that if they had not written them down we would not have known what Jeremiah said? I know that in those days memory was good when writing was a little known art, except among those who had had a special education. Memory passed down folklore and sayings very accurately in any period, but God wanted something even more reliable than memory.

The Chinese have a proverb that the weakest ink is stronger than the strongest memory. I have learned that in my daily life as I guess you have. Make a list and then you won't forget. Now the circumstances in which the spoken word became the written word in Jeremiah's life are very interesting. Before I describe them for you, let me contrast the spoken word and the written word. Both have advantages and disadvantages. The spoken word is usually more immediately effective than the written. It has greater impact; it comes with tone of voice. It comes through the personality; black and white print does not. You don't get the feel of a person when reading from text but you do when you listen to his voice. You know how he feels when he is speaking. So the spoken word has immediate impact. That is why God so often uses the spoken word to achieve miracles. He caused this world to come to be with a spoken word. He said "Let there be" and there was. He just had to say it and it was as good as done. So his spoken word is powerful and that is why preaching the Word of God will never be out of date. Announcing the good news person-to-person is God's way of achieving miracles of new birth and new lives.

Having said that, God also wanted us to have his written Word because there are disadvantages to the spoken word. One is that as soon as it has been spoken, it is finished. You can't take it all home. Those who hear me preach in person probably take home about two or three percent of what I say. That doesn't worry me a bit. The preacher is there to let God speak to you at some point. If he says just one sentence to you that you take home, it has been worth it. That is why I put a lot of different thoughts into one sermon – not to cram each hearer's head, but so that a greater variety of different people can get one thing to take home. The rest of the spoken word is quickly forgotten. Like a river in the Negev, it filters away into the dry sand.

There are other disadvantages to the spoken word. One is that you can only get a little bit at a time, whereas when it is printed and written you can get the thing as a whole. You can read it right through and then go back and read parts of it again. You don't just get the little fragments that keep coming in the existential moment.

God knew all this and so he caused his Word to be written, and then people would get it whole. Then they have all of what he has said to mankind, so they don't get it in fragments. Even if they forget it, they can then go and read it and recall it and refresh their minds. God knew that if he relied on the spoken word then he relied on the presence of the man, and anything could happen to that man. If you are not where he happens to be speaking you will not hear. If the person is ill or dies then the message stops, but if it is written down then these handicaps are overcome. The book can go where the messenger can't. The message will spread, going where the man can never go. Here we are, reading the book of Jeremiah. Why? Because somebody wrote it down. The written word becomes God's spoken Word to us and God goes on speaking through the words he said, because it was written.

In our day, praise God, inventions are coming which are enabling us to encapsulate the Word of God even more effectively. Gutenberg invented movable print so that the Bible could be spread more quickly and more cheaply and more easily. Since we have had printing, the Word of God has gone to places no missionary had been to, and churches have sprung up without a single preacher because they have had the written Word. A man in a New York subway car was a pickpocket and he put his hand in somebody's pocket, felt some leather and thought it was a fat wallet full of notes. He pulled it out, got off the subway, dashed around the corner and looked at it – and it was a New Testament. He was about to throw it away but took it home and decided to read it. That man became one of the most prominent preachers in the United States. His life was transformed.

In the twentieth century came cassette tapes. I praise God for that invention because it has the best of both worlds. It is not only in permanent form so that you have got the whole so that you can refer to it; not only can it go where man cannot; it not only survives a man's illness or death, but it enshrines the impact of the spoken word. We praise God for that invention which brought together the spoken and the written Word in a most effective form. That invention, of course, has been followed by digital recording on other media.

Jeremiah chapter 36 describes how his words came first to be written. The circumstances were these: the year was 604 BC. Little Israel was in the middle of the world, the crossroads of the continents of Africa, Asia and Europe. I have pointed out before that if you live in the crossroads you will get run over again and again – and they have been. Israel was trapped between two powers, east and west: Egypt and Babylon. As with so many little nations, they were wondering which one to back, which one to play off against the other, and King Jehoiakim put his money on Egypt, thinking it would be the biggest power in the world, and so wanting to be friends with them. He was mistaken. In 604 BC there was an almighty battle between these two big powers, which was decisively settled on the banks of the Euphrates at a place called Carchemish. At that battle the Egyptians were routed.

Israel found herself trapped in her own political intrigue in the realm of foreign policy. Babylon was to the northeast, they had to come around the river from the Fertile Crescent, so they would enter Israel from the north. Jeremiah had been saying for years that a great power would come from the north and trample right through the land – as the Bible says will happen again one day.

Now Jeremiah began to say who the power would be: Babylon. All his predictions of twenty-one years were now coming true. Jeremiah realised, as others did, that the battle of Carchemish in 604 BC was the beginning of the end. They realised this was the end of Israel, or what was left of it. There were only two tribes left, under the name of

Judah. The second was Benjamin. A little pocket of Israel was left and Jeremiah knew that Babylon was coming and that it was all over.

He did not know then that he would be the only man (or one of the only two men) who would be left free, but he was concerned about the Word of God. This is how his mind worked. He remembered how, not long before, when he predicted that the land would be taken, he had gone to a lawyer's clerk called Baruch. He said to him, "Will you arrange for me to buy a field in my native village Anathoth from my relative? He wants to sell and get the cash." So he had said to Baruch, "Will you arrange the title deeds and then will you take the two deeds – the two copies – and then will you put them in a jar and seal it and bury it so that it is safe? So that one day my descendants can come and claim those title deeds when Israel gets the land back." That clerk duly saw the sale of the land through and buried the title deeds. Jeremiah thought of Baruch again and God said, "Go and use him again and this time write down all that I have said through you and get him to look after that too." So off he went to Baruch and he said: I have another job for you. It's going to take a little longer, this one. I want you to write down everything I have said over the last twenty-one years for this one.

You can imagine Baruch's eyes. For one thing there is a miracle of memory involved here. How will Jeremiah be able to remember what he said? I can hardly remember what I said last Sunday! How could Jeremiah remember everything he had said over twenty-one years? Well, it would not be a question of God having to repeat himself. It would be a question of the Holy Spirit releasing memory. One of the things now known is that you remember everything you have said, everything you have done, and everything you have ever felt and thought. Did you know that? I think that you must know from time to time memories are stirred by a circumstance – memories which you have not thought about in twenty-five years. I visited my home town where I was born and bred. The first thing I saw when I got there was a barrage balloon and parachuters were jumping from it. My stomach turned because I was a boy during the Battle of Britain, crouching in an Anderson shelter, listening to the crack of shells and the thump of bombs, and that barrage balloon brought back feelings that I had not had in years. I knew then that I had not forgotten, I had just been able to recall. The Holy Spirit can release memories. This is what happened to Jeremiah, and a miracle of recalling came. Do you remember that, on the last night before he died, Jesus said to his disciples, "Now I have told you a whole lot of things but it's alright you will remember them, the Holy Spirit will bring them to remembrance" – they would be able to speak them out, write them down and share them. That is how we got our New Testament. The Holy Spirit recalls a memory, releases the things that are there, locked up in that filing cabinet, pulls the drawer out and gives you the thing that you need. That is how you are able to use the sword of the Spirit, which is the Word of God. That does not mean the Bible, that means a recalled Word of God which you pull out, by the Spirit, to use. Jeremiah was to dictate, and this he did. It was the last despairing effort to reach the conscience of his countrymen. He had preached and preached and they had taken no notice for twenty-one years. If Jeremiah wrote it all down and they got it all in one fell swoop, and they got the whole lot in one day, would they listen?

After the Yom Kippur war, the chief Rabbi in Jerusalem called Israel to repentance, preaching a sermon calling the nation to repentance and reminding them of the sins he believed had contributed to the defeat on that occasion. But he knew that his sermon would be quickly lost so he took a page from the Jerusalem Chronicle and other papers and listed the sins of Israel. Number five was their bad driving on the roads. They learn in tanks, you know, and it tends to follow through. He listed some twenty-five sins and the impact of that list was pretty powerful.

Baruch sat down to write out, word by word, what we know as chapters 1–25 of the book of Jeremiah (some scholars say 1–35). Can you imagine the tedium? In those days a reed sharpened with a penknife was used for such a task. Then Jeremiah could not go to the house of the Lord, having been banned. We don't know how or why that had happened. I guess it was after he had that little argument with the high priest and Pashhur put him in the stocks. From then on, prophet and priest were so far apart that Jeremiah could not even step inside the temple. So he waited until the next big national fast. For, especially with the world powers pushing them around, this tiny nation, wondering if it could hold on to this piece of land, had national days of prayer and fasting.

In the middle of December, on the next national occasion when people came from all over Judah to pray and fast and say, "Lord, can we not keep this land?" Jeremiah said to Baruch, "Now go and read all this." Baruch stood there and must have put on an extra overcoat – it was a very cold day. The King was shivering over a fire in his palace. Baruch brought cold comfort to those people. He went right through everything we have read and studied, and the people listened. It must have been quite a feat for Baruch to read all that through. I have found that if I read two chapters or three even once, I am getting tired at the end. There was a meeting at the time of a local aristocracy, the local governors, the council – not the priests. They didn't like it one bit, but the council heard about it and said, "Baruch, come and read it to us." So, for the second time that day, Baruch read it through. The council were afraid. Now what were they afraid of? I just wish they had been afraid of God, but they were not, they were afraid of man. That comes out in what they said, "Baruch how did you get this? Did that man dictate it to you?"

Yes, he dictated every word."

"Baruch, for your own safety, your own skin, get out of here quickly, get Jeremiah and go into hiding because we will have to tell the king. It will come back to his ears. He will say, 'Why wasn't I told about this document?' and we are scared of how he will act, because if this document is right the king has been wrong. If Babylon is going to be the big power, the power of the east, and we have been relying on the west, our whole foreign policy has been wrong and it is the King who has been telling us it is the west that will win. What he will do when he hears this, I do not know; get out of here quickly."

Those poor councillors were torn with fear of men. They wanted to protect Jeremiah. They half agreed with him. On the other hand, they didn't want to fall out with a king and they showed a typical political expediency. So they took the document in to the king and they read it again. The king listened and he was furious, unwilling to face the truth because this document was saying: you are wrong; you are not only wrong, you are evil and that is why you are wrong.

For a man, especially a man in a high position, to admit his mistakes and say, "I am wrong and I am evil" takes a lot of grace, and Jehoiakim didn't have that grace. He took the knife that he used to sharpen his pen and he took that penknife. Now the scroll would be a very long piece of paper rolled up at either end and you would read it by unrolling one end and rolling up the other. The Hebrew would be in columns up and down, read from right to left. As each column was read he would say, "Give me that", and he would tear it with penknife and throw that piece on the fire, and then another piece – until all that work was gone.

But you can't destroy God's Word. You can fight against it, you can burn it, you can do anything you would like with it, but: "My Word shall not pass away." We know that the only result was that it was written again. How different from his father who had read to him the law that had been discovered in the cupboard in the temple when there was spring cleaning. When Josiah had heard that, he had said, "We are finished unless we repent," and he called the whole nation to repent. He said that he had been wrong, the people had been wrong, and he called the nation to say sorry to God. But when his son Jehoiakim heard the same message from God through this document, he was so furious, and I think he showed that he knew it was wrong because, you know, when you are fighting against the truth you get more and more cross.

When the word about what had happened got back to Jeremiah, God said, "Jeremiah, dictate the whole thing again and add some more about Jehoiakim," and he added some more: "Jehoiakim, you will not have a royal line to follow you." It came true to the letter. His son did come to the throne and within three months was off that throne and into exile. No other descendant was ever on the throne of David again. If you fight against God's Word, you are the one who suffers. If you are hurt by it, if it is saying, "You're in the wrong," and you are in the wrong because you are wrong, you may get rid of it, you may cut it out mentally; you may burn it up and as soon as you get outside the church forget what is said. But God will simply write some more, and that may be pretty devastating. You can't fight against the truth. And so it was repeated.

Spare a thought for Baruch. We shall see in chapter 45 that he got fed up with this. Writing out chapters 1–25, reading them twice in one day, having it burned and then setting down the next day to have it all happen again – can you imagine his feelings? We will come to that, but first, let me tell you that this book is feared as it was then. God's written Word is feared by those whose policy is wrong. That is why it is so difficult to get the Bible into some countries.

Why are they so afraid of a book? Because it shows their policy is wrong. It shows their policy toward Israel is wrong, so they fear this book. But there was a day, even in this country, when men were so afraid of this book that they burned it. If you have ever been to Smithfield Market where they butchered and sold meat wholesale, remember that you stand on the spot of the Smithfield bonfires. On that spot, copies of the Bible were burned by the hundred, and the men who were caught reading it were burned with it.

Not far from the house where we lived in Buckinghamshire there is a stone monument just outside Amersham, up on a hill in a field at the edge of a wood. On that monument are the names of twenty-one men and women who were burned alive on that spot. Their own children were made to light the bonfire. They were burned alive for this crime: they were caught reading the Bible in that little wood. There was a time when if people had not smuggled Bibles into this country the truth would not have got here. So think of that when you think about those who smuggle it elsewhere. It was smuggled into Britain wrapped up in cotton bales and it came in through King's Lynn, Norfolk. Then it was secretly spread.

Jeremiah was told by God: "Write down in the book all that I have said through you. Perhaps, perhaps if people get it in written form they will turn from their evil way and be forgiven." That word "perhaps" comes twice in the next chapter. So I spend my time reading this book to my hearers and proclaiming it far and wide, because there is a "perhaps" and so often that "perhaps" happens: somebody listens and it makes them wise to salvation; they say, "Now I see what life is all about. Now I know what is wrong with me. Now I know why I am not fulfilled. Now I know why I don't have a sense of purpose; now I understand" – and they turn and are forgiven. This book is the great "perhaps". God in heaven said, "Let's get my word written down, perhaps they will turn and be forgiven", and that is what it is all about.

Now let us finish off this study with chapter 45, just five little verses. A young man is frustrated with his affliction and his ambition. Both were things that God had to deal with. First of all, his affliction. It was a two-fold affliction—the depression that came on him through having all of Jeremiah 1–25 on him in one go. Can you imagine writing all that out, and the pressure of it on your soul, the doom and the gloom of it? That was his pain. As he wrote, he thought: why was I born with these people, in this land, at this time? Having written all that out and being told that he would have to do it all again—that is enough to discourage anyone.

I think of a brilliant aircraft designer who was a church secretary, and he designed Britain's biggest helicopter. He came home, switched on his television and learnt that after working seven years on this project, the news said the government had scrapped the helicopter. That was the end of seven of the best years of his life – all wasted. You can get very discouraged when your work is destroyed.

Baruch had really laboured. Jeremiah must have dictated it slowly, word by word, and then it was burned, and Baruch couldn't take it. He was a young man, though not as young as Jeremiah, and he said, "Lord, why do you have to add sorrow to my pain? It was painful to write it once; it's a sorrow to write it again. I am just weary. Why do you give me no rest? I'm fed up with doing this." So God spoke to him. God knew that behind this complaint lay ambition and that the ambition was to get on. This young man with ability had been born at a time and in a place where there was no scope for a career. The land was shrinking and looked likely to disappear, and if Jeremiah was to be believed, he had no future. This young man is ambitious and he is complaining because he cannot see any further. It is a dead end. Was he going to finish up as Jeremiah's clerk for the rest of his life? God could say to him: Baruch, I too know what it is to have my work destroyed. I planted this land, now I am plucking it up. I built this land, now I am destroying it. Baruch, I understand what it is to see your work destroyed.

I will never forget the time I met my sister in-law at Heathrow. She had been in Angola for six or seven years. Then, in the Portuguese troubles out there, all the people in the churches had to flee into the bush. The churches had been destroyed. All their missionary work had disappeared. She came through the barrier at London airport – blank, with staring eyes. Her work had gone.

God knew how Baruch felt. He had planted that land of Israel, had built the people up, and now they were destroyed. He had hoped that his people Israel would be good. He wanted them to stay forever. He wanted them to live a holy, healthy life and now he had to destroy it all because it was gone. Baruch, I'm discouraged too – wasn't that a lovely word from God? How sympathetic.

God knew that Baruch's ambition had been frustrated, that he wanted to do some great thing. But he said to him: "I will give you your life". Thank God you are alive—that is the biggest blessing. "In all the evil I am bringing on all flesh," says God, "I will give you your life as a reward for being a faithful secretary." The fact is that when the Babylonians finally overran Jerusalem, the people were taken away in chains, and two people were left free: Jeremiah and Baruch. They both died of old age down in Egypt, and God had said, "I will give you your life in whatever country you go to." Are you seeking great things for yourself? Don't. Just count it the great blessing of God to be alive – for life is to be alive; not to achieve, but to be alive in God's world and to be faithful even if the job you are given is humdrum.

READ JEREMIAH 37–38

We are now into the narrative section of Jeremiah, which describes things that happened to him rather than things he said. It is fascinating to study the Bible. There are two fascinations about it. There is on the one hand the fascination of how it came to be written and then there is the fascination of reading it. The fascination of how it came to be written is a story in itself. Nobody knew they were writing the Bible. It was written, as I have mentioned, by forty different people over at least fourteen hundred years and at least three different languages and not one of them realised he was writing the Bible. A shepherd strumming on his guitar, a king writing a passionate love poem, a man whose hobby is collecting folk sayings, an ex-rabbi who loved writing letters – all these people were putting together the Bible, and here we have this remarkable collection. Jeremiah realised that the end was very near and he wondered how his word was going to go on being felt and heard.

We have seen how God dealt with Baruch. He must have accepted this, first because he wrote it down for us, and if he had not accepted that then he would never have written it, but secondly, I know that he dealt with that matter of ambition because he began to do something else. Having finished writing out the prophecies, Baruch now began to keep a diary so that he could complete the account of Jeremiah. It is interesting that at this point, where Baruch enters the picture, Jeremiah is spoken of as "he" rather than "I". So

Baruch set himself to do for Jeremiah what later Boswell did for Dr Johnson, and was content to be in the background keeping a diary, as later Doctor Luke was content to keep a diary about Paul's missionary journeys.

Thank God for those in the Bible days who kept diaries about other people, and that is how we got so much of our Bible. Some were content not to have great experiences themselves but were content to write down the experiences of God that others had, so we can share them. Well now that is the fascination of the writing of the Bible, but for us personally there is even more fascination in reading the Bible. I never get tired of it and I hope you don't. The fascination for me is twofold. On the one hand, the Bible tells me more about the divine nature than any other book if I want to know what God is really like. How does he really react to things? How does he really feel? Most people believe there is a God but the important question is: "If there is a God, what is he like? Does he like me or does he not? Does he love me or does he hate me or doesn't he care anything about me?" I must know what God is like. The more I read scripture, the more I get into his heart, the more I understand how he reacts to me, to the world that he has made, to the things that happen in it. I can begin to anticipate how he will act, what he will do, how things will turn out, and I find security in finding out more and more about God and understanding him. That is one side of the fascination of reading the Bible, but as I read these two chapters the fascination is that you discover more about human nature than from any other book. You discover more about yourself and about other people. No psychologist has ever been able to produce a book which helps people to understand themselves as well as the Bible does. Our modern ideas about human behaviour as individuals and as groups – whether in psychology or sociology—are nothing compared with scripture. This is the one book that enables you to see yourself as you really are, to see human nature in the raw, to see real people behaving as we might behave in that situation. Therefore this book becomes not only a window through which we see God, it becomes a mirror through which we catch a reflection of ourselves, and you see both at the same time. It is like walking past a shop window. You see what is behind the glass and you see yourself in front of it. As I read this book I see the God who is behind everything – it opens a window in heaven and I can see. "So that's what you're like, God." Then as I look I see a reflection of someone else and the Word becomes a mirror. The Bible says that if you read the law of God it is like looking into a mirror, and tragic is that man who looks into the mirror, sees what he is like, and then goes away and forgets what he has seen. For then the mirror has been a waste of time. This section, chapters 37–38, is a mirror to mankind so that you can see clearly the folly of disobedience and the blessing of obedience. So in this study I am not going to talk about God much, I am going to look at the two men who have a strange love-hate relationship, the two men whose natures reflect everybody. You are either nearer to Zedekiah or nearer to Jeremiah.

You see Zedekiah, a man who is typical of a man of the world, even though he believed in God. In Jeremiah you will see a man of the Word. We see how in Zedekiah his fears overcame his faith. That put him on one side of the picture. In Jeremiah we see a man whose faith overcame his fears, and that put him on a totally different side of the picture. Notice that they both had faith and they both had fear, but in one his fear overcame his faith and in the other his faith overcame his fear. That splits the human race right down the middle, and that is the different between the world and the church. It is not the difference between those who don't believe in God and those who do. It is not the difference between those who go to church and those who don't. It is the difference between those whose fears overcome their faith and those whose faith overcomes their fears.

We look first at Zedekiah, the last king of Judah, who really was not fit to be a king. Indeed he had no royal blood. He was just chosen as a puppet king. The Babylonians had already been and taken Jerusalem once. They had taken away some ten or twelve thousand of the top people – all the aristocracy, even the skilled craftsmen – and they had left the nobodies, and from those nobodies they chose a nobody to be a puppet, a kind of caretaker, and they called him "king" just to give him a little incentive to look after the rest. This was Zedekiah, the last king of Judah, a weak, irresolute man, a petty politician who lived by expediency and not by principle.

He thought he could play off a big power against another big power. In a sense, he could have done. The only mistake he made was to choose the wrong big power, which is a pretty big mistake. In Zedekiah, like many big men and big fish in little ponds, a little power went to his head and he decided that he would get his independence and that he would become the big man. So Zedekiah said, "I'm going to appeal to Egypt" – to come and get rid of this big power Babylon, even though he owed his position to Babylon. He turned against them. So Zedekiah turned against those who had given him his position, got involved in political intrigue and played off one against the other. The biggest gamble he took was to ask Egypt to come against Babylon. The name of Pharaoh, the king of Egypt at that time, was Nephora.

He ought to have known better. The silly fool went and did it and he marched against the Chaldeans or the Babylonians. They were Chaldeans from Babylon actually, but the names are interchangeable. He marched against them and the Babylonians were by this time besieging Jerusalem for the second time, to bring Zedekiah to heel.

When they heard the Egyptian army was on the move, the Babylonians left Jerusalem and went to meet them. Zedekiah said, "There my politics have paid off. The siege is lifted. We're going to be free. We're going to be independent."

Jeremiah said, "Zedekiah, you're absolutely mistaken. The Chaldeans have just withdrawn and they will deal with the Egyptians and they will be back within weeks and this city will be burned," and Jeremiah was absolutely right.

Now let us look at Zedekiah in this situation, for what we read in these chapters takes place during that interval while the siege was lifted and the Babylonians were away. In the middle of this siege being lifted, Zedekiah and Jeremiah had quite a few chats. It is in these conversations that we see the men as they really are. We won't go through the conversations—I just look at each man and his side of the conversation. Look at Zedekiah first. There was no doubt that he had a faith, that he believed in God and that he believed in the power of prayer. It may not have been a strong faith but after all he was king of Judah and he believed in the true God of Israel. Here is a man whose faith is strong enough to go to Jeremiah and say, "Will you pray for us? Will you pray that this siege being lifted will be permanent? Will you pray that they will not come back? A man would not say that unless he had some faith. But isn't it fascinating? He believed in prayer but he did not believe in prophecy, and that shows how far his faith didn't go. Putting it simply, he was perfectly willing to talk to God and to have others talk to God for him, but he was not willing to listen to God and did not want God to talk to him – and that is the picture of a worldly man. Worldly people will pray. I have spoken to people who would never go near a church. One was a housewife who said, "I know I don't go to church, but I pray every night."

I asked her, "Do you read your Bible?"

"No."

"How does God speak to you?"

That is the question. It says, "Neither Zedekiah nor his servants nor the people of the land listened to the words of the Lord which he spoke." Then, "Zedekiah said to Jeremiah: pray for us to the Lord our God." Now that is the kind of one-way conversation that belongs to worldly religion. It is the outlook that wants God to *serve* us but doesn't want God to *save* us. It is the outlook that wants to get out of distress but doesn't want to get out of disobedience. It is the outlook that wants to be saved from sickness but doesn't want to be saved from sin. It is the outlook that wants material prosperity from God but not moral reformation – and you can see it all there: pray for me but don't preach to me. Speak *to* God but don't speak *from* God. I am not listening; I want to talk. It is the mark of a worldly person, even if they believe in God and go to church, that they are praying for themselves and want others to pray for them, but listening to what God has to say to them and doing what God tells them is unknown to them. Does Zedekiah reflect for you something terribly common? Many people say they believe in God, and the majority of those claim that they pray. But do they listen to God? Are they interested in the Word of God – what he has to say to them? Their Bible remains unopened on the bookshelf, the preachers remain unheard. Zedekiah had faith. But it was only a one-way faith, a belief in prayer as a last desperate resort: "Will you pray to God" – it was almost a faith that Jeremiah's prayers would be more effective. It was a willingness to have somebody with a stronger faith pray for you, but that is not a strong enough faith to overcome your fears.

Let us look at Zedekiah's fears. They were all horizontal, not vertical. I mean that all his fears were fears of men; he had

394

no fear of God. That is why his fears overcame his faith. The fear of the Lord is the beginning of wisdom, and the fear of man is the beginning of folly, and it was the second fear that he had. He had two fears. The first was a very understandable one: a fear of the Babylonians. In those days when a nation was defeated, as a symbolic act of degradation its king was brutally mutilated and then executed. Zedekiah knew that this was what would happen to him if the Babylonians came. He had rebelled, he was in a state of siege, and he knew that the day the Babylonians got inside the city he would be tortured and put to death. That was his first big fear and he had a right to have it. But the funny thing is that he had another fear, which came out in one of these conversations, and this was a fear of some of his own people – Jews who had taken Jeremiah's advice and deserted to the enemy: that they would abuse him, mock and ridicule him and say, "That's the king who landed us in all this trouble. That's the king who didn't know how to play politics. That's the king who caused the destruction of Jerusalem. He thought he was the great clever politician, look at him now." He was more afraid of the ridicule of his fellow countrymen than he was of the torture of his enemies. But in all his conversation there is not one trace of fear of God. Jeremiah said, "If I tell you the truth, you won't listen. You won't do anything about it," and he was absolutely right. Zedekiah did nothing.

There is an intriguing little verse and I wonder if you noticed it. Zedekiah said to Jeremiah, "Now come on, tell me the truth. What's going to happen?" Jeremiah said this: "Look, if I tell you, how can I be sure you won't put me to death, because you won't like it one bit. If I tell you, you won't listen to me anyway." Zedekiah said, "I promise you, I won't put you to death." Did you notice he didn't say, "I promise you I'll listen"? Did you get that little omission? The things that are not said in scripture are just as interesting as the things that are said. Zedekiah said, "I promise not to put you to death." If only he had said, "I promise to do what you tell me" – but he wouldn't. His ears were deaf to God, and yet there was that fascination. He was like many people I have known who are fascinated to hear the Word of the Lord and yet they are going to do nothing about it. They are fascinated to hear a preacher unveil what is going to happen, but they are going to do nothing about it. They may promise not to do anything antagonistic but they won't promise to listen and obey. Yet they are fascinated with the future—and that is why horoscopes are so popular.

This was Zedekiah's position, a man who believed in God, but a worldly man whose faith was a one-way faith and whose fear of man was greater than his fear of God. Therefore the man finished, as you know, being taken captive. He had his eyes gouged out. He did have his life but he remained a blinded man who had to be led around by the hand for the rest of his life.

It is a wonderful liberation when you can say with that writer in the New Testament, quoting the Old, "I will not fear what man can do to me." In fact, I was brought up on a little saying – my father kept saying it: "If you fear God you will fear no one else." It is the horizontal fears of man that overcome what faith we have: fear of what the neighbours will think, fear of what my friends will think, fear of what my social set will think, fear if I go all the way with God, fear of where he might lead me, fear that I might suffer, fear that I might lose my friends, fear of all kinds of things, and it is all horizontal fear. If you are governed by horizontal fear then your faith will not be strong enough to see you through, and the end is disaster, even if you believe in God, even if you go to church.

Let us turn from Zedekiah to Jeremiah. Now Jeremiah was not very good for public morale. A remarkable parallel is

John Knox. Do you remember the occasion when John Knox was in St Andrews, Scotland and the French were besieging that town? His words are almost identical with Jeremiah's here. Knox said, "The only possible course to save your lives is to surrender to the French. You will be taken into exile into France," and indeed John Knox himself was. He said, "You'll be taken into exile but you'll save your lives. It is no use calling on England to come and save us. England will not come and will not be able to save us – and why? Because the lives of the citizens of St Andrews are corrupt." It is intriguing that he was almost repeating Jeremiah word for word. It was a parallel situation and Knox was as unpopular with the leaders of St Andrews as Jeremiah was unpopular with Zedekiah and the princes. It is bad for public morale, when you are fighting for your lives, with backs to the wall. What every human being with any guts responds to is the call of Masada: we will go down dying. We'll fight to the last ditch if it means the death of all of us. That stirs the heroism in us, but Jeremiah was going around saying, "If I were you, I'd get out." He literally was saying that. When the king would not listen to his advice he went round to individuals in the streets and said, "If you want to save yourself, desert to the enemy. Get out, go to the Babylonians, and you'll live." It was these deserting Jews that Zedekiah was so afraid of, but many took Jeremiah's advice.

So he was regarded as a traitor. You imagine if during World War II a preacher had gone around every town in England saying, "Give in to the Germans." Do you think he would have been left alone to do that indefinitely in a nation under threat, determined to fight on the beaches? Do you think that is going to be a popular message? No. Jeremiah was lowering public morale but I must say this for Jeremiah: he did not himself desert. He could have done, but he was going to stay, and until the very last he was going to tell people: "Get out, desert." So we can say Jeremiah was no coward. He was going to stay until the bitter end and he did. In fact, he was imprisoned for the last year or so of the siege.

The Bible is an honest book. It portrays Jeremiah here with fears. It doesn't say he was a great hero or was afraid of nothing and no-one. Indeed, one of the marks of inspiration is that an account of heroes will be truthful. Jeremiah didn't like what happened to him. Indeed, he was afraid of it. It got on top of him. I am so glad the Bible tells us that when he got the chance to plead with Zedekiah he went on his knees and said, "Please don't send me back to that." Zedekiah put him back in the court of the guard under surveillance. I am glad that Jeremiah is revealed as a man who hated every minute, who couldn't cope with it and said "Please get me out."

But there was another, even deeper fear that Jeremiah had. It led him to tell a lie. It was the fear of a violent death. It came out when he had been in the dungeon then back to the court of the guard, then they put him in the cistern. It was the powerful princes who had now got on top of Zedekiah. They came to Zedekiah and said: "This man must be put to death – he must be put out of the way altogether." Zedekiah, like the weak king he was, said, "I can't stand up against you. He's in your hands."

So they threw him into that slimy cistern to die. It was an Ethiopian eunuch who took pity and pulled him out with the ropes under his armpits—fancy that, not even a Jew. Truth is stranger than fiction but Jeremiah was afraid of being put into that cistern because he knew sooner or later he would get so tired he would slip down into that slime and suffocate and it led to a lie. After one of those secret interviews when Zedekiah again asked him, "Have you any word of the Lord?" Jeremiah told him the truth yet again. Jeremiah said, "I can't face that cistern again." Zedekiah said, "I'll tell you what then. Don't you dare to mention what we have talked about. They will ask you what we have been talking about. Tell them that you just came to plead with me to get out of the cistern. Don't tell them what you have said." It says in the Bible at the end of chapter 38 that they did ask Jeremiah what had been talked about. Jeremiah said, "Well, I only asked him if I could be out of this cistern."

Now there are many people who feel uncomfortable at this point and they say, "Oh dear, I'm sure there must be some explanation as to why Jeremiah said that. I am sure it was love for Zedekiah, to protect Zedekiah's life." But we can't get around it. The simple fact is that Jeremiah told a lie to save his skin, and I want you to notice two things. God didn't tell him to tell that lie, so we are not being encouraged to do the same. It is not being told to us as an example. I also want you to notice that God did not reprove him for telling the lie. God is very understanding and he knows when someone is really being pushed to their limits, and God did not rebuke him. It doesn't say it was right. It is put there to tell you that Jeremiah was a real man, a man of passions like ours, who couldn't take it, and a man who therefore entered into complicity with the king and lied.

I mention that to show you that there were real fears in Jeremiah's life. He was afraid of the dungeon, he was afraid of death, but Jeremiah stands as a man of the Word not because he didn't have fears, not because those fears didn't lead him to do things that were wrong, but because faith in God was stronger than the fears, because his faith was the kind of faith that listened to the Word of God; that spoke what God had to say. That didn't bring a lot of prayer requests to get out of trouble but said, "God is going to bring trouble." He had the kind of faith that listened to what God had to say and then told it the way it was. It was the kind of faith that was built on truth and not on illusion, the kind of faith that said, "God, what are you going to do? What do you say about this?" – then faced reality, however unpleasant it was to face it and to share it. That is the kind of faith that will ultimately triumph over the fear and produce a man of the Word and a man of God. It is like the difference between hell and heaven. The man whose fears overcome his faith is the man heading for hell. The man whose faith overcomes his fears is the man heading for heaven.

Jeremiah's faith was in God who said: "This city will be burned." So his faith stood firm as disaster came nearer. It is not the faith built on the illusion that everything will turn out all right. That faith will crash. Everything will not turn out all right. This world is not going to get better and better. It will get worse and worse according to the Bible. Says Jesus: "There will be earthquakes and famine on an increasing scale and nation will rise against nation and there shall be wars and rumours of wars before the end comes." Now a real faith that listens to God will not be shaken when these things happen. A real faith based on listening to God will not be shaken, but a faith that is simply "pray for us that we may not have any troubles" – that faith will go and the fear will take over.

Jeremiah believed that Jerusalem would fall. He believed the worst and therefore he was able to see beyond that and to see the hope for the future and to see the best beyond, because he was realistic. He faced the darkest facts—Jerusalem will be burned and you will all be taken away — but beyond he could see that God would not give up and the dawn would come. The other side to his faith was not just that Jerusalem would be vandalised but that Yahweh would be vindicated. This was the ground of all his political judgments. A nation that turns away from God is finished. Faith believes that history is *his story*. It is a faith that in the last analysis, government is in the hands of God.

God will be vindicated, and if God is just, then without a

vision the people perish, and If righteousness exalts a nation then its opposite degrades it. "If God is God" – that was Jeremiah's faith. Let God be true and every man a liar – that God is true. This is what overcame his fears. Jeremiah had his very real fears. He hated prison and he feared a violent death at the hands of men who hated him. But his faith was in a God who would vindicate his Word, a God who meant what he said.

Could those two swap places? Must Zedekiah remain a Zedekiah and must Jeremiah remain a Jeremiah? Is our fate fixed that certain men are like this and certain men are like that by temperament, by heredity, by environment, so that we can't help being a man or woman of the *world* or of the *Word*? People have said to me you only preach because your dad and your granddad were preachers. Oh, if they only knew! My conscience is captive to the Word of God. I have *got* to preach. Is it that we are just born this way? Well, as Shakespeare put it, "The fault dear Brutus is not in the stars but in ourselves." It is not fate that determines your destiny. Therefore don't bother to read your horoscope. It is faith that determines your destiny.

The most important word to me in chapters 37 and 38 is a word of only two letters: "If". Jeremiah said, "Zedekiah if...." Even now, though they were in the last months of siege, although the siege had just been lifted temporarily, even though they were within months of the final disaster, Jeremiah said: "If Zedekiah...." *If* it was the last conversation they were to have.... If you will listen and do it, you will live and your life will be spared and the city will not be burned and God will see to it because God is God. But if you do not, you fear the ridicule of the men who deserted, I prophesy that you will be ridiculed by women. That, to Zedekiah, was quite an insult. Jeremiah said, "The women will laugh at you and say look his feet are in the mire. He's got us in this mess." It is the women who will taunt you as a totally inadequate ruler.

What a lovely touch. Jeremiah had just been pulled out of the cistern. He was caked in mud and he was saying: they will say your feet are in the mire, you're in the mess, and it will be the women who will laugh at you. It was a tremendous appeal to Zedekiah. He was afraid of ridicule and Jeremiah is laying it on thick, trying to get through to that man with the biggest "if" there is: If you will listen and obey everything will be all right but if you do not, you remain a Zedekiah.

Jeremiah was in chains standing before Zedekiah, but who was the prisoner? Zedekiah was free then but he spent the rest of his life in captivity. Jeremiah would be in captivity for the rest of the days of Jerusalem and then he would be set free and would be free for the rest of his life. That is the difference. The man of the world is free here; he will be in captivity for the rest of eternity. The man of the Word may be in captivity here but he knows that in the next world he will be free.

READ JEREMIAH 39–41

The theme of this passage is how human nature copes with crisis, tragedy and sudden events which shake the very roots of our lives. How we respond in the crisis is a test of character, and it is lovely when you discover in the crisis that God can see you through. For example, I was driving down to Cornwall one day and quite suddenly a mini car right in front of me stopped so quickly, then turned right without warning. I knew I could stop in time but in my driving mirror I saw a couple of motorbikes tearing along, hard on my tail, and there was just time to send up a flash prayer, jam the brakes on and swerve – but then thump, a motorbike was into the back of my car and its rider was on the road. Yet in a crisis like that you find that God gives you a serenity, peace and ability to deal with what needs dealing with.

One of the reasons why we may find it hard to identify with this passage is that England has not been invaded by a foreign army since 1066, so we don't know what it is to have our land taken over by someone else. We don't know what it is to see the town in which we live burned to the ground. If you go to the Channel Islands, you find that their residents understand, for they came under a foreign power. They reacted in exactly the ways that these people who are mentioned in Jeremiah reacted. Some collaborated, some resisted, some said the way of peace is to do what the authorities tell us, and co-operate with them. Others said, "No, we will try and attack them and undo them as much as we can." One of the tragic effects of being invaded is that often there is a greater tension among the people invaded than between those people and the occupying forces. It has happened in many other countries. Sometimes the greatest tension is between those churches who register with the state and the fellowships that are underground and who do not register, meeting unofficially. That is one of the tragedies of being invaded – morale is sapped by the tensions that arise among people who ought to be brothers. Does that give you a little of the feel of the situation?

We are going to look at seven different people, at how they reacted, and what ultimately happened to them in this situation of being invaded. Ask God for the gift of imagination to try to get inside the skins of these people. Try to understand why they did what they did and how they reacted as they did. Maybe you do know what it is to have your country overrun, and know all the problems as to what to do and where to go and who to identify with, and whether to try to fight, whether to take to the hills or to collaborate.

When a crisis like this is upon you, your true motives are revealed – whether you really trust in God or whether you run around from person to person saying, "What shall we do?" If England were ever invaded again and occupied by a foreign power, we would have to decide, we would have to examine our own hearts. We would find what we really were.

These are national events. A capital city has fallen and a vast imperial power called Babylon is swallowing up satellite states. Yet the Word of God focuses on seven individuals. That is how God sees our world – not the big newspaper headlines but how individuals respond to crises. Do they put their trust in him or do they panic? How does Zedekiah react? How does Ebed-melech react? How does Nebuzaradan react? How does Ishmael react? God still looks at individuals. He looks at you. He would notice whether you have had a crisis this week and how you reacted. Have

you felt trapped this week? How did you respond? Have you felt you have got into a situation where everything caved in and your little world had collapsed? How did you react?

As we look at each of these seven individuals in turn, we are going to ask one question about each of them: how did they relate to Jeremiah in the crisis? Because he was God's mouthpiece – God's man. Their relationship to him was like their relationship to God. Your relationship to the Lord is revealed by your relationship to the Lord's people. Every time: inasmuch as you did it or did it not to the least of these his brethren, you did it or did it not to him. Therefore you can tell what their relationship to God was by their relationship to the man of God, and we shall see that in every single case their ultimate destiny depended on their relationship to Jeremiah, the man who brought them the Word of God.

Let us take Zedekiah first—he is the first individual mentioned in chapter 39. We know that he knew Jeremiah well. We know that he was interested in hearing him preach. We know that he asked him about the Word of God for the future of his nation. We know that Jeremiah gave him advice. We know that Jeremiah told him exactly what to do, and we know that Zedekiah never did it. Here was this man who knew the Word of God, who knew what to do, who knew what God was saying, and did nothing about it. So what happened? Quite typically, when he realised they had broken through the wall in the northern part of his city he escaped through the southern gate through the king's garden and went down the Kidron Valley. That leads through the wilderness right down to the deep Rift Valley where the Dead Sea and the Jordan lie, called the Arabah. He fled.

The leader of this people ran and left them to it. It shows what he was made of. He had more fear of man than fear of God. He could have remained on the throne had he listened to Jeremiah, had he done what the Word of God said, but he panicked.

They caught him. It is a pretty rough thing and our sensitivities are offended by the crudeness of it. They held him there in chains and in front of his eyes they took each of his own boys and slaughtered them. Then they took all his nobles, all his cabinet ministers, and they killed each one. Then, to make sure that was the last thing he did see, they gouged his eyes out. He was blind. From the man who had been in a position to lead, he became a man who had to be led. You didn't see a blind king on the throne. He could not lead troops into battle. He could no longer be the leader. It was a profound punishment for him. Now to us this is a very cruel and bloodthirsty situation. What a thing to do! In fact, I want to point out that he was treated leniently. It would have been perfectly normal for him to be executed too, but Jeremiah, though he didn't tell him he would be blinded, had said, "Your life will be spared."

So then Zedekiah lived – blind. In a sense, there was poetic justice in this. The man who refused to see finished up blind. Jeremiah had read the signs of the times and had told him what to see, but this king refused to see, so there came a day when he couldn't see, and if you refuse to see God's Word and see what is coming then there will come a day when you will not be able to see either, for hell is pitch black and you will see nothing in hell if you refuse to see now. You will be blinded.

We turn, secondly, to Nebuchadnezzar himself. Now the trouble is that most of us have got our main impression of this man from the book of Daniel and certainly when you read about Nebuchadnezzar in the book of Daniel, the man is a megalomaniac. The ruler went mad and his hair became long, his nails became like claws, and he lived in a field and ate grass like the animals because power went to his head.

Lord Acton said, "Power tends to corrupt and absolute power tends to corrupt absolutely," and that was what happened to Nebuchadnezzar. But I want you to remember that Nebuchadnezzar began as a fairly tolerant humane imperialist as most dictators do. Many tyrants start as men who want to do good for their nation but power goes to their heads and they become megalomaniacs. Now Nebuchadnezzar, when he took Jerusalem, was in his early days. He was a man who had some respect for those he conquered. He treated them tolerantly, and though he had been fighting against Jerusalem for eighteen months before he had finally breached the walls, and that had cost him a lot of money and a lot of time, nevertheless he did not do what many others would have done in those circumstances in those days. He did not kill the people in that city. He took them away so that they could not live in it. He burned their city but he took them away alive. He did not kill the king.

Then he gave the land to the very poor—a remarkable little touch. He looked around for the beggars who had nothing. He looked around for the peasants who were little better than slaves and said: "I am going to give you a governor from your own people." He looked around for a good man, and he found a good man in Gedaliah. He said, "You be governor for me over these poor people. Behave yourselves and I won't trouble you. Pay me taxes but just behave yourselves and you can have the land."

Nebuchadnezzar was a very tolerant man in the early days, before it went to his head and he built great statues of himself and had people bow down, before he thought he was a god and said, "Mine is the kingdom. Mine is the power. Mine is the glory." That is what he said in Daniel 4, and if you say that and don't say, "Thine is the kingdom, thine is the power, thine is the glory"– as soon as you say *mine* instead of thine – you go mad because you think you are God. But he treated the conquered leniently. Above all he said, "Now get hold of Jeremiah. Set him free from the prison. Look after him. Give him anything he asks for but look after him carefully."

That is remarkable. Why did he do that? Some would say it was because Jeremiah had been on his side. Jeremiah had been advocating that people surrender, but I think there is a deeper reason. Deep down in Nebuchadnezzar was a religious streak that recognised God – and therefore a man of God. Do you remember what Nebuchadnezzar said to Daniel years later? Daniel, your God is the God of gods. Your God is the ruler of kings. Nebuchadnezzar knew that when he met the real God, and so when he met Jeremiah he knew that he was meeting a man of the real God, and he said, "Look after him carefully." So Jeremiah went back home. I think his feelings must have been very mixed, going back to the little village where he had been a boy and he had been away forty years. It was only eight miles but he had never gone home. He had bought a field there but had never gone to see it. He had tried to but he had not been allowed out. He had been arrested, and during the last few years of Jerusalem he had been imprisoned, and how extraordinary, how his heart must have felt mixed with feelings – imprisoned by his own people, set free by the invader. He had to spend forty years of his life trying to save a city, and now it was gone – every house burned to the ground. He is going back home. He is now fifty-seven years of age. All this preaching has been for nothing. Can you imagine his feelings? Nebuchadnezzar said, "Let him go home." That was after forty years of preaching, warning the city that it was not holding out against Babylon they should be concerned about, it was the fact that they were holding out against God. He had pleaded, then finally the city had fallen. He must have thought his ministry was over and that he could settle down in the village and retire, but his work was not over. Events were to overtake him even in his home village.

Thirdly, let us look at Ebed-melech. When Jerusalem fell, there was in Jerusalem a foreigner living among the besieged—his name Ebed-melech. His home country was what we now call the Sudan but in biblical days it was called Ethiopia. His skin was black. Who would look after this man when the city fell? Who would protect him? No-one. He was a foreigner in a strange place, and of all people he would be surely one of the first to be killed. This man was afraid and Jeremiah had a special word from the Lord for this single immigrant. How like God this is – to think of the stranger within the gates. It is such a lovely touch of God: Jeremiah, I've got a message for you – not for the Babylonian empire, not for the people of Jerusalem, not for the king, but for that little immigrant Ebed-melech. I want you to go to him and say, "God is going to do all the evil that he said he would do to this city, but you don't need to be afraid. You will live." –Why? Well, do you remember what Ebed-melech once did when Jeremiah had been cast into the cistern and was up to his waist in slime and filth and darkness so that he couldn't sit down or rest, and got no food? When he thought his life was ended it was a little taste of hell. When Jeremiah was in that pit, Ebed-melech got some ropes and some rags and he let the rope down and said, "Put the rags under your armpits. We'll get you out of there, Jeremiah." That is all he had done. But you can never get God in your debt. Even a cup of cold water given to one of his disciples is noted in the book. God will pay for it. That is all that Ebed-melech did. He got the man of God out of the slime—and God never forgot. The things that you have done for people of God are remembered. That is why in the last day Jesus will say: "I was in prison and you visited me. I was sick and you came. I was a stranger and you invited me home for lunch."

"When did we do that Lord?"

"You did it for one of my brethren and I haven't forgotten

it."

Isn't God lovely? "Ebed-melech, I've got a word for you. You will live. I will repay," says the Lord and this man from Africa lived.

There were two people in Jerusalem who were set free and stayed on in the land: Jeremiah and Ebed-melech. Remarkable, isn't it?

Let me move on to personality number four—Nebuzaradan, Nebuchadnezzar's Captain of the Guard. That is a very polite translation of the Hebrew. Literally it says, "Chief butcher," but then the people who translated the English Bible usually rendered the impolite things rather more politely for Gentile congregations. Yet he wasn't a butcher—he was a very remarkable man.

You know, some of the finest Christians have been professional soldiers. If you had gone to one little Baptist church you would have seen a man singing choruses, lifting his hands praising God, and you would not have looked at him twice, but if you did then you would have been looking at an Admiral who was Commander in Chief of the NATO forces for the whole of the Mediterranean. The Holy Spirit filled him and he was a fine Christian.

There are those who say, like the centurion in Capernaum, "I also am a man under authority. So you can say, 'Be healed and it will be done.'" They are used to obedience and that is one of the fundamental virtues of human nature. It would be a bold person who would say that there has been greater respect for authority and greater obedience among young people since National Service ended.

Here was this man Nebuzaradan. There is a little bit of a mystery between chapters 39 and 40. In chapter 39 he is told to look after Jeremiah carefully and give him anything he wants. In chapter 40 he is leading Jeremiah in chains to Babylon. I am not quite sure how to resolve that one. I have read all the commentaries but none of them satisfies me, so I am going to wait until I get to heaven and get hold of them both and ask what exactly happened. Maybe one is a condensed account, pulling together the beginning and the end of the relationship and omitting the little bit in between. But let us go back. Do you remember in an earlier chapter in Jeremiah a voice is heard in Ramah – Rachel weeping for her children? When Nebuzaradan was leading away the captives to Babylon in chains, Jeremiah was among them, though he was carefully looked after, and when they reached Ramah they heard the voice of a woman weeping and it came from the grave of Rachel. Somehow this touched this soldier and he turned to Jeremiah and said, "Take those chains off. I give you a free choice. You can come with me to Babylon and I will look after you, or you can go and live with your own people, but you are free." But here is the remarkable thing – this Babylonian officer said to Jeremiah: It is God who has done this to your land, isn't it? It is God who said he would do it. Your God is a God who keeps his word, isn't he? It is a remarkable statement. This pagan soldier recognised the true God through Jeremiah – as, later, Cornelius would recognise the true God. Searching after God, fearing God – there is something about this man Nebuzaradan that really gets me. Where had he learned all this from – about God's predictions concerning Jerusalem? I think that as he marched his prisoners north he had been chatting to them and they told him, "You know, Jeremiah told us that you would come."

"Oh did he? How long ago?"

"He's been telling us for forty years."

"Forty years? How did he know forty years ago that we would come?"

"Well, God told him."

"God? Which God?"

"Our God, the God of Israel" – and this pagan officer

recognised authority and said, "Your God commanded the fall of this city and it has happened. I recognise authority when I see it, so you are free. I dare not take you in chains. You serve a greater authority than Nebuchadnezzar." That was how he reacted.

Fifthly, let us now look at Gedaliah—chosen for one of the most difficult assignments a man can ever have. It happened in Jersey during the war. It happened in Paris. It happened in Norway. The man chosen to be governor of an occupied territory, a man from among the people, will be under suspicion both from his own people for collaborating and from the occupying forces, wondering whether he is playing tricks behind their backs. It is an unenviable position, yet Nebuchadnezzar chose well. He chose a good man, a man who knew how to negotiate, a man who knew what was best for his people, and he chose this man Gedaliah, a Jew. What was Gedaliah's relationship to Jeremiah? Simple—he agreed with every word Jeremiah said. Gedaliah knew that Jeremiah had been right all along and that the way of safety, the only hope of a future, was to surrender and to collaborate, and so now he and Jeremiah became partners. They did not try to rebuild Jerusalem. That would have been folly. The Babylonians would simply come and knock it down again.

So they moved just a few miles north, to a hill called Mizpah, which you can see today, and there they began again. Gedaliah said, "Now gather around everybody. Let's gather what few Jews we've got left and let's plant vineyards and sow corn. Let's believe that God will bless us and let's just co-operate with the Babylonians. Let's not fight." All around the hills were guerilla bands who were going to go on fighting. Their leaders and the guerillas heard that Gedaliah was governor and they all came and said, "We're with you. We're not going to fight. We'll plant instead of fighting." That year they had the best harvest in years, and God blessed them. In the autumn, when they gathered the corn and the grapes, they were astonished at how much they harvested. If only those people had listened to Jeremiah two years earlier they might still have had the Temple and they might still have had Jerusalem. They had not listened. But now there was a man in charge who did listen, and Gedaliah understood that Jeremiah spoke the truth, and so they settled the poor in the land. Gedaliah himself was poor, and a good man. He had only one fault and it was to prove fatal. It is a fault that other good men have too. It is the fault of naïvety. It is the fault of believing that there is only good in good people, and it is a very big mistake. Jesus never made this mistake—it says in John 2 that Jesus trusted no man because he knew what was in man. That is a very solemn statement. When did you last hear a sermon on that text? You see, you can have too rosy a view of human nature or you can have too cynical a view. The cynic says don't trust anybody, they will always trick you. Then you have the naïve view, which Gedaliah had: "Well, these poor people are not such bad sorts after all. I'm sure they wouldn't do anything to upset the apple cart now."

Johanan said to Gedaliah, "Do you know that one of those guerilla leaders who has come and surrendered, and who is living among you, is in league with another nation, Ammon, over on the other side of the Jordan, and the king of Ammon is paying him to kill you?"

Gedaliah said, "You lie. He wouldn't do that to me." He was naïve and had too optimistic a view of human nature. You see, when you know your heart well and you know God well, you know that there is evil in the best of us as well as good in the worst of us. Gedaliah made the mistake that other rulers have made since: he failed to realise that his own safety was the key to his people's safety. He was being brave as he said, "No, I don't believe that story is true." But it was true, and Gedaliah is a warning to us not to be too naïve about human nature but to be alert, to be aware of evil, to be aware that there is always somebody who will do the wrong thing, always somebody who can destroy what is being built up. It can happen in a church and we ought to be aware that one church member can wreck a situation. One church member who is apparently supporting a church can undo the work that God is doing – building up so that the harvest is coming in. Leaders must never be over-naïve, they must be realistic. As soon as they hear of a possible threat they must take it seriously. They must realise that the devil can use somebody even within. The devil can use someone within a little group who are seeking to reap a harvest – to wreck that harvest. It was only just after they had gathered in the harvest that Ishmael came with his guerilla band and they came and sat at the dinner table with Gedaliah.

So now our attention turns to the sixth person – Ishmael. Why did he do it? Was his the sort of temperament that cannot accept defeat? Had he ambitions for himself? There is one clue in the Bible: he had royal blood in his veins. His mind was saying, "Why should Gedaliah, a peasant, be the governor and I have got royal blood?" Satan worked on this jealousy and resentment and so built it up that he accepted the support of the king of Ammon, enemy of Judah. Why did the king of Ammon want him on the throne? Well, I expect he thought he could make him a puppet king and extend the empire of Ammon. I don't know why. I know that in the Middle East to kill someone after you have accepted their meal is the worst crime of all. Hospitality is the unwritten fundamental commandment in the Middle East. You must give hospitality to anyone who needs it. You must look after any stranger in your home, and when you accept hospitality you must do so graciously. To kill your host is terrible, and yet Ishmael did it to his fellow countrymen, then proceeded to take the people there off with him to Ammon. What was

Ishmael's relationship to Jeremiah? None. Jeremiah is not mentioned once during the whole of the story of Ishmael. Here is a man who lived without any reference to the Word of God at all, and it was this man whom Satan used to undo the good that was being done. It was this man who wrecked the rebuilding of the little nation of God.

Finally, number seven, we look at the one man who tried to redeem the situation. His name was Johanan. He was another guerilla leader, but he was one who really meant it when he agreed with Gedaliah about co-operating. He was the very man who had come to warn Gedaliah about the plotted assassination. So Johanan pursued Ishmael and rescued his captives. Ishmael escaped with eight men and got to Ammon, but Johanan brought the others back. What was he to do with them? He had a few soldiers, a few women, a few children, a few eunuchs—a bit of a motley crew. What should he do? Johanan was in perplexity and he said, "If we go back to Mizpah, as soon as Nebuchadnezzar hears that his governor has been assassinated what is he going to do? He is going to come and wipe out the rest of us. Where shall I go?"

Mizpah was in the land of Benjamin, four or five miles north of Jerusalem. So Johanan took the remaining crew about three miles south of Jerusalem. He took them to some sheepfolds outside a little village called Bethlehem and said, "I think we'll have to flee to Egypt." But thank God that before he did he said, "But hold on a moment. Let's ask Jeremiah first. Let's ask what the Lord thinks." So he didn't panic. What did the Lord say? Did Johanan obey what the Lord said? We shall return to that later.

We have the great advantage of reading the Old Testament through the New. Do you know history never repeats itself? That is not a biblical idea. The Greek concept of history is that it goes around in circles. but the Hebrew concept of history is of a one-way line that goes from past to present to future, and history never goes back. Having affirmed that, it is remarkable how often things that happen at one point on the line reflect things that happen later. As I look at these seven men I think of people in the New Testament, for when Jesus was born in Bethlehem of Judea the land was occupied by a foreign army – not the Babylonians but the Romans. You had a parallel situation. When I read about Zedekiah, the puppet king of Babylon, I also think of Herod, the puppet king of Rome. Herod was interested in Jesus. Herod was glad to see Jesus. He hoped to see a miracle performed by Jesus. But Herod had no intention whatever of obeying the words of Jesus. Herod was another puppet king with no intention of being obedient. When I look at Nebuchadnezzar I think of a benevolent imperialist, Augustus Caesar. You know, time and time again they tried to get Jesus to join the resistance movement, and they said, "Should we pay tax to Caesar?" Jesus held up a coin and said, "Whose image is that?" The implication was: you benefit from their coinage, you benefit from their protection, you use their money, then co-operate. If a Roman soldier compels you to carry his bag one mile (as he could), then carry it a second. It wasn't popular. When I read of Ebed-melech, who do I think of? He was an immigrant who did a small service for Jeremiah and was rewarded by the Lord. I think of an African who just did one thing for Jesus. He carried his cross when he could not carry it himself. Was he rewarded? Most certainly. He was given two Christian sons, Rufus and Alexander. There it is in the Bible. I think, too, of a dying thief who, in our Lord's utter loneliness on the cross, when others were mocking and cursing him, said: "This man has done nothing wrong." Jesus said, "Today, you will be with me in Paradise." You can never get the Lord in your debt. When I look at Nebuzaradan I think of the Roman centurion whom I have already mentioned: I also am a man under authority therefore I recognise God's authority in you. When I look at Gedaliah I think of Pontius Pilate and a man who knew what was right, who tried so hard to keep the two sides together, but couldn't.

I think of Ishmael, who actually slaughtered eighty pilgrims who came to mourn over the Temple, with beards shaved, their bodies gashed and clothes torn. He went out to meet them, weeping. They were crocodile tears and he slaughtered those pilgrims. When I think of Ishmael I think of Judas. Judas: do you come to me with a kiss? The one man right in the band of disciples; the one man who Satan entered into, who wrecked the whole thing and betrayed Jesus for his own motives. When I look at Johanan I don't know quite who to think of. Nicodemus, who tried to do something at the end? I leave you to think of someone.

There are strange echoes all the way through. Jesus was born at Bethlehem and his parents were told to flee into Egypt from Bethlehem. Did you think of that? Or of Jesus predicting the fall of Jerusalem and saying:

"O Jerusalem, Jerusalem, killing the prophets and stoning those who are sent to you. How often would I have gathered your children together as a hen gathers her chicks beneath her wings, and you would not. Now your house is left to you desolate and you won't see me again until you say, Blessed is he who comes in the name of the Lord."

"Jerusalem shall be trodden down of the Gentiles until the time of the Gentiles be fulfilled."

Did you get echoes of that? In AD 70 it was all burned down to the ground again. When I hear Jesus speak the Sermon on the Mount I hear these amazing words: the meek shall inherit the earth. When Jerusalem fell and it seemed as if the end of the world had come, who got the land? The poor in the land were given it. When the end of this world comes, who will inherit the earth? The meek – those who have not grabbed it.

Most of all, as I read these chapters I thought of the disciples of Jesus and remembered that one of the Twelve was Matthew, a tax collector, a collaborator with the enemy occupying forces, and I thought: another of them was Simon the guerilla, the zealot, the leader of the resistance movement. I thought: only Jesus can bring all those people together. Only Jesus can bring together in a crisis those who have completely opposite reactions. Only Jesus can bring all people out of their panic, their rush, their human ideas, and into his kingdom. I thought: if only Jesus had been on earth when Jerusalem fell in 587 BC he would have sorted it all out. Why are there so many parallels between then and now? There are two very simple reasons. First: human nature doesn't change. Even though you may not have been able to identify with one of these seven people, I would guarantee that if your town were invaded by an enemy you could read these chapters and see yourself in one of those seven somewhere. You too would have to decide as in some countries today: would you go with the underground church or would you join the state registered church? You might then start criticising each other as can happen even among Christians —that is the tragedy of it. Human nature doesn't change.

The other reason why there are echoes through history is that divine nature doesn't change either. The God who dealt with these people is the God who deals with us. The God who saw through the international events and saw individuals reacting is the God with whom we have to deal. When the greatest catastrophe of all comes and this world ends, when all around us billions of people are losing their lives, chaos is around us and the very heavens are falling and being rolled up like a curtain – when all that is happening, God will see individuals and how they respond, and whether they are still and know that he is God.

READ JEREMIAH 42–44

This is a very solemn passage. We can see that the situation could hardly have got worse. A once proud nation – a once proud empire – has dwindled and crumbled to a handful of people who are seriously considering abandoning their land and becoming refugees. Such is the nation that loses God. After nine hundred years of independence and prosperity of a land they could call their own, a handful of people has gathered in fear near Bethlehem.

They have moved from Mizpah after the assassination of Gedaliah, the governor appointed by Babylon. They moved south of Jerusalem, on the road to Egypt, and there they are considering whether they should run. One of the reasons they were afraid of reprisal from Babylon was that they had been unable to apprehend the assassin Ishmael. They feared that Nebuchadnezzar would come and say: "So you assassinated my governor and you let the murderer go free, then I will come and kill the lot of you. You are not to be trusted."

Human instinct wanted to run. When you are afraid of people, your instincts take over and you panic, and you generally think of doing the wrong thing. In the Shetland Islands there was a village where there were many more women than men and nearly all the women dressed in black from head to foot. I once asked why – what lay behind this strange thing? I was told that one night thirteen ships set out from that village to fish for herring and a storm of tremendous ferocity came. Twelve ships were lost from one village with most of the men who lived there. One ship got back. Why was one ship saved? Because twelve ships ran from the storm and one ship turned and faced it, and that one came through it and got back home. Instinct says: run, panic. When you are in a situation of threat and danger, you get away from it. But, as we shall see, God was telling the people to stay right where they were – he was with them. What more could you ask? You are safe where I am, and I am staying. It was an extraordinary thing for this little motley crew, this surviving remnant of the once proud nation to consider going to Egypt. First they would have to go *down* to Egypt. Have you noticed that little word "down" whenever Egypt is mentioned? Living up in the Judean hills you can see that the road to Egypt goes downhill, and you go down from healthy hills to a disease-ridden swamp. There may be food there, but there is disease there too. When God had brought them out of Egypt, he brought them into a holy land, and the word "holy" means "healthy". He brought them into a healthy land and he promised them that none of the diseases of Egypt would follow them up the hills.

They were going to go down from cool, fresh mountain air into that swampy, sultry Nile Delta. Not only were they going to go *down* to Egypt, but to go to Egypt was to go *back* to Egypt. Nine hundred years earlier, God had got them out of that place and they were considering going back to it. It is incredible that human nature can behave as if the whole history of redemption has never occurred and can go back to where they started from. Nations as well as individuals can finish up right back where they started as if nothing had happened in between. Think of the trouble God had taken to get them out; think of the forty-year struggle he had to get them to keep coming out. Then think of all that God had done to get them into their own land, and now they said, "Let's go back to Egypt. There's peace and plenty there."

The choice was utterly simple and it was between material

prosperity and moral purity. Alas, we often make the wrong choice. On what grounds did you choose the house where you live at the moment? Ask yourself that question absolutely honestly before the Lord. Was it because that is where the Lord wanted you to be, or for other reasons? I think that if many of us are honest we would say it was for other reasons we chose to go and live where we did. We may not be living in the house God intended us to live in. Ask the Lord: where do you want me to be living? You may find yourself moving house as a result of this.

Chapters 42 and 43 describe the stage of *disobedience* – when God told them what to do and they disobeyed. It isn't long before a person in the state of disobedience moves into a phase two, of *defiance*, where he not only disobeys God but is in fact insolently defiant of God because he is fighting against the truth. Even the women became so degraded that they insolently defied the Word of the Lord. It is one thing for men to do that, but when their mothers, wives and daughters defiantly refuse the Word of God, then you can say that nation is finished.

Let us look first at *disobedience*. They came to Jeremiah— this little remnant—and said to him: "Will you pray for us and ask the Lord to show us the way we should go?" Now that sounds as if they had had a change of heart, but I am afraid it is deceptive. It sounds as if at last they were going to ask God what to do. It sounds as if at last they had learned their lesson and were actually going to seek the will of God, but Jeremiah was not fooled for one minute.

As 42:21 states quite clearly, Jeremiah says, "You have not been obedient in one single thing I told you. I can't believe that you're going to start now." So he made a promise to them and they made a promise to him in return. His promise to them was: all right, I've heard you, I will pray to the Lord, but I promise you I will tell you everything he says and exactly what he says. They said: that is fine, we make a promise in return: whatever he says we will do.

There is an old hymn: "Trust and obey for there's no other way; Where he sends I will go, what he says I will do...." Do you mean it? If he told you to move house, would you do so? Well, they said: "God bear witness against us if we don't do what you say." So Jeremiah went away to pray. Now in fact their request was loaded, and so often the requests for prayer we bring are loaded. We have already made up our minds and we are simply asking God to rubber stamp our plans.

In this chapter they said: "Pray to the Lord for the way we should go." Do you notice the way the wording of the prayer is loaded? It is not pray to the Lord as to whether we shall go or remain but about *where* they should go. Have you noticed that? They are not contemplating that the answer might be: stay where you are. I have noticed this both in my own life and in others. Someone comes and says they are seeking guidance as to what they should be doing. I ask, "What are you doing now?"

"Well I'm here, but I'm unsettled and I'm not very happy in my job so I'm seeking guidance."

The way they phrase the question about seeking guidance shows they are not open to the possibility that God may say, "Stay right where you are in that job and go on serving me there, because that's where I am."

I think of one girl who came to me and said, "I've been converted a few months. I'm the only Christian in the office and I'm unhappy and they're getting at me. I've had the offer of a job in a Christian firm where everybody's a Christian." She wasn't the first to make the mistake of thinking that sounded like the Promised Land. So she said, "I'm seeking guidance and I'm praying that the Lord will tell me whether it's this job or not." But, you know, the Lord wanted her to stay where she was. Alas, she didn't stay. She moved and she found out the new place wasn't the Promised Land. Working with just Christians is not necessarily all fun and fellowship. God had called her in the office where there was no witness, and he wanted a witness in that office.

The other way it was loaded came out later, when Jeremiah gave them the answer. Their minds were already made up and they were simply seeking God's confirmation of what they had decided to do. Jeremiah was not fooled, but he said, "I'll go and pray." He prayed for ten days before he got the answer. I find that very comforting. Even great saints like Jeremiah don't always get an immediate telegram back. It is as if God gives us time. The best test of guidance is time. The devil loves us to rush because he knows that if we rush into a thing we don't give the time to discern between satanic impulses, our own impulses of the flesh and the impulses of the Spirit. Therefore sleeping on it is jolly good, and sleeping on it ten days is even better. In fact, if you get an impulse and you think the Lord is telling you to do something, give it the test of time.

When I felt called to the ministry I went to see my minister and told him: I want to be a minister, can you sort of tell me how I set about it? He said, "Right, go away for eighteen months and come back and see me then." I did just that. I came back in eighteen months and said: "Look, I have got to be a minister."

He said, "Right I'll help you now."

If a thing is of God, time increases the sense of call until you feel you are going to be disobedient if you don't obey, whereas impulses of the flesh die quite quickly and impulses of Satan vanish fairly quickly because he goes to another tack – but if God is calling, time is a good test. So Jeremiah spent ten days getting the answer, and the answer when he came was crystal clear. Unfortunately, during those ten days the people had made up their minds ever more firmly as to what they were going to do anyway, but they listened to him.

So we now come to the next section, the prophecy of vv. 7–22 following the prayer of 42:1–6. The message was: stay where you are and I will look after you. You are safer with me in Judah then in Egypt without me. Haven't you yet learned that all the troubles that came on this place came because I brought them, and I have now repented of all the evil that I brought? I have changed now my outlook, and from now on there will be no more punishment of people who stay in this land. I will bring mercy on you, even through Nebuchadnezzar. I brought the punishment; I will bring the mercy. I am in charge of the situation. Or, to put it in very simple language: do you fear man more than you fear me? That is the question. That will determine where you live. Is it human factors or divine factors that are uppermost in your mind?

Jeremiah spelled it out positively and negatively. Positively: if you will remain in the land I will plant you, not pluck you up; I will build you, not break you down. Then negatively: but if you go, then I foretell physical and mental suffering on a scale you have never yet seen.

I don't know which is worse – physical death through famine, war or disease—the greatest three killers of mankind–or the mental anguish of being an execration, a horror, a taunt and a joke. But he says: you will suffer mentally and you will suffer physically, if you go to Egypt. That was the straight choice. Stay where you are and be planted and built up, or go and suffer mentally and physically. That was the prophecy and the answer to the prayer. It was in 42:1–7 that we found that prejudice in the minds of his hearers. Do you know what prejudice is? It is to pre-judge a question. It is to make your mind up before you have considered all the facts. They said, "Jeremiah you're telling a lie. We don't believe you. You never got that from

God. Where did you get it from? I bet you got it from your secretary Baruch. We know he's pro-Babylon. We know he wants us to stay." It tells us something of the sad, desperate state of their minds that they could rationalise the situation to this degree. They thought Jeremiah was getting on for sixty and that the young man Baruch was a much clearer thinker and had been persuading the old man to give them that message.

It is a terrible state of affairs and yet their mind is so made up that they are not open to reason. They are not open to revelation. Their minds are closed and yet they dare to say: "Whatever he says we will do."

The only way around that one is to say that he is not saying it. They say, "You're telling a lie."

Off they set for Egypt, and they dragged Jeremiah and Baruch with them. What a sorry little procession. Can you imagine the feelings of Jeremiah's heart as he trailed down that desert route, down from the healthy hills, down to the steamy delta, to a place called Tahpanhes (which has now been discovered). They went to that frontier town on the Nile delta. Jeremiah had a heavy heart and they asked the Lord to tell them. It is the same old story. They make their own minds up and just want God to rubber stamp their plans.

I think we are getting the message, aren't we? We need that message as individuals, as churches and as nations: not to ask God's blessing on what we plan, but to say, "Lord show us..." – not even the way we should go but whether he wants us to stay or go, and to be totally open to the Lord's will. So, in 42:8–13, Jeremiah makes a prediction – one of his acted-out parables. He has done some funny things in his time to get the truth across. Whenever he is desperate, whenever the people are so hard-hearted that their minds seem closed, he seems to resort to this under God's guidance. Since they are so hard and tough, he gets up one morning and goes out into the desert, and they see him staggering back with little boulders until he has got a heap of stones. He has smashed pots, he has worn a yoke, he has buried his underpants by the Euphrates River. He has done some extraordinary things to get the truth across, but now he has got these big boulders and he goes very boldly to the royal palace. We know that Pharaoh Hophra, the ruler of Egypt whose protection the Jews were seeking, had a frontier palace at Tahpanhes. He didn't live there very often so it was probably deserted, but it was still bold of Jeremiah. He went and dug up the pavement in front of the palace, in the very courtyard where Pharaoh used to sit to be greeted by people at the frontier. Actually it was made of brick. He pulled up some of the bricks and then he dug a hole, put the boulders in the hole, and put soil back on top and replaced the bricks.

By this time there was quite a crowd around Jeremiah. Has the old boy gone a bit? What's he doing? What's the point of that? Jeremiah turns around, and with a voice like a whiplash he says: "You bury yourselves in Egypt to get away from Nebuchadnezzar. I tell you, Nebuchadnezzar will put his throne on this very pavement and spread his canopy over – and you who buried yourselves in Egypt to get away from him will feel the full weight of Babylonian might here." What a lesson; what a parable.

Toward the end of the nineteenth century, an archaeologist found Tahpanhes. First, he found there was a Pharaoh's palace, second he found the pavement, and third he found the stones. People may say this is a book of myths and fairy tales. They have not studied the evidence. Do you know that in the year 568 BC, just twenty years after Jeremiah buried those stones, Nebuchadnezzar sat on that pavement, not facing outwards like the Pharaoh did to meet visitors to the frontier, but facing inwards, looking at Egypt which he had conquered. He went through the length and breadth of

Egypt, from north to south, and looted it. Jeremiah had said: "He will loot Egypt like a shepherd picks lice off his coat, as easily as that." A vivid picture. Prophets never mince their language. They use everyday metaphors. Jeremiah's prophecy came true to the letter. Nebuchadnezzar came and sat on that pavement, he looted the cities of Egypt and the Jews died. If only they had listened to the word of the Lord.

Now we move on to chapter 44. I want you to realise that this little remnant that found its way down to Tahpanhes was not the first bunch of Jews from Judah to go to Egypt. By the way, the word "Jew" is a shortened form of "Judah" and in fact it only begins to be used when the nation shrank to the tribe of Judah. So there were Jews down in Egypt already. They had gone in the earlier part of the troubles, just as in the 1930s Jews in Germany were planning how to get out, how to transfer their treasures. They had a certain foresight at the practical level. A number of Jews had already gone down to Egypt, so they were not only the last little remnant at Tahpanhes, but there were some scattered at Memphis, Heliopolis, some right down in the south or upper Egypt. So there were little pockets, actually four colonies, which are mentioned at the beginning of chapter 44. Tahpanhes was the last to be established. From time to time all the Jews got together for religious festivals. Jeremiah was present at the next festival, and the Jews from the other three centres further south came north, and they met up with this latest group of refugees for a religious festival. It was a big crowd, men, women, children all there – a great occasion. But there was only one snag: they did not meet to worship the King of heaven; they met to worship the queen of heaven. I wonder if that means anything to you. Do you know that throughout the ancient world you find traces of the worship of female deities? Around the whole Mediterranean coast, and through to the Tigris-Euphrates basin, pagan religions so often said

God was "she" not "he".

I remember a phone call one Thursday morning, when Granada Television in Manchester said, "Will you come and take part in a recording of a discussion for Sunday evening on the future of Christianity?"

I said, "Look, I'm in Guildford. When is this recording?"

"This afternoon."

"It's hopeless, I can't get to Manchester in one day."

They replied, "We'll fly you up. We'll have a car waiting for you at Manchester airport." So I went.

I got there and found the whole thing hollow. The first person I was introduced to was John Allegro who thought that Christianity started with a drug from a mushroom. Do you remember *The Sacred Mushroom*? Best book he ever wrote! No-one has taken him seriously ever since. The next person I was introduced to was the then Bishop of Kingston, Montefiore, who believed Jesus was homosexual. Then I was introduced to a Buddhist – an atheist. I thought: what is this – a discussion of the future of Christianity?

We got into the studio and the discussion went from bad to worse. The question master or anchor man had said, "When I want you to come in, I'll look to you and say, 'Now what do you think?'"

Well, after about three minutes the discussion left Christianity and was on to Buddhism. Within another two it was on to atheism, and then in a very short while the anchor man said, "Now for the big surprise of the evening: we have with us two real live witches." On came two women painted up to the nines and they said, "Well, all the discussion is wrong because God is feminine, God is she not he."

From then on I just began to pray that the Lord would blot me out, and forty minutes went by and the programme closed down. The anchor man looked across at me and said, "Oh, I forgot to bring you in" – just like that. I praise God it was such utter tripe and I wouldn't have had a chance to say much because he was cutting everybody off after half a sentence as usual. The thing was pure sensationalism. So I did accept my airfare back to Guildford, but I didn't accept any fee. The whole thing was so hollow. It was supposed to be a discussion about Christianity but was nothing of the kind.

Jeremiah turned up for the Jewish festival and he expected that they would worship the King of heaven. Instead they worshipped the queen of heaven. In Babylon that was the star Venus. In Canaan it had been the goddess Astarte. In Egypt it was another female god, but they all shared the same title "queen of heaven" and, ever since, this has been a pressure even on Christianity. I believe that this is the source of the title "queen of heaven" for the virgin Mary. It was the influence of the Mediterranean world creeping through, and even to Christian circles. There are still people who wish that it was a female up there instead of a male – and especially the women. Why? Because the worship of Venus or Astarte, or whatever other name she was given, consisted in baking cakes and that was something the women felt they could do. If you recall, way back in Jeremiah chapter 7, Jeremiah said, "Your children go out and collect sticks, your husbands light the fires, and you bake the cakes to the queen of heaven." The cakes were a kind of hot-cross bun. Just as at Easter we have buns with a cross on, they had little cakes with an image of the Astarte or Venus on them. When he got to Egypt he thought, "Surely, when they have lost their land and saw Jerusalem desolate and empty, they would have stopped this rubbish." But he found out that the women had kept it on, and that the husbands had not dared to stop them.

May I make a strong plea to Christian women? You have untold power in your hands. You can lift men to great heights and you can drag them to great depths. You can bring out and reinforce in men what is there. So often a family owes its very character to a good mother. But when their mothers go wrong, something serious happens in a nation. They said to Jeremiah, "Well, it was with our husband's approval." But it was the wives who took the initiative and they worshipped the queen of heaven; they baked their cakes and they offered them to the queen of heaven.

To his horror Jeremiah saw this whole Jewish crowd gathered for a reunion hoping to one day go back to the land of Yahweh, the land of Judah, and look at them all baking cakes with the image of Venus on them. So out came one of the strongest sermons he had ever preached. It is full of unanswerable questions. He says, "Why, you know what happened to Jerusalem. You've lost your land. Have you not learned your lesson? Why are you hurting yourselves?" Do you know, that is the perplexing question: why are you hurting yourselves? His second question: why are you hurting God, why are you provoking him to anger?

These are the two questions that God asks of people who do not worship him, a people who go away from him, "Why do you hurt yourself, and why do you hurt me?" That is what you are doing. I notice the loving order of those questions. God is even more concerned about them than himself. The positive commands of God are: love the Lord your God with all your heart soul and mind and strength, and love your neighbour as yourself. The negative questions of God are: Why do you hurt yourself? Why do you hurt me? Then Jeremiah says, with great poignancy: "Have you forgotten?" Five times in one sentence he uses one word – wickedness. Have you forgotten the wickedness of your nation? Have you forgotten the wickedness of your kings? Have you forgotten the wickedness of your fathers? Have you forgotten the wickedness of your wives?

The truth was that they had never really thought of it or

remembered it. Could you go through a national disaster and still not think of it? Yes, you can. People can go right through a summer drought and still not ask the right question. They will still put it down to natural causes, dismiss it and say, "We'll manage." But the right question is, "Why do you hurt yourselves and why do you hurt God?"

So Jeremiah has to say: "You may hope to go back to Judah but not one of you will go except those who run away now – a few fugitives." How accurate the predictions of God are. He knows the future exactly. In other words: a few of you who run away from Egypt will get back, but for the rest, you will die here. So that was his prognosis of their problem and we now come to the most disturbing part of it, vv. 15–19: the women. They were saying: we will not listen to you – apart from anything else you're not married and you don't understand women. Can't you hear them shouting? The insolence, the impudence of it! Now we have an extraordinary kind of logic. This is what sinful logic (masculine and feminine) does with facts. Jeremiah has appealed to the history of the last twenty-five years of their nation, and he says, "Haven't you learned the lesson?" They said, "Yes, we have learned the lesson and we'll tell you what it is. While we were baking cakes to the queen of heaven we were prosperous. As soon as King Josiah told us not to, it was then that our troubles began and we've had nothing but trouble ever since." Isn't it extraordinary – the same facts of history and Jeremiah puts one interpretation on them and the women put exactly the opposite interpretation on the facts. All the facts of nature and history are open to opposite interpretations. It is true that you can make history say anything you like by selection and by interpretation. The important question is: which interpretation is the right one? For example, there are those who say that drought and natural disasters have nothing whatever to do with the moral quality of our nation—there is no connection. There are those who could argue that when we were permissive in the sixties we were affluent and prosperous. Our troubles have only come in later. To show how wrong this argument is, I would use a very telling and appropriate illustration. You have seen the details of the awful disease asbestosis – the growth that comes in the lungs through breathing the dust, and it is a killer. Now supposing you met a man in one Yorkshire village where so many have been affected, and supposing he wheezed and gasped for breath as he spoke to you, as one of them did when interviewed on television. Supposing he said, "All the time I worked in the asbestos factory. This has only started since I retired. It's my retirement that's to blame. If only I'd gone on working in the factory I'd be fit and well. I was fine while I worked there, but now look what's happening." You can apply it very directly. Take smoking. Think of someone every few minutes taking in smoke which can lead to cancer. You can tell them, "Look, the evidence is there." I used to see doctors in their surgeries smoking, with ashtrays full on their desk. They knew, yet some did not learn. Try to teach your kids to brush their teeth. You might say, "You know, in twenty years from now you will wish you had." Why don't we learn? I'll tell you why, it is because there is a time lag. That fools us. It is true of nature. It is true of history that cause and effect are usually separated by some years, and that is why we can deny the connection. If the moment you worship the queen of heaven you were stricken with disease you would not do it, would you? If the moment you lit up a cigarette you got lung cancer, you would not do it, would you? If the permissive sixties would have been punished immediately, people would have stopped some of what they were doing. But there is a time lag and it applies as we pollute nature. We will find out after the time lag. This is the problem. We don't learn our lessons because of the time lag. The only lessons flesh will learn are lessons that have an immediate result in health or sickness.

So these women could argue: when we were worshipping the queen of heaven we were prosperous. It was only after we stopped that the troubles began. But Jeremiah put a proposition to them. The troubles, when they began, were they not God's remembering what had gone before? Was it not the time lag of God's patience? God has a long memory. God does not settle his accounts every Friday. If he did, everybody in town would be in church on Sunday. So we gamble on things not happening after the time lag, and we don't learn our lesson because the effects are not experienced immediately. It is as simple as that.

So we think we have got away with something in the immediate future and we have, but in the ultimate we have not. The flesh can only learn immediate lessons. It takes the spirit to learn ultimate lessons because it takes the spirit to say by faith, "I believe this will lead to that." It takes faith for a doctor to stub out his cigarette and say: I believe in twenty years' time I'll pay for doing this. It takes faith. It takes a step of confidence in the future, not just a response to the present to learn lessons.

These people had drawn the wrong conclusion because they had expected God to act immediately and he doesn't. God is very longsuffering. God is slow to anger. God is patient. This is the problem of Psalm 73. In that problem Psalm, David goes to the Temple and says, in effect: "God, I just don't understand it. The wicked prosper – they die in peace in bed. They have good lives. It doesn't pay to be good. Here I am, I have cleansed my heart in vain and I just suffer all the time. It doesn't pay. I don't get it." Then, in the house of the Lord, he worshipped God and he said, "Oh I do get it. For now I perceive their end and truly you have set their feet in slippery places."

You learn long-term lessons in the spirit. It takes the spirit to grasp heaven. It takes the spirit to understand the rewards available for those who live by God's will here. You may not prosper here. Honesty may not be the best policy here. In the short term, dishonesty can make more money than honesty. In fact, because the police are failing to find even fifty per cent of the criminals who commit crimes, crime does pay in England. You stand a better chance of not being found out – but in the long term it does not pay. It is the short term and the long term.

The women defied Jeremiah. So he put the proposition to them: let's test with time. The world rushes after the latest idea, the latest philosophy, and time proves them hollow and empty. But as an American preacher often said: "The trouble is I'm in a hurry and God isn't." The mills of God grind slowly but they grind exceeding small.

Jeremiah is saying: I propose to give you two tests as to whether your word will stand or mine; whether your interpretation of history is right or mine. Here are the two tests. Firstly, the name of God will disappear from Jewish lips. That has been true now for two thousand five hundred years. I tried in conversation with a Jew, every way I knew, to get her to use the name of God so I would know what the Hebrew pronunciation of it was. I could not get her to say it. Go to any Jew, and even if he or she is not an orthodox Jew, they won't use the name. They will even refer to God as "the Name" and will say, "Pray to the name. The name will help you." We have a better name; we have the name of Jesus, and that name is not disappearing from our lips. But Jeremiah said: here is the first test as to whether my word or yours is true – the name of God will not be used by Jews. The simple fact is that if you are getting away from God you use his name less and less, until there comes a time when it becomes a superstition and you dare not use it. That is what it has become even among Jews who don't worship God in Israel – they are so superstitiously afraid of mentioning his name they do not use it.

The other test that Jeremiah gave as to whether his interpretation of history or theirs was true was this: this Pharaoh, whom you have come to for protection, will be delivered into the hands of those who seek his life. Less than twenty years later, just a few years after Jeremiah said it, Pharaoh was assassinated by his own cousin. You need to be pretty bold when you give a specific test like that. Whose word is true? So Jeremiah left them with this question: who is reading history rightly – you or me? You explain it one way and I explain it another. Let history decide, and history is *his story*.

This is the last recorded utterance of Jeremiah. As far as we know, he said no more. He finished by delivering them to a reprobate mind. He said, "You vowed to perform libations to the queen of heaven, then perform your vows. Get on with it." There comes a point where people are so stubborn, so hard-hearted, so closed-minded, that the only thing you can do is say: then get on with it; go your way. It happened on the night before Jesus died. There was a man who had lived with him, eaten with him, slept in the same room, walked with him, talked with him for three years, but that night Jesus said to him, "What you have to do, do it quickly." Get on with it. You have made your decision, then go – and Judas went out and did it.

There comes a point where, if we refuse to listen to God's interpretation of history–where we close our hearts against the spirit of truth – that God says: then perform your vows; go off to the queen of heaven, I am finished with you and you will never use my name again. Romans 1 says that God delivered them over; men gave God up so God gave men up to a reprobate mind. You can say: to a closed mind. There comes an awful moment where, if you give God up, God gives you up to a closed mind.

I feel for Jeremiah at this point. He has faithfully preached the Word of God for forty years and he has ended in total failure. He has pleaded with them for forty years through disaster after disaster, "Listen to God; this is what God says...."

They have said, "No. We will not listen to you. You're lying." He has been through all their bad choices with them. He had the choice to go to Babylon where he would have met up with people like Ezekiel, Daniel and Nehemiah, and probably lived to a good old age, but he chose to stay in Judah to try to rebuild the little poor remnant that remained.

Now he is with them in Egypt and he chooses not to run from them. He is going to die there and he is never going to see his own land again. His last word to them is a word of hopelessness: "Perform your vows." Their mind is closed. Fancy ministering the Word for forty years and finishing with total failure, even the last little remnant of your congregation refusing to listen. Yet Jeremiah stands out to me as a spiritual giant who had the honesty both with himself and his God to go on speaking the truth, even when the Word of God came at Tahpanhes. He was a man who was courageous enough to say what he did against all public opinion. Again and again, democracy triumphed over him and public opinion outweighed his conviction. But he went on speaking as long as he could.

One of the saddest, loneliest paths a man has ever been called to tread is to preside over the collapse of a nation and to warn that nation repeatedly that it was not inevitable. We don't know anything more about Jeremiah. The rest of the book contains prophecies that he uttered earlier.

As far as we know, Jeremiah died shortly afterwards in Egypt. It may be significant that the very next chapter (45) was the little one about Baruch that we took earlier because it referred to something much earlier. But it may be that Baruch finished chapter 44 and just slipped in a little bit about himself. "Baruch, don't seek great things for yourself. If you have your life, that's something." Maybe Baruch was the only one left after Jeremiah died who still knew the truth of the Word of God and he wrote it down.

From the depths of Egypt we have this book and we can read it now. The Word of God is still true and history has shown that it was not the Jewish interpretation of history. It was Jeremiah's that was true. There is just one lesson that I draw out from this passage: when you ask for guidance, really ask for it with an open mind or you will finish up where you started. Whether to stay or to go — obedience brings blessing. But we finish now with the people of God out of the Promised Land. The majority have gone into compulsory exile in Babylon, the minority have gone into voluntary exile into Egypt, but it is interesting they have all gone back after nine hundred years to where they came from. The majority has gone to where Abraham was originally when God said, "Come out and be with me." The minority has gone to Egypt, where God said to Moses, "Come out and be with me."

They have gone back. You make up your mind where you are going to live on your own basis. You decide your own life and then ask God to rubber-stamp it with his blessing, and I tell you, you will finish up where you started. It may not happen immediately for God is slow to anger, but making plans and asking God to rubber stamp them is tantamount to disobedience and will lead you to defiance, and defiance will lead you to disaster.

READ JEREMIAH 46–49

When we study the story of the fall of Jerusalem following the predictions of Jeremiah, there is a certain sense of unreality about it, because it was so long ago and so far away. However, it is intensely important for us to be reading these things and studying them, because the same God who dealt with Israel is dealing with us. God is alive and real, and Jeremiah was not only told to speak to his own land, and to be an ambassador in Israel, he was told to be God's ambassador at large to all the nations of the world. This came out in the day of his call, way back in chapter 1: "Then the Lord put forth his hand and touched my mouth and the Lord said to me, 'Behold, I have put my words in your mouth. See, I have set you this day over nations and over kingdoms to pluck up and to break down, to destroy and to overthrow, to build and to plant.'" What you may not yet have fully realised is this: not only did Jeremiah *predict* the disaster that befell his land, his word *produced* that disaster.

Now this is a concept of prophecy which many do not grasp. They feel that the prophets were given divine inspiration to predict events that would happen, but what they have not realised is that God produced those events by their word. The word of God is powerful, sharper than any two-edged sword. It doesn't return to God void; it accomplishes that which he pleases. It doesn't just announce it, it accomplishes it.

Therefore, Jeremiah had more power than Nebuchadnezzar. "Behold," said God, "I have set you over the nations; to pluck them up and to plant them, to break them down, and to build them up." Because when God's Word is in someone's mouth, that person is not only able to predict God's activity but is able to produce it.

Therefore, when Jeremiah said "Jerusalem will fall" he was not just predicting the end of his nation, he was producing it. He was saying, "My word will damn this nation" – and it did. God used his words to produce the effect, and so, in the same way, the Word of God today produces the effects. It does not return to him void; it accomplishes, not just announces – it accomplishes what he pleases. As I preach his Word, not my words, but whenever my word is his Word, it will *produce*, not just predict – not just preach; it will *accomplish* (not just announce) what God wants to accomplish in your life now, provided you are willing to respond and co-operate. And so to preach is not simply a mind-to-mind operation; lives are changed.

In this passage we are going to get a sense of the greatness of God, and we are going to see in the events of Israel over two thousand miles away and two thousand years ago, a microcosm in which we see how God is going to deal with all the nations. You find that prophet after prophet in the Old Testament not only spoke *to* Israel, but spoke *through* Israel to all the nations of the then-known world. Read Isaiah 1:3 – 2:3, and he goes through seven different nations and speaks to them; read Isaiah chapters 13–23, and you will find Isaiah is not speaking to Israel but to other nations. Read Ezekiel and you will find that he spends twelve chapters speaking to nations other than Israel.

In Jeremiah now we have come to the section which collects together the messages he gave not to his own people but to every nation in his known world. He went right through every nation and said, "This is what God will do to you." So Jeremiah speaks, and still speaks, for he said that

God is going to deal with you because you are neighbours to Israel, and your attitude to God's people reveals your attitude to God. I say that today, in a world that has become a global village with instant, universal communication – all of us have become neighbours of Israel. All of us will be judged by God for our attitude to that nation. If we fail to stand up for Israel, that is going to prevent us from fulfilling our relationship with God's people. This is a relevant word, and in chapters 46–49 Jeremiah is saying: because of your attitude to Israel, the God of Israel will deal with you as a nation, and you will be finished. Therefore, it is most relevant; it is as up-to-date as today's news reports.

Now let us say a few things about God, because the main purpose of reading the Old Testament is to find out about him. The God of the Old Testament is the God of Jesus. He told people to search the scriptures, which would mean the Old Testament – because there was truth, and the scripture cannot be broken. There was the God who was the Father of our Lord Jesus, and those who dismiss the Old Testament God as an unchristian God have to reckon with Christ, who believed in this God because he was this God's own Son. So here are five things I would underline about God, which come out of chapters 46–49.

First: God is *real*. There may be mystery in God, but there is no myth. There is no fiction, only fact. This God really does exist and he is the one with whom we have to do, because he is real. No man or woman on earth can escape having dealings with him, because they are always in his presence, and one day will meet him face to face.

Secondly, God is *universal*. We tend to think, reading the Bible, that God is somehow local or national; that he was the God of the Jews; that he was confined to that little area and to that small people. But the God mentioned in chapters 46–49 is the God who deals with all nations. He is the God whom Paul announced in Athens as the God who made all nations of men of one blood to dwell together on the face of the earth. There is no other God. Other gods do not exist; they are figments of the imagination, which is another way of saying they are images. God is real, and God is universal, therefore we have a solemn duty to tell every nation about this God. If God was simply local or national, and if one religion was as good as another, then there would be no call for missionary endeavour. But, because God is universal, every nation needs to hear his true Word.

The third thing I would declare about God is that he is *moral*; right and wrong matter to him. God is a God of justice; a God of fairness. That comes out in one particular verse: "For thus says the Lord, 'If those who did not deserve to drink the cup must drink it, will you go unpunished?'" Which means that God is fair; he has a sense of justice. What security lies in that fact? If we believed in an arbitrary God, who was not bothered about injustice – who didn't mind if the wicked prospered and the innocent suffered – then life would indeed be terrible; we would be led to despair. But even though there is injustice in this world, as the book of Ecclesiastes shows so clearly and faces so honestly, behind this world we know there is a God of justice, to whom right and wrong matter, and who is fair, and he deals fairly with the human race and with nations.

The next thing I want to affirm is that he is a *penal* God. I mean by this that he is a God who punishes. This is a fact that we must never forget: God punishes everyone without exception, whether you belong to his people or not. If you belong to his people, then God punishes you because he loves you. If he does not punish you, then you are a bastard, says the New Testament in Hebrews 12; you are not his son. But if his own family get punished, how much more will other peoples? He is a punishing God, and he punishes his own people as well as every other people. We need to remember this. If you study the history of Israel, you are looking at God's own people, and look how he punished them! Why? Because he loved them, and therefore, God is a penal God, and if you think that God is a nice, old grandfather kind of God, who never punishes, then think again. If you think that because you are one of his people, he will never punish you, then think again. Read the Old and New Testaments, and it is as clear as daylight. There is one verse in the first section which is a very difficult verse for some people to accept. Before I come to that, note another verse from chapter 46: "That day is the day of the Lord of Hosts; a day of vengeance to avenge himself on his foes." That is a thought which is uncongenial to human nature.

The idea is that when every nation has had its day, God will have his day. The "Day of the Lord" is a concept running through all the prophets and the New Testament – that one day, which is already fixed in the calendar, God will say, "Now it is my day!" At the end of the day, it is the day of the Lord. He is a penal God; he is the Judge of all the earth, and it is the judge who has the last word in any court case.

That brings me to something which will be even more difficult for some people to accept: that God is a *historical* God. I mean by this that history is *his* story. I mean by that also, and this is the difficult one to swallow, that he is a God of war. He is described as that in the scriptures, in both the Old and New Testaments. In the last four thousand years, only three hundred years have been free from war. Therefore, if history is his story, then God is a God of war, and he brings wars to pass upon the earth.

The concept behind chapters 46–49, which is the biblical philosophy of history, is that the prime instrument which God uses to judge nations is to raise up an imperial tyrant who will bring war on the nations whom God is disciplining.

The key word in these chapters is "sword": I will bring the sword against Egypt; I will bring the sword against Philistia; I will bring the sword against Ammon; I will bring the sword against Moab, against Edom, against Damascus, against Kedar, against Hazor, against Elam, against Babylon. God is a God who brings the sword. A nation that forgets him and becomes complacent and at ease, and turns away from God's principles, is a nation inviting itself to be invaded militarily. Now this is the hard teaching of the Word of God. It gives a sense of the greatness of God. It means that as we read history, which is just one succession of tyrant after tyrant arising, and with imperialist ambition to conquer the world, bringing war to nation after nation, we see God's hand. We see God dealing with nations. We see him bringing complacent nations to humility, teaching them again those values that get lost in times of peace and prosperity. Few nations grow in character during affluence. Our deepest moral qualities are developed in adversity, not in prosperity.

God, in his mercy, uses war as his instrument, and describes a man called Nebuchadnezzar, who was no believer in God, as "my servant". He describes a conqueror like Cyrus as "my servant", and we may therefore say that the Hitlers of this world, the Napoleons of this world and the Caesars of this world are all encompassed by God's historical power and purpose. It is in this way that he brings nations to their knees. Now if this is uncongenial to you, then I am afraid it is the Word of God. It is here in Jeremiah, and we read what Jeremiah has to say about nine nations. The first and the third are the longest, and then they get shorter. We start with chapter 46. Now Egypt had been the greatest world power throughout Israel's history, and if you have visited that land or seen pictures of the pyramids and the ruins of the cities, you will know that Egypt was great, but not now. What happened to that greatness? What happened to those pharaohs? I will tell you what happened. First, they made the mistake of oppressing Israel, and Israel never forgot their captivity; they still don't. Every year at the *Seder*, at the Passover, they remember: "We were slaves in Egypt." No nation caused so much suffering to Israel as Egypt. They made the second mistake of thinking they were God, or thinking that their gods could give them world dominion. So that empire grew and grew, until in the time of Jeremiah they said, "It's time that we took over the world," which in those days meant the Fertile Crescent – stretching from the Nile through to the Tigris and Euphrates.

Egypt marched. On the way round the Fertile Crescent, the last good king of Israel, a mere youth, Josiah, who was trying to reform his land, met Pharaoh, tried to stop him, and was killed at Megiddo. They marched on like a great horde, rising like the Nile in flood, says Jeremiah: "You rose like the Nile in flood; you flooded around the Fertile Crescent. You reached Carchemish on the banks of the Euphrates; you killed its inhabitants and you settled there and you said, 'Now Egypt stretches to the Euphrates.'"

Within the year, the famous battle of Carchemish took place – 605 BC. It ranks with the Battle of Hastings and the Battle of Waterloo as one of the greatest turning points in human history. The battle of Carchemish found the Egyptians between Nebuchadnezzar and the river Euphrates and they had no boats to cross, so they were trapped. Jeremiah had predicted that defeat and described it in detail. Jeremiah decided the outcome of that battle, for his word produced, not just predicted it. He said, "Nebuchadnezzar will invade Egypt and you will go into exile."

When God speaks to a people, he always uses language they understand. This comes out in these messages to the nations, as it does in the seven letters to the churches in Revelation 2 and 3. God always knows categories of language which people understand, and so he talks about heifers, bulls, gadflies and locusts. He says, "When Nebuchadnezzar comes, your bull will run." Now that in itself is quite an amazing story if you have had anything to do with bulls, but the next picture is even more understandable. If you are driving through the countryside, and you suddenly see a cow, a heifer, with its tail straight up in the air, charging across the field, you will know it's being attacked by a fly that will burrow into its skin. The Nile delta was full of cattle. Their god was in the form of a golden bull — that was where Aaron got the idea of a golden calf from. Their god was the god of Cyrus, and they made a bull. "Your bull has fled, and your nation is like a heifer being attacked by a gadfly." It is a vivid picture to anyone who has been farming.

Then he says: "There will come upon you the hordes of Nebuchadnezzar like locusts." You can only imagine that if you have seen a locust swarm. The only one I have ever been in was in northern Nigeria, and the locusts were flying past at ten miles per hour. You could run and keep up with them, yet for three-quarters of an hour at midday the sky was blotted out, and the insects are small. "They will come upon you like locusts" – and Egypt always dreaded the locusts. "And you will slither away like a snake" – keeping a low profile, hidden. How vivid these pictures are! You have to live in Egypt to understand the impact of this message of Jeremiah.

So Jeremiah predicted: even though you are at this moment thinking you are on the way to conquer the world, you will be defeated at Carchemish; by the river Euphrates your army will be trapped, then Nebuchadnezzar will come back, and he will invade you and you will go into exile and your greatness will be over. These events came true to the letter, not just because Jeremiah had predicted it but because he produced it.

When God speaks, it happens. That is true from the very

beginning. When God said, "Let there be light," the lights were switched on. He said, "Let the land be divided from the sea," and it was so. Therefore, when God says, "You will be defeated by the river Euphrates", it was so. The Word of God produced the result and Jeremiah was doing it. ("I have set you over the nations....") As later Jesus would teach his disciples: Go, I have given you authority; use my name, but you have the authority; you have the power. It is an amazing concept of the Word of God.

So much for Egypt, and there is that little final thing, a little note at the end which says: "And afterward, it will be inhabited again." So it has proved, and Egypt today is not deserted as other lands; it has people living in it – no longer a great people; no longer building pyramids, but inhabited again. When God says something, that happens to the letter.

We turn to a shorter word to the Philistines: chapter 47. Between the hills of Judea and the Mediterranean there is a flat plain, and there lived the Philistines. They knew that they were vulnerable, for they were the highway between Babylon and Egypt, but they had allies in the north. Further up the coast there were the Phoenicians in Tyre and Sidon, and they had a pact that either would come to the other's aid if they were attacked. Living on a plain as they did, the one thing they feared was a flash flood, which could sweep down from the Judean hills and swamp the plain.

So God speaks to this people: "I see an enemy coming from the north like a flood over the plain, cutting you off from your allies up in Tyre and Sidon, and causing you such panic that fathers will run without even looking at their own children." Did that come true? The answer is that it did. For when the remnant of the Egyptian army came back to their homeland, unable to defeat the larger foe, they decided to wreak their frustration on the smaller land of Philistia. God said they were to vanish forever, and they have done. There is nobody in the world today calling themselves a Philistine. That nation had been an enemy of Israel right through the period of the Judges—read the stories of Samson, of Saul; finally, David managed to bring them into subjection by defeating Goliath—but this nation has disappeared. The only trace left is in the name "Palestine".

Now the Arabs use the name of the Philistines as the token of their homeland—that is all that is left, because they attacked God's people. "Inasmuch as you did it to the least of these, my brethren, you did it to me." This is the lesson we are going to have to learn here. Our attitude to God's people is our real attitude to God. Whatever else we may say or do, if a man says he loves God and hates his brother, he is a liar.

In chapter 48, Moab is spoken of. Now this prophecy is a long one but I want you to notice especially certain verses. First of all, the verse that tells us most clearly that God is a God of war, v. 10 – "Cursed is he who does the work of the Lord with slackness." Now there is quite a motto for you. It is a good text to have on your desk at work: "Cursed is he who does the work of the Lord with slackness." But what is the work of the Lord here? Listen, "And cursed is he who keeps back his sword from bloodshed." There are times when that is the work of the Lord, and cursed is he who is slack in that.

Moab was on the east side of the Dead Sea. It was one of three nations: Ammon, Moab, Edom, which were just into Transjordan. Moab was famous for its wine; its vineyards were noted. If you really wanted to give somebody a nice drink you gave them a cup of Moabite wine. It was prepared from the grapes, and carefully matured; it had to be frequently poured from one vessel to another and disturbed, or else it was contaminated by its dregs. That is the picture and it is in that language that God speaks to Moab, saying: "Moab, you are like wine that has not been poured from vessel to vessel. You have never been invaded; you have never been disturbed; you are complacent; you are comfortable; you are at ease, and therefore you are contaminated with the dregs of your society."

Here is a philosophy of history. God is saying: that nation which is never disturbed, which never finds itself at war, which is never poured from vessel to vessel, never defeated, never deported; that nation will be contaminated by its dregs. It will be like wine that is not poured from vessel to vessel to mature properly, and Moab was such a nation. It had never been invaded. It had grabbed land from Israel; it had grabbed land from the Reubenites; it was secure. The crowning condemnation was that Moses and Israel had passed through Moab on their way to the Promised Land and had told Moab of the true God. This nation had the chance to know the truth and instead they chose a pagan god, Chemosh. God says here: "Chemosh will not be able to help you." Moab is to be punished, but – and here it comes again – not desolated. Afterward, it shall be inhabited again – and it was.

May I draw out the two types of punishment that come from God? It is important to recognise both. One is what I might call disciplinary punishment, in which the person survives, chastened; the other is destructive punishment, in which the person or nation does not survive. If you like, it is the difference between corporal punishment and capital punishment. Corporal punishment is reformatory; capital punishment is retributive. With corporal punishment, the person survives – we hope a better person. With capital punishment, the person does not survive; it is a hopeless situation. God uses both forms. He is saying to some of these nations: your punishment will be disciplinary and you will survive. Egypt and Moab will survive. But other nations—Edom, Kedar—will not survive because their punishment is capital punishment, and no man will live in those lands. No man has, ever since. So, God has two kinds of punishment and the good news is that for God's own people the punishment is always disciplinary; for others, the punishment is destructive. This is the lesson we must learn: God punishes everyone but he punishes his own children out of love, that he may discipline and reform them; it is corporal punishment. But sinners are punished with capital punishment. As we read these prophecies against the nations, put them into categories — is he destroying this nation utterly, or is he going to discipline them with the loss of their land and then allow them to come back chastened, as he has disciplined his own people as well?

We move on to the Ammonites. They lived just north of the Moabites. Moab was where Moses had died on Mount Nebo, and just north was Ammon, and in fact, the city which they had as their capital is still there – it is now called Amman, the capital of Jordan. God has said here that it would continue to be inhabited; it would not be deserted. Some decades ago I heard of Arabs becoming Christians in Amman and of plans for a Bible bookshop there because of a demand for the Word of God. We are now reading Jeremiah's prophecy about Amman—the Ammonites. Isn't history fascinating? The same God who promised that they would not be wiped out is working by his Spirit through a Spirit-filled Arab evangelist in modern times.

The Ammonites shared Moab's complacency. If there is one thing God cannot stand it is a complacent nation that says "Everything is alright." To use the words here: "a nation that trusts in its treasure". A nation that has an arsenal bigger than others and therefore is confident; a nation that has more missiles than anybody else—this is offensive to God. A nation, therefore, that becomes proud. "He is very proud; his loftiness, his pride, his arrogance, and the haughtiness of his heart; I know his insolence," says the Lord about Moab.

That is the danger of a nation that is affluent, that has peace, that has a good army and plenty of money—that nation becomes proud, arrogant, defiant, insolent; and Ammon was such a nation. "Why do you boast of your valleys, O faithless daughter, who trusted in her treasures saying, 'Who will come against me?'"

They did one other thing: Ammon took from the tribe of Gad land that God had given to Israel, as if Israel had no right to it. And so God says, concerning the Ammonites, "Has Israel no sons? Has he no heir? Israel shall dispossess those who dispossessed him," says the Lord. Sure enough, that came true of Ammon to the letter. At 49:7 a word about Edom begins. Have you visited or seen pictures of Petra? That is what we are thinking about. I will never forget my journey there, riding on horseback through a narrow crack in the mountain, at times ten to twelve feet wide and 150 feet deep. So impregnable was the land of Edom, the descendant of Esau, twin brother of Jacob, that a handful of men could hold the entire country. They could be poised on the cliff-tops with rocks to drop down this gorge. When you come through it, you come to a remarkable sight: a huge, open area; acre upon acre; temples, treasuries and government buildings carved out of the solid rock, some of them as high or higher than sixty-five feet—carved into the solid, red sandstone; cavernous places. You have never seen anything like it! In the middle of this open area, hidden inside the mountains and accessible only through this crack, there is one huge hump—Mount Seir, a thousand feet high. There on the top lived Edom—proud and prosperous. God said: O, Mount Seir, I know your pride! You are right up on the top of the rock where the eagle makes his nest, but I'll bring you down, and no man will ever live there again. The striking thing as you look at these magnificent buildings, the remains of the streets, the columns and the marketplace — and I have never seen such magnificent buildings hollowed out of the solid rock – every piece carved, and from the pinnacles of the roofs you could see as far as the Red Sea – it was deserted! No-one is living there; Edom is finished.

I remind you that the last remnant of the Edomites of whom we know was a family by the name of Herod. Yes, his family left Petra, they went to live in Israel and he persuaded the Romans to make him king—Herod the Great, the Edomite. He had the infamous family of Herod Agrippa, and the other Herods – it was a terrible family. The last member of it died eaten up with worms.

Now Damascus. It is a beautiful city, nestling between the mountains of Syria and the desert. There are two beautiful, clear blue rivers, Abana and Pharpar, coming down from the mountains, through the city and into the desert, where they dry up. There, where there is fresh water, the city grew up, on the main trade route between Egypt and Babylon. It is still a beautiful city, nestling there as it does. Yet that beautiful, famous city, which everybody knew, God said it will be burned with fire, and it was burned.

We do not know what its sin was. We are not told here, but that it sinned against God is quite clear, for God is just and he said, "Damascus will burn." But God did not say it would remain empty. Had it remained empty, Saul of Tarsus would not have gone there, and we would not have had the world's greatest missionary. But Damascus was inhabited again after it was scorched, and Saul of Tarsus made his way to this very city, and another burning, blinding light—the fire of God—blinded him, and he became the apostle of grace.

Kedar and Hazor are Arab nomads, descendants of Ishmael, the other son of Abraham. We do not know where either of these places are. There is no trace of them on the map—we can trace many of the cities of the Old Testament, but these two are lost beyond recall. Somewhere in the sands of the desert lie these two settlements, Kedar and Hazor, and they have gone. God said of them both, "No man will dwell in you forever."

Why? What had they done? Listen, "You dwell securely" – that is all. "Therefore I will bring calamity upon you." Now to you that may be a strange thing for God to say, but they had become complacent, proud, self-sufficient – afraid of no man and therefore not afraid of God either. It is nations like these that God cannot stand, for men are without excuse; the power and deity of God is clearly manifest in the things he has made. A nation that thinks it can defend itself is without excuse. A nation that becomes secure and complacent is a nation that has forgotten its Creator. God will deal with that nation and remove it from the face of the earth.

Finally, the very last prophecy mentioned here is about Elam. We began with Egypt, in the west of the then-known world; we have gone right to the far east of the then-known world, Elam. Even though they are so far from Israel, God still deals with them; the God of Israel knows about them. He says: "You too will have war. I will send the sword to you but in the latter days I will restore the fortunes of Elam." Do you know, that latter promise came true so literally that Elam was one of the nations that finally defeated Babylon, which was the nation that had been used to defeat all the others we have mentioned? Do you know that Elam is now Iran? The man who was Shah of Persia in the twentieth century was one of the richest men in the world and he gave himself the title "king of kings, lord of lords". I tremble for that country now. But God kept his word and Elam's fortunes were restored.

Can you see the picture? When God says, "This place will be inhabited again but without greatness," you can see it coming true in Egypt. When God says, "This place will be inhabited by no man forever," you can visit Petra and find not one solitary soul living there, though it is an ideal place to live. When God says, "This land will have its fortunes restored," you look at Iran and you see its wealth. What is God going to say about Britain? For whatever he says about it will be our destiny and his Word produces the result.

We have learned a great deal as we have looked at this serious passage. It is not the kind of passage that is anybody's favourite; I daresay there is not a verse in all four chapters that you could quote from memory. There are few promises that you cling to. You might have known the words, "Cursed is he who does the word of the Lord with slackness" – it is often quoted – but the second half of the verse is never added. This has been a stern passage; it is a deep passage, but I have been giving you the philosophy of the Bible about history.

All these nations fell – Egypt, Philistia, Edom, Ammon, Moab, Damascus, Kedar, Hazor, Elam. There are three ways of looking at history. You can say, simply, they fell because they were overcome by a stronger military power, and that would be true, but it would be only one level of history. You could probe a little deeper and say, "Even before they fell by military conquest from without, they had already succumbed to moral corruption within," and that was also true of every one of them. Pride had crept in. You can probe deeper still and say, "These nations fell because God is God," and he is the universal God, the God of all the earth, the Judge of all the nations.

The Bible is the book that gives you the true interpretation of history. You can read history books, and the kind of history I did at school was all about the military powers. I could draw those little diagrams of the Battle of Waterloo with all the little red squares and the blue squares, and the arrows showing the way they moved. They did not tell me at school that moral corruption preceded military defeat. They certainly did not tell me that God was a God of war, and that he was working his purpose out as year succeeds year, but I am giving you that history now because we are part of that history. We are living in it, and so we need to learn the lessons of history.

The lesson is that history is *his* story and God has his hand on the nations. That is why Jesus said, "There shall be wars and rumours of wars" – because he knew that God was in control, and that war is God's way of dealing with wayward nations. War is God's way of bringing proud people to their knees. But he only sends military defeat where there has been moral decay first, for he is moral and just.

There is one final thing to mention, about two vital verses: 46:27–8. In the middle of all these terrible messages for other nations, there is that little message for God's people, Israel. The other prophecies include the word "terror" or "panic" or "fear". But there is this little word to Israel, God's own people, and it came true literally. Part of Israel was taken in captivity to Assyria. Where is Assyria today? You will find most of Assyria in the British museum. The rest of Israel was taken to Babylon. Where is Babylon today? Buried under the mud and silt of the Mesopotamian valleys. Where is Israel today? She is back in her land. She does not yet have the quiet and the ease that God has promised here, and she won't until she gets back to her God, but she is back. God's people are told, "You need not fear a full end," and that is also true of the church. Britain may disappear; England, Scotland, Wales, and Ireland may go the way of all nations, and their names may disappear from the map, but while empires rise and fall, the church of Jesus constant will remain. You will remain and you will have quiet and ease. You will be brought to your land, the Father's house, and there you will settle down again in quiet and ease. "But I will by no means leave you unpunished. I will punish you in just measure." Whom the Lord loves he chastises – that is the message here.

I close this study with two quotations from the New

Testament. The first is where Paul is talking about the future restoration of Israel: "The gifts and the call of God are irrevocable" (see Romans 11:29). This means that, having called Israel, he will never let that nation go. The other is this: "For the time has come for judgment to begin with the household of God, and if it begins with us, what will be the end of those who do not obey the gospel of God?" (See 1 Peter 4:17).

READ JEREMIAH 50–51

If you go to the city of Jerusalem, to the Church of the Holy Sepulchre, and you look in the floor, there is a silver star, to which people will point and say, "That is the very centre of the world," and it is. That star was put there by the Crusaders. Jerusalem is the centre and all other cities are secondary to it. The famous *mappa mundi* (made circa 1300) shows the city of Jerusalem in the middle of the known world, and Jerusalem is what catches your eye. Then, as you look further, you find that there is only one other city on the map. It is about halfway between Jerusalem in the centre and a representation of Christ at the top of the circular map, on the throne, looking down at that world, and he is judging it. The only other city on the map is Babylon. That map tells us that there are only two cities in the world that really matter in the last analysis, in the final day. Jesus, the Son of Man, is seated on his throne, all the nations are gathered before him, and there are only two cities in which he is interested. They are not London, Peking, Washington, wherever; they are Babylon and Jerusalem. He will say to those who belong to the city of Babylon: "Depart from me, you are goats," and to those who belong to Jerusalem, "Come, my flock." Everyone holds a passport – not an earthly one, but a heavenly one – to one or other of those two cities. You cannot have dual citizenship; you either belong to Jerusalem or Babylon. Jesus on the throne looks down at two cities in the world and says: to which do you belong?

We think primarily about Babylon as we look at this

passage, but these two chapters constantly switch. You look at Babylon, then Zion; Babylon, then Zion. Then in chapter 51 the name Zion changes to Jerusalem, and you look at Babylon then Jerusalem.

At the end of Jeremiah's life, Babylon was at the very peak of its career. Magnificent Babylon was the greatest city the world had ever seen. It was at the peak of its might and its glory, and at the end of Jeremiah's life Jerusalem lay in absolute ruin; its buildings had been torn down, were charred and burnt, and not a soul was living there. Yet Jeremiah said that these two situations would be totally and permanently reversed. Jerusalem shall rise again and Babylon will become a desolation where no man will even spend the night. I can testify to the truth and accuracy of God's Word. I could take you to Jerusalem and show you a living city, full of people, with a future. Then I would take you hundreds of miles to the northeast, to Babylon. We would have to get some Arab guides, some Iraqis, to take us to that desolate spot. We would have to watch out against hyenas, and when the sun began to go down our Iraqi guides would say, "Come on, we must be going. No man spends the night here. The *jin*, the evil spirits, dwell in these ruins, and we do not spend the night here."

Even the camps of archaeologists have had to be outside the city of Babylon for that reason. So we are studying things you can go and look at with your own eyes. It is remarkable that Jeremiah, at the end of his life, when Babylon was magnificent, crowded, the greatest city in the world, and Jerusalem lay in absolute ruin and desolation, said that this was not going to be God's last word. The two cities would change places. Babylon would fall, and Jerusalem would rise again. It took faith to make a statement like that in that situation; but he made it and it has come true to the letter.

That is giving you the end from the beginning. The great

empire of Babylon lasted seventy-three years and then fell. Jerusalem lay empty and ruined for just seventy years, then they came back and they began to rebuild it and it is still there. It just took one lifetime for the position of those two cities to reverse. That is only like the blink of an eyelid to God, for a day is as a thousand years and a thousand years as one day.

Let me give you a bit of the history of Babylon. It began in a flat plain where man said: Let's make us a name. Let's have some national pride about us. Let's build a building that you can see for seventy miles. Let us build a tower that reaches right up into the sky – and they built the Tower of Babel. "Babel" is the word, and it means confusion, misunderstanding – babble. When there is babble you cannot hear what is going on; you can't make sense of the noise.

God looked at man's proud attempt to build a city that reached up. The tower was built of brick and bitumen. In the Mesopotamian basin, that great flat plain of silt and clay, there is no rock or stone. You have to bring materials from the mud and the slime to build, so they took the clay and baked bricks, and clay is simply wet dust. They took the dust of the earth, the clay and the silt; and they took the bitumen, the slimy, black dirty stuff that comes out of the bowels of the earth; and they stuck the bricks together with the slime; and they built up – and that is man's pride.

Man uses brick, but there has been a bye-law in the city of Jerusalem that brick cannot be used to build. Jerusalem must be built of rock – God's materials, not from the bowels of the earth; not black and slimy, but white, golden, lovely rock from the top of the hills. The contrast is marked. Brick is clay, and we are clay; and we are made of dust and we go back to the dust. Jesus said, "Peter, you are the rock, and with this rock I'm going to build my church." God builds with rock. He doesn't make clay for bricks and bitumen to stick it together. No, there is brick and rock – Babylon and Jerusalem.

It is interesting that down in Egypt, an unhealthy, steamy, silty delta, the Hebrews had to make bricks. It is the difference between the city of God and the city of man – rock and brick. We, of course, have now discovered reinforced concrete and can imitate rock. We have our own version of it.

That Tower of Babel survived some time, but at that place God created language; he created the different dialects. He created us so that, if we live away from someone else for a time, our speech develops differently from theirs, and when we come together we don't understand each other. He deliberately did that so that mankind could not be united without him; could not have fellowship unless they had the fellowship of the Spirit. God mercifully gave us many languages so that we would not be able to achieve a united human race without him. There are now six thousand tongues, and we just don't understand each other. Even when we use the same language, we don't seem to understand each other. So God has deliberately confused us. He has even subjected the whole creation to futility so that even creation itself cannot be fulfilled until the sons of God are redeemed; until God is back in the centre. How merciful of God to confuse human pride in this way, so that we couldn't do without him.

Babel was destroyed by a man called Sargon, and it lay ruined for a time. Then an extraordinary thing happened. Think of the right-hand side of the oblong Arabian peninsula, the Persian Gulf, where much of our oil comes from. At the head of the Gulf, where the Tigris and the Euphrates enter it, there is a big delta. In that area lived a group of people called the Chaldeans, or the Chaldees. They were busy experimenting with building, and their model city was Ur. It was a pretty good city, built of brick stuck together with slime. It was so progressive, that I have shown photographs of some of the rooms to people, and they have thought they were looking at modern buildings that had just fallen empty. They had running water in the bedrooms and central heating – highly sophisticated. The Chaldeans were saying: we have had a good city in Ur, let us build another, bigger one on a better site. They moved up the river Euphrates some hundreds of miles and found a spot where there had been a city before – and they rebuilt the tower of Babel. Around it they rebuilt the most magnificent city, and so Babylon was founded.

It all came from a city called Ur. Does that hit you? It was from that very city that another man, an old man called Abram—we know him better as Abraham—left that same city and went up the Euphrates looking for a city, but not that one. While his fellow countrymen settled on the old Babel, rebuilt it and formed Babylon, he kept on going, right up the Euphrates. He got to a place called Haran, a little town of mud huts. Still he moved on, up into the hills of Judea among the limestone. He lived in a tent until the end of his days, and the only bit of real estate he ever owned was a cave in which to bury his wife – the cave of Machpelah at Hebron. Yet this old man said, "I'm looking for a city". He was looking for one a good deal better than Ur, and not one that I believe man can make, but one that I believe only God can make – a city whose builder and maker is God. Abraham spent the whole of his life looking for that city. He knew it was there, and he went looking for it.

Does that set the scene? Does that help you to realise why Jerusalem and Babylon are the only two cities that really matter? You see, the Chaldees went looking for a city, and most of them built their own at Babylon; but one man said, "We'll never build the ideal city; God will have to build it. I am going to live in a tent because I look for that city." This gets me very excited; the whole tie-up of history—to see God's purposes being worked out.

The man who really built Babylon up more than any other was Nebuchadnezzar (or Nebuchadrezzar, it doesn't matter which you say). He was the man about whom these chapters were written. During the twenty-five years or so that he was king of Babylon, he said, "This is going to be the greatest, because I am the greatest." It sounds familiar, doesn't it?

I can scarcely begin to describe that city for you. Its walls were seventeen miles long, and they were so wide that chariots could pass on the top. The gates were high and you can see one of them today – the Ishtar gate, which has been reconstructed. He built a wide processional way a thousand yards long, and it had something like 575 statues of bulls or lions or dragons down it in glazed blue brick. His throne room was about 180 feet long and sixty feet wide, and that was just the room in which he received people on his throne.

His wife was from Persia. She was a Mede. When she came to live with him she said, "Well, it's a lovely city, but I do miss the hills and the mountains. I do miss seeing those slopes covered with greenery."

"Right," he said, "I'll build you some hanging gardens," and he did. The Hanging Gardens of Babylon became one of the Seven Wonders of the World. This fantastic pyramid of gardens, with greenery tumbling down the slopes in the middle of the plain was a man-made mountain with flowers and trees.

He built a canal system. The Euphrates went right through the middle of the city and the canal system irrigated the area inside the walls. Archaeologists have unearthed many temples there. That was Babylon, and Jeremiah said it would be dust. A time would come when no man would even spend the night there, but the little city up in the hills that had been destroyed would rise again. What faith! So we turn from this tremendous picture of Babylon to chapter 50, where Jeremiah begins to predict the fall of Babylon, when it was at that peak. Can you imagine somebody walking through the streets of New York and saying, "The Empire State Building will fall." Can you imagine somebody walking through Brasilia and saying, "It'll all vanish and nobody will live here," or even somebody walking through London and saying, "One day this will just be a wasteland. Nobody will live here." You begin to get the feel of what Jeremiah dared to say.

Jeremiah had been predicting the fall of Jerusalem for forty years. At first, he didn't name the cause of the fall, but later, as the Lord revealed it to him, he said, "The trouble will come from the north." Later still he said, "I know now it's going to be Babylon." That was strange because at that time power number one was Egypt. Babylon destroyed Egypt at Carchemish, so it was Babylon's turn to be top dog.

We have already noticed that in almost every case it was Babylon that destroyed the nations: Moab; Edom; Ammon; Egypt itself; Kedar; Hazor; Damascus – all of these fell to Babylon. Those chapters said Babylon was the rod of God's anger, and that God had raised up Nebuchadnezzar as his servant to deal with these other nations and to punish them, and that is the biblical philosophy of history, and it means that God raises up Napoleons and Hitlers to deal with nations with whom he is displeased. Therefore when a dictator arises or when a world power arises, you ask: "What have the nations done to deserve this? Have they forgotten God? Have they become proud and self-sufficient? What has gone wrong?" We always have to ask that when a new, big power is arising. "Why is God allowing this dictator to cause fear and dread? Why are countries being overrun? What was wrong with them before?" It is a very important question to ask but – and here is the big "but" – the problem is that when God raises up a man and gives him the power to deal with other nations, it goes to the man's head. He thinks that because he has the power to punish others he must be alright himself – that is when things go wrong, and that is what Babylon was saying.

Babylon's attitude was: we are not guilty for what we have done against Israel. They sinned against their Lord, their true habitation, the hope of their fathers. So we are alright you see; God has used us. Babylon knew that God was using them; claimed that God was using them, as Hitler did, incidentally. But Babylon made Hitler's mistake too. It went to Nebuchadnezzar's head. As Lord Acton observed, power tends to corrupt, and absolute power tends to corrupt absolutely. Because you have been used to punish another, that does not mean that you are right yourself.

At the very smallest scale, within the family: parents, fathers, mothers, because you have been given the divine calling of from time to time punishing your children when that is necessary, it doesn't mean you are alright because you can spank your kid. In fact, it should have the opposite effect on you. It should make you say, "What have I done wrong that makes my child do that?" You should not be silly enough not to punish; that is a foolish attitude. A parent who says, "Because I'm not a perfect saint, I have no moral right to punish my children," or a policeman who says, "Because I'm not a perfect saint I've no right to arrest that burglar" would cause chaos. When you are used to punish someone else, that is when you need to remember that God is God, and that he puts you in the scales as well. When Winston Churchill was called to the Admiralty during the First World War, the Prime Minister of Britain asked him to go and stay with him. He went to stay in the Prime Minister's house and, just before he turned out the light to go to sleep, he noticed a Bible on his bedside. That was in the days when an English Prime

Minister kept a Bible by every bedside. Winston Churchill had been given the task of controlling His Majesty's navy, and in those days Britannia ruled the waves; therefore, being given this tremendous position of responsibility and power to deal with enemy fleets, before he went to bed that night, he picked up the Bible, almost by chance, and let it fall open. It fell open at this passage: "Do not say in your heart, after the Lord your God has thrust them out before you, 'It is because of my righteousness that the Lord brought me in to possess this land,' whereas it is because of the wickedness of these nations that the Lord is driving them out before you. Not because of your righteousness or the uprightness of your heart are you going in to possess their land, but because of the wickedness of these nations the Lord your God is driving them out before you." Churchill never forgot that; it was as if God put the word in his heart from the very beginning: because I will use you to win a war, don't you think that you are any better than those you defeat. I wonder if Churchill recalled that in 1945.

God spoke: "Babylon, I have used you to deal with Egypt; with Israel; with Edom; with Ammon; with Moab; with Kedar; with Hazor; with Damascus; but don't you think it is because you are righteous; it is because they are wicked!" Do you understand? That is the message, and Babylon made the mistake. So Jeremiah makes specific predictions. He says, "There's a great army coming from the north of many nations." When the war came, it did not come from one, but many; and all the nations on the northeast borders of Babylon united to attack. They were led by the Medes and the Persians, but there were others. The Elamites joined in, and many another joined in, and they all came and Jeremiah had said they would. Jeremiah had dared to say, "Your idols will be embarrassed." The first thing the invading army did was to go to the temples, grab the idols, take them away and say, "Now they are on our side." Cyrus, the leader of the invading troops, made the great mistake of saying, "It is the god Marduk" (which was the god of Babylon) "who has given us the victory, because he's now with us." Cyrus had the god Marduk in his tent, an idol, and that is why Cyrus didn't last either.

How history reveals that God is God. There is only one true God, and all others are idols. The difference between God and idols is this: idols are made; God makes. The portion of Jacob is the one who formed all things, whereas these idols, you have had to form them. This is the difference between the only true God and all other people's ideas of god. Their ideas they have made; but God made them. He is the great unmade. If a Sunday school child thinks they are being clever and says to a teacher, "Who made God," there is a very simple answer to that, and that is no one, because God never was made; he is the Maker. So the question, "Who made God?" is a nonsensical question; it is like saying, "What is a square circle?" or "Why is an oven when it's hot?" It just doesn't make any sense to say "Who made the Maker?"

He dared to call their idols by a rather uncomplimentary name. The word in Hebrew for idol is a word that means dung pellet. Isn't that extraordinary? To you: cowpat. That is the word Jeremiah uses all the way through here, "Your cowpats will be ashamed." Doesn't it put the thing in perspective? The Hebrew is always blunter than the polite English versions and it gets the truth across. Here are things to avoid – watch out that you don't step into idolatry. That is what Jeremiah is saying. There are word plays on Babylonian places here. He calls a place "double rebellion" and "visitation" but, when you boil it down, what he says in chapter 50 about Babylon summed up the problem. The reason why God was going to destroy them is revealed in vv. 31-2, "Behold, I am against you, O proud one", and in the next verse: "The proud one shall stumble and fall."

We don't know that Babylon was terribly immoral. We don't know if there was a lot of dishonesty or immorality in that city. The only thing we do know about the city of Babylon was that it was filled from end to end with pride. It started at the top with the king, and he used to strut in his gardens, from which you could see this magnificent city, and he used to say, "Is not this great Babylon which I have built by my power for my glory?" You notice his prayer: "Mine is the kingdom, and the power, and the glory; forever and ever, amen." We can see how he thought; but seventy-three years would see it out.

If you listen to Hitler's speeches you get the same tone. It begins as national pride, and then it becomes personal pride. That is the deadliest of all the seven deadly sins. The way we treat it, you would not think so. We can have pride in our little domain. You can have pride in your family that is not a godly pride; pride in your car; your house; your garden; your job; your qualifications; your exam results – and it can all be godless pride instead of thankfulness to God for enabling you to do it.

Pride is deadlier than other sins because the trouble is that if you manage to deal with all the others, you finish up with this one. Have you ever noticed? That is what happened to the Pharisees. Because they managed to deal with the other sins, they finished up by saying, "What a good boy am I" and slipped right into the worst one of all. That was what was wrong with Babylon, and therefore a Christian has to be on his guard against national pride. That is a very subtle thing, and wars have been waged in its name. National pride is a form of projected pride. Babylon was the proud one, with its hanging gardens, its temples, its walls and its buildings, its bricks and its bitumen. That is the main thing that is wrong, and so there comes this tremendous poem about the sword, and Babylon is put under God's ban. God said, "This mighty city, no one will dwell in her!" That is a remarkable thing to say about a big city.

It was ruined. One day there came to that place a young Greek man who by the age of thirty-one had conquered the then-known world. Everybody called him Alexander the Great. He came to Babylon and said, "We are going to rebuild Babylon, and this will be my eastern capital." They got as far as clearing the old rubble and foundations out of the way for Alexander to rebuild it, and before the first brick was laid Alexander was dead. I think he died because he tried to do something that God said must not be done. He died quickly and suddenly at a young age. So, if you will take my advice – if you want to see your pension, don't start rebuilding Babylon. Don't make the mistake Alexander made.

Now let us look at the message of chapter 50 for Israel: you are my lost sheep; out of all this you are going to come running home to the fold weeping – you are going to want to spend the rest of eternity with me; you will want to make an everlasting covenant with me. O, Israel, you are my lost sheep, living among these goats! Come out; flee; get out of that city; come back home! When this trouble comes to Babylon, see you are not in that city, or you will go down with it. Get out of that city while you can! Get all the ties broken and get back to Zion, and there talk about my greatness; there praise my vengeance; but get back to Zion.

The loveliest phrase for Israel is this, "Remember your Redeemer is strong." Now the Hebrew word "Redeemer" there means redeemer-kinsman. It means the Hebrew relative who had to take justice into his hands and avenge his relative. So if my nephew was murdered, I became the kinsman-redeemer who had to go and find the murderer and kill him. That is the meaning of the word Redeemer: Israel, your Redeemer is strong, and he will come and deal with Babylon. Babylon has slain your young men; Babylon's young men shall be slain. So it happened.

I turn briefly to chapter 51. If chapter 50 concentrates on the destruction of Babylon, chapter 51 says that God will raise up a destroyer – a spirit of a destroyer, which means supernatural powers to destroy. Every dictator who has managed to conquer his known world has had supernatural power, a spirit within him. Hitler certainly had; he began to dabble in the occult about 1937, and the signs of the possession came shortly after. "I will put the spirit of a destroyer in the Medes." They are named. Here is Jeremiah writing history beforehand. He had said that Babylon would come and destroy Jerusalem, and it did. Now he says the Medes will come and destroy Babylon – and they did. Fancy writing history in such detail. To predict a downfall is one thing, but to say who will do it and how! He puts emphasis on archery, but the most extraordinary prediction in chapter 51 is that the waters of Babylon will dry up. It is mentioned four times. Now when Cyrus and the Medes arrived at Babylon, they looked at those massive walls which were so high that you could not scale them, they were so thick and so strong. That very night, Belshazzar's feast was going on. They were so secure, so safe, so self-sufficient, so confident in their own impregnability, that Belshazzar was getting drunk inside that banqueting hall. Cyrus said, "How do we get in?" Like a brilliant strategist he said, "Where is the gap in the walls? It is the great river Euphrates, which cuts right through." The two half-circles of wall were cut by that great river and so he said, "Right. We divert the river and we go in there." His army dug a new canal out into the desert and back into the river, and they diverted the mighty Euphrates. They had a dry river bed leading into the heart of the city, and in the middle of Belshazzar's feast Babylon fell.

Jeremiah had said, "Your waters will be dried up; the enemy will come in like locusts", and it was a magnificent description. If ever you have seen locusts come, you will know that. "They'll come in like locusts, but behind the locusts is God like a lion." This is vivid language – the lion is sending the locusts, and they will come in; "Your waters will dry up, you will fall in a day; your young men will lie slain in the streets. There are some modern Old Testament scholars who do not believe prophecy or prediction is possible and do not believe in the supernatural, and who say this chapter must have been written after the event and therefore could not have been written by Jeremiah – it is too accurate. We will leave the scholars with their lack of faith, and we will believe in a God who knows the end from the beginning, and a man of God who therefore knows the end from the beginning. In the middle of this chapter 51 is this tremendous contrast – the God who makes is the God who breaks. Let that be the message that stays with you. The God who made the heavens, who made space, who made planet Earth; the God who makes the wind and the rain and the lightning – the God who has a dynamic storehouse of energy – is the God who breaks. That is the God with whom we have to deal. He made Babylon and breaks Babylon. God says to Babylon, "You are my hammer with which I break" ... "but now I break you, Babylon – you are no more than my hammer". You know, you can break a hammer; you have probably done it. You have been hammering away, and then the shaft of the hammer goes, flying off at all angles. It is just a hammer so you buy another one. God is saying: I am buying another hammer – the Medes. I hope they will remember that they are just the hammer in my hand, no more. I make; I break.

In chapter 51 what does it say to Israel? "Get out while there is time. If you are still in Babylon when this happens, you have had it. Their judgment has reached up to the skies.

What a vivid picture! As I explained earlier, like the Tower of Babel, their sin had been building up. It was simply the sin of pride. It had built up until it had reached the heavens, and the heavens' lightning was striking.

Now comes one of these little touches. Remember Jeremiah was a good visual aid teacher, who used object lessons. He used a yoke, a potter's wheel, a jar to break, and his old underwear which he buried by the Euphrates; now he is going to use his last. Chapters 50 and 51 he wrote down in a book and he gave it to his secretary's brother. His secretary, you remember, was Baruch, and Baruch had a brother, Seriah, who was a quartermaster in the army of Zedekiah. So he gave the book to Seriah and said, "Go with Zedekiah to Babylon. When you get there, read the book, then tie it to a heavy stone and in the presence of the public [so everybody knows about it] throw that book and that stone into the river Euphrates and say, 'Thus shall Babylon sink.'" Though that scroll must have rotted away by now, we can be thankful to God that somebody kept a copy of it, or we could not read it now. Somebody must have kept a copy, though the stone still lies at the bottom of the muddy river Euphrates.

The biggest building in Babylon was a stepped temple called a ziggurat. Its bottom platform was 290 feet square and 160 feet high. That was just the bottom layer, like a wedding cake. The next tier up was sixty feet high. It was the most extraordinary thing that you have ever seen. If you want to find it today, do you know what you will find? If you go there today, you will find a pit the exact size and shape of that ziggurat, as deep as it was high. It has happened through a number of strange things; partly because people have taken away the bricks and built other things elsewhere; it is partly because the Euphrates River flooded in; it is partly because the water table rose and other things happened; but today it is known as "the pit". That great ziggurat, reaching up to heaven, is now a great pit, reaching down to hell, and so God's Word comes true.

Jeremiah spoke the truth — God's word is the rock on which the hammer is broken. We have noted that at the end of the New Testament, as at the end of the book of Jeremiah, there are only two cities: Babylon and Jerusalem. People have commented on the Babylon in Revelation, which is clearly about the future: does that mean that ancient Babylon will be rebuilt? I do not believe so, because God said it never will be inhabited. So where is Babylon going to be? The answer is that the spirit of Babylon has moved on into other cities. Even in the days of the New Testament, the word "Babylon" was applied by Christians to Rome. Peter wrote in a letter: "Those who are in Babylon salute you," but he was writing from Rome. The spirit of Babylon moved on from Rome to other capitals. Where is Babylon today? You will find Babylon today in Beijing, Brussels, New York, London, Moscow. But one day there is going to be one Babylon that is bigger than all of them. I don't shout "Hallelujah" to that one, because I will shout "Hallelujah" when it is destroyed. The "Hallelujah Chorus" comes with the fall of Babylon. One day there is going to be a pinnacle of human civilisation, a city whose human architecture and power will surpass any other city there has ever been, and God's message is: Get out of that city before it falls. Have no part in her. She is a prostitute. She will seduce you with the glamour, the money, the opportunities. The big city promises so much and delivers so little, and does it for material gain. This city is the scarlet woman, the harlot, the prostitute. Come out of her. Don't find your life so tied up with Babylon that when Babylon falls, you fall. But rather think of the Chaldean called Abram who set out to look for another city.

I believe there will be a new Babylon somewhere. It may be one of the existing cities of the world or it may be a totally new city which Antichrist will build for himself. It may be in the middle of the deserts of the Middle-East. Who knows? I don't know where it will be. When it comes, I will know. I know that the new Babylon will fall. It will be somewhere near the sea, because the ships at sea will see the smoke arise from Babylon and they will bewail that they have no port to sail to, and that the commerce of the world has crashed. You can read all about the details in the book of Revelation. It ties up so clearly with Jeremiah.

I also know that there is going to be a new Jerusalem, a new city whose builder and maker is God. I can't wait to see the designs, apart from anything else – perfect town planning. It will be a city constructed out in space, not on earth. It will not be a city built up from brick and slime, from the earth built up – it will be coming down out of space. Nowadays we are talking about building cities in space. God has had plans on the stocks for a very long time. There is nothing new under the sun. He thought of it first.

Putting it simply then, in which city does your citizenship belong? The big city with its commerce, its science, its architecture and its art, which is all godless; or the city of God, the perfect city which makes every other city just look nothing, which makes you feel that your home city is like a station waiting-room that we are just passing through. You will either go down with Babylon and lose everything you have, or you will go up with Jerusalem and keep everything worth having.

The Son of God left the eternal home of glory, and came into human civilisation, into "Babylon". When they put him to death, they wrote in the languages of civilisation — Greece, Rome, even of Israel. They wrote the inscription in Greek, Latin and Hebrew, and put him to death, and because of that death you may one day go to live in the new Jerusalem forever.

READ JEREMIAH 52

It is a very strange ending, isn't it? A little bit of history, clearly not written by Jeremiah himself but added by someone else, probably his secretary Baruch. It is out of place in time – incidentally, most of the book is, as we have discovered. The technique is known in the cinema as "flashback" but Jeremiah discovered it long before and there is this constant moving around. This chapter belongs with chapter 39 which describes the fall of Jerusalem.

I believe that not only did the human editor add this chapter, but that the divine editor behind him wanted this book to finish on this rather flat, historical, mundane note, without a single mention of the prophet Jeremiah. The only time the name "Jeremiah" occurs it is someone else, as you may have noticed. Without a single word from the Lord in it, it is nevertheless part of the Word of God and the ending to one of the greatest books of the Bible, certainly the greatest in size and one of the greatest in message.

Let me summarise the chapter briefly. It describes the last days of a once great nation. It is therefore a very sad chapter. It describes what happened to its king, its buildings, its leaders, its people, even its furniture and treasures. It begins with that puppet king Zedekiah, a pure politician trying to play off the great powers one against another and coming badly unstuck. Zedekiah managed to escape from the city when he realised all was lost. He went out of the one part of the city wall that they were not guarding because it was a garden rather than houses – the king's garden. Right at the bottom end of the spur of the hill of Zion, he escaped out through that garden with his troops. They deserted the civilians, which is a comment in itself, and they went down the valley towards that deep rift in the earth's crust, called the Arabah, in which lies Jericho and the Dead Sea, and there they were caught.

As we have seen, they did three things to Zedekiah. First of all they made him hopeless by destroying all of his sons in front of his eyes. He would therefore know that the royal line he hoped to found was finished. Secondly, they made him helpless by gouging out those eyes that had watched his sons' assassination. From now on he had to have everything done for him and had to be led around. Thirdly, they made him harmless by shutting him up in prison where he could not even talk to his own people. He spent the entire rest of his life in a Babylonian dungeon with time only to think. One can only guess at Zedekiah's thoughts, I would like to guarantee that most of his thoughts were centred on another man called "Jeremiah", who was still free.

How he must have wished that he had listened to Jeremiah. By a strange coincidence, his own grandfather had the same name—it seemed as if this name was going to haunt him all his life and it is mentioned here: "Zedekiah, the grandson of Jeremiah". To distinguish that one it says "Jeremiah of Libnah", whereas our Jeremiah was of Anathoth. But there he must have pondered on the strange coincidence that he would not have been in the world at all but for one Jeremiah and he might still have been on the throne if he had listened to another. This man spent the rest of his days thinking that one through.

The second section of the chapter talks about the buildings. After three days, the captain of the guard of Babylon came with orders for systematic demolition of that entire city. Kathleen Kenyon's excavations have abundantly proved the truth of every part of this narrative. On the hill of Zion there is hardly the remains of a single house. There are a few Arab homes there, but there is no point in looking now. Most of the ancient city of Jerusalem has gone. Modern Jerusalem, even medieval Jerusalem, is further to the north.

The third thing that is described in this chapter is what happened to the people. Most of them were taken off to Babylon. Zion was not a huge city and the total number recounted here, 4,600, figures as the population of that city. They were all taken off, except a few of the very poorest who were left to keep the vineyards and the fields going. For the rest, the city was evacuated.

The next thing that is described is what happened to the temple fittings. Most of them were of precious metals and they were taken off—the gold, the silver. Some of them were huge. The great bronze "sea", as it was called, was a gigantic basin supported by four bronze bulls on a bronze pedestal, and that was smashed with sledgehammers. The great columns, the two great bronze hollow columns outside the holy of holies, the holy place, were also smashed and carted off. The metals were precious. So those Jews had to watch Solomon's beautiful temple, the house of God, systematically smashed and taken away.

The next part of the chapter describes what happened to their leaders. In those days, when a nation was defeated it was automatic that its leaders, both religious and political, were killed so that they could never lead again. Rob a nation of its best brains; rob a nation of its best thinkers. Take the leaders and it will be years before they recover. That has been known in modern times also. Remove the leaders and you make the people that much slower in their recovery. So the leaders were assassinated.

Finally, there is a very careful account of the numbers that were taken away, showing – as we know, right through the Bible – that God is interested in numbers and keeps careful records. You notice that it is not just about three thousand, it is 3,023, which shows, because it is in the Word of God, that it isn't "about so many" at a meeting. God has already counted the people at a church service because he knows every individual. He knows where they are. He counted these particular people because he wanted to bring some of them back to the land. God keeps his eye on his people. If there are ninety-nine safe in his fold and one who isn't, then God has got his eye on that one.

Concluding the summary, there is a little statement that a previous king of Judah, one of Zedekiah's predecessors who had been deported after reigning only three months at the age of eighteen and had been imprisoned in Babylon, was released. He was now treated very well – not by Nebuchadnezzar, but by his son Evil-Merodach who only reigned for twelve months. We know that Evil-Merodach was a good deal less of a tyrant than his father and he felt that Jehoiachin had been badly treated because he had not fought against Nebuchadnezzar but had surrendered. So it was put right and he was allowed to sit at the king's table and given a daily allowance.

Such is the amazing confirmation of the Bible through archaeology that when they dug up the remains of the Ishtar Gate in Babylon, they found Jehoiachin's ration book. They found a tablet with Jehoiachin's name written on it and his daily allowance. Those who doubt the truth of God's Word – it is these little things. You cannot invent a fact like that. Doesn't it give you confidence in the rest of God's Word— that the last little paragraph of this book, with a seemingly irrelevant statement, has nevertheless been proved to be absolutely correct?

So much of the Bible has been demonstrated this way that I find no difficulty in accepting the rest of it. It has been said: accept all in the Bible you can on the basis of reason, accept the rest on the basis of faith, and you will live and die a happier person. That is not a bad basis in approaching the Bible. You do not need to leave your reason behind, but it won't take you all the way.

Why is this final chapter there? At the climax, why should we get into this kind of history after such dramatic words from God? Part of the flatness is that there is more excitement in anticipating something than in it happening. Have you noticed that? This is the sense we get in this chapter when we get to it. I am going to give you one general reason and then some particular reasons. You can either take all of them or take your pick; I will leave you to judge. The general reason is something that is true of the whole Bible: this book is not just a record of the *words* of God; it is a record of the *deeds* of God and either without the other becomes meaningless. If we had only the words of God in this book but not his deeds, then people could say, "Words, words, how do we know it's true?" If we had only the deeds of God, then people would be free to put whatever interpretation they like on the history, and people do that. What we have in the Bible is history, which is the deeds of God, and we know these historical events to be the deeds of God because they are accompanied by the words of God. The words explain the deeds and the deeds take meaning from the words, and the two belong together. That is why the Bible is a mixture of what God says and what he does; it is a mixture of preaching and history. We have got to have the history to prove that God means what he says. That is what this chapter tells us. Let me give you one example. Jeremiah has spoken frequently about the anger of the Lord, and the vast majority of people in Britain do not believe that is true. They say it is only words and that God does not get angry but is like a nice grandfather – benevolent, loving, and he just wants us to be happy and pat us on the head and say, "There; there." This picture is found within the church. Some years ago, a group of representative Christian leaders met together to discuss a united outreach to Britain. There was one man there who said, "I do not believe that we are sufficiently united yet to do this together." They said, "Rubbish; we all believe in the same God."

He said, "We do not."

"What do you mean?" they asked.

He said, "Well, may I tell you what God I believe in?" That man took his New Testament and he opened it at Romans 1. He said, "The wrath of God is being revealed from heaven. Men have given God up so God is giving men up and his anger is revealed in disobedience to parents, homosexual relationships, a spirit of rebellion, and this is a sign in our society of the anger of God."

Leader after leader said, "No, we don't believe in a God like that. We don't believe in a God of wrath. We don't believe in a God of anger," and that meeting came to absolutely nothing.

But the Bible is full of teaching on the anger of the Lord. It is also full of the teaching of the love of the Lord, but I am using this as an illustration. Jeremiah is full of the teaching of the anger of the Lord and the New Testament, too, is full of the teaching of the anger of the Lord. Even Jesus himself was angry, and a study of his anger is a most revealing study. Yet people say, "I don't believe it. I don't accept that God is like that. I don't believe that God could be angry with Britain and that the troubles we are going through could be a sign of his wrath." The only thing said about God in chapter 52 of Jeremiah is this: "Surely because of the anger of the Lord things came to such a pass in Jerusalem." Now do you see? It is one thing for Jeremiah to say, "God is angry," but the

proof of it is in the deed of God. How do you know when a
person is angry? Because of what they do about it. How did
you know that Jesus was angry? Well, you knew that he was
angry because he took a whip and turned the moneychangers
out of the temple—that's how you knew. It is not enough for
someone to say, "I'm very cross with you." You will know
they are cross with you by what they do. That is why the
Bible never makes a statement about God without backing it
up with a deed of God that proves that he means what he says.

Jeremiah had been saying for forty years: "God is angry
with this nation; he's angry with this city." So chapter 52 tells
us: this surely proves it. In plain, matter of fact terms, with
no purple passages, no emotional phrases, no adjectives – in
simple nouns, subjects, verbs and objects, the statements are
made. The king had his sons killed, was blinded, and was
put in prison. The people were deported, the houses were
demolished, the leaders were assassinated, the furniture was
broken up and taken. It is writing underneath all of God's
Word: Amen. It is true. God means what he says, and if God
is angry he will prove it.

That is why I am glad that this is a book of history. I find
other religious books are not. The Koran is not history. The
books of other religions are not history. And they are words
without deeds. They have no history in them; they cannot
prove the truth of what they say. They cannot point to this
event and that. They cannot point to a ration book dug up
in the gates of Babylon. That kind of detail is missing from
other religious writings, but I praise God that it is here in
this book. History is *his story*; it is not just words. What is
true of the anger of the Lord, praise God, is also true of his
love. To say, "God is love" could be just words unless one
day a cross was erected on a hill outside Jerusalem and God's
own Son was put to death on it.

So chapter 52 had to be there. If God has said something

then he is going to do it. His Word acts; it produces results. He said, "Let there be light," and there was light. When God says, "Let there be darkness," there is darkness. When God says, "Let there be death," people die. When God says, "I forgive your sins," the sins are forgiven. So the deeds must be there as well as the words — that is the general reason. It is the reason, incidentally, why the Apocrypha is not in the Bible and shouldn't be. I am sorry it was included in both the *New English Bible* and the *Jerusalem Bible*. The Apocrypha is historically interesting – part of the history of Israel and the Jewish people, but it was written during four hundred years when God didn't have a word to say. There was not a prophet from Malachi to John the Baptist; not one word came from heaven. Therefore that block of history was without meaning. Interesting? Yes. Courageous? Yes. The story of Judas Maccabeus has inspired music and song and inspired heroism today in Israel. Yet it does not belong to that history which gives meaning to life. The only history included in this book is that segment of history that is interpreted by God's words, those deeds of God that are clearly seen to be his acts because he said so.

That is why the Bible covers some history but not all. It doesn't even cover all the history of Israel. It covers that bit when God was speaking, right from the first time God said, "Let there be..." through to Malachi. Then for four hundred years Israel had to wait for a word from God and the scribes mulled over what had already been said, but there was no new word from God. Then one day, after waiting four centuries, a man appeared in Elijah's clothes and began to say "Thus says the Lord" again. That is a phrase which occurs 3,808 times in the Old Testament, but does not occur once in the Apocrypha.

Over a quarter of the verses of the Bible contain a specific prediction about something that will happen in the future.

Now that is a pretty bold book. It contains altogether 737 different predictions. A man would be pretty bold to make 737 predictions. Even those who claim to tell the future do not dare to risk that number of predictions. Jeremiah almost holds the record. He is second only to Ezekiel for the number of verses that contain a prediction. He is second only to Isaiah in the number of events he predicts. He predicts 90 and Isaiah predicts 111. Jeremiah has the greatest number of verses about one event: 222 times. For actual amount of words of prediction, Jeremiah holds the record. These statistics may be of interest to you or maybe not, but the vital one is this: 737 – get that fixed in your mind – events are predicted in the Bible, Old and New Testaments. How many of those have come true? Let me tell you: 593 have already come true; 80.5 per cent have already happened. That does not mean the Bible is 80 per cent accurate; it has been 100% accurate thus far, for many of the rest of the predictions are concerned with the end of the world. Here is something even more striking: out of 737 separate events predicted in the Bible, not only have 593 already happened, there are only seventeen more to happen before Jesus comes back to planet Earth. If the Bible has been right in 593, I can trust it for the rest. Do you? This is exciting. This is God's Word and God's deed linking together. What God says he means, and what he means he does.

Now that is the general reason why I believe God inspired the editor of Jeremiah to add this chapter – to confirm. It vindicated Jeremiah, but it vindicated Yahweh too. It vindicated that God is a God who means what he says. You dare not trifle with his words and you dare not gamble on him being wrong. You dare not risk God being a liar. "Let God be true and every man a liar" is the only safe way.

Now I give you particular reasons. Here is the first, a perfect lead in to the very sad poem called Lamentations.

The next few pages in the Bible are wet with tears and they are funeral dirges which are still sung by modern Israel once a year when they remember the fall of Jerusalem. I would like them to remember the reasons for the fall as well as they remember the fall. But still to this day the book of Lamentations and its poignant phrases of agony speak to the depths of our sadness. "Is it nothing to you? All you that pass by, is it nothing?" I recalled those words spoken when standing and looking at the ruined walls of Jerusalem uncovered by Kenyon. Doesn't it move you to your depths that a great nation sank to this?

If we left the book of Jeremiah at chapter 51 there would be no continuity into the book of Lamentations. I believe the editor added this chapter to tell you what they are weeping over in Lamentations, to be a continuity link with that next book. I was tempted to go on into Lamentations. Following the study in Jeremiah it seems to follow so easily. The Lord told me, "No, keep it for the day that Britain falls," and I am going to keep it for then. I pray that I will not need to expound that book in my lifetime. But he said, "That's a book you cannot understand until your nation has fallen, so keep it.

So chapter 52 tells you the facts. The king had his eyes gouged out and was put in prison; imagine what you would feel if that had happened to Queen Elizabeth. When you have seen your houses systematically demolished, when you have seen all but a few very poor people taken off to a land and know that they will never see their own country in their lifetime, though their children may come back, then you will weep and you will understand Lamentations.

Let us go back to its context the other way. Chapter 52 certainly leads into what follows, but it also perfectly completes what precedes it. What was the theme? It was the fall of that enemy Babylon, the fall of the greatest power the world had then seen. It was very moving to see that fall. But, you know, it is a very dangerous thing for us spiritually to end rejoicing over the downfall of our enemies. It is dangerous because we should be examining ourselves and our own destiny. I am afraid all of us can be so glad at the downfall of our enemies. I remember V.E. Day. There was singing and dancing. Hitler was dead. This country was shouting "Hallelujah" then, but we needed to be thinking about ourselves and our destiny. It seems to me that the editor, under divine inspiration, knew that it would be absolutely wrong for Israel to read Jeremiah's words and be left with a thought of Babylon falling. He knew that they must be challenged, and remember and learn from their past – that it was Jerusalem, the city of God, that fell. That was the greater tragedy; that is what they must learn from. Those who do not learn from history are condemned to relive it. So we are left with this thought: that judgment began with the house of God; that judgment began with Jerusalem. It went on to Babylon, but it began with Jerusalem.

That is where we must stay; that is where we must abide in our memory as we read Jeremiah, not thinking about even Jeremiah, or Jerusalem, or Babylon, but thinking about our church and thinking about ourselves. So, in this very interesting way, the editor of this book brought Jewish readers back to themselves: remember this was your nation, your king, your temple, your houses, your people; even though Babylon is to fall, learn the lesson of history about yourself rather than about your enemies.

That came home to me very forcibly as I watched the military parade on the twenty-fifth anniversary of the State of Israel, as they rejoiced over the Six Day War not long before. I trembled for them and I remember saying to someone, "I wonder how soon it will be before God humbles this people," little dreaming that it would be within six months. God would say: learn the lesson of history; put not your trust in missiles and tanks (or horses and chariots) – put your trust in me.

It means that we live in a moral universe and that God deals with sin even in his own people. Why "even"? I should express it as: *especially* in his own people. That is surely the message of Jeremiah. Yes, God will deal with evil in Babylon, but the whole of Jeremiah shows that he deals with it even and especially in his own people. That is the message we must be left with: not Babylon, but Jerusalem; not pagans, but God's own people. He deals with them, for he is a moral God in a moral universe—that is the final word.

Alas, I have to tell you that Israel, though it came back, did not learn and was, therefore, occupied, and reoccupied, and reoccupied again by Egyptians, by Syrians, by Greeks, by Romans. It was during the Roman occupation that at last, God did something radical and stepped back into the situation and sent not a prophet this time, but his own Son. They had dealt with prophet after prophet: O Jerusalem, Jerusalem, you stone the prophets; I sent servant after servant to you, but would you listen to my son? God sent his Son, Jesus, to this city that had not learned from its own tragic history.

I want now to explore briefly the amazing connection between Jesus and Jeremiah. Separated in time by over five hundred years, they nevertheless show such affinity. When Jesus was born, the country was ruled over by a Roman puppet king who was a descendant of Esau, a hated Edomite, one of those mentioned in the later chapters of Jeremiah – one of the nations. This Edomite was so jealous for his own position that he would do a number of things to safeguard it. He built that remarkable place at Masada to protect himself not only from Cleopatra in Egypt, but from the Jews themselves, in case they turned nasty. But to try to appease the Jews he said: I'm going to rebuild your temple and build it bigger and better than ever. I will give you the best temple you ever had; Solomon's will be nothing on the one I'm going to give you. He started rebuilding it. You can see today the huge foundation stones that he laid to impress this nation with his apparent concern for their welfare.

Jesus came into that very situation when Herod was rebuilding the temple. It was being rebuilt and Jesus was born. The other thing that Herod did was this: he safeguarded his throne by assassinating every potential rival. He was Herod the Great in more senses than one. When Jesus was born in Bethlehem of Judea, Herod, who had a castle just outside Bethlehem on a man-made hill which you can see to this day, said, "There's a king born. Kill every boy under two years." Of all those boys, the future generation of Bethlehem, one escaped—his name Jesus.

Matthew, telling the story, quotes Jeremiah and writes of the weeping of Rachel for her children. Jeremiah wrote it when his fellow countrymen were being deported and were being led away to Babylon, past Rachel's tomb. One escaped because at Rachel's tomb Nebuzaradan said, "Jeremiah, you can go free", and one escaped. The parallel is clear – that is why Matthew used the prophecy. The voice of Rachel "crying for her children", but one escaped and his name was Jesus, as the one who escaped when that word was said previously was Jeremiah. Then, later in the account of Jesus, you find contact after contact. You find that when Jesus cleansed the temple he did it twice, once at the beginning, once at the end, when this magnificent new building was still going up. He went in with a whip and was angry. What words did he use? He used the words of Jeremiah, "You made my house into a den of robbers." He could find no better words than those words of Jeremiah.

When you think of Jesus on the Palm Sunday riding in from the Mount of Olives, you see Jeremiah. "Oh Jerusalem,

Jerusalem, how often would I...?" Then Jesus went on to predict the identical thing that Jeremiah had predicted of that city, "... Jerusalem, a siege works will be cast up about you and you will be destroyed and not one stone left on another." That is exactly what Jeremiah had predicted. From Jeremiah's first prediction to its actual happening was exactly forty years, and from Jesus' prediction of it happening to its fulfilment was also exactly forty years.

When Jesus was arrested and taken for trial, the parallel between his own imprisonment and the things they said and did to him is almost identical with the trial and imprisonment of Jeremiah. I say it carefully, but I believe that, to a degree, Jeremiah also shared the sufferings of Jesus – he knew what it was to be despised, rejected of men; knew what it was to want to gather that city, Jerusalem, to God, and find that they did not want it; he knew what it was to be alone, knew what it was to cry out to God: why have you left me?

It is out of that lone experience of suffering that I think Jeremiah comes to us today. I now reach my conclusion of these studies: to help us, for in his lonely walk with God, thrown out of the temple, out of the public worship, out of the ritual, Jeremiah discovered a personal walk with God. He discovered a new religion – a religion of the heart. He discovered a religion that could be written inside a man that was not dependent upon external support. He discovered a walk with God. It is at this point of loneliness and suffering that I think Jeremiah can help you most.

I finish then with just three things which Jeremiah helps us to cope with. I am quite sure his book will have spoken to you. First, Jeremiah helps us to cope with disaster. His is the book for a nation sliding downhill. It is terribly difficult to cope with this, and the way most people do is to deny that it is happening. That is the way we shield ourselves. We say, "Don't worry, it may never happen." The teaching in Jeremiah can help us through disaster – to be honest and face reality – because Jeremiah sees a hope at the end of the tunnel. You might feel like Jeremiah at times and say, "God, why was I brought forth from the womb to see all this?" But Jeremiah got through it. When you read his book, he will help you through it, with understanding and with a word for others and with help for them.

The second thing he will help you to cope with is the depression that is the effect of such doom. Depression is something we all have to cope with. For most of us, it is centred around very personal things that happen to us, but there is a general mood of depression that could come over this country. I sense it already, a feeling of helplessness. A feeling: what is the point of trying to save your money for the future; what is the point of planning for the future? Many think there isn't any point, so let us just make the best of the present. Jeremiah helps us to cope with that. He had a thankless task. He had to preach for forty years and know that people would not listen. He had to watch his own nation dissolve, yet he kept going. Somehow, out of his very depression, there came such a close walk with God that he had no choice but to go on telling people that the light would one day return, that dawn would one day break. When you are depressed with a situation, go back to Jeremiah.

Read about the times when he was depressed, but read on and see how God challenged him, picked him up, set him on his feet and told him to go and tell the people – and keep on doing it. You know, Jeremiah did it without any hope of the resurrection. There is not a mention of an afterlife in Jeremiah, yet he could see it through. We have got a life before us that is wonderful. We have the resurrection as part of our faith. Can we not cope with depression if he could? He was able, without a single thought of surviving the grave, to cope, and he came through with God.

Finally, Jeremiah helps us to cope with the disobedience that causes the depression, for that is the real point of the book. Disaster isn't arbitrary; it isn't a matter of luck or chance. Disaster is related to disobedience. God has made this world a lawful world. His laws protect us, so thank him for his laws. You cannot break his laws, you can only illustrate them. Do you think that if you walk off a cliff, you will break the law of gravity? No, you will illustrate it. You cannot break God's laws, they break you. That is the truth. It is the same with health. There are laws of health. If you break the laws of physical health, you don't break them, they break you.

That is the heart of the message – the disobedience – and that is the heart of our problem. "Can the leopard change his spots?" says Jeremiah, "Or the Ethiopian his skin?" He was utterly realistic with human nature and he recognised, as he put it, that sin is written into our hearts and that we cannot change ourselves and that we are like this and we are rebellious and disobedient.

The thing that is most vividly in my mind after this study is the picture of the potter with the clay. We have discovered that the usual interpretation of that passage is the opposite of the true one. The usual interpretation is that the potter decides what shape the clay should be, but in fact, we saw that it was the clay that decided, and that the clay would not mould to the shape the potter wanted. So he had to bang it into a lump and make a poorer vessel out of it, a vessel which Jeremiah later smashed. The problem is with the clay. We are clay that will not mould to the potter's hand. That was the lesson Jeremiah learned. We are like the leopard who cannot change spots or the Ethiopian who cannot change skin. We are the clay that will not respond to the potter's hand.

If it were left there then the message of Jeremiah would be unbearable, but he did not leave it there. In chapter 31

he said something so profound that it became the name of
the other half of the Bible, for our word "New Testament"
is the Latin translation of "new covenant". It was Jeremiah
who first coined that phrase. So our very New Testament is
named after that phrase from Jeremiah. He saw something
new happening – he saw forgiveness. He saw a change
in human nature. He saw a new kind of religion in which
the commandments were not written in stone but written
somewhere much better – written in the heart so that our
heart wants to keep the law.

He saw a whole new covenant, a whole new relationship,
and a whole new religion. He saw it from a distance; it didn't
come for another five hundred-odd years, but he saw it. He
was in effect declaring: I can see that what my people need
is a new religion, a new nature, a new relationship with
God, not like the one they had with the God who brought
them out of Egypt (which they still remember every year,
incidentally). They need something quite new. They need a
new relationship with God.

One night a Jew called Jesus took a loaf of bread and
he broke it and he took a cup of wine and he gave it to his
disciples and said, "Drink of this; this is my blood" – of
what? He quoted Jeremiah. "This is my blood of the new
covenant". When Jesus died, the new relationship became
possible. It became possible to know God intimately – from
the least to the greatest. It became possible to keep his laws.
It became possible for sins to be forgiven rather than simply
overlooked. It became possible for God's people to enjoy
God's blessings forever.

At first many Jews responded to Jesus. All the early
followers of Jesus were Jewish, but many others would
not listen. They went on with their old religion, their old
relationship, though it did not work. In AD 70 what Jesus
predicted came true yet again, and Jerusalem was razed to

the ground. The house of the Lord was burned – it had only been finished for six years. It was pulled down stone by stone, and there is nothing but the stone platform left today. This relationship was thrown open to us Gentiles—Hallelujah! We came into Jeremiah's blessings.

Do you know that one of the first big battles in the Christian church, which involved calling a whole council together in Jerusalem, was the battle: should Gentiles come into this faith which is Jewish? They had a big debate and one of the apostles stood up and quoted the Old Testament to show that Gentiles were included. Who did he quote? Jeremiah. At that council it was settled forever that we, Gentiles, can be part of Israel without becoming Jews and that we are part of Israel. That does not mean that the old Israel has lost out. God intends to bring them back in, make no mistake.

When Paul talks about the ingathering of Israel back to the fold, who does he quote in Romans 9? Jeremiah. So I could go on. There are forty-one different quotations from Jeremiah in the New Testament; twenty-six of them in the book of Revelation. You see what Jeremiah was teaching: my people, Israel, need a changed heart, a new relationship, a new covenant, a new religion with the same God. He discovered it himself, in his own heart, because he had been robbed of the temple, of his people, of everything, but he had found God and he knew God. He taught: that is what the people need; one day they will get it. And they have done. When I taught my church about the passage which included the phrase "the leopard and its spots", somebody jotted down one sentence on a piece of paper and pushed it into my hand at the door. It said: "A leopard cannot change his spots, but I know that my spots have been healed by his stripes." That is the new covenant. A leopard can't do it, but Christ can do that for a believer.

For more of David Pawson's teaching,
including DVDs and CDs, go to
www.davidpawson.com

FOR FREE DOWNLOADS
www.davidpawson.org

For further information, email
info@davidpawsonministry.org

CPSIA information can be obtained
at www.ICGtesting.com
Printed in the USA
BVHW061722260820
587362BV00004B/57

9 781911 173762